Chinese Linguistic

Chinese Linguistics

An Introduction

GIORGIO FRANCESCO ARCODIA (馬振國)
BIANCA BASCIANO (白夏儂)

OXFORD
UNIVERSITY PRESS

OXFORD
UNIVERSITY PRESS

Great Clarendon Street, Oxford, OX2 6DP,
United Kingdom

Oxford University Press is a department of the University of Oxford.
It furthers the University's objective of excellence in research, scholarship,
and education by publishing worldwide. Oxford is a registered trade mark of
Oxford University Press in the UK and in certain other countries

Italian edition *Linguistica cinese* first published by
Pàtron Editore S.r.L © Pàtron, Bologna 2016

English translation © Giorgio Arcodia and Bianca Basciano 2021

The moral rights of the authors have been asserted

First Edition published in 2021

Impression: 1

Published in the United States of America by Oxford University Press
198 Madison Avenue, New York, NY 10016, United States of America

British Library Cataloguing in Publication Data
Data available

Library of Congress Control Number: 2021948430

ISBN 978–0–19–884783–0 (hbk.)
ISBN 978–0–19–884784–7 (pbk.)

DOI: 10.1093/oso/9780198847830.001.0001

Printed and bound by
CPI Group (UK) Ltd, Croydon, CR0 4YY

Contents

Preface to the English edition

This book is a revised edition of our 2016 Italian language monograph *Linguistica Cinese* (Bologna, Pàtron). The rationale for writing it then came from a simple, but perhaps surprising, realization: despite the steady growth of Chinese studies and of students of Chinese as a foreign language over the past twenty years, an up-to-date introductory book on Chinese linguistics for a Western audience is not easy to find. Five years later, this still appears to be true. What is perhaps the most popular and authoritative introduction to Chinese linguistics, Jerry Norman's *Chinese*, was published in 1988 and has never had a revised edition; a glut of encyclopedias and handbooks on the subject have seen the light in the past few years, but none of them can be used as a primer on Chinese linguistics for the benefit of students and scholars, including non-specialists of Chinese.

Compared to the first edition, the main difference in the composition of the volume lies in the introductory chapter, which was not included in the Italian version; also, we updated the references to include some new publications in the field, and we streamlined the historical and typological overview of Sinitic (Chapter 2). Lastly, we added a case study on an emerging phenomenon in Chinese word formation in Chapter 5 (§ 5.3.2), and a section on subjecthood in the chapter on syntax (6.2.1). As to the presentation, we adapted some passages in order to make them more easily understandable for an English-speaking audience (e.g. by making reference to English and to the situation in anglophone countries).

In this volume, we chose to use traditional Chinese characters as a default; however, in direct quotes from a source in simplified characters, we also use the latter for consistency. As to the transcriptions, for Modern Standard Chinese we use *Pinyin*, which is nowadays almost universally accepted in the Chinese-speaking world and in the scientific community; for Cantonese, we use the Yale romanization, while for Taiwanese we use the Taiwanese Romanization System (Taiw. 臺羅拼音 *Tâi-lô Phing-im*). For Japanese and Korean we use, respectively, Hepburn romanization and the Revised Romanization of Korean. For all other languages and varieties, we use the transcriptions provided by the sources. For previous historical stages of Chinese, we transcribe the examples with the *Pinyin* romanization for Modern Standard Chinese, as is customary in Chinese studies; whenever appropriate, we also provide reconstructed forms. For Old Chinese, reconstructed forms are starred, whereas for Middle Chinese they are not (see Baxter 1992); we use as a default the Baxter-Sagart reconstruction, quoting other proposals when needed. For the sake of simplicity, we modified Baxter-Sagart's notation as follows: we removed square brackets, which indicate uncertainty as to the nature of the reconstructed sound, but we kept parentheses, which indicate uncertainty as to the presence of the sound itself; we also follow their conventions of using a dot (.) to indicate pre-syllables and angle brackets (< >) for infixes (see Baxter and Sagart 2014).

Also, whenever quoting from the classical literature, we add the original title of the work between parentheses (at first mention only). The names of dynasties are in toneless *Pinyin*, with the exception of 'Jìn' and 'Jīn', which would be undistinguishable otherwise; for characters, complete transcription, and dates the reader is referred to the periodization presented after the list of abbreviations. As to place names, we provide Chinese characters (at first mention) only for minor cities and counties; the same goes for personal names. When quoting from the literature, we chose to use both surnames and names of Chinese authors *when there is only one author*, instead of surname only: thus, we use e.g. (Chappell 2015a) and (Liu and Tao 2016), but (Dong Xiufang 2004). This choice is motivated by the extremely high frequency of common Chinese surnames (e.g. Wang, Li, Zhang, etc.), which are even less differentiated in their transcription (e.g. 高 *Gāo* and 郜 *Gào* are both rendered as 'Gao'): to avoid ambiguity, we use the full name.

The glosses follow the general guidelines of the Lepizig Glossing Rules <http://www.eva.mpg.de/lingua/resources/glossing-rules.php>; in the list of abbreviations we therefore include only additional glosses.

For academic purposes, Giorgio Francesco Arcodia is responsible for Chapters 2, 3, and 4, and Bianca Basciano is responsible for Chapters 1, 5, and 6.

To conclude, we would like to express our heartfelt gratitude to our colleagues and friends who contributed in many different ways to the preparation of this volume. First and foremost, we would like to thank Magda Abbiati, Giulia Baccini, Emanuele Banfi, Clara Bulfoni, Martina Codeluppi, Sara D'Attoma, Franco Gatti, Paolo Magagnin, M. Silvia Micheli, Anna Morbiato, Marie-Claude Paris, Luisa M. Paternicò,

Waltraud Paul, Chiara Piccinini, Emanuele Raini, Chiara Romagnoli, Carlotta Sparvoli, and Serena Zuccheri for their friendship and for their continued support throughout the difficult (and tiresome) process of putting our ideas in writing. We would also like to thank Attilio Andreini, Wolfgang Behr, Hilary Chappell, Katia Chirkova, Amedeo De Dominicis, Zev Handel, Guillaume Jacques, Henning Klöter, Alexis Michaud, and Alain Peyraube for providing crucial references, and for the many enlightening discussions. Last, but not least, we would like to thank Julia Steer and Vicki Sunter of Oxford University Press for their effort in the production of this book: it is no exaggeration to say that, without their patience and dedication, the publication of this volume would not have been possible.

List of abbreviations

ATT	attenuative
BSOL	Baxter-Sagart Old Chinese reconstruction (on-line version 1.1, 20 September 2014)
Cant.	Cantonese
CMC	computer-mediated communication
CONT	continuous
CRS	Current Relevant State
DOR	Direct Object Restriction
EMC	Early Middle Chinese
EMPH	emphatic
EXH	exhortative
EMSEA	East and Mainland Southeast Asian
Eng.	English
EXP	experiential aspect
It.	Italian
Jap.	Japanese
Kor.	Korean
LMC	Late Middle Chinese
MC	Middle Chinese
MOD	Marker of modification (的 *de*)
MSC	Modern Standard (Mandarin) Chinese
N	noun
OC	Old Chinese
OM	Old Mandarin
PREF	prefix
P	preposition
REC.PST	recent past
SFP	sentence final particle
SUFF	suffix
Taiw.	Taiwanese (Taiwan Southern Min)
V	verb

Periodization of Chinese history

Xia Dynasty (夏 *Xià*; XXI–XVI cent. BC)

Shang Dynasty (商 *Shāng*; XVI cent. –1046 BC)

Western Zhou Dynasty (西周 *Xī Zhōu*; 1046–771 BC)

Spring and Autumn Period (春秋 *Chūnqiū*; 771–476 BC)

Warring States period (戰國 *Zhànguó*; 476–221 BC)

Qin Dynasty (秦 *Qín*; 221–207 BC)

Western Han Dynasty (西漢 *Xī Hàn*; 206 BC–24)

Eastern Han Dynasty (東漢 *Dōng Hàn*; 25–220)

Three Kingdoms (三國 *Sānguó*; 220–65)

Western Jìn Dynasty (西晉 *Xī Jìn*; 265–316)

Eastern Jìn Dynasty (東晉 *Dōng Jìn*; 317–420)

Northern and Southern Dynasties (南北朝 *Nán-Běi Cháo*; 420–589)

Sui Dynasty (隋 *Suí*; 581–618)

Tang Dynasty (唐 *Táng*; 618–907)

Five Dynasties and Ten Kingdoms period (五代十國 *Wǔdài Shíguó*; 907–60)

Northern Song Dynasty (北宋 *Běi Sòng*; 960–1127)

Southern Song Dynasty (南宋 *Nán Sòng*; 1127–1279)

Liao Dynasty (遼 *Liáo*; 916–1125)

Jīn Dynasty (金 *Jīn*; 1115–1234)

Yuan Dynasty (元 *Yuán*; 1271–1368)

Ming Dynasty (明 *Míng*; 1368–1644)

Qing Dynasty (清 *Qīng*; 1644–1911)

Republic of China (中華民國 *Zhōnghuá Mínguó*; 1912–49 on the mainland; from 1949 in Taiwan)

People's Republic of China (中華人民共和國 *Zhōnghuá Rénmín Gònghéguó*; from 1949)

1

Introduction

1.1 What is 'Chinese linguistics'?

Chinese linguistics may be broadly understood as the scientific study of Sinitic languages, or even of any language of China, from virtually any perspective: historical, typological, sociolinguistic, etc. The field of Chinese linguistics is therefore defined on the basis of its object, i.e. Sinitic languages, or the languages of China belonging to any family.

In this broad sense, Chinese linguistics is a subject of interest both for specialists in Chinese studies and for linguists working in other areas. As to the latter, for instance, typologists will be interested in the diversity which may be found within China and the Chinese-speaking world; specialists in historical linguistics will be both puzzled and fascinated by the unique situation of Chinese, a language with four millennia of uninterrupted documentation, but in a script which gives little clear phonological information; scholars of writing cannot but be interested in what is the only logographic script currently in use to write a national language (including Japanese); also, the research in the field of Chinese linguistics is (or, perhaps, should be) intimately connected with the research on applied linguistics and language teaching. At the same time, language is the main device through which Chinese culture has expressed itself, and many topics related to language, including e.g. the genesis of the national language, the status of dialects, or the

Chinese Linguistics: An Introduction. Giorgio Francesco Arcodia and Bianca Basciano, Oxford University Press.
© Giorgio Arcodia and Bianca Basciano 2021. DOI: 10.1093/oso/9780198847830.003.0001

complex relationship between speech and writing, are undoubtedly of the utmost relevance for many, if not most, China scholars.

Perhaps paradoxically, Chinese linguistics may be regarded both as an established and as an emerging subfield of linguistics and Chinese studies. The indigenous tradition of reflection on language and writing began even before the Imperial Age in China, and had a major development in the first centuries of the first millennium of the Common Era, when the Indian tradition of phonological analysis reached China (see Casacchia 2006); foreign scholars, many of whom missionaries from the West, started writing grammars and treaties on Sinitic languages at least since the sixteenth century. There is hence no doubt that linguistic studies on the languages of China have a very long history, and thus they easily qualify as an established field of learning. On the other hand, the field has experienced momentous growth and development in the past thirty years, and perhaps even more strongly since the beginning of the third millennium: while the nineties have seen the positive effects of the policies of 'reform and opening-up' (改革開放 *gǎigé kāifàng*) in the P.R.C., leading to more dialogue between Chinese and foreign academics, and the establishment of major international scholarly associations for Chinese linguistics,[1] the past decade has witnessed a steady growth of conferences, journals, courses, and publications specifically dedicated to Chinese linguistics. Besides, the tremendous rise in the number of language students (mostly learning Modern Standard Chinese; see the figures in Liu and Tao 2016) and teachers, and in the number and variety of courses in Chinese language and culture offered (especially since the beginning of the Confucius Institute programme in 2004), has contributed both to the growth of research in applied linguistics, again with the establishment of scholarly associations abroad,[2] and to the interest in the broader field of Chinese linguistics.

---

[1] The International Association of Chinese Linguistics <http://www.iacling.org/> (last access: 22 May 2020) was established in 1992; the European Association of Chinese Linguistics <http://chineselinguistics.eu/> (last access: 22 May 2020) was established in 1998; the North American Conference on Chinese Linguistics series <https://naccl.osu.edu/> (last access: 22 May 2020) began in 1989 (as *Northeast* Conference on Chinese Linguistics for the first two years).

[2] While in the US, a Chinese Language Teachers Association <http://clta-us.org/> (last access: 22 May 2020) has been in existence since 1962, the European Association of Chinese Teaching <http://www.ouhanhui.eu//> last access: 22 May 2020) had its inaugural symposium only in 2017; the Chinese as a Second Language Research <http://www.caslarcenter.com> (last access: 22 May 2020) project was launched in 2010, and led to the publication of the eponymous journal two years later.

2

1.2 Aims and scope of this book

As illustrated in the previous section, the strong rise in the interest for Chinese linguistics from a diverse audience invites a book like the present one: its declared aim is to provide an accessible general introduction to key topics in Chinese linguistics both for China scholars and for linguists, including those with little or no previous knowledge of Chinese. Thus, we chose to rely as much as possible on works in European languages, in order to enable direct access to the sources for those who do not read Chinese with ease. While nowadays an impressive range of reference works on the languages of China is available in English (and other European languages), they are generally aimed at an audience with a background in the subject, and typically provide detailed treatments for each topic: a neophyte looking for an overview would probably feel lost. This book is instead conceived as something which can be read with ease from beginning to end, in order to obtain a general grasp of linguistic studies on Chinese. In our intentions, it could be used, for instance, as a background reading, or even as a main textbook, for courses in Chinese linguistics at MA or PhD level, or as support material for course designers. As hinted at earlier, further potential readers include linguists specializing in other areas, in need of a quick and accessible introduction to one or more general topics in Chinese linguistics, and scholars in Chinese studies, especially in the fields of literature, history, and education, who want to gain a better understanding of current issues in the domain of language studies.

It is important to stress the fact that this is not a book about (Modern Standard) Chinese, but about Chinese *linguistics*: it is not meant to be an aid to language learners, or just as an introduction to the language *per se* (such introductions, incidentally, are never in short supply). Thus, we tried to provide as much data as possible from nonstandard Sinitic varieties, i.e. the so-called Chinese 'dialects'; we also make reference to other languages of East and Southeast Asia which share many crucial typological features with Sinitic. Moreover, we tried to present the data on modern Sinitic languages also taking into consideration the diachronic side, whenever appropriate. We hope that this will be appreciated by those readers who are looking for a comprehensive view of Chinese both in a typological and in a historical perspective.

However, it goes without saying that packing all of the above in a reasonably sized book is no easy feat: we had to make some inevitable choices as to what to include, and what not to include. Thus, for instance, almost nothing is said on the many non-Sinitic languages spoken in China; the same goes for the fascinating history of Chinese linguistics, which has a very marginal place in the present volume. Given the vastness of the subject, striking a balance between readability and comprehensiveness is extremely difficult: while we tried to provide the broadest possible subject coverage, we also had to make choices, and some topics are only briefly mentioned, or even simply left out. For instance, those looking for an introduction to semantic and pragmatic issues relating to Chinese will be disappointed, since they have almost no place in this book; on the other hand, despite the lack of a dedicated chapter, many topics in sociolinguistics have been dealt with, but in an unsystematic fashion, wrapped into discussions on language history, writing, etc. Also, while non-Sinitic languages of China are occasionally mentioned in different parts of the book, we decided to limit our scope to the Sinitic family of languages, opting in a sense for a 'narrow' definition of the field. Needless to say, the choices we made as to what to include reflect our own views on what is more important for a general understanding of the subject.

1.3 Organization of this book

The remainder of this book is divided into five chapters. The second chapter sets the stage, providing a thorough overview of the key issues concerning the history, classification, and typology of Sinitic languages. After having defined the object of our study, i.e. 'Chinese', in Chapter 2, we sketch a brief history of the evolution of Sinitic languages from the earliest attestations up to the genesis of a national language, and we introduce the main issues concerning the genealogical collocation and classification of Chinese, as well as its typological features and areal ties.

In Chapter 3, rather than moving to the description of Sinitic languages *per se*, we propose an overview of Chinese writing, including: general issues on the nature and role of logographic writing in the Chinese-speaking world; a concise history of Chinese characters, and of proposed alternatives to logographic writing; a short discussion on how Chinese writing has been used to write languages other than the 'official' one, i.e. Chinese dialects and non-Sinitic languages of the Sinosphere.

The topic of Chapter 4 is the phonology of Chinese. The first part of the chapter is devoted to historical phonology, with a presentation of the methodology and limits of this branch of Chinese linguistics and an overview of the phonology of the main historical stages of Chinese; the second part focusses on synchronic phonology, with a brief description of the phonology of Modern Standard Chinese and of each branch of the Sinitic family.

Chapter 5 deals with morphology and the lexicon. The first part provides a general overview of the morphology of Chinese, including the earlier historical stages of the language, with a separate focus on each major word formation device (compounding, derivation, etc.); dialect data has been included whenever relevant. We then move to the topic of the introduction of foreign lexical items in Chinese, with a focus on the post-Opium Wars period, and we discuss some recent trends in Chinese word formation, including internet neologisms and 'buzzwords'. We close the chapter with a brief presentation of some significant differences in the lexicon of different branches of Sinitic.

The last chapter is devoted to syntax. Given that an adequate summary of this subject could hardly be achieved in a book chapter of reasonable length, we chose to present only some key topics in Chinese syntax: word order, again including both historical data and contemporary dialectal variation; topichood and subjecthood; serial verb constructions; tense and aspect; argument structure; and word classes.

2

Sinitic languages

A historical and typological overview

2.1 'Chinese', 'dialects', and 'Sinitic languages'

A common issue in language studies is that the terminology used for languages and varieties in a specific context may be misunderstood by those who are not familiar with that situation. The first example which comes to mind is 'dialect', which has a very different meaning when used with reference to the English-speaking world if compared, for instance, to Italy, where dialects are in fact sister languages of standard Italian. The same goes for language names, especially in situations of diglossia: for instance, 'Arabic' is often seen as the language of some 313 million people (Simons and Fennig 2018), divided into several 'dialects', as e.g. Moroccan Arabic; however, these 'dialects' are, for all intents and purposes, separate languages, at least in their spoken form, with no or limited mutual intelligibility with other Arabic 'dialects'. The standard variety, i.e. Modern Standard Arabic, is used in writing and in formal speech, and it is acquired through formal education: this entails that not everybody has the same degree of command of the language, and that the varieties acquired spontaneously during early childhood are, in fact, the dialects (see Ryding 2011). Hence, to say that a Moroccan person speaks 'Arabic' *par défaut* as a mother tongue might be incorrect and even misleading.

Chinese Linguistics: An Introduction. Giorgio Francesco Arcodia and Bianca Basciano, Oxford University Press.
© Giorgio Arcodia and Bianca Basciano 2021. DOI: 10.1093/oso/9780198847830.003.0002

Very similar issues are met in the case of Chinese. The English term 'Chinese' (as well as e.g. French *chinois*, or Spanish *chino*, among others) is commonly used to refer to Modern Standard Mandarin Chinese (henceforth, MSC), i.e. the official language of the People's Republic of China and of the Republic of China (Taiwan),[1] as well as a co-official language of Singapore: this is the variety which is normally (though not exclusively) taught in language courses and which dominates the media in most of the Chinese-speaking world. Nevertheless, this term may actually be ambiguous, as it might refer, in principle, to just *any* Sinitic language, i.e. to any language belonging to the same family as MSC. Sometimes the word 'Mandarin' is used in English to distinguish the standard language from other Chinese varieties, but this is again not very precise, as 'Mandarin' is the designation of a whole branch of Sinitic, as we shall see later. Moreover, 'Chinese' is often used also to refer to earlier historical stages, or when discussing phenomena which have characterized 'Chinese' all along. See, for instance, Norman (2003: 72): '[f]or want of a better term, I will also refer to the totality of all forms of Chinese, ancient and modern, local and standard, as Chinese'. In the present work, we follow this practice and use 'Chinese' in statements which are generally valid for Sinitic languages, both in synchrony and diachrony; in all other cases, we use the specific term for the variety at issue (e.g. 'MSC', 'Cantonese', 'Early Modern Southern Min', etc.).

In MSC as well, there are several names which (roughly) translate as 'Chinese' (for an overview, see Harbsmeier 2001; Wiedenhof 2017). Arguably the most commonly used one in ordinary conversation, and even in written usage, is 中文 *Zhōngwén*, lit. 'writing of China'; originally, it was supposed to refer specifically to the written language (Lü Shuxiang 2002 [1942]), but it is nowadays commonly used both for the written and for the spoken language (as e.g. in 中文配音 *Zhōngwén pèiyīn* 'Chinese dubbing'). 中文 *Zhōngwén* is also a very good example of the ambiguity inherent in many language names: for instance, the Chinese name of the Chinese University of Hong Kong is 香港中文大學 *Xiānggǎng Zhōngwén Dàxué* (Cant. *Hēunggóng Jūngmàhn Daaihhohk*). Here 中文 *Zhōngwén* indicates the choice of standard written Chinese

---

[1] The political status of Taiwan is a very sensitive issue. As is known, the Republic of China (R.O.C.) is recognized only by a small group of countries, whereas the vast majority of the world's countries recognize the P.R.C. as the only legitimate government of China. However, since the Mainland and Taiwan are *de facto* controlled by different governments, we believe it is appropriate to mention both areas as far as language policies are concerned.

as the language of the university (besides English): however, classes are given not only in MSC, but also in Cantonese (Wang Hui 2013: 313). In scientific works and in language learning materials, it is customary to refer to MSC as 漢語 *Hànyǔ*, lit. 'the language of the Han (people)'; the Han are the overwhelming majority (more than 90%) of the population in China (see Fn. 11), and this name originally had an ethnic connotation (the language of the Han as opposed to the languages of the other ethnic groups, i.e. the minorities; see Norman 1988: 137). However, 漢語 *Hànyǔ* may also be used to refer to Sinitic languages; in point of fact, the Chinese name for the Sinitic family is 漢語(語)族 *Hànyǔ(yǔ)zú*; in the broad sense, 漢語 *Hànyǔ* is the term to which all historical stages and all Sinitic languages are associated. Yet another name, 華語 *Huáyǔ*, is often used in Chinese-speaking communities in Southeast Asia (especially Singapore), again to refer to MSC; however, the above-mentioned *Chinese University of Hong Kong* offers courses teaching MSC to 'Chinese speakers', indicated in Chinese as 華語人士 *Huáyǔ rénshì* 'speakers of *Huáyǔ*',[2] which here obviously cannot mean MSC. And, incidentally, the fact that speakers of other Chinese varieties (in this case, mostly Cantonese) choose to attend a course to learn MSC is indicative of the vast differences which exist between them. Thus, just as said before for Arabic, classifying someone as a 'speaker of Chinese' is potentially ambiguous, and may actually mean different things for different individuals.

Interestingly, the native terms which indicate unambiguously the national standard language, i.e. MSC, have been coined under the influence of Japanese. 國語 *Guóyǔ*, i.e. 'national language', was adopted as the name of MSC at the beginning of the twentieth century following the Japanese usage of 国語 *kokugo* (see §2.2.4), and is nowadays still in use in Taiwan. As to the P.R.C., since 1956 the official designation for MSC or, better, specifically for its spoken form, is 普通話 *Pǔtōnghuà*, lit. 'common speech'. This term was also created following a Japanese model (namely, Jap. 普通語 *futsūgo*; Kaske 2004: 282, Fn. 47; 2008: 212–13) and unequivocally designates the standard spoken language, as opposed to other Sinitic varieties. The fact that these terms emerged only in the twentieth century and are based on a foreign model is revealing of the traditional Chinese attitude towards language, and especially about

---

² <http://www.cuhk.edu.hk/clc/placement_evening_P4C.htm > (last access: 12 July 2021).

the notion of a unitary spoken language; things changed during the past hundred years, and the building of a unified national language, in fact, became an essential part of China's 'quest for modernity' (Liu and Tao 2016: 123). We will get back to this later (§2.2 ff.).

Thus, to sum up, just as 'Chinese' appears to be an ambiguous term in English, in Chinese too there are a number of names for the language(s), each of which has its own nuances and preferential context of usage. But even a term which is universally accepted in the Chinese linguistic tradition, i.e. 'dialect' (方言 fāngyán, lit. 'local/regional language'), has been an object of much debate for non-Chinese scholars (see e.g. Mair 1991). In the Chinese tradition, 方言 fāngyán is a term used for Sinitic languages other than the national standard, whereas in scientific works written in European languages, these are often referred to as (Sinitic or Chinese) 'languages' (see e.g. Chappell 2015a). It goes without saying that, in 'pure' linguistic analysis, the distinction between 'language' and 'dialect' is often not very relevant; however, here it is worth discussing how these labels are applied in the Chinese context, in order to gain a better understanding of the (socio)linguistic history of Chinese, and of language attitudes and policies in contemporary China.

As hinted at at the beginning of this section, the English term 'dialect' may be used with reference to two very different situations. In English, it is customary to refer e.g. to American English or Australian English as 'dialects' of English; in China, just as in Italy or in the Arab world, 'dialects' are actually just sister languages of the national standard. From the historical point of view, while e.g. Australian English emerged as a distinct variety from British English, in China the derivation goes the other way round: as we shall see in greater detail later (§2.2 ff., 2.3 ff.), *after* the split of Sinitic into different branches and languages, the standard emerged from the Mandarin branch. To draw a parallel from Europe, we may think of the rise of Romance languages from Latin: in Italy, for instance, several local vernaculars were spoken, and in the Renaissance a variety of literary Tuscan emerged as *the* Italian language, after which all other local languages came to be considered as dialects. If one takes mutual intelligibility as a criterion, according to which speakers of dialects of a language should be able to understand each other (a very debatable criterion; see e.g. Chambers and Trudgill 2004), then we could probably speak of hundreds of Sinitic languages, given that mutual intelligibility between dialects is often quite low

(Norman 2003: 72).[3] As Chappell (2015a: 4) puts it, 'the Sinitic languages are, *grosso modo*, as distinct from one another as European languages'. Note that, sometimes, the term 'language' is used in the literature to refer to whole branches of Sinitic; even in a major reference work as the *Ethnologue* (Simons and Fennig 2018), dialect groups as Wu, Xiang, or Gan are listed as 'languages'. This is obviously misleading, and to treat, for instance, Wu or Xiang as languages is not unlike treating West Germanic or South Slavic as languages.

Thus, from a strict (descriptive, historical, comparative, etc.) linguistic perspective, Chinese 'dialects' should not be understood as varieties *of* MSC, but rather as sister languages, just as German is to English; however, Chinese linguists almost invariably treat Sinitic languages as dialects of Chinese (漢語方言 *Hànyǔ fāngyán*; see Kurpaska 2010: 2). In fact, from the sociolinguistic perspective, there are good reasons to treat Sinitic languages other than MSC as 'dialects': put very simply, this is because they have no official recognition (with the partial exception of Cantonese in Hong Kong and Macao, and of Taiwanese and Hakka in Taiwan; see §3.3.1), and they are not standardized. In other words, the choice of the label 'dialect' may be based only on extralinguistic facts. Moreover, the choice of the label 'dialect' rather than 'language', in the Chinese context (as in many others), has political and ideological connotations. In Kurpaska's (2010: 2–3) words:

Calling the varieties of Chinese 'dialects' (方言 *Fāngyán*) rather than languages does have a strong political undertone, as it serves the unity of the Chinese people. If a vast majority of inhabitants speak one language, the country is also unified. [...]

The choice between the terms 'dialect' and 'language' is not merely a political question, but can also interfere in the sense of ethnic identity [...][4]

Besides, in linguistic circles, the idea of the fundamental unity of Chinese dialects found support in one of the most influential works in the history of modern Chinese linguistics, namely Yuen Ren Chao's *A Grammar of Spoken Chinese* (1968). In Chao's grammar, he speaks of a

---

[3] On a proposed measure of the degree of mutual intelligibility among Chinese dialects, see Cheng Chin-Chuan (1996).

[4] See also Baxter (1992: 8): '[s]ince having its own language is one of the normal characteristics of a 'nation' or *mínzú* [民族], to regard, say, Cantonese and Mandarin as different languages, merely because they are mutually unintelligible, would seem to imply that Cantonese and Mandarin speakers belong to a different *mínzú*—a conclusion which would be both historically inaccurate and politically unacceptable'.

'universal Chinese grammar' (1968: 13) which is shared by all Chinese dialects; in his view, the differences among dialects are mostly limited to their phonology and, to a lesser extent, to the lexicon. This erroneous view is best explained by a peculiar phenomenon which has been termed 'ditaxia' (Matthews 1996; see §2.2.2): in Chinese dialects, it is often possible to create 'hybrid' structures based on the grammar of MSC, but with dialectal phonology. These hybrid constructions represent the literary, formal register of a dialect, which is grammatically and lexically very close to MSC; dialectal grammar and lexicon are instead found in the colloquial register. Thus, for instance, in Cantonese one finds two alternative comparative constructions, one closely corresponding to the MSC construction (compare 1a and 1b), and one which is 'truly' Cantonese (2; Matthews 1996: 1277):

(1)   a.   我比佢高。
           ngóh béi   kéuih gōu
           1SG   compare 3SG   tall

      b.   我比他高。
           wǒ   bǐ   tā   gāo
           1SG   compare   3SG.M   tall
           'I am taller than him.'

(2)   我高過佢。
      ngóh   gōu   gwo   kéuih
      1SG   tall surpass 3SG
      'I am taller than him.'

The construction in (1a) is the literal equivalent, word by word, of the MSC construction in (1b): this is representative of the literary register of Cantonese, and it is used by more educated speakers, typically in formal speech. This is the type of parallel which might suggest that the grammars of Chinese dialects are indeed virtually identical. However, if we look at the authentic, colloquial register, here exemplified in (2), the idea of a 'universal Chinese grammar' appears as empirically untenable: the informal Cantonese construction belongs to a completely different type from the Mandarin one, with different word order and a different marker of comparison ('surpass' instead of 'compare'; see §6.1.3). In addition to that, we may remark that scholars like Chao were concerned with the standardization of the language, and hence downplaying the differences among dialects was in line with their agenda (Matthews 1999: 221–2).

11

Lastly, there is one more reason which justifies the treatment of Sinitic languages other than the standard as 'dialects': namely, the tradition of having a unitary written language which, differently e.g. from Latin, makes use of logographic characters (see §3.1) and hence is largely independent from dialectal and diachronic diversity (Norman 1988: 1–2). For most of Chinese history, this written language was 'Classical Chinese', i.e. the language of foundational works of Chinese culture from the late Spring and Autumn Period to the Han Dynasty: for instance, Confucius' *Analects* (論語 *Lúnyǔ*), the *Mencius* (孟子 *Mèngzǐ*), and the *Commentary of Zuo* (左傳 *Zuǒ Zhuàn*), among others. Later, and until the beginning of the twentieth century, the role of prestige written language was inherited by the so-called 'Literary Chinese' (文言 *wényán*), modelled after the Classical language, which had rougly the same role as Latin in Medieval Europe (Norman 1988; Pulleyblank 1995a).[5] Educated Chinese were part of this written tradition, independently of their native dialects, which was supported by a central authority (i.e. the Imperial Court), and mastery of this written language was crucial for social promotion, especially to become an official. Moreover, as we shall see in the next section, in China there has never been a flourishing of local literary traditions comparable to that of European vernaculars, which could support the independence of local dialects (Norman 1988: 2–3; Yuan *et al.* 2001: 16; see §3.3.1). Thus, in short, the 'dialectal' status of non-standard Sinitic languages comes also from their lack of a written form and from the lack of recognition for spoken languages as 'official' until relatively recent times.

To conclude, we must mention the fact that, needless to say, the standard language varies considerably in different regions of China, partly because of the influence of the underlying dialects. This type of diversification, which might confusingly be termed as 'dialectal' in English, has been recognized in the recent literature: local varieties of MSC are generally termed 地方普通話 *dìfāng Pǔtōnghuà*, lit. 'local Putonghua' (Chen Ping 1999: 42; *vernacular varieties* in Saillard 2004); these are in fact dialects *of* Chinese ('tertiary dialects' in Coseriu's 1980 classification), just as Texan English is a dialect of (American) English; however, they are not normally considered as such in the linguistic literature.

---

[5] Note that 'Classical Chinese' and 'Literary Chinese' are sometimes both referred to as 'Classical Chinese', particularly by non-specialists.

In this section, we introduced some basic terms which are used in the analysis of Sinitic languages. However, to put those notions into context, a (brief) overview of the linguistic history of China is necessary. This is the topic of the next section.

2.2 A short history of Chinese

As hinted at in the preceding section, the linguistic history of China has been characterized by a tension between, on the one hand, 'high' prestige varieties and spoken (national and regional) varieties and, on the other hand, written and spoken languages.

The Chinese language has one of the longest uninterrupted written traditions; the earliest documents in a Sinitic variety date to the fourteenth century BC, and the writing system was already mature by then (see §3.2.1). While one cannot deny that there is indeed a connection between these early attestations and modern Sinitic languages, the evolution of Chinese is far from linear and involved interactions among different diatopic, diastratic, and diamesic varieties, as well as highly complex historical stratification, as we shall see later.

2.2.1 Language in pre-imperial China

The oldest available Chinese texts are the Shang Dynasty oracle bone inscriptions (甲骨文 *jiǎgǔwén*). The corpus of oracle bone inscriptions is made of more than 150,000 pieces of tortoise shells and ox bones, on which about 26,000 sentences have been carved (Djamouri and Paul 2009: 196, Fn. 1). The texts are part of the rituals of plastromancy and scapulomancy: oracle bones were first heated, and the cracks caused by the heat were interpreted by the diviner.[6] The question and the response of the oracle were then carved on the bone itself (Abbiati 2012: 28). See this very short example of a response from the oracle bone corpus (from Djamouri and Paul 1997: 236; tones added):[7]

---

[6] Note that the characters 卜 *bǔ* 'divine' and 兆 *zhào* 'omen' contain graphic elements reminiscent of the cracks in oracle bones.

[7] Following our sources, here we use the current shape of the characters, which is often different from that used in paleographic texts.

(3) 王勿伐
    wáng *wù*   *fá*
    king   IMP.NEG attack
    'The king should not attack'

The representative texts of the following period in Chinese history, namely the Zhou Dynasty, are bronze inscriptions (金文 *jīnwén*), i.e. words and sentences engraved on bronze artifacts. See the following example (Djamouri 1991: 22; our transcription):

(4) 吏牆夙夜不豙
    lì   *qiáng* *sù-yè*   *bù* *suì*
    officer Qiang day-night   not fail
    'Officer Qiang never failed'

While these two paleographic corpora are of paramount importance for the history of Chinese, they also suffer from a serious shortcoming: because of their nature and functions, the language of the inscriptions is very formulaic; the lexicon is limited, lacking many common words; many syntactic patterns and function words appear rarely (Boltz 1999; Behr 2017). Because of this, in research on language history and philology, much importance has been attached to texts written on bamboo and wooden strips (respectively, 竹簡 *zhújiǎn*, or 簡牘 *jiǎndú*, and 木牘 *mùdú*) and on silk (帛書 *bóshū*). Generally speaking, all paleographic materials are of the utmost relevance for historical research, if compared to contemporary works which have been more or less tampered with in later epochs (Baxter and Sagart 2014; see §4.1.1), as many texts from the so-called 'preclassical' period (Norman 1988; Pulleyblank 1995a; Boltz 1999), like e.g. the *Classic of Poetry* (詩經 *Shījīng*). This is true also for many works from the classical period, whose received editions have often undergone substantial changes throughout their textual history.

While here we speak, generically, of early 'Chinese' texts, this does not necessarily entail that there was just *one* Chinese language at this stage: as pointed out by Branner (2000: 24), 'there does not seem to have been a time when Chinese was not diverse'. Even for early attestations, we may speak of some degree of variation. Oracle bone inscriptions likely reflect, in a condensed form, the language of the Shang capital 殷 *Yīn* (close to present-day Anyang, Henan province); it has however been proposed that even the language of the inscriptions was not uniform, and that e.g. the variation in the order of direct and indirect object could be the result of dialect(/language) mixing (Yue and Takashima 2000).

The foundation of the Zhou Dynasty is considered to be the beginning of the feudal age in China, and the resulting fragmentation ushered in linguistic variation (Chen Ping 1999: 7):[8] scholars generally believe that there was a prestige language in use at the Zhou court, referred to as 雅言 *yǎyán* (lit. 'elegant language'), which is mentioned, for instance, in Confucius' *Analects*. Historical documents suggest that noblemen and officers from different regions could communicate using this 雅言 *yǎyán*, apparently without the aid of interpreters; we may thus infer that this variety was diffused at least in the Zhou period *élites* (Coblin 1994: 5; but cf. Mair 1994: 729). The relative uniformity of bronze inscriptions, which came from all the pre-Qin Chinese-speaking world, further attests to the diffusion and prestige of the written form of the 雅言 *yǎyán* (Behr 2010: 573–4). This 'elegant language', probably deriving from the one used at the Shang court, was based on a variety from central China (中州 *Zhōngzhōu*), i.e. the area around present-day Henan province (Chen Ping 1999: 8; nowadays the term 中原 *Zhōngyuán* 'Central Plains' is used to indicate this region);[9] as we shall see later, the varieties associated with the 中州 *Zhōngzhōu* area played an essential role in shaping prestige varieties of Chinese for many centuries.

The very notion of 雅言 *yǎyán* entails that there was already awareness of linguistic diversity at the time; as a matter of fact, in the classical literature we find many references to linguistic differences not only between the Chinese people (referred to here as the 夏 *Xià*, i.e. Zhou China; Behr 2010) and others, but also among the different states in which the Chinese-speaking world was divided then. For instance, in the *Commentary of Zuo*, in relating events of 614 BC, reference is made to the lack of mutual intelligibility between the languages of the neighbouring states of 秦 *Qín* and 晉 *Jìn* (Coblin 1994: 4; Branner 2000: 6). In a frequently cited anecdote from the 尹文子 *Yǐnwénzǐ*, a philosophical work of the Warring States period, it is said that the word 璞 *pú* meant 'raw jade' in the state of 鄭 *Zhèng*, while in 周 *Zhōu* it was the name for uncured rat meat (Branner 2000: 5; Behr 2010: 575). Another often-quoted

---

[8] On dialectal and linguistic diversity from Zhou to Jìn times, see Hua Xuecheng (2007).

[9] Incidentally, the current name of China, 中國 *Zhōngguó* 'Middle State', was originally used to indicate this area, which was surrounded by the 'Four Barbarian Tribes' (四夷 *sìyí*) at the borders of the Chinese world.

reference to linguistic diversity in pre-imperial China comes from the *Mencius*:

(5) 孟子曰：否。此非君子之言，齊東野人之語也。

    Mèng-zǐ   *yuē* *fŏu* *cǐ*   *fēi*   *jūnzǐ*   *zhī*   *yán*
    Meng-master say no this NEG gentleman POSS word
    Qí dōng *yě*   *rén*   *zhī*   *yǔ*   *yě*
    Qi east coarse person POSS language PRED
    'Mencius said: "no, these are not the words of a gentleman, it is the language of a coarse person from Eastern Qi".'

This passage may be interpreted as referring either to dialectal variation between territories in the Warring States period (You Rujie 1992: 92) or to a sociolinguistic (diastratic) difference (Behr 2010: 570). In both cases, it clearly appears that the attitude towards diversity was far from neutral.

Thus, the idea of a prestige variety has been part of Chinese culture since the ancient times; however, the 'standard' languages of different periods were based on different varieties, following the changes in the political and cultural scenario of Chinese-speaking people(s). While the relative uniformity of the literary language somehow obscures this variation, in works from the Classical period we may find evidence of diatopic and diachronic variation. For instance, Pulleyblank (1995a: 3) individuates at least four (macro-)varieties of Classical Chinese:

- a. an archaic variety, probably based on a central dialect, represented in texts like the *Commentary of Zuo* (IV cent.) and the *Discourses of the States* (國語 *Guó Yǔ*; fifth century BC);
- b. a variety from the state of 魯 *Lǔ* (part of present-day Shandong province), represented in Confucius' *Analects* and in the *Mencius* (the latter being more innovative);
- c. a dialect from the 楚 *Chǔ* state (roughly, part of present day Hubei and Hunan), represented e.g. in the poem 離騷 *Lí Sāo* by Qu Yuan (屈原 *Qū Yuán*, 340–278 BC);
- d. a variety of the third century BC, represented in the philosophical works *Zhuangzi* (莊子 *Zhuāngzǐ*), *Xunzi* (荀子 *Xúnzǐ*), and *Han Feizi* (韓非子 *Hán Fēizǐ*).[10]

---

[10] However, compare Norman (1988: 83): '[l]ike most literary languages, Classical Chinese here and there revealed local and temporal variations; these variations were not, however, so great as to be termed different dialects in any meaningful sense of the term'.

The end of this period is marked by the establishment of the first imperial dynasty, i.e. the Qin dynasty; needless to say, this is a juncture in Chinese history which had a tremendous impact on Chinese culture, including language, as we shall see in the next section.

2.2.2 The Qin unification, language, and writing

With the unification of China under Qin rule, and even more so under the following Han dynasty,[11] we may appreciate two major developments in the history of the language. On the one hand, we see a gradual fossilization of the literary language, which becomes more and more detached from spoken varieties. On the other hand, the events leading to the split of Chinese into separate branches are set into motion. Moreover, this is the period during which Chinese characters are standardized and assume the form they mostly keep to the present day (excluding of course the simplification they underwent in the twentieth century), as we shall see in greater detail later (§3.2.2, 3.2.3). In fact, the beginning of the Han Dynasty is a major watershed in the history of Chinese writing: suffice it to say that the Chinese term 古文 *gǔwén* 'ancient writing' (also 古字 *gǔzì* 'ancient characters') indicates the forms of writing preceding this period (Norman 1988; Qiu Xigui 2000).

As to the written language, the 'canonization' of the classical texts of Confucian doctrine as the basis of education for the ruling class under the Western Han dynasty (Loewe 1994: 154), which remained almost unchallenged until the beginning of the twentieth century, contributed to the fossilization of the written language (Pulleyblank 1995a: 4). However, besides 'orthodox' Literary Chinese (正統文言 *zhèngtǒng wényán*), which was anyway not entirely immune from contaminations from the spoken varieties, there was also a parallel and more 'vernacular' style of Literary Chinese (通俗文言 *tōngsú wényán*, lit. 'popular Literary Chinese'), mostly used in letters, contracts, and in popular religious and literary works; while this popular style of writing was still firmly anchored in the classical tradition, it could include more colloquial features (Lü Shuxiang 2002 [1942]: 4–5). During the Eastern Han

---

[11] While the names for 'China' in Western European languages are mostly based on the name of the Qin dynasty, the Han dynasty has come to be used as shorthand for 'Chinese' in most of East Asia, including China itself: 'Han' is the name of the majority ethnic group in the Chinese-speaking world (see §2.1), and it is found e.g. in the name for Chinese characters (漢字 *Hànzì* 'Han characters') and for Chinese studies (漢學 *Hànxué* 'Han studies').

period, we already find Buddhist texts, including translations and adaptations of Indian works,[12] as well as popular poetry and tales, which
contain vernacular elements (on the so-called 'Buddhist Chinese', see
Lock and Linebarger 2018; Zhu and Li 2018); moreover, the dialogues in
historical and narrative works, as well as theatre plays, might somehow
reflect the spoken languages of that period (Norman 1988: 7). Starting
from the Tang Dynasty, and even more clearly from the Song period, we
find texts in which vernacular elements become dominant: this is the
style of writing which later came to be known in Chinese as 白話 *báihuà* (lit. 'simple/vernacular language'), and it was mostly based on
Northern Chinese varieties, to which we would nowadays refer to as
'Mandarin'.[13] While vernacular Chinese was generally seen with contempt by the political and cultural *élites* of the time, it was a very effective style of writing for all those works which were aimed at an audience
with limited formal education, because of its greater adherence to
(some) spoken varieties (Chen Ping 1999: 69).

The 文言 *wényán* vs. 白話 *báihuà* dichotomy was a stable feature of
Chinese culture until the first half of the twentieth century, and even
today some knowledge of the classical language is important for reading and writing MSC, because of the use of words, idioms, and constructions from Literary Chinese even in contemporary writings.[14] It
goes without saying that for historical research on Chinese, especially as
far as syntax is concerned, vernacular texts are far more important
than those written in 'pure' 文言 *wényán*, given that the former reflect
more closely developments in spoken varieties (Peyraube 1996; Sun
Chaofen 1996). Some examples of key vernacular texts for the history of
Chinese grammar are the 世說新語 *Shì Shuō Xīn Yǔ* ('A New Account
of the Tales of the World'; ca. 420), the Buddhist 'transformation texts'
(變文 *biànwén*; ca. 850–1015), and the 祖堂集 *Zǔ Táng Jí* ('Anthology of
the Patriarchal Hall'; 952), among many others. We will get back to the
history of 白話 *báihuà* in §2.2.4.

---

[12] On the role of Buddhism in the rise of vernacular writing in East Asia, see Mair (1994).
[13] Note that, originally, 白話 *báihuà* could also be used to indicate 'any idiom considered
representative of any given dialectal group', as e.g. Cantonese; it developed its current meaning of 'Northern/Mandarin vernacular literary language' in the twentieth century
(Masini 1993: 3).
[14] Actually, literary expressions may be found even in certain contemporary speech
styles; Harbsmeier (2001: 394) uses the term 'oral *wenyan*' to designate a spoken register of
MSC replete with classical elements.

As to the spoken language or, better, the spoken languages, the changes in the distribution of the population occurring during this period led to a strong increase in linguistic diversity, often the result of language contact. The establishment of the Qin empire was followed by a large number of waves of migration of Chinese-speaking people from the Yellow River basin (the cradle of Chinese civilization), mostly southwards, towards the south of the Yangtze River (長江 *Cháng Jiāng*); these areas were then inhabited by non-Sinitic ethnic groups, speaking Austroasiatic, Hmong-Mien, and Tai languages (collectively referred to in Chinese sources as the 百越 *Bǎi Yuè* 'hundred Yue'; Zhou and You 1986; LaPolla 2001; Chappell 2004b).[15] Moreover, during the Han dynasty, the empire expanded its influence over the Western regions, i.e. present-day Gansu, Ningxia, and Inner Mongolia, with the forced migration of some 580,000 people of different origins: thus, the 'colonization' of the West did not bring just one Sinitic variety into the new territories but, most likely, a number of different dialects, with a strong central (i.e. 中原 *Zhōngyuán*) flavour (Coblin 1994: 4–7). After the end of the Han dynasty, there were even more 'irregular' movements of people in Northern China, to which we must add more waves of migration (more or less) forced by the political situation or by local conflicts; it has in fact been proposed that the relative uniformity of modern Mandarin dialects is best explained by the admixture which occurred during this period (Zhou and You 1986; You Rujie 1992; Coblin 1994). Moreover, the influx of non-Sinitic (mostly, Altaic-speaking) peoples also influenced the development of Northern Sinitic varieties (LaPolla 2001; see §2.3.1).

This is the scenario in which the modern dialect groups were formed. Interestingly, the current term for 'dialect' comes from the (abbreviated) title of the first work on dialectal(/linguistic) diversity in China, i.e. Yang Xiong's (楊雄 *Yáng Xióng*; 58 BC–18 AD) 方言 *Fāngyán*, which dates to the Han period. In an Eastern Jìn commentary to the 方言 *Fāngyán*, Guo Pu's (郭璞 *Guō Pú*) 方言注 *Fāngyán Zhù* 'remarks on the *Fangyan*', the term 北方話 *Běifānghuà* 'Northern speech', i.e. present-day Mandarin dialects, is used for the first time (You Rujie 1992: 94–5; Chappell 2004b: 10); on the other hand, in the 方言 *Fāngyán* itself, the term 通語 *tōngyǔ* 'common language' is used, suggesting again that

---

[15] On the ethnic and linguistic composition of the 百越 *Bǎi Yuè*, see Yue Anne Oi-Kan (1991: 294–9).

some form of language common to the empire did exist at the time (see Casacchia 2006: 359), although almost certainly with regional differences in the phonology (Harbsmeier 2016: 487–90). Another interesting remark contained in the 方言 *Fāngyán* is that the varieties of 秦 *Qín* and 晉 *Jìn* are presented as a single dialect (Yuan *et al.* 2001: 19), which may be seen as evidence of the convergence within Northern China; as seen in §2.2.1, in the seventh century BC, the dialects of these two territories were still different enough as to lack mutual intelligibility.

According to Chappell (2004b: 7–9; see also Zhou Zhenhe 1991), in the long period between the Qin and Song dynasties, there were at least four waves of migration which deeply influenced the development of Sinitic languages. The first one was directly planned by the first Qin emperor, who dispatched some 500,000 soldiers to Southeastern China to support the Chinese presence in border regions; the colonization of the South continued in the Eastern Han period, thus laying the foundations for the establishment of the six oldest dialect groups (Min, Wu, Yue, Gan, Hakka, and Xiang; see §2.3.2). Later, between the Eastern Han and the Sui period, migrations from North to South continued, especially following the fall of the Jin capital, Luoyang, to the Xiongnu (匈奴 *Xiōngnú*) 'barbarians' in 311. Northern noblemen fled to Jinling (金陵 *Jīnlíng*), i.e. present-day Nanjing, which remained the capital almost until the end of the sixth century, leading to the 'mandarinization' of the local Wu dialect (LaPolla 2001: 228). Also, migrants from the Central Plains and from present-day Shandong, Shanxi, and Shaanxi, speaking both Central and Eastern Mandarin varieties, moved to Southern Jiangsu and Zhejiang (Coblin 2002a: 530). Generally speaking, the division between Northern and Southern China and the political fragmentation of this period, without a central authority which could impose a linguistic model to the whole of China, favoured the diversification of Sinitic (Norman 1988: 185–6).

Two more waves of migration of great importance took place during the Tang Dynasty and towards the end of the Northern Song Dynasty. During the Tang Dynasty, the massive influx of Northern migrants in Southern China led to the contamination of local varieties, which were sometimes overwhelmed by the Northern vernaculars; this was a crucial time for the formation of Southern Sinitic languages, as well as for the differentiation of Mandarin dialects in the South (Zhou Zhenhe 1991: 39–40). Moreover, according to one widely adopted view of the history of Sinitic, during this period migrants helped spread the Northern *koinè*, which represented a model for contemporary spoken varieties (Norman 1988: 186).[16] Then, similarly to what happened during the Western Jìn period, at the end of the Northern Song Dynasty the Chinese ruling class left Kaifeng *en masse*, and the imperial capital was moved southwards: first to Nanjing, and then to Hangzhou (1138). Perhaps unsurprisingly, the Wu dialect of the new centre of the empire received strong influence from the varieties of the newcomers from the North: in fact, the present-day Hangzhou dialect has been classified as either 'semi-Mandarin' (Zhou and You 1986) or even just as a Mandarin dialect (VanNess Simmons 1999a-b; see §2.3.2). Generally speaking, the Mandarin-speaking 'incursions' into Wu territory have led to some degree of convergence of the latter varieties with the Northern type, as we shall see in greater detail later (§2.3.2, 4.2.3).

At the end of the Southern Song period, the situation of Chinese dialects was largely the same as today (with the exception of Hui dialects, which separated later). From the Yuan Dynasty on, migrations of Chinese-speaking people followed mostly the East-West route, spreading Northern dialects in the Southwestern border regions (i.e. present-day Sichuan, Yunnan, Guizhou), in the West of China, and also in the Northeast; moreover, the massive immigration from rural areas to cities led to dialect admixture and, consequently, to the restructuring of several urban varieties (Zhou Zhenhe 1991; Lee and Wong 1991). We shall get back to the role of migrations in the formation of modern Sinitic languages in §2.3.2.

Note that the Northern Sinitic varieties which expanded their influence in Southern and Western China were far from homogeneous, needless to say. Northern immigrants came from different areas and were thus speakers of different dialects (Coblin 2002a); moreover, each period had its own prestige varieties (both in a national and in a local

---

[16] For the sake of conciseness and readability, here we do not mention the opposite view of Chinese linguistic history. In the only approach discussed here, attributed to Bernhard Karlgren and Edwin Pulleyblank (1984, 1998; see §2.2.5), there was a Tang period *koinè* which replaced almost completely pre-Tang Sinitic varieties; all modern Sinitic languages (with the exception of Min) derive from this *koinè*, in this view. Norman and Coblin (1995) propose instead a radically different reconstruction: they suggest that there has never been such a *koinè*, for which there appears to be no historical evidence, and that the modern dialects are the product of complex historical stratification, associated with the waves of migration briefly presented here (see also Zhou Zhenhe 1991; Handel 2014). Here we cannot elaborate on the merits and demerits of these two opposite proposed versions of the history of Chinese; we will get back to this *vexata quaestio* in §2.3.2.

context), and the varieties spoken in different times belong to different diachronic strata. This stratification is apparent in the phenomenon known in Chinese linguistics as 文白異讀 *wénbáiyìdú*, lit. 'different colloquial and literary readings': this happens when in a given dialect a character has a 'colloquial' reading, i.e. a reading which reflects the developments in the phonology of that dialect, and one or more 'literary' readings, which are in essence borrowed from another Sinitic variety (typically, a prestige Mandarin variety; Norman 1988: 41; You Rujie 1992: 111–12). For instance, in the Xiang dialect spoken in Hanyin (漢陰 *Hànyīn*), Shaanxi, initial aspirated voiceless affricate and plosive consonants (see 4.2.4) in the literary stratum correspond to unaspirated sounds in colloquial pronunciation: the former is the product of language contact with Southwestern Mandarin varieties, while the latter reflects the regular evolution of those sounds in Xiang dialects (Wang Futang 1999: 29–30). In Northern Wu dialects, literary readings often correspond to the colloquial readings of the same characters in Jiang-Huai Mandarin dialects; this stratum derives from the speech of the above-mentioned Northern immigrants of the Song period, which is preserved in some Wu dialects (Coblin 2002a: 535–6). In the Southern Min dialect of Chengmai (澄邁 *Chéngmài*, Hainan), one finds a more complex stratification: for instance, the character 學 'to learn' (MSC *xué*) has the 'conservative' literary reading *hiak*[3] (compare MC *haewk*; BSOL), the 'new' literary reading *hiok*[3], and the colloquial reading *o*[33]; the 'new' literary reading is said to be the product of the influence of the surrounding Yue dialects (compare Cant. *hohk*; Ho Dah-an 1981, qtd. in You Rujie 1992: 112). Moreover, even colloquial readings may be stratified, reflecting different historical stages of a variety: for instance, in Wenzhounese, there are at least three diachronic strata of colloquial readings (Zhengzhang Shangfang 2008: 101). Even in the Beijing dialect, which is often regarded as the basis of MSC (but see §2.2.4), we may distinguish literary and colloquial reading for some characters: for instance 色 'colour' may be read as *sè* (literary) or *shǎi* (colloquial); 擇 'choose' may be read as *zé* or *zhái* (Baxter 1999: 8). Lastly, stratification in dialects is not limited to phonology: as seen earlier (exx. 1-2), sometimes there are 'parallel' words and constructions belonging either to the colloquial (i.e. truly dialectal) or to the formal (i.e. based on the standard language) register. This stratification is evident in hybrid constructions (as 1a), combining colloquial and 'literary' elements.

In this section, we have shown that the historical development of Sinitic languages has been characterized since the beginning by language contact, both within the family and with neighbouring non-Sinitic languages, and by the influence of (national and regional) prestige varieties (Pulleyblank 1998), which led to stratification at all levels. Because of this, a classical *Stammbaum* representation of the relationship among Sinitic languages appears to be inadequate, as we shall see later (§2.3.2).

2.2.3 'Standard' varieties in imperial China

In the last two sections we hinted at the fact that the 'standard' varieties (or, better, the national prestige varieties) of Chinese were virtually always based on Northern dialects; however, the exact dialect from which the prestige variety emerged was not the same all along. This entails that, often, we cannot treat the historical data from different epochs as the product of a linear pathway of evolution: this is indeed of the utmost relevance for diachronic research, especially as far as phonological reconstruction is concerned (Coblin 1994; 2002b; see §2.2.5).

In the history of 'high' varieties of Chinese, the names which are met most often are those of the cities of Luoyang, Chang'an (present-day Xi'an), Nanjing, and Beijing:[17] these have all acted as capitals of imperial and/or of Republican governments. However, until the Yuan Dynasty, our knowledge of which varieties were considered the 'standard' is incomplete. As said in §2.2.1, it is generally believed that the 'elegant language' (雅言 *yǎyán*) of Zhou times was based on a 中州 *Zhōngzhōu* variety: the prestige of Central Plains Chinese grew when Luoyang became the imperial capital (Eastern Zhou Dynasty). Luoyang was the capital also during the Eastern Han and Western Jin periods, and its dialect spread into Wu territory at the fall of the Jin, as mentioned before. Until the Song period, the main competitor of the Luoyang dialect was the variety of Chang'an, an imperial capital during the Qin, Western Han, Sui, and Tang Dynasties. Interestingly, however, the varieties associated with Luoyang and Chang'an did not develop independently: in the *Book of the Later Han* (後漢書 *Hòu Hàn Shū*), a fifth-century historical work, it is said that in 190 AD the warlord Dong Zhuo

---

[17] Also known with different names in Chinese history.

relocated millions of people from Luoyang to Chang'an, thus creating an environment for language contact (Zhou and You 1986: 88); Chang'an was then soon abandoned and its population, as well as their dialects, dispersed (Coblin 1994: 6). Large-scale migration from and to Chang'an and the surrounding area (known as 關中 *Guānzhōng*) occurred again in the following centuries, and it is very likely that these population movements deeply influenced the development of the local dialects: it has been indeed proposed that the similarities between modern Northwestern Mandarin and Central Plains dialects are best explained by the population admixture in those areas (Coblin 1994: 15; see also Zhou and You 1986).

A very important source of information on what was perceived to be the 'standard' pronunciation for reading literary texts (but, crucially, not on spoken languages; we will get back to this later) in different periods of Chinese history comes from the so-called 'rime books' (or 'rime dictionaries'; 韻書 *yùnshū*) and 'rime tables' (等韻圖 *děngyùntú*). Rime books and rime tables use a peculiar system of notation (discussed in §4.1.1) which provided indications as to how to 'correctly' read aloud characters in literary works. The most important (and most studied) rime book is the 切韻 *Qièyùn* (601), compiled by Lu Fayan (陸法言 *Lù Fǎyán*, 581–618) in Chang'an, then capital of the Sui Dynasty; however, perhaps surprisingly, scholars mostly agree that the phonological system recorded in the 切韻 *Qièyùn* was not that of a Chang'an dialect, but rather a sort of compromise between the literary pronunciations of Nanjing (then Jinling) and of the Central Plains varieties of Ye (鄴 *Yè*) and Luoyang. In fact, none of the 'consultants' which assisted Lu Fayan in his selection of 'correct' readings was a Chang'an native (Norman 1988; Baxter 1992; Norman and Coblin 1995, among others).[18] In the oldest extant rime table, the 韻鏡 *Yùnjìng* (lit. 'mirror of rimes'), the original version of which is said to date to the ninth century (see Coblin 1996: 349), the system described is obviously younger than that of the 切韻 *Qièyùn* and, also, appears to be based on a different dialect: while Pulleyblank (1984, 1998) suggests that it reflects a standard of the Chang'an area, Norman and Coblin (1995) and Coblin (1996) believe that it is very difficult to say which dialect(s) the 韻鏡 *Yùnjìng* is based on. Be it as may, it is almost certain that, in the years between the 切韻 *Qièyùn* and the 韻鏡 *Yùnjìng*, the basis of the 'standard' (at least for

[18] For a different interpretation of the 切韻 *Qièyùn* data, see Pulleyblank (1984, 1998).

literary pronunciations) had somehow changed. In the Northern Song period, with the establishment of a new capital in Kaifeng, not very far from Luoyang, there may have been a new eastward shift of the prestige variety, although the details are still unclear (Pulleyblank 1984: 3; Chen Ping 1999: 10; Coblin 2007a: 15).

Note that, in this context, we use the terms 'standard' and 'prestige' variety with reference to what appears to be but a system of learned readings for Chinese characters. This is obviously quite different from the notion of 'standard language' which we have today. For Premodern China, Pulleyblank (1984: 2) defined the standard as 'an accepted norm for pronunciation among educated speakers in the country as a whole at any given time': thus, the only aspect that matters for the definition of the high, prestige variety is phonology (Chen Ping 1999: 9). Note that, for instance, in Ming times the closest concept to 'standard/official language' was arguably that of 正音 zhèngyīn, i.e. 'correct pronunciation' (Coblin 2000a: 541, 2000b: 269). As a matter of fact, according to Harbsmeier (2001: 377), even the 雅言 yǎyán mentioned in the Classical literature (see §2.2.1) is but an educated norm for pronunciation, rather than a real language. Interestingly, this perception of the 'standard' as, essentially, a phonological norm for reading has continued (*mutatis mutandis*) to the present day: the teaching of 普通話 Pǔtōnghuà in primary education is often focussed on standard phonology (Saillard 2004: 155–6). An institution which had an important role in the definition of the standard as a set of literary readings is the system of imperial examination for civil service (科舉 kējǔ), established in 605, and abolished only thirteen centuries later (1905): since rhyming writing was a crucial skill required to pass the examination, an educated norm for literary pronunciation was essential to enable candidates to identify which characters actually rhymed (Chen Ping 1999: 9); rime dictionaries were compiled also for this use.

However, there is also another sense, closer to the current one, in which 'standard language' may be used with reference to the situation of Premodern China: this is the administrative *koinè* which was supposedly used in communication between civil servants (as well as, arguably, other social groups) from different regions of China. While it is hard to pinpoint the exact nature of this *koinè*, it is likely that it was some sort of compromise among dialects with 'floating norms' (Norman and Coblin 1995: 581), constantly negotiated and modelled on the specific needs of interdialectal communication, and whose basic structure was Northern (Chen Ping 1999: 11–12).[19] In all likelihood, before the Contemporary Age, the standard spoken languages of each period were in fact second languages for the vast majority of the Chinese population, who had one or more dialects as their mother tongues (Coblin 2000a: 549).

A crucial juncture in the linguistic history of China is the establishment of the Yuan Dynasty and the rise of Dadu (大都 *Dàdū*), what is now called Beijing, as the imperial capital. As said in §2.2.2, at this stage (almost) all modern dialect groups had already separated: this is then conventionally seen as the beginning of Mandarin *stricto sensu*. The English term 'Mandarin' translates MSC 官話 *guānhuà*, lit. 'speech of the officers (mandarins)',[20] which was used to refer to the administrative *koinè* of the Ming and Qing periods; however, scholars also use 'Old Mandarin' (早期官話 *zǎoqī guānhuà*) to indicate the (hypothetical) Yuan Dynasty standard language (Coblin 2000a: 537; see §2.2.5). As hinted at earlier, in current usage 'Mandarin' indicates either MSC, or the group of Northern dialects (北方方言 *běifāng fāngyán*) as a whole.

Our knowledge of Old Mandarin mostly relies on the fourteenth-century rime book 中原音韻 *Zhōngyuán yīnyùn* ('Rhymes of the Central Plains'), based on the language used in the popular and colloquial 曲 *qǔ* verse and on the corpus of texts written in a contemporary phonographic alphabet, the 'Phags-pa script (Norman 1988: 48–52; we will get back to 'Phags-pa in §3.2.2 and 4.1.1). However, not all scholars agree that the 中原音韻 *Zhōngyuán yīnyùn* and the 'Phags-pa corpus reflect the same language. The former might be either based on a variety of the Yuan capital Dadu (大都 *Dàdū*), i.e. present-day Beijing, or on the phonology of the Luoyang-Kaifeng area, or even on one or more Northern *koinai*; the latter probably reflects a compromise among the learned literary readings of different regions of the empire, being thus different from the 中原音韻 *Zhōngyuán yīnyùn* 'language' (Coblin 2007a: 18–22; see also Coblin 1999).

While it is hard to pinpoint the exact background of the varieties reflected in the representative texts of Old Mandarin, it clearly appears

---

[19] We may suggest a comparison with present-day English, a polycentric language with many dialects and varieties: despite the differences, e.g. between Scottish English, American English, and New Zealand English, especially in the phonology, communication is normally unproblematic: films and TV series, for instance, are distributed in any English-speaking territory in the same form.

[20] Probably from Portuguese *mandarim* < Malay *mantari* < Sanskrit *mantrín* 'counsellor'.

that, despite the fact that the capital had been moved to Dadu/Beijing, during Yuan times the Beijing dialect was not necessarily the prestige variety; oral communication within the Chinese *élites* still relied on a heterogeneous system, mostly based on Central Plains varieties. Interestingly, despite the widespread belief that the dialect of the current imperial capital had always played an essential role in shaping the standard, and that 官話 *guānhuà* has been based on a Beijing variety since its early days, historical research has convincingly shown that, from Ming times until the mid-nineteenth century, the Jiang-Huai Mandarin dialect of Nanjing was the basis of the prestige variety (Chen Ping 1999; Coblin 2000a, 2000b, 2002b). If we compare the phonology of the standard from the mid-fifteenth century and the early seventeenth century, which has been reconstructed on the basis of phonographic transcription in Korean and missionary sources (see §4.1.1), we see an evolution from a central variety with Southern features, arguably deriving from the late Song administrative language, towards a system with a Jiang-Huai Mandarin-type phonology (Coblin 2000a, 2000b, 2002b, 2007b, 2007c). The dominance of Jiang-Huai Mandarin in this context may be explained (among other factors) by the presence in this subbranch of archaic distinctions which had already been lost in Mandarin dialects to the North; Southern Mandarin was hence, in a sense, closer to the classical language (Kaske 2008: 41–2).

Does this entail that 官話 *guānhuà* and the Nanjing dialect are one and the same thing? Probably not, since the phonology of 官話 *guānhuà* was, again, arguably a compromise among different varieties, as shown by the inclusion of Northern Mandarin, non-Jiang-Huai features in it (as e.g. the distinction between initial [n] and [l], absent in Nanjing; Coblin 2000a: 541–2). The linguistic dominance of Nanjing over Beijing well into the nineteenth century is explicitly acknowledged also in foreign sources, as in Robert Morrison's *Dictionary of the Chinese Language* (1815, qtd. in Coblin 2002b: 29):

The pronunciation in this work, is rather what the Chinese call the Nanking dialect, than the Peking. [...]

What is called the Mandarin dialect, or 官話 Kwan hwa, is spoken generally in 江南 Keang-nan and 河南 Ho-nan provinces

We may thus conclude that, until at least the first half of the nineteenth century, the 'Mandarin' described by Western missionaries was the expression of a large area, which included the low Yangtze and Henan province, in the Central Plains.

To sum up, the Mandarin in use in Ming and Qing times, just as all other *koinai* discussed before, is in fact a system with a compromise phonology, which was based more or less on the dialects of a specific area in different times, but never equal to an individual variety (Coblin 2002b: 31–2). Moreover, this 官話 *guānhuà* varied in different regions, and those diatopic differences were recorded in descriptions, mostly by foreign authors. For instance, in the Japanese textbook 唐話纂要 *Tōwa sanyō* (1716), the 'Mandarin' described includes Wu features, and closely resembles the Hangzhou dialect: as a matter of fact, the Japanese considered the Hangzhou variety of of 官話 *guānhuà*, as a prestige variety, together with Nanjing Mandarin (VanNess Simmons 1997; Coblin 2000a). Beijing 官話 *guānhuà* itself is mentioned, for instance in the *Arte de la lengua mandarina*, a Mandarin grammar by the Spanish missionary Francisco Varo (1703; manuscript revised in 1793; Coblin and Levi 2000); in the *Arte*, Beijing Mandarin is treated as a diatopic variety of 官話 *guānhuà* (Coblin 2003: 239–40). Incidentally, this entails that even the adoption of Beijing 官話 *guānhuà* as the 'official' language of the court rituals around the mid-eighteenth century did not have immediate consequences for its status, as opposed to Southern Mandarin (Kaske 2008: 52–3).

By the second half of the nineteenth century, the Beijing variety seemingly became the standard for 官話 *guānhuà*: for instance, the 'Chinese' textbooks by Joseph Edkins (1864) and Thomas Wade (1867) describe precisely the Mandarin of the imperial capital (Coblin 2003: 199). Two important factors in the rise of Beijing 官話 *guānhuà*, apart from its status in the imperial court, were the opening of the foreign legations in the capital, turning the Beijing variety into the *de facto* language of diplomacy (Kaske 2008: 67), and the decline of the city of Nanjing following the devastations occurred during the Taiping Rebellion (1850–62; Chen Ping 1999: 11; Coblin 2002a: 540). However, it still appears that, even at this time, Nanjing 官話 *guānhuà* remained the most commonly used variety of Mandarin in use in the Qing Empire (Coblin 2000a: 541; Kaske 2008: 54); as we shall see in the next section, Beijing Mandarin was held in low esteem by many Chinese intellectuals up until the first half of the twentieth century. Moreover, note that this shift in the standard towards Northern Mandarin was mostly limited to phonology and, to a lesser extent, the lexicon (including function words); the syntax is instead very close to the 官話 *guānhuà* of previous times (Coblin 2000a; 2002b). It is also important here to stress that 'Beijing 官話 *guānhuà*' is not actually the same as 'Beijing dialect': in the above-mentioned *Grammar of the Chinese colloquial language commonly called the Mandarin dialect* (1864), Edkins specified that, in Beijing, one could hear two varieties: Beijing Mandarin (北京官話 *Běijīng guānhuà*) and the Beijing dialect (京話 *jīnghuà*, lit. 'speech of the capital'), which were distinct from one another (Coblin 2003: 237–8).[21]

To conclude, the history of 官話 *guānhuà* may be seen as the slow evolution of a Southern Mandarin, Jiang-Huai-type system towards a phonology with more Northern Mandarin features: the result of this process has been described as 'a complex tapestry of phonological, lexical and grammatical features, woven from strands taken from southern GH [官話 *guānhuà*], received northern standards, and the local northern dialects' (Coblin 2003: 240). This variety is the backbone of Modern Standard Chinese: following the 'National Conference on Script Reform' (全國文字改革會議 *Quánguó Wénzì Gǎigé Huìyì*) and the 'Symposium on the Standardization of Modern Chinese' (現代漢語規范化學術會議 *Xiàndài Hànyǔ Guīfànhuà Xuéshù Huìyì*) in October 1955, the new national language, namely the above-mentioned 普通話 *Pǔtōnghuà* (§2.1), was defined as the standard form of Chinese having the 'Northern' (i.e. Mandarin) dialects as its base dialect, with the Beijing dialect as its standard for phonology and modern works in the 白話 *báihuà* vernacular as the grammatical norm (§2.2.2; Chen Ping 1999: 23–4). However, the process of the fixation of the norm for Modern Chinese was far from linear. In the next section, we will briefly discuss the key aspects of this process, which are crucial for our understanding the role of language ideologies in the shaping of the Chinese language.

2.2.4 The birth of a national language

As said earlier, a fundamental dichotomy which has characterized Chinese culture since its early days is that between written and spoken language. Suffice it to say that there is no traditional term to indicate

---

[21] Moreover, even Beijing 官話 *guānhuà* was not a homogeneous language: there was a more colloquial form, termed 'true Mandarin' (真官話 *zhēn guānhuà*), and a more ornate form, used in ceremonial settings, termed 'cultured speech' (文話 *wénhuà*; Coblin 2003: 237–8).

'language' as a whole, but rather one for the written language, 文字 *wénzì*, and one for the spoken language, 語言 *yǔyán* (Kaske 2008: 32): they were then joined to create the expression 語言文字 *yǔyán wénzì* 'spoken and written language'. On the other hand, even the written language had, so to say, a 'spoken' side, i.e. it could be read aloud; but, again, the phonology of reading the literary language had an indirect relation with actual spoken language, as already mentioned.

In fact, until the end of the eighteenth century, imperial governments were virtually only concerned with the norms for reading and writing in Classical Chinese, the language of Chinese culture *par excellence*, as well as the gateway to a succesful career in the administrative *élite*: the purpose of rime books and tables, as mentioned before (§2.2.3), was basically that of sanctioning the 'correct' pronunciation for classical texts. Generally speaking, that was the case for all native Chinese prescriptive works on language until relatively recent times: the first grammatical description (again, of Literary Chinese) produced by a Chinese linguist was Ma Jianzhong's (馬建中 *Mǎ Jiànzhōng*, 1845–1900) 馬氏文通 *Mǎshì Wéntōng* 'Mr Ma's Grammar', published only in 1898, and under evident foreign influence (see Mair 1997). And, interestingly, native scholars seemed to be aware of the chasm between literary norms and actual spoken norms in phonology: for instance, in the mid-eighteenth century, the philologist Jiang Yong (江永 *Jiāng Yǒng*) distinguishes the notions of 正音 *zhèngyīn* 'correct pronunciation' (see §2.2.3) and of 官音 *guānyīn* 'official/Mandarin pronunciation', i.e. the phonology of the administrative *koinè* (§2.2.3); in the well-known Kangxi Dictionary (康熙字典 *Kāngxī Zìdiǎn*, 1716), we find also the 'current' reading of the characters, but still in a conservative phonological framework. Also, note that the system of pronunciations of the Kangxi Dictionary was considered an important reference until the end of the Qing Dynasty, almost two centuries later (Kaske 2008: 43–9).

Thus, the diffusion of a norm for the spoken *koinè* was almost never part of official language policies until recent times. A notable exception is represented by a 1728 edict of the Qing emperor Yongzheng (雍正 *Yōngzhèng*), who imposed the requirement of learning the 'correct pronunciation' of 官話 *guānhuà* to officials from the Southern provinces of Fujian and Guangdong, whose dialects were very distant from the Mandarin-based *koinè*: to this end, a system of 正音書院 *zhèngyīn shūyuàn* 'academies for correct pronunciation' was established. However, this requirement quickly turned into a mere recommendation (1737), and most academies closed shortly after (Kaske 2008); in 1840, English interpreter Robert Thom wrote that the linguistic situation in Guangdong was in essence unchanged, if compared to one century earlier (Masini 1993: 4). For the common people, especially in Southern China, the knowledge of 官話 guānhuà was probably very limited, or even non-existent. Again, interesting insights on the topic may be found in the writings of foreign observers, as for instance in those of British consul Henry Gribble: having arrived in Xiamen (Fujian) in 1843 with two interpreters from Guangzhou, he soon realized that they could not understand either the local dialect or 官話 guānhuà, and thus had to hire two more translators, 'one who spoke the local dialect and knew a little English having lived in Singapore, and the other to translate the dialect into guanhua' (Masini 1993: 13). In 1888, Presbyterian mission-ary Absalom Sydenstricker (Pearl Sydenstricker Buck's father) com-plained that, as to phonology, there was no 'universal' 官話 guānhuà in China: if the lexicon and syntax of the koinè were quite uniform, the differences in phonology were so vast that, in his words, 'Nanking dia-lect is not understood in Chinkiang [鎮江 Zhènjiāng] (40 miles)' (qtd. in Kaske 2008: 72); thus, dialects remained a very important means to spread the Christian faith among the commoners.[22]

As to the written language(s), literature in the 白話 báihuà vernacu-lar (§2.2.2), which was surely closer to spoken varieties, enjoyed great popularity in Ming and Qing times: the so-called 'Four Great Novels' (四大名著 Sì Dà Míngzhù), among the most popular and influential works of Chinese literature (including the *Journey to the West* and the *Dream of the Red Chamber*), were written in 白話 báihuà, rather than in Literary Chinese. Nevertheless, until the beginning of the twentieth century, 白話 báihuà remained a low prestige variety, a *Schreibdialekt*, also (or, perhaps, mostly) because it had no role in imperial examin-ations; as a matter of fact, it was also referred to as 俗話 súhuà, lit. 'vul-gar/popular speech' (Kaske 2008: 32, 106). Thus, 文言 wényán, which was largely divorced from the spoken languages, was the only written language taught systematically in formal education, which was anyway

---

[22] However, some Catholic missionaries of the sixteenth and seventeenth century sug-gest instead that 官話 guānhuà was used in all social groups (see Coblin 2000a and Raini 2010). The different pictures painted may be explained by the contexts in which Western merchants, diplomats, and missionaries worked in the nineteenth century: namely, Southern provinces, rural areas, and minor cities, where the koinè was arguably less dif-fused (see Masini 1993: 8–9).

a privilege of a minority of the population (see the data in Kaske 2008: 33–4).

However, China's disastrous defeats in the Opium Wars (1839–42 and 1856–60) and in the Sino-Japanese War (1894–5) led to profound changes in the Chinese political and cultural landscape; language was no exception. The humiliation suffered at the hands of the Western powers and Japan, which until then was considered to be 'more or less a Chinese cultural colony' (Masini 1993: 89), brought a sense of great uncertainty within the Chinese *intelligentsia*, who realized the weakness of China, facing the threat of the great world powers of the time. Thus, the modernization of the country came to be regarded as crucial for its survival; since Japan has already gone through a successful season of reforms and 'Westernization' of the country, the so-called 'Meiji renovation' (Jap. 明治維新 *Meiji ishin*, 1868–90; also known as 'Meiji restoration'), it easily became a model for Chinese reformers.

In the debate on the modernization of the country, two tightly connected issues came to the forefront: the reform of the educational system, then regarded as one of the main reasons for China's backwardness, and the language issue (Kaske 2008: 78). Parallel to this was the problem of the burden of logographic writing in the process of teaching literacy to the masses: plans for the substitution or integration of Chinese characters with phonographic writing were also part of the debate (Chen Ping 1999: 165–6). The history of the different positions and movements on issues related to education and language during this period is very complex and we cannot present it extensively here (the reader is referred to Chen Ping 1999 and Kaske 2004, 2008); in what follows, we will just propose a brief overview of the most relevant intellectual and political trends, and we postpone the discussion of proposals on the reform of writing to §3.2.3.

In the mind of many progressive thinkers, as e.g. Huang Zunxian (黃遵憲 *Huáng Zūnxiàn*, 1848–1905) and Liang Qichao (梁啟超 *Liáng Qǐchāo*, 1873–1929), among many others, Japan's success in mass education and literacy was tightly connected with the outcomes of the 'Movement for the Unification of Spoken and Written Language' (Jap. 言文一致運動 *Genbun Itchi Undō*), a current of opinion in favour of the adoption of a national written language based on the spoken language; as a consequence, the parallel Chinese expression 言文合一 *yán wén héyì* became very popular at this time. As already mentioned, in 1905, a few years before the dawn of the Republic (1912), the system of imperial examinations was abolished: this entailed that 文言 *wényán* lost much of its relevance, as it was no longer the gateway to a career in the administration. Between the end of the nineteenth century and the early twentieth century, vernacular publications written in some form of 白話 *báihuà* flourished: while the Northern variety was dominant as always, dialectal works from the South of the country were far from marginal (see Fn. 13); we will get back to this in §3.3.1.

Nevertheless, the newly established national educational system (1904), designed after the Western and Japanese models, still had the Confucian doctrine at its core, taught through rote memorization of the classics; thus, Literary Chinese remained the dominant written language in schools. Confucianism was still perceived by imperial authorities, as well as by many intellectuals, as crucial for the cultural identity of the country, and, obviously, the language of the foundational texts could not be forsaken (Kaske 2008: 233–4). The only concession towards spoken varieties in education was the introduction of a style of writing termed 普通文 *pǔtōngwén*, lit. 'common style' (< Jap. 普通文 *futsūbun*; Kaske 2008: 276), which was somehow a compromise between Literary and Vernacular Chinese. Even the many translations of European and Japanese works which appeared during this period were mostly written in 文言 *wényán*: in point of fact, one of the most important translators of the time, Yan Fu (嚴復 *Yán Fù*, 1854–1921), used to write in a very archaic language which was hard to understand for his contemporaries, even though he dealt with modern themes and made ample use of neologisms (Masini 1993: 114–5).

Towards the end of the first decade of the twentieth century, the growing opposition to Literary Chinese found support in the so-called 'New Culture Movement' (新文化運動 *Xīn Wénhuà Yùndòng*), and in the 'May Fourth Movement' (五四運動 *Wǔ-Sì Yùndòng*, 1919),[23] in which some of the most influential individuals in modern Chinese history were involved: Hu Shi (胡適 *Hú Shì*, 1891–1962), Chen Duxiu (陳獨秀 *Chén Dúxiù*, 1879–1942, co-founder of the Chinese Communist Party) and Lu Xun (魯迅 *Lǔ Xùn*, 1881–1936). Both movements supported the modernization, opening up, and democratization of China, and it was believed that the substitution of 文言 *wényán* with 白話 *báihuà* was required to spread education and culture among the masses,

---

[23] The 'May Fourth Movement' started as a student protest following the transferring to Japan of the German concessions in Shandong set out in the Versailles Treaty.

and to leave behind Chinese traditional culture, considered to be a burden for the progress of the country (Chen Ping 1999: 72, 79); the 'Literary Revolution' (文學革命 *Wénxué Gémìng*) promoted by Hu Shi and by other members of the 'New Culture Movement' in 1917 contributed to the growing prestige of 白話 *báihuà* in the Chinese *intelligentsia* of the time, including many conservative figures (Kaske 2008: xix–xx). Besides, the end of the Empire and the establishment of the Republican Parliament gave to the reformers more opportunities to contribute to the renewal of school curricula; in 1920, the Ministry of Education of the young Republic of China mandated the use of 白話 *báihuà* in textbooks, and advised to limit the presence of 文言 *wényán* in education. Within a decade, Vernacular Chinese took the place of 文言 *wényán* both as the standard written language (Chen Ping 1999: 76–7) and as an element of national unity (Kaske 2004: 283).

However, at his stage 白話 *báihuà* was still a fuzzy entity, and it was not fully developed as a comprehensive and effective instrument for written communication (Chen Ping 1999: 78). As hinted at before (see Fn. 13), 白話 *báihuà* was a label which could be applied, in principle, to any written style based on a spoken variety, with considerable variation within Sinitic; moreover, vocabulary items and constructions could be drawn from Literary Chinese to a lesser or greater extent, especially (and perhaps unexpectedly) for neologisms (Masini 1993: 119–20; see §5.2.1). Thus, the so-called 'new 白話 *báihuà*', i.e. the various styles of vernacular writing of progressive authors, was actually quite removed from contemporary spoken varieties (Chen Ping 1999: 76–7): this is perhaps unsurprising, given that, at the time, a standard for the spoken language was not precisely identified, and competence in this ill-defined standard was not very widespread. Moreover, even the most progressive intellectuals involved in language reform had been in fact educated in the traditional curriculum, based on the classics. This perception of 白話 *báihuà* as inadequate led to a continuous stylistic elaboration in the following years: Modern Written Chinese was thus born out of the 白話 *báihuà* of traditional popular literature, which was mostly based on Jiang-Huai and Northern Mandarin dialects, to which other dialectal items, words and idioms from 文言 *wényán*, and lexical and syntactic calques from European languages were then added (Chen Ping 1999: 82–7).

The other major issue which had to be faced on the road to modernity was, obviously, the standardization of the spoken language, in order

34

to provide a unified medium for education and for nationwide communication. Just as for the reform of the written language, in this case too the model for China came from Japan, where a 'National Language Research Committee' (国語調査委員会 *kokugo chōsa iinkai*) was established in 1902: as said in §2.1, the term 國語 *Guóyǔ*, which had been previously in use in China to refer to the language of the Manchu Qing rulers (or, anyway, to languages of non-Sinitic people; Norman 1988: 133; Mair 1994: 727), acquired its current meaning of 'national language' following Japanese usage. Until the very end of the Empire, the obvious candidate for the role of national language was still referred to as 官話 *guānhuà*, defined in essence as a phonological standard; for the written language, at this stage a sort of 'modernized' Literary Chinese, the label 國文 *Guówén* 'national literature' (< Jap. 国文 *kokubun*) was introduced (Kaske 2004). The publication of the 國語教科書 *Guóyǔ jiàokēshū* 'a *Guóyǔ* coursebook' in 1910, and its official adoption in the school curriculum, is a turning point for language reform: arguably for the first time in Chinese history, a unitary notion of 'language', both spoken and written, was accepted. Interestingly, however, the longstanding tradition of separating 文字 *wénzì* from 語言 *yǔyán* was so entrenched in Chinese culture that the above-mentioned modernized version of Literary Chinese, 國文 *guówén*, was still in use in the administration and education until the 1950s (Kaske 2004: 295–9). Again, this was also (perhaps, mostly), an ideological issue: rejecting Literary Chinese (even in the form of 國文 *guówén*) was tantamount to rejecting, in a sense, the Confucian tradition, while defending 文言 *wényán* meant also defending the traditional heritage (on language ideology in China between the nineteenth and early twentieth century, see Kaske 2008). The demise of Literary Chinese came only after the establishment of the P.R.C.: in fact, words, idioms, and constructions from Literary Chinese are more common in the written styles of Taiwan and Hong Kong, if compared to Mainland China, even to the present day (Chen Ping 1999: 88).

Just as seen earlier for the written language, the definition of the national spoken language was also achieved only after a long and intense debate, focussed on phonology in this case. While by the beginning of the twentieth century Beijing 官話 *guānhuà* was seemingly regarded as a prestige variety, the above-mentioned first 國語 *Guóyǔ* coursebook still reflected a composite phonological system, a compromise between Northern and Jiang-Huai Mandarin: many of the intellectuals, educators, and officials involved in language reform were of Southern Chinese origin and would not easily accept a wholesale shift to Beijing phon-ology. In fact, during the first half of the twentieth century the Beijing variety was far from unchallenged: other dialects, as those of Nanjing, Wuhan, and Shanghai, were proposed as base varieties for 國語 *Guóyǔ*; another option on the table was a compromise variety, which obviously had to include non-Beijing features in its phonology (Chen Ping 1999: 14). This is apparent in a key reference work produced in this period, the 'Dictionary of National Pronunciation' (國音字典 *Guóyīn Zìdiǎn*), published in 1919 following the indications of the 'Commission for Unifying Reading Pronunciation' (讀音統一會 *Dúyīn Tǒngyī Huì*): while the phonological system described in this dictionary largely over-laps with the Beijing variety, it retains archaic Northern traits, as well as features of other dialects, mostly Wu and (non-Northern) Mandarin. Thus, it does not correspond precisely to any single individual dialect (Chen Ping 1999: 17–18); the inclusion of historically and diatopically inconsistent features meant that this 'standard' was not well suited for actual use (Dong Hongyuan 2014: 132).

Another turning point in the history of spoken Mandarin was the publication of the revised edition of the aforementioned dictionary in 1932.[24] The 'New National Pronunciation' (新國音 *xīn guóyīn*) sanc-tioned in this version was entirely based on the Beijing variety: hence, for the first time what was standardized was not an artificial system, mostly based on literary readings of characters, but, rather, an actual dialect in its current form (Chen Ping 1999: 21–2). However, up until the mid-fifties, there were still attempts at 'watering down' Beijing Mandarin with elements from other dialects: in the debate for the def-inition of the norm of 普通話 *Pǔtōnghuà*, there was still support in favour of retaining phonological distinction already lost in Beijing (Chen Ping 1999: 24). Also, one should not forget that 普通話 *Pǔtōnghuà* is still not a synonym of 'Beijing dialect': while the two varieties largely overlap, there are still important differences at all levels, including phon-ology (see §4.2.1). As pointed out by Zhou Minglang (2012: 3), 普通話 *Pǔtōnghuà* 'was an imagined standard language for a growing modern nation in the 1950s' and started out 'without any native speakers'.

To sum up, in this concise presentation of the key events in the his-tory of Chinese we highlighted an essential trait of Chinese linguistic

---

[24] With the revised title 國音常用字彙 *Guóyīn Chángyòngzì Huì* 'A lexicon of Frequently Used Characters with their National Pronunciation' (Chen Ping 1999: 20).

ideology: namely, the strong separation between the written language and the spoken language, and between the officially sanctioned literary language and informal writing. Only Literary Chinese, modelled after the classical language, was considered to be worthy of the designation of 文 *wén* 'written sign' (Kaske 2008: 31), as the vehicle of transmission of Chinese culture and a symbol of national unity. This 'sacred' status of the classical language was challenged after the encounter with the major world powers in the nineteenth century: however, the radication of Literary Chinese in the tradition was so strong that it could somehow resist until roughly the first half of the twentieth century, when it was superseded by (written) Modern Standard Chinese. The devotion towards the literary tradition was reflected also in the attitude towards spoken varieties: until recently, 'spoken standard(s)' corresponded, in essence, to a norm for the correct reading of literary texts. We had to wait until the twentieth century to witness the development of a new, comprehensive conception of 'language', both spoken and written, and grounded in actual use. To conclude this overview of Chinese linguistic history, we now move to the topic of the debate on the periodization of Chinese.

2.2.5 The periodization of Chinese

Chinese thinkers were aware of the fact that language changes from very early on (Branner 2000: 6); nevertheless, the beginning of research in Chinese historical linguistics is conventionally associated with Qing period philologists, who studied the pronunciation of classical texts in order to correctly interpret them (Norman 1988: 42). As to periodization, the first proposal had to wait until the twentieth century, and it came from a Swedish scholar, the well-known sinologist Bernhard Karlgren (1889–1978; Tai and Chan 1999). Karlgren was also the first to propose a complete reconstruction of Old Chinese (see §4.1.1); since, just as his Chinese predecessors, he was concerned with phonology, his periodization is based only on this level of analysis. The tendency to elaborate periodizations based only or mainly on one aspect of language (mostly, phonology or syntax) is common also to many later proposals: this explains why there are so many differences among them. For reasons of space, here we shall not discuss Karlgren's periodization (see Norman 1988: 23); we will rather introduce some more recent schemes for periodization.

In current, non-specialistic usage, the most commonly used labels for the main historical stages of Chinese are 'Old Chinese' (上古漢語 *shànggǔ Hànyǔ*), 'Middle Chinese' (中古漢語 *zhōnggǔ Hànyǔ*),[25] and 'Modern Chinese' (現代漢語 *xiàndài Hànyǔ*, lit. 'Contemporary Chinese'); we may add to these a less common term, 'Early Mandarin' (近代漢語 *jìndài Hànyǔ*, lit. 'Modern Chinese'), used to refer to the language from the Song period to the mid-nineteenth century. In Chinese usage, both Old and Middle Chinese are sometimes subsumed under the generic label 古漢語 *gǔ Hànyǔ*, lit. 'Old Chinese', here loosely referring to all premodern forms of Chinese. However, these periods are very long, and far from homogeneous; moreover, there is no general agreement on their definition. Besides, many different proposals for the periodization of Chinese have been made, with a strong dividing line between phonology-based and syntax-based periodization (with the lexicon playing a minor role).

In research on historical phonology, the Old Chinese period, in the broadest sense, is defined as the language from the earliest attestations up to the third century of the Common Era. Some set Qin unification as the limit for this stage (Baxter and Sagart 2014: 2), while more restrictive definitions include only the language of the first half of the Zhou Dynasty (Handel 2014: 578). Other scholars (including Karlgren) base their definitions of each historical stage of Chinese on the specific documents which they use for their reconstruction (see §4.1.1). Thus, for instance, Pulleyblank (1984, 1991, 1998) defines Old Chinese as the language of the *Classic of Poetry*; Middle Chinese is divided into an Early phase, associated with the 切韻 *Qièyùn*, and a Late phase, associated with the 韻鏡 *Yùnjìng* and other Song Dynasty rime tables; Early Mandarin is the language represented in the rime book 中原音韻 *Zhōngyuán Yīnyùn* (see §2.2.3; see also Baxter 1992: 15).

Many scholars (Norman and Coblin 1995; Tai and Chan 1999; Handel 2014) have already pointed out the shortcomings of such an approach to periodization: besides the fact that, needless to say, a periodization which takes into account only phonology is inevitably relevant only for phonology, rime books and dictionaries, as said in §2.2.3, reflect an 'artificial', learned tradition of readings which did not correspond to any

---

[25] In research on historical phonology, some choose to adopt Karlgren's conventions and use 'Archaic Chinese' for 'Old Chinese', and 'Ancient Chinese' for 'Middle Chinese' (Handel 2014: 577; see §4.1.1).

spoken variety of the time; thus, the systems reconstructed on the basis of rime books are not 'real' languages (but cf. Pulleyblank 1984: 130). Other authors proposed periodizations based on the most important phonological changes (e.g. Ting Pang-hsin 1996), which are however based on reconstructions, rather than on actual language data; given that there is no agreement on many aspects of the reconstruction of previous stages of Chinese, as we shall see later (§4.1.2, 4.2.3), this approach to periodization is heavily dependent on the underlying hypotheses on reconstruction (Tai and Chan 1999).

Syntax-based periodizations, on the other hand, have had a smaller impact in the field, if compared to phonology-based ones. This is explained by the relatively short history of research on diachronic morphology and syntax in Chinese linguistics (Peyraube 1996: 161–2), and by the uncertainty in the dating of many morphosyntactic innovations, also because of the strong influence of the literary model on Vernacular Chinese (Tai and Chan 1999). Also, there may be significant differences in the dating of an innovation because of discrepances in the definition of the innovation itself: some scholars look for the very first attestation of a given construction, while others take into consideration only the attestations which are close, or identical to, the modern usage of a given construction (Shi Yuzhi 2002: 23–5). An extreme case is that of the resultative construction (see §5.1.2): according to Shi Yuzhi (2002: 23), the datings which have been proposed in the literature for this construction range from the Shang period to the Tang Dynasty, a time span of almost two millennia.

In order to provide a rough picture of the disagreement among different proposals for the periodization of Chinese, we offer here a brief comparison among some models. Let us take as a starting point for our comparison the periodization proposed by Alain Peyraube (1996: 164; see Peyraube 1988 for the details), who identifies four major historical stages for Chinese, with three more transitional periods and two further subdivisions, yielding a total of nine substages:

a. Pre-Archaic Chinese, i.e. the language of the oracle bone inscriptions (fourteenth–eleventh century BC)
b. Early Archaic Chinese (tenth–sixth century BC)
c. Late Archaic Chinese (fifth–second century BC)
d. Pre-Medieval Chinese (first century BC–first century AD)
e. Early Medieval Chinese (second–sixth century)

    f. Late Medieval Chinese (seventh–mid-thirteenth century)

    g. Premodern Chinese (mid-thirteenth–fourteenth century)

    h. Modern Chinese (fifteenth–mid-nineteenth century)

    i. Contemporary Chinese (from the mid-nineteenth century on)

In Aldridge's (2013a) proposal, which is based on Peyraube's, the label 'Middle Chinese' is used instead of 'Medieval Chinese', and the period is considerably longer than Peyraube's Medieval Chinese, ranging from the second century BC to the end of the Tang Dynasty: this is because, she suggests, the main grammatical innovations characterizing Middle Chinese may be already found in Han Dynasty texts. Sun Chaofen (1996: 3) and Shi Yuzhi (2002: 21) also identify four major stages, but while Sun uses 'Early Mandarin' for the period between the beginning of the second millennium and 1900, and uses 'Modern Mandarin' for the language from the twentieth century on, Shi believes that 'Modern Chinese' begins in the sixteenth century, while the period from 901 to 1500, termed 'Premodern Chinese', is the time in which 'almost all of the grammatical changes which characterize Modern Chinese happened'. Moreover, both Sun and Shi date the beginning of Old Chinese considerably later than Peyraube's Archaic Chinese. A yet completely different proposal may be found in Lü Shuxiang (1985, qtd. in Tai and Chan 1999), who identifies only two (macro-)stages in the history of Chinese: namely, Old Chinese (古代漢語 *gǔdài Hànyǔ*), i.e. the language up to the tenth century, and 'Modern Chinese' (近代漢語 *jìndài Hànyǔ*). Interesingly, according to Lü, the contemporary language is not distinct enough from his 'Modern Chinese' to consider it as a separate stage in the history of the language; thus, in stark contrast with Shi Yuzhi's view, Lü Shuxiang does not seem to attach much importance to the changes that occurred between the tenth and the fifteenth century. According to Tai and Chan (1999), the most important changes in Chinese grammar occurred between the end of the Han Dynasty and the early Tang period, with the diffusion of classifiers and the genesis of several nominal affixes, and between the late Tang and early Song periods, when several modern syntactic constructions, and verb suffixes, emerged: thus, just as Lü Shuxiang (1985), Tai and Chan believe that the most important innovations in the grammar of Modern Chinese were introduced significantly earlier than what Shi Yuzhi (2002) proposed.

In short, even a brief overview as the present one, already shows that there appears to be no agreement on many non-trivial aspects of the history of Chinese grammar, regarding both the dating of morphosyntactic innovations and their relative importance in the definition of the historical stages of the language. As to the lexicon, we already mentioned that it had a minor role in the periodization of Chinese: in their overview of the issue, Tai and Chan (1999) mention only Pan Yunzhong's (1989) proposal, which is anyway primarily based more on major periods in Chinese history, rather than on developments in the lexicon. Tai and Chan (1999) actually propose their own (sketched) lexicon-based periodization for Chinese, distinguishing between native and foreign lexical items. For the native lexicon, they identify three historical stages, mostly based on changes in processes of word formation: pre-Qin, from late Han to early Tang, and late Tang and Song; for the imported lexicon, the two key moments are, again, the period from the late Han to the early Tang Dynasty, when many lexical items from Central Asia and Buddhist terms were introduced in Chinese, and the period following the Opium Wars, when a huge number of words of foreign origin flooded the Chinese lexicon (we shall get back to this in 5.2.1).

Not all scholars, however, have focussed only on one aspect of language in their periodization schemes. What is probably the best known attempt at a comprehensive periodization of Chinese is the one by Wang Li (1980 [1958]: 35). He identifies four major stages, separated by three transition periods:

a. Old Chinese (上古漢語 *Shànggǔ Hànyǔ*), from the earliest attestations to the third century AD
(transition period: third–fourth century)
b. Middle Chinese (中古漢語 *Zhōnggǔ Hànyǔ*), fourth–twelfth century
(transition period: thirteenth–fourteenth century)
c. Early Mandarin or Premodern Chinese (近代漢語 *jìndài Hànyǔ*), fourteenth century–1840
(transition period: 1840–1919)
d. Modern (or Contemporary) Chinese (現代漢語 *xiàndài Hànyǔ*), from 1919 on

Note that the first transition period coincides with the collapse of the central imperial authority under the pressure of the 'barbarians' from the North, which brought about all the consequences discussed earlier (§2.2.2), while the third and last transition period is the time between

the Opium Wars and the May Fourth Movement, one of the most crucial times in the history of Chinese (§2.2.4). The most interesting aspect
of this proposal is that, while being primarily based on syntax, it also
takes into account phonology and the lexicon. However, as highlighted
by Tai and Chan (1999), the relative weight of each component of language is not consistent: while Old Chinese is defined on the basis of
syntactic and phonological features, Middle Chinese is defined primarily on morphology and syntax, Early Mandarin exclusively on phonology, and Modern Chinese on syntax, morphology, and the lexicon. If
we were to consider only grammatical aspects in this periodization, we
would have to conclude that Modern Chinese grammar largely coincides with twelfth-century 白話 *báihuà* (i.e. Wang Li's Middle Chinese),
with the later addition of some syntactic constructions modelled after
European languages (Wang Li 1980 [1958]: 35).

On the basis of an analysis of a fairly large sample of schemes for
periodization, some of which were discussed in this section, Tai and
Chan (1999: 237) propose a periodization of Chinese including only two
(macro-)stages, following Lü Shuxiang's (1985) above-mentioned model:
an early stage, termed 'Classical Chinese' (古代漢語 *gǔdài Hànyǔ*), followed by 'Premodern Chinese' (近代漢語 *jìndài Hànyǔ*), which includes
also Contemporary Chinese. A key argument for their proposal is that
the period from the late Tang to the early Song Dynasty, i.e. their
Premodern Chinese, constitutes a major watershed in the history of
Chinese, in phonology, morphology, syntax, and also the lexicon.

However, given the problems with the reconstruction of the phonology of earlier stages of Chinese, the uncertainties concerning the dating of major grammatical innovations, and the relative independence of
lexical developments, we suspect that a periodization which takes
equally into account all of the above is probably not feasible. Tai and
Chan's approach, which is based on the individuation of one or more
moments of major changes at all levels, looks more promising; nevertheless, any proposed periodization is inevitably based on reconstructions and textual analyses which are far from uncontroversial, and
hence it is anyway hard to reach a general consensus on the subject.

Moreover, here we discussed the periodization of 'Chinese', but it
goes without saying that it is simply impossible that, for instance, Wang
Li's Old Chinese was a homogeneous language for more than fourteen
centuries, and diatopic variation was also part of the picture, in all likelihood (Baxter and Sagart 2014: 2); however, dialectal diversity, while

acknowledged by scholars, has not had any significant influence in the periodization of Chinese, especially as far as Old and Middle Chinese are concerned (Handel 2014: 578). More generally, the fact that, as seen in §2.2.3, the 'standard' (i.e. the prestige variety) was different at different times, with considerable admixture of varieties (and sociolects), means that we cannot take the historical stages of Chinese as the product of a linear process of evolution, especially for phonology (see Matisoff 1991: 472). Take, for instance, the two substages of Middle Chinese identified by Pulleyblank: Early and Late Middle Chinese are known to be based on different varieties which, in all likelihood, did not reflect any spoken variety of the time, as mentioned in §1.2.3: they are the product of a composite literary tradition, and probably include many archaisms. Nevertheless, for the purposes of reconstruction, Late Middle Chinese is treated *as if* it were derived from Early Middle Chinese (Pulleyblank 1984: 129–30).

To conclude, while we recognize that any proposal for periodization involves some arbitrary choices, in this book we chose to follow Wang Li's model, which seems to have gained some degree of acceptance in the field. However, given the above-mentioned limitations of this scheme, we provide explicit temporal indications (e.g. 'tenth century', 'late Tang', etc.) whenever appropriate. Also, we would like to stress the point that here we discussed only the history of Chinese starting from the earliest attestations of the language; however, Karlgren's original model, for instance, included a 'Proto-Chinese' stage, predating the earliest documents. According to Baxter and Sagart (2014: 2–3), it is likely that a hypothetical Sinitic protolanguage was not very distant from the oldest attestations and, hence, it is not easy to make a meaningful distinction between Proto-Chinese/Sinitic and Old Chinese. Due to reasons of space, here we shall not discuss the matter any further, and we shall focus on the attested history of Sinitic.

2.3 The classification of Sinitic languages

The debate concerning the classification of Sinitic languages revolves around two fundamental issues: the genetic position of Sinitic as a whole, and its internal structure. While both questions have been, and still are, controversial, the latter has been the object of a particularly intense scholarly debate, especially in recent times (see e.g. Branner

1999, 2000; VanNess Simmons 1999a-b; Norman 1988, 1999, 2003; Baxter 2006; Kurpaska 2010; Chirkova 2013). Also, the issue of the genetic affiliation of Sinitic inevitably overlaps with that of its areal typology: both aspects must be taken into consideration for a proper understanding of the history and present of Chinese languages.

2.3.1 Sinitic languages: genealogy and typology

The current shape of Sinitic and, generally speaking, of the languages of East and Southeast Asia has been determined to a significant extent by contact, as briefly mentioned in §2.2.2. A particularly important factor in this connection is, obviously, the Chinese colonization of the South, which led to the creation of a fertile ground for language contact (and acculturation) with speakers of Tai-Kadai, Hmong-Mien, and Austroasiatic languages.

With the application of the comparative method, researchers have convincingly argued that Sinitic is related to Tibeto-Burman: the family to which they belong is generally termed 'Sino-tibetan' (漢藏語系 *Hàn-Zàng yǔxì*). As is standard in historical-comparative linguistics, the genetic relationship among Sino-Tibetan languages is argued on the basis of shared lexicon and morphology. As to the lexicon, a handy diagnostic is the form of the lexemes 'five', 'fish', and 'I', which should all be traceable back to a form close to *ŋa* (Handel 2008: 425): compare, for instance, Written Tibetan *ŋa* 'I' with Old Chinese *η^{ς}aj? (BSOL), Bodo *aŋ*, Chang Naga *ŋò*, (Jianchuan) Bai *ŋo³¹*, Guiqiong *ŋø³⁵*, and Jingpho *ŋai³³* (and Proto-Tibeto-Burman *ŋa; see Table 1 in Handel 2008: 425); the reconstructed Proto-Sino-Tibetan etymon for this is *ŋa-y (Matisoff 2003: 605).[26] As to morphology, these are some of the affixes which are commonly considered as characteristic of Sino-Tibetan (and see §5.1.2):

(6)   The causative (also 'denominative' and 'intensive') prefix *s- (Mei 1989; Sagart 1999b; Pulleyblank 2004): OC *mə-lək (MSC 食 *shí*) 'eat' vs. *s-m-lək-s (飼 *sì*) 'feed'; Jingpho *lòt* 'run away' vs. *šəlòt* 'to free' (with palatalization of *s–; Matisoff 2003: 101); Written Tibetan *grib* 'shadow' vs. *sgrib-pa* 'darken (trans.)' (LaPolla 2017: 40)

---

[26] A list of lexemes which may be used as a diagnostic for Sinitic may be found in Norman (2003: 72–5).

(7)   The alternation of voiceless and voiced initial consonants, corresponding to a valency change (transitive/intransitive; LaPolla 2003;
Jacques 2017a): MC *paejH* 'defeat' (OC *pˤrat-s) vs. *baejH* 'be
defeated' (OC *N-pˤrat-s; MSC 敗*bài*; BSOL); Bahing *kuk* 'make
bent' vs. *guk* 'be bent', Bodo *pheŋ* 'make straight' vs. *beŋ* 'be straight'
(LaPolla 2017: 41)

(8)   The nominalizing suffix *-s (Sagart 1999b; LaPolla 2007; Matisoff
2003): Old Chinese *s-tˤrek 'demand a payment' (MSC 責 *zé*
'demand') vs. *s-tˤrek-s 'debt' (MSC 債 *zhài*; Sagart 1999b: 133);
Qiang *nə* 'sleep' vs. *nəs* 'bed'; Written Tibetan *graŋ* 'count' vs.
graŋ-s 'number' (Matisoff 2003: 466–7; see §4.1 and 5.1.2)

However, it clearly appears that the typological profile of modern
Sinitic languages is much closer to that of Thai or Hmong, for instance,
rather than to Tibeto-Burman languages as Tibetan or Jingpho (see
Norman 1988: 11). Besides, the number of lexical items of Chinese origin in some East and Southeast Asian languages is far from trivial, even
in the basic vocabulary: for instance, Thai numerals from 2 to 10 all
derive from (Old and Middle) Chinese (Thai *sǎam* 'three' < MC *sam*;
Thai *hâa* < OC *C.ŋˤaʔ; Suthiwan 2009; BSOL).[27] This has led some to
propose that Sinitic may be related to Tai-Kadai, Hmong-Mien, and/or
Austroasiatic and Austronesian; in fact, some have suggested that
Chinese might be part of an even broader genealogical grouping, as we
shall see later.

Currently, the most widely accepted position among scholars sees
Sinitic as an independent branch of the Sino-Tibetan family. However,
there is no universally accepted definition of this family, in terms of its
internal structure and of the affiliated languages; Handel (2008: 423)
even suggests that there is no conclusive proof of the existence of a
Sino-Tibetan family, and there may be alternative (non-genetic) explanations for the similarities between, for instance, Chinese and Tibetan. A
key problem in Sino-Tibetan linguistics is that different scholars have
taken as the basis of their research different reconstructions, especially
for Old Chinese (Norman 1988: 14); this has been highlighted, for

---

[27] For further examples of (early) Chinese loans in the languages of the area, see the
World Loanword Database <http://wold.clld.org/language/211> and <http://wold.clld.org/
language/248> (last access: 26 April 2018). For the notation used here for Middle and Old
Chinese, see §4.1.

instance, by van Driem (1997: 461, 2005a: 301–2), who notes that, for instance, Baxter and Sagart's reconstruction of Old Chinese is much more 'Tibeto-Burman-like' than Karlgren's early proposal (see §4.1.2). Moreover, as said earlier, a solid argumentation for a genetic relationship should include some evidence of shared morphological processes, and not only shared lexicon; as modern Sinitic languages have a strong isolating profile, with a (nearly) total lack of inflection, comparison may be based only on reconstructed Old Chinese morphology, thus providing an uncertain base for comparison (Pulleyblank 1995b; Branner 2002; Jacques 2017a; see §4.1.1, 5.1.2). Reconstruction and comparison are further complicated by the great diversity displayed by Tibeto-Burman languages, with historical data available only for a small number of them; and, again, the dramatic decomplexification undergone by many languages and branches of Tibeto-Burman caused a loss of the kind of morphological evidence on which solid classification should be based (DeLancey 2015: 61). Needless to say, a thorough discussion of the problems in the classification of Sino-Tibetan is well beyond the scope of the present volume; here we shall just focus on the main issues concerning Sinitic languages.[28]

Put very briefly, a widely accepted model sees Sinitic and Tibeto-Burman as the two major branches of the Sino-Tibetan family; however, there are competing models, though not as widely accepted (see Matisoff 2003; Thurgood 2017). For instance, Van Driem (1997) proposed that Sinitic is closer to Bodic (≈ Tibetan) languages, and the two constitute a 'Sino-Bodic' branch of the 'Tibeto-Burman' (rather than 'Sino-Tibetan') family; while the reception of this model has been lukewarm (Jacques 2017a), it had the merit of calling into question the position of Sinitic within the broad family (Handel 2008: 431). In fact, given our limited knowledge of the history of Sino-Tibetan languages, some prefer an 'agnostic' family tree, with tens of independent branches.

---

[28] A much debated issue in Sino-Tibetan linguistics which is directly relevant to Sinitic is the position of Bai (白語 Báiyǔ), a minority language (with three main dialects) of Southwestern China. While some treat Bai as genetically closer to Tibeto-Burman, others suggest that it might be actually Sinitic, particularly because of the astonishingly high number of morphemes and words of Chinese origin even in its basic lexicon (Norman 2003; Wiersma 2003; Wang Feng 2005). Due to reasons of space, here we mention just a recent paper by Lee and Sagart (2008), who show how Sinitic lexical items in Bai actually belong to three distinct diachronic strata. Moreover, some key basic lexemes, as the numerals a^{21} 'one' and ko^{33} 'two', are clearly Tibeto-Burman: compare e.g. (Taoping) Qiang a^{31} 'one', Jingpho $la^{55}khoŋ^{51}$ 'two'). According to Lee and Sagart, this is evidence of the fact that Bai is a Tibeto-Burman language, although strongly influenced by Chinese.

While this is an unlikely scenario, it allows for an open debate on the structure of Sino-Tibetan (van Driem 2005a-b; Jacques 2017a). For the sake of simplicity, here we stick to the label 'Tibeto-Burman' to indicate all non-Sinitic Sino-Tibetan languages; however, these languages have profound differences among them, and although common innovations for the non-Sinitic languages of the family have been proposed in the literature (Sagart 2017), until Sino-Tibetan phylogeny has been investigated on a level of rigour comparable to that of Indo-European, it is unjustified to assume that they form a proper subgroup of the family.[29]

An alternative view (made popular by a very influential article by Li Fang-Kuei (1973 [1937]; see Zhengzhang Shangfang 1995), which sees Sino-Tibetan as a much larger family, including also Tai-Kadai and Hmong-Mien languages, still enjoys some support among Chinese scholars. The inclusion of these two groups in the Sino-Tibetan family is based on shared lexicon and on their similar typological profile: isolating morphology, a tendency towards monosyllabism, and the use of lexical tones, which are seen as characteristic of the family; the morphology of Tibeto-Burman languages is thus seen as innovative. However, it has been convincingly argued that lexical tones and the tendency towards monosyllabism are relatively recent innovations in Sinitic and in other languages of the East and Southeast Asian area (Haudricourt 1954a-b; Sagart 1999a; Michaud 2012; see §4.1.2, 4.1.3). Also, some of the proposed shared etyma between Sinitic, Tai-Kadai, and Hmong-Mien look more like borrowings, as proven by their close correspondence with Middle Chinese (rather than Old Chinese) lexemes: compare e.g. Proto-Tai *dɔːŋ 'bronze', MC *duwŋ* and OC *lˤoŋ (Jacques 2017a). Moreover, it seems unlikely that the type of irregular and opaque morphology which may be found e.g. in Tibetan may be a recent evolution out of an isolating matrix (Jacques 2017a). However, on the basis of this enlarged view of Sino-Tibetan, some Chinese linguists have proposed an even broader 'Sino-Austric' family (華奧語系 *Huá-Ào yǔxì*), including also Austroasiatic and Austronesian (Pan Wuyun 1995; Zhengzhang Shangfang 1995).[30]

---

[29] We thank Guillaume Jacques for helping us to clarify this issue. Interestingly, in a very recent paper by Sagart *et al.* (2019), it is suggested that Sinitic is the most likely 'outgroup' in the Sino-Tibetan family, based on phylogenetic estimates.

[30] A similar proposal is that of an East Asian family (Starosta 2005), including the same languages as Sino-Austric, which in this view derive from a common ancestor named 'Proto-East Asian' (van Driem 2005a: 321–4).

A recent proposal, put forth by Laurent Sagart, suggests that Sino-Tibetan and Austronesian derive from a common ancestor language, namely 'Proto-Sinotibetan-Austronesian'; in this hypothesis, Tai-Kadai languages are a subgroup of Austronesian, while Hmong-Mien and other East Asian languages have no genetic relationship with Chinese (Sagart 2005a-b; see also Sagart 2004a). Sagart's proposal is supported by shared etyma, as proto-Austronesian *punuq, OC ᵃnuʔ (nˤuʔ in BSOL) and Tibeto-Burman *(s-)nuk 'brain', and the distributed action/object infix *-ar-: compare Paiwan k-ar-akim 'search everywhere' (vs. kim 'search') and OC 話 *gʷˤrat-s 'speak' (vs. 曰 *Gʷat 'say'; Sagart 2005a: 163, 170–1; BSOL). For a critical assessment of Sagart's proposal, see Blust (1995), Li Paul Jen-Kuei (1995), and van Driem (2005a).

A less recent hypothesis was made by Sergej Starostin (see the references in van Driem 2005a: 308), who proposes that Sino-Tibetan, North Caucasian, Yenisseian, and Burushaski all belong to a macro-family called 'Sino-Caucasian'. As many as 1,361 shared etyma have been identified and reconstructed for this family, as e.g. Proto-Sino-Caucasian *cwǎjŋĕ 'liver, gall' > Proto-Sino-Tibetan *sĭn (compare MSC 辛 xīn 'bitter, pungent'), Proto-North Caucasian *c_wǎjmĕ, Proto-Yenisseian *seŋ, Proto-Burushaski *sán.[31] However, differently from Sagart's Sino-Austronesian, the Sino-Caucasian hypothesis is not supported by shared morphology (van Driem 2005a: 314–415; Jacques 2017a); moreover, as remarked by Jacques (2017a), a plausible historical background for the family is lacking.

Lastly, starting from the second half of the nineteenth century, several scholars have suggested that there might be a remote genetic relationship between Sino-Tibetan and Indo-European. The most interesting proposal is the one by Pulleyblank, who provides lexical and morphological evidence for such a connection, based on his own reconstruction of Old and Middle Chinese: for instance, according to Pulleyblank (1995b: 179–80), the Sino-Tibetan forms for 'dog' as EMC kʰwɛn (MSC 犬 quǎn; OC *kʷʰˤenʔ; BSOL), Tibetan khyi, or Burmese khwè could be related to the Indo-European root *kʲwon–, *kʲun– (Sanskrit śvǎ, śvan–, Ancient Greek kúōn, kunós, Gothic hunds, etc.). For a brief discussion of proposed historical background for the common ancestor of Sino-Tibetan and Indo-European, see Pulleyblank (1995b: 163–4).

---

[31] See the database on the web page <http://ehl.santafe.edu/main.html> (last access: 26 May 2020).

Independently from the hypotheses on the genetic affiliation of Sinitic, there is no doubt that, as hinted at earlier, the typological profile of (most) modern Sinitic languages belongs to the East and Mainland Southeast Asian (EMSEA) type (Matisoff 1991; Enfield 2005; DeLancey 2010). The EMSEA area is a *Sprachbund* which includes Sinitic, Hmong-Mien, Tai-Kadai, Mon-Khmer, and some Tibeto-Burman (as Bai and Karenic) and Austronesian (Chamic) languages; a long history of contact among speakers of EMSEA languages has led to significant convergence not only in their languages, but also in their cultures (Matisoff 2001; Enfield 2005). Note, however, that the narrow definition of the EMSEA area includes only Southern China, i.e. not all of Sinitic: in fact, as we shall see later, many differences between Northern and Southern Sinitic languages may be explained by the stronger influence of the EMSEA type on the latter.

We already mentioned some features of the EMSEA type: the use of lexical (and grammatical) tone, the tendency towards monosyllabism (*sesquisillabism* for some languages), and isolating/analytic morphology. Some other salient features of EMSEA languages are (Matisoff 2001; Enfield 2005; Goddard 2005; Ansaldo 2010):

a. lack of agreement for number, gender, case, etc.
b. verb-medial, head-modifier order, use of prepositions
c. the use of serial verb constructions
d. the use of lexical morphemes with grammatical functions
e. lack of obligatory arguments (zero anaphora)
f. topic-prominent syntax
g. the use of (modal) sentence-final particles
h. the use of classifiers
i. prominence of aspect over tense
j. rich vowel inventories

Many of the above-mentioned typological features which characterize EMSEA languages are tightly interconnected and have important consequences for the development of these languages. The almost total lack of inflectional morphology, i.e. the lack of morphological markers which may help in the identification of syntactic relations between the constituents of a sentence, and the (tendential) non-obligatoriness of aspect and mood markers, together with the dropping of arguments and with the pragmatic-based organization of utterances, all lead to the characteristic 'indeterminatedness' of EMSEA languages (Bisang 2004:

111–12; Enfield 2005: 188).[32] See the following MSC example (LaPolla and Poa 2006: 276):

(9) 沒有人可以問問題。
     méi-yŏu   rén   kěyǐ wèn   wèntí
     NEG-exist person   can   ask   question
     a. '(There is) no one (who) can ask questions.'
     b. 'There is no one to ask questions of.'

The sentence in (9) allows at least two radically different interpretations, in which 人 *rén* 'person' represents different arguments ('subject' vs. object—but see §6.2.1), as well as different thematic roles (agent vs. recipient/addressee). Moreover, the situation described in (9) could be located, for instance, in the past ('there *was…*'), or it could be the protasis of a conditional sentence ('*if* there is…'): the absence of markers of person, number, case, tense, and mood, and the pragmatic-based organization of the utterance, makes all these intepretations (as well as others) possible.

Furthermore, the almost total lack of inflection, combined by some degree of flexibility in word-class identity, somehow favours the reanalysis of lexical morphemes as grammatical functors; often, this happens to verbs in serial constructions (Bisang 2001a: 204; Enfield 2006: 314; Bisang 2009; see also §6.3, 6.3.1), which are typically found in languages without morphological markers of dependency (Matthews 2006: 84). A nice example of this type of process of grammaticalization is that of dative constructions based on the verb 'give', attested in Sinitic, but also in Lao, Thai, and Vietnamese:

(10) 我要打電話給她。
      wŏ   yào   dǎ   diànhuà   gěi   tā
      1SG   want   hit   telephone   to   3SG.F
      'I have to call her.' (MSC)

(11) 我細佬寄咗封信俾我。
      ngóh   sailóu   mail-jó   fūng   seun   béi   ngóh
      1SG   brother   send-PFV   CLF   letter   to   1SG
      'My brother mailed me a letter.' (Cantonese; Matthews and Yip 2011: 155)

---

[32] See also Kibrik (2001: 1127): '[…] zero anaphora is particularly typical of East and South-East Asia, and West Africa, and these are two areas where the isolating morphological type is highly common; there may be a connection between zero anaphora and isolation. Gundel (1980) attempted to connect zero anaphora with "topic-prominence", another typical feature of East and South-East Asia […]'.

(12) laaw2 nùng1 khaw5 haj5 khòòj5
3SG.F steam rice for 1SG
'She steamed rice for me.' (Lao; Enfield 2007: 481; glosses altered)

(13) tôi sẽ làm cho ông
1SG FUT do for 2SG
'I will do it for you.' (Vietnamese; Thompson 1987 [1965]: 232)

The verbs 給 gěi, 俾 béi, haj5, and cho are still used with their original lexical meaning, i.e. 'give'. However, in examples (10–13), their function is that of marking a recipient, and they are usually analysed as prepositions; the grammaticalization of these verbs occurs in a serial verb construction (for more examples, see Matthews 2006: 85 and §6.3.1). This is but one of the many cases of lexical items with the same meaning (here, 'give') which develop the same (or very close) grammatical function in EMSEA languages: Bisang (1998: 17) even suggests that a convergence area might arise also from the diffusion of patterns of grammaticalization (see also Bisang 1996; Chappell 2001).

Needless to say, as for any other linguistic area, not all EMSEA languages possess all the traits of this areal type. This is true also for Sinitic: for instance, the overwhelmingly dominant order throughout the family is modifier-head, rather than head-modifier, although some Southern Sinitic languages do have a few cases of left-headed modification structures (as e.g. in a Cantonese compound as 魚生 yùhsāang 'fish-raw, raw fish'; compare MSC 生魚 shēngyú, with the opposite order; Ansaldo 2010: 940; Matthews and Yip 2011: 56; see also §5.1.3.1). Moreover, some EMSEA features are actually found also in neighbouring areas, as e.g. numeral classifier constructions, common also to Korean and Japanese, among others (see Comrie 2007: 39; Gil 2013).

As noted earlier, a stronger convergence towards the EMSEA type is visible in Southern Sinitic languages, namely the varieties which developed in closer contact with Tai-Kadai, Hmong-Mien, and Mon-Khmer (§2.2.2); Northern China, on the other hand, was (and still is) inhabited also by speakers of Mongolic, Turkic, and Tungusic languages, including Manchu as the ethnic language of the Qing emperors (LaPolla 2001: 230; Ansaldo 2010: 920; for a brief overview on language contact in Northern China, see Cao and Yu 2015; see also Zu Shengli 2013). These languages, traditionally referred to as 'Altaic', have a very different typological profile from EMSEA languages: they are typically verb-final, place modifiers before the modified element, and they mostly make use of agglutinative morphology. Thus, unsurprisingly, while Southern Sinitic languages are very close to the EMSEA type, Northern Sinitic possesses many North Asian (Altaic) features (Comrie 2008: 1). These differences were indeed interpreted by Hashimoto (1976, 1986) as the product of the 'Altaicization' of Northern Sinitic and of the 'Taiization' of Southern Sinitic (Thai being perhaps the best representative of the EMSEA type; Comrie 2007: 44–5). In Table 2.1, we propose an overview of the main points of opposition between the Northern and Southern Sinitic type.

Table 2.1   Main differences between Northern and Southern Sinitic according to Hashimoto

North	South
Stress-based and fewer tones	More tones
Higher proportion of polysyllabic words	Higher proportion of monosyllabic words
Simpler syllable structure	More complex syllable structure
Smaller inventory of classifiers	Larger inventory of classifiers
Preponderance of modifier-modified	More instantiations of modified-modifier
IO-DO word order for ditransitives	DO-IO word order for ditransitives
Preverbal adverbs	Possibility of postverbal or clause-final adverbs
Marker-standard-adjective order in the comparative construction	Adjective-marker-standard order in the comparative construction
Passive markers based on causative speech act verbs	Passive markers based on the verb 'give'

(adapted from Chappell 2015b: 17)

The different features presented in Table 2.1 are to be seen as tendencies, rather than rules. For instance, while belonging to Southern Sinitic, Southern Min dialects do not generally align with the DO-IO word order; they are rather closer to the Northern model (Chappell 2015b; Peyraube 2015; see also Lin Philip T. 2015). On the other hand, the Southern order is found also in several Northern Chinese dialects, e.g. in some Mandarin dialects of Hubei and Anhui (Peyraube 2015: 72–3). Nanning Pinghua, a dialect spoken in the Southern Chinese province of Guangxi, seems to have a dispreference for monosyllabic nouns, just as Mandarin (De Sousa 2015: 174). Moreover, as we shall see in greater detail in the next section, Norman (1988, 2003) convincingly argued that a Central transitional zone between Northern and Southern Sinitic, with hybrid properties, can be identified.

While the idea of a North-South divide within Sinitic is generally accepted in the field (see e.g. Ansaldo 2010: 920), Hashimoto's proposal of an Altaic origin for the above-mentioned Northern Sinitic characteristics has come under criticism (at least since Bennett 1979, and more recently in McWhorter 2007); and even some features of Southern Sinitic traditionally identified as of Tai/EMSEA origin, as DO-IO word order for ditransitives, might also be explained as internal developments, rather than as the product of language contact (De Sousa 2015; Peyraube 2015; we will elaborate on this in §6.1.3). Moreover, recent typological research has shown that, for some specific phenomena, as e.g. differential object marking or agent markers, there are more areal divisions within China which, interestingly, sometimes cross-cut the North-South border (Chappell 2015b). On this basis, Chappell (2015b: 45–6) proposes a refinement of Hashimoto's and Norman's typology, with as many as five different areas:

a. Northern
b. Central Transitional
c. Southwestern
d. Far Southern
e. Southeastern

The Southwestern area includes the provinces of Sichuan, Guizhou, and Yunnan, as well as parts of Hubei and Western Hunan: this is the region where Southwestern Mandarin dialects are spoken. The Far Southern area has its core in Southern Guangdong and is best represented by Yue, but includes also the Hakka and Pinghua dialects of Guangdong and Guangxi. The representative varieties for the Southeastern area, on the other hand, are the Min dialects of Fujian and Taiwan, but it includes also some Southern Wu dialects to the North. In the Central Transitional area, spanning over Zhejiang, Jiangsu, Anhui, Jiangxi, and Hunan, we find most Wu dialects, as well as Gan, Xiang, Hui, and Jianghuai Mandarin varieties.

In essence, Chappell's revision better accounts for the variation attested in Southern and Southeastern China, while retaining the general idea of two distinct Northern and Central areas: as we shall see in the next section, Southern China, and especially Southeastern China, are also the regions with by far the highest genealogical diversity within Sinitic. However, Chappell also points out that, despite the relatively high degree of homogeneity within the Northern area, there are two 'aberrant' enclaves within it: namely, the Jiaoliao and Ji-Lu subgroups of Mandarin, mostly spoken in Eastern Shandong, which possess some important non-Northern features, and a region of Northwestern China (mostly Qinghai and Gansu), overlapping with the historical Amdo Tibetan region, where Mandarin dialects have developed in close contact with speakers of Bodic, Mongolic, and Turkic languages, developing Altaic-type features (see §6.1.3). She also stresses the fact that the features found in the Central Transitional zone are not just a combination of Northern and Southern patterns: constructions which are independent from either model are also attested, such as the use of 'wait' verbs as passive markers (Chappell 2015b: 51).

Lastly, in a recent paper, Szeto, Ansaldo, and Matthews (2018) analyze a sample of forty-two Chinese dialects, twenty-six of which belong to the Mandarin group, based on twenty-one typological features (including phonological, lexical, and morphosyntactic features). Consistently with Chappell's (2015b) proposal seen before, they show that there is a rather strong North-South divide even within Mandarin dialects; also, while Northern Mandarin dialects tend to be fairly homogeneous, Southern varieties are much more diverse, and tend to cluster areally (rather than forming a consistent subgroup of Mandarin).

2.3.2 The structure of the Sinitic family

As hinted at earlier, the internal subdivision of the Sinitic family is a much debated topic, especially outside China. The 'traditional' partition of Chinese dialects was inspired, again, by the above-mentioned seminal paper by Li Fang-Kuei (1973 [1937]); in this widely accepted classification, there are seven major groups of Chinese dialects/languages (Yuan *et al.* 2001):

    a. Mandarin ('Northern') dialects (北方方言 *běifāng fāngyán* or 北方話 *běifānghuà*), spread over Northern, Western, and Southwestern China, native to roughly 900 million people (Sun Chaofen 2006: 29)

    b. Wu dialects (吳方言 *Wú fāngyán*), spoken in Zhejiang, part of Jiangsu, and in the Shanghai Metropolitan area

    c. Xiang dialects (湘方言 *Xiāng fāngyán*), spoken in Hunan and in some counties of Northern Guangxi

d. Gan dialects (贛方言 *Gàn fāngyán*), spoken in Central and Northern Jiangxi

e. Hakka (or Kejia)[33] dialects (客家方言 *Kèjiā fāngyán*), scattered over several areas of the country (Hunan, Sichuan, Hainan, Guangxi), with a strong presence in (Northeastern) Guangdong, Fujian, and Jiangxi, as well as in Taiwan (see §3.3.1).

f. Yue (or Cantonese) dialects (粵方言 *Yuè fāngyán*), spoken in Central and Southwestern Guangdong, Southeastern Guangxi, Hong Kong, and Macao

g. Min dialects (閩方言 *Mǐn fāngyán*), prevalent in Fujian and Taiwan; the so-called 'Taiwanese language' (台[or 臺]語 *Táiyǔ*) is a Southern Min variety (see §3.3.1)

Note that here we use 'Yue', rather than the more familiar term 'Cantonese', to refer to the whole Yue branch of Sinitic; while 'Cantonese' is sometimes used also in this sense, it more properly refers to the prestige variety of Yue dialects, i.e, the dialect of the provincial capital Guangzhou/Canton and Hong Kong, known in Chinese as 廣東話 *Guǎngdōnghuà* (Cant. *Gwóngdūngwá*) or 廣州話 *Guǎngzhōuhuà* (Yue Anne Oi-Kan 1991: 294; Matthews and Yip 2011: 3). Accordingly, here we use 'Cantonese' in the latter sense, to refer to a specific Yue dialect.[34]

More recently, a revised version of the seven-branch model has been proposed (Li Rong 1985; 1989), including three more dialect groups:

h. Jin dialects (晉方言 *Jìn fāngyán*), the only non-Mandarin dialects of Northern China, whose heartland is Shanxi province; Jin dialects are also scattered through Henan, Hebei, and Inner Mongolia

i. Pinghua dialects (平話 *Pínghuà*), mainly spoken in Guangxi

j. Hui dialects (徽方言 *Huī fāngyán*), spoken in Anhui and in some areas of Zhejiang and Jiangxi

---

[33] The name 'Hakka' comes from Cantonese 客家 *haakgā* 'guest people/families' (MSC *Kèjiā*) and was apparently coined to distinguish Hakka speakers from the 'indigenous' speakers of Yue dialects (Cant. 本地 *búndeih*, lit. 'local, native'; Chappell and Lamarre 2005: 4). It is the only denomination for a Chinese dialect which is not based on a toponym.

[34] Note that there are some (relatively minor) differences between the Cantonese spoken in Guangzhou and in Hong Kong, and there are also distinctive varieties of Cantonese spoken by Chinese communities abroad (Matthews and Yip 2011: 3). The language data used in this book are of the Hong Kong variety, chosen for its prestige and for the availability of reference works.

Moreover, there are some varieties whose status is still uncertain, as e.g. the so-called Shaozhou *patois* (韶州土話 *Sháozhōu tǔhuà*; Chappell 2004b: 7; Kurpaska 2010: 72–3; see §4.2.9).

However, if the first seven dialect groups are widely accepted, there is no consensus in the field on the status of the latter three. For many scholars, Jin is but a subgroup of Mandarin, Pinghua belongs to the Yue branch, whereas Hui dialects are often seen as either part of Wu or Mandarin (see Kurpaska 2010: 74–6; we shall get back to this in §4.2.9). Be it as may, it clearly appears that diversity is not equally distributed over China: in fact, the highest degree of diversity is seen in a relatively small area of the country, i.e. the Eastern and Southeastern regions, while the rest of China is dominated by Mandarin dialects.

Needless to say, this is just a first-level partition: each major branch (referred to as 方言 *fāngyán*, i.e. 'dialect', in Chinese) contains sub-branches or subgroups (次方言 *cì fāngyán*, lit. 'subdialect'), which in turn may include several 'local vernaculars' (土語 *tǔyǔ*), each vernacular possibly having more 'accents' (腔 *qiāng*). An alternative geographical taxonomy involves the notions of 'supergroup' (大區 *dàqū*, lit. 'macroarea'), 'group' (區 *qū*), 'subgroup' (片 *piàn*), 'cluster' (小片 *xiǎopiàn*), and 'local dialect' (點 *diǎn*, lit. 'point'; Yuan *et al.* 2001: 24; Li Rulong 2001: 1, 31; Kurpaska 2010: 63–4). For reasons of space, here we cannot present the internal structure of each branch of Sinitic (see Kurpaska 2010, and Chapter 4); we will just mention some particularly important subdivisions, namely:

a. the Northern, Central Plains (中原 *Zhōngyuán*), Jiang-Huai (江淮 *Jiāng-Huái*), and Southwestern subgroups of Mandarin
b. the Central (閩中 *Mǐnzhōng*), Northern (閩北 *Mǐnběi*), Eastern (閩東 *Mǐndōng*), Southern (閩南 *Mǐnnán*), and Puxian (莆仙 *Púxiān*) subgroups of Min (Yuan *et al.* 2001: 235); besides, another important distinction within Min is that between 'inner' (i.e. Central and Northern) and 'coastal' (Eastern, Southern, and Puxian) dialects (see Chappell 2004b: 14; Lin and Fan 2010: 661)
c. 'New' and 'Old' Xiang dialects (新湘語 *xīn Xiāngyǔ* vs. 老湘語 *lǎo Xiāngyǔ*; Yuan *et al.* 2001: 101).

If Northern Mandarin dialects, as mentioned in §2.2.2, are relatively homogeneous and have a fair degree of mutual intelligibility (although this is not necessarily the case for Southern Mandarin), the Min group is arguably the most diverse of all Sinitic: as Norman (1988: 188) put it, within Min, 'in some cases even neighbouring villages use forms of speech that are totally mutually unintelligible'. As for Xiang, the 'New' dialects appear as closer to Mandarin than the 'Old' dialects, because of the influence of Southwestern Mandarin on the former: thus, for instance, the 'New' Xiang dialect of Changsha has converged towards Southwestern Mandarin to the point that speakers of the two varieties can communicate with relative ease (Yuan *et al.* 2001: 101; Chappell 2004b: 11).

The proposals for the classification of Sinitic languages presented here are all based, in essence, on phonological criteria. This is because phonology is often seen as the component of language which is more stable and less subject to external influence (compared to lexicon, morphology, and syntax; see VanNess Simmons 1999b: 209). Specifically, the traditional approach to the Sinitic family heavily relies on a single criterion for dividing dialects into (major) groups: namely, the evolution of Middle Chinese voiced obstruents (Norman 1988; Chirkova 2013; Handel 2014). In this model, Min dialects have a very special position, since their phonological system, showing archaic features, cannot be derived from Middle Chinese (see Handel 2010, among others); thus, Min is the only branch in the family tree of Sinitic languages which detached before the Middle Chinese stage, as shown in Figure 2.1.[35]

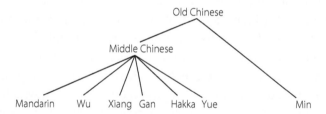

Figure 2.1 Family tree of Sinitic languages

Note: For the sake of simplicity, here we include only the commonly accepted seven branches.

We defer the presentation of the criteria for the individuation of each branch to Chapter 4; in the remainder of this section, we will rather discuss the limits of the 'traditional' approach to the classification of Chinese dialects and the alternative approaches.

Firstly, it has been pointed out that relying on a single phonological criterion for the identification of language groups has limited predictive

---

[35] On the relationship between Old Chinese and Min, see Handel (2010).

value, as the groups are not always homogeneous enough, and poses problems for the classification of varieties with hybrid features. A case in point is the Hangzhou dialect (see §2.2.3), which has been seen (and is still seen by some scholars) as a Wu dialect because it retains the three-way distinction (voiced, voiceless, and aspirated voiceless) for initial obstruents, traditionally considered to be the defining characteristic of Wu. However, as shown by VanNess Simmons (1999a-b), this is actually one of the very few features which Hangzhou shares with Wu; its phonology and lexicon are actually much closer to Mandarin dialects.[36] To overcome this weakness, VanNess Simmons proposes a 'multidimensional' approach to classification, which takes into account a fairly large number of features, and which allows for different 'degrees' of affiliation (see §4.2.3): in his view, the Hangzhou dialect is primarily a Mandarin dialect, but shows affinities with Wu (VanNess Simmons 1999b: 219–20). Similar cases have been discussed in the literature: see e.g. Yue Anne Oi-Kan (1991) for Yue and Branner (1999, 2000) for Min. Moreover, Norman (1988: 189–90) highlighted that some branches are more clearly distinct than others: thus, for instance, while Wu and Min are easily distinguished, the borderline between Xiang and Mandarin is not as strong (see §4.2.4).

A more general problem in the classification of Chinese dialects is that the choice of criteria determines the outcome of the taxonomy, and conservative and innovative features are sometimes treated as equally valid; however, the identification of a branch of a language family should be primarily based on common innovations, as pointed out time and again in the literature (Sagart 1998, 2002; Yu Zhiqiang 1999; Baxter 2006; Chirkova 2013). In this connection, Baxter (2006: 75) proposes an approach based on the analysis of phonological fusions, which are seen as innovations. Through the application of his method on a small sample of dialects, Baxter concludes that the above-mentioned Hangzhou dialect and Changsha ('New') Xiang could both derive from a hypothetical 'Proto-Macro-Mandarin', which is also the ancestor of Mandarin dialects (see also Baxter 2000).

An alternative model for the classification of Chinese dialects has been proposed by Norman (1988, 2003). Norman's taxonomy is based on fifteen phonological and lexical features, as, for instance:

---

[36] Moreover, voiced obstruents are not retained as such in Hangzhou, but are rather realized with breathy voice, and only when the syllable has a low-register tone (VanNess Simmons 1999b: 215–16; see §4.2.3).

a. the third person pronoun is *tā*, or a form with the same etymon
b. the copula is *shì*, or a form with the same etymon
c. velar consonants are palatalized before high front vowels

Languages with all (or nearly all) the fifteen traits belong to the Northern dialect type (i.e. Mandarin), while languages with none (or almost none) of those features belong to the Southern type (i.e. Yue, Hakka, and Min); dialects of the Central group (Wu, Gan, and Xiang; see §2.3.1) have both Northern and Southern features.

Secondly, the idea that all Chinese dialects (except Min) somehow derive from Middle Chinese is not universally accepted in the field. As hinted at before (Fn. 16), the existence of a Tang period *koinè* which replaced (or anyway heavily influenced) the Chinese dialects of the time has been questioned, for instance, by Norman and Coblin (1995; see also Branner 2000). Norman and Coblin propose a comparison between the historical evolution of Chinese and that of Romance: *mutatis mutandis*, the status of the 切韻 *Qièyùn* 'language' (§2.2.2) is more or less analogous to that of Classical Latin, while, as is known, Romance languages derive from a form of *sermo vulgaris*; similarly, modern Sinitic languages more likely derive from a spoken variety which was different from the language represented in the 切韻 *Qièyùn* (Norman and Coblin 1995: 582).[37] Moreover, the high degree of diversity of Chinese dialects suggest that they parted ways much earlier than the eighth or ninth century, and, probably, the groups did not split all at the same time: thus, for instance, while Wu (and, needless to say, Min) could have already been formed by Han times, Yue, Xiang, and Gan probably separated in the Sui and Tang periods (Chappell 2001: 334).

In addition to that, according to several scholars, not all dialect groups developed independently. For instance, it has been proposed that Hakka and Southern Gan both evolved from a 'Proto-Southern-Gan' (Sagart 1988, 1993, 2002; see §4.2.5, 4.2.6), or that Hakka, Yue, and Min descend from an 'Old Southern Chinese' language (Norman 1988: 210); or, even, that Gan, Yue, and (most) Hakka dialects belong to a 'Gan-Yue' dialect group (贛粵語區 *Gàn-Yuè yǔqū*; Lau Chun-fat 2002: 90–2). Yet others propose 'Proto-Wu' or 'Proto-Wu-Min' as a possible

---

[37] Sagart (2002: 138) uses the term *Common Chinese* to indicate the common ancestor of all Chinese dialects, roughly defined as 'the standard language in Northern China at the time of the Chinese conquest of the South, Early Han'.

common ancestor of Wu and Min (You Rujie 1992: 99; see §4.2.3). A family tree which takes into account all these partitions, on which there is however no consensus (see Norman 1988; Chappell 2001; 2004b), would obviously be way more complex that the traditional *Stammbaum* seen before (Figure 2.1).

Another fundamental objection to the traditional approach(es) to dialect classification concerns the very nature of the Sinitic family. As seen in §2.2.2, Sinitic languages developed in a situation of prolonged contact, both within the family and with unrelated languages, with the 'superimposition' of different historical strata and diatopic varieties of Northern Chinese on Central and Southern dialects. The traditional *Stammbaum* model thus appears inadequate for the representation of the relationship among Chinese dialects, which could be seen as fuzzy entitities, the characteristics of which have been shaped to a significant degree by language contact; an areal approach (see §2.3.1) could provide a better account of the structure of the Sinitic family (Sagart 1998: 298–9; see also Norman 2003; Chappell 2004b). According to Chappell (2001: 353), if the family tree model is fairly adequate for phonology and for some aspects of morphology,

[...] this only accounts for a small part of a much more complex linguistic picture: the family-tree model is unable to capture the effect of successive waves of Mandarinisation of Southern Sinitic languages, stratifying lexical and syntactic components [...].[38] Hence, a more delicate and subtle treatment of the question of genetic affiliation is needed.

The current situation of Sinitic is well explained by the linguistic history of China: particularly, by the contact among dialects *after* the separation of the main groups (Chappell 2001: 334–5: see also Dixon 1997; François 2014). Norman's classification seen before, as well as Chappell's revised version (§2.3.1), reflects these trends in Chinese linguistic history: Central varieties, located between Northern and Southern dialects, have been subject to stronger Mandarin influence than Southern Sinitic (Norman 2003: 76).

To conclude, an increasing number of scholars insist on the relevance of contact and phonological, lexical, and syntactic stratification in the formation and evolution of Sinitic languages. Moreover, we showed that

---

[38] The so-called 'stratology' (層次學 *céngcìxué*) approach in Chinese dialectology focusses on the analysis of phonogical and lexical strata of Northern Chinese in dialects (Handel 2014: 596).

the identification of a common ancestor of modern Chinese dialects and the relationship among them are both much debated issues, once again in reaction to a traditional approach which is seen as inadequate by many specialists. We shall get back later to many of the issues discussed in this section, as they concern several fundamental aspects of the history of Chinese.

3

Chinese writing

3.1 Chinese characters

Writing is one of the most fascinating aspects of Chinese (and Japanese) culture, and it can be very attractive (but, also, overwhelming) for the language learner. The Chinese writing system is one of the oldest in the world, and it is also the only non-phonographic script currently in use for a national language. The complexity of Chinese writing often impresses people with no background in Chinese, and there are many common misconceptions concerning the relationship between writing and language, i.e. among sounds, meanings, and characters (see DeFrancis 1984: 141–3). In this section, we shall first clarify the possible relations between graphemes and units of language in the Chinese tradition. We shall then present some quantitative data on Chinese characters, also in order to assess the 'burden' of writing for language users.

3.1.1 The classification of Chinese characters

In non-specialistic language, Chinese characters are often referred to as 'ideograms', while specialists prefer the generic term 'characters', a direct translation of Chinese 字 *zì* (or 漢字 *Hànzì* 'Chinese characters'). While sometimes the word 'ideogram' is used without any specific implicature as to what characters actually represent, in many other cases by 'ideogram' it is implied that Chinese characters represent ideas, concepts,

Chinese Linguistics: An Introduction. Giorgio Francesco Arcodia and Bianca Basciano, Oxford University Press.
© Giorgio Arcodia and Bianca Basciano 2021. DOI: 10.1093/oso/9780198847830.003.0003

rather than just units of language (on the 'ideographic myth', see DeFrancis 1984; Boltz 1994; Hansell 2003).[1] In this interpretation, Chinese characters are not unlike graphic representations as, for instance, the biohazard symbol (☣): this symbol has a conventional-ized meaning, but it does not directly reflect units of language. In point of fact, the biohazard symbol can be associated with different words in different languages, as e.g. German *Biogefährdung*, or Italian *biorischio*. However, as aptly pointed out by Coulmas (2003: 41),

[...] it is doubtful that there ever was a writing system that expressed ideas, as this term [ideographic] would seem to suggest. [...] In the threefold relation between objects, concepts and words it has not been possible to design a writing system that operates on the level of concepts regardless of language.

Let us take as an example the characters 紅 *hóng* and 赤 *chì*, both meaning 'red'. Now, if these were actually ideographic, there would be no need to have *two* symbols for the same referent (Hansell 2003: 157). Besides, treating them as ideograms overlooks the fact that these char-acters represent two distinct Chinese *words* (*hóng* and *chì*), rather than a chromatic notion independent from language. Note, also, that several psycholinguistic studies show that phonological (and not only seman-tic) activation is very important in character reading: see e.g. the refer-ences cited in Perfetti and Liu (2006), Leong Che Kan (2006), and McBride-Chang and Zhong (2006; but cf. Taft 2006).

Incidentally, an argument which is often used to support the idea that Chinese writing represents 'ideas', referents, (almost) without the medi-ation of language, is that Chinese characters are actually used to write other languages and dialects, just as if those 'ideograms' could convey meanings independently from the units of a specific language. Thus, for instance, the character 赤 is *chì* in MSC, but it is also read as *chek* in Cantonese, and as *akai* (or *seki*) in Japanese, while conveying the same meaning, i.e. 'red'. However, this argument is based on an erroneous understanding of the difference between 'script' and 'orthography' (Hansell 2003: 157): the Chinese *script* may be used to write Cantonese and Japanese, just as the Latin alphabet may be used to write English, Portuguese, or Finnish, but each language has its own *orthographic* con-ventions. Thus, while it is true that a literate Japanese could read a word

---

[1] Specifically, on the historical origin of the notion of 'ideographic writing' and on its application to Chinese characters, see DeFrancis (1984: 133-6 and 141-3). On the 'false myths' about Chinese writing, see also Unger (2004).

or a simple sentence written in Chinese, in order to do this s/he would still have to associate those graphemes to a unit of the Japanese language (i.e. a word, or a morpheme), rather than to a meaning only. And, on the other hand, speakers of Chinese and/or Japanese without a specific training cannot easily read a text in Classical Chinese, just because they know Chinese characters (see Boltz 1994: 7–8). Moreover, note that Chinese characters have been often used to write words of other languages just for their sound value, rather than for their meaning, as we shall see later (§3.3.1, 3.3.2).

Thus, to sum up, the Chinese script, just as any other writing system, is a tool for rendering in written form language, rather than 'ideas' without linguistic substance. The term most often used in the literature to describe Chinese writing is 'logographic', i.e. 'writing of words': this is the label we use also in the present volume. However, since Chinese characters generally represent morphemes, but not always words, and almost always correspond to a syllable, DeFrancis (1984: 125) suggests that the term 'morphosyllabic' (1 grapheme = 1 morpheme = 1 syllable) may be more appropriate (see §5.1.1).

Another common misconception, connected to the 'ideographic myth' discussed earlier, is that characters should be iconically related to their meaning, i.e. they look like what they depict: hence, they might be understood even without knowing the word they represent. In the earliest attestations of *bona fide* Chinese writing, namely oracle bone inscriptions (甲骨文 *jiǎgǔwén*; see §2.2.1), there actually are quite a few iconic characters, very close to a pictographic representation of their referents and with no clues as to the sound shape of the word they represent. For instance, let us see the early shapes of the characters 魚 *yú* 'fish', 上 *shàng* 'above', and 集 *jí* 'gather', shown in Figure 3.1:

Figure 3.1 The characters 魚 *yú*, 上 *shàng* and 集 *jí* in oracle bone inscriptions

At this stage in the evolution of the Chinese script, we may quite easily recognize the image of a fish in the character 魚 *yú*, even though this is no longer evident in its current form. The character 上 *shàng* 'above' is used to convey a more abstract, relational concept, and it is therefore arguably less transparent than 魚 *yú* 'fish': nevertheless, the iconic motivation of the character is anyway visible. The third character, 集 *jí* 'gather', combines two pictographic symbols to designate yet another referent: originally, this character represented birds gathering on a tree (Hu 2012) (ZYZD).

However, besides the fact that these characters almost entirely lost the iconic connection with their referents in the evolution of the Chinese script (see §3.2.2), they are anyway not representative of Chinese writing. Indeed, characters with a pictographic origin are but a small fraction of the inventory of Chinese graphemes, as we shall see later. In the traditional classification of Chinese characters, which was first set out in the second-century dictionary 說文解字 *Shuōwén jiězì* 'Explaining simple characters and analyzing compound characters'[2] by Xu Shen (c. 55–c. 149), characters are classified into six categories (the 六書 *liù shū* 'six forms of writing'). These are (Boltz 1993; 1994; Qiu Xigui 2000):

a. 象形 *xiàngxíng* 'pictographs', i.e. graphic depictions of concrete referents, as the above-mentioned 魚 *yú* 'fish'
b. 指事 *zhǐshì* 'indicatives', i.e. iconic representations of abstract or relational notions, as the above-mentioned 上 *shàng* 'above'
c. 會意 *huìyì* 'etymonic compounds' (lit. 'joined meanings'), i.e. combinations of two graphic components which, taken together, have an iconic connection to another notion, as the above-mentioned 集 *jí* 'gather'
d. 形聲 *xíngshēng* 'phonetic compounds', i.e. composite characters made up of a constituent indicating the (broad) semantic area to which the word(/morpheme) belongs and a constituent suggesting its pronunciation, as e.g. 粉 *fěn* 'powder, flour', from 米 *mǐ* 'rice' (semantic) and 分 *fēn* 'divide' (phonetic)
e. 專注 *zhuǎnzhù* 'graphically and etymonically related pairs of characters' (lit. 'reversed and annotated'), the meaning and definition of which is very controversial; it is exemplified by Xu Shen

---

[2] The translation we gave here for the 說文解字 *Shuōwén jiězì* is based on the traditional understanding of the meaning of the terms 文 *wén* and 字 *zì* in Xu Shen's work: namely, that 文 *wén* are simple characters, which cannot be divided into constituent parts, while 字 *zì* are compound characters, made of more than one constituent, and can thus be 'analyzed' (解 *jiě*; Boltz 1993: 431). However, this interpretation of the meaning of 文 *wén* and 字 *zì* is challenged by Bottéro (2002), who notes that in the text of the 說文解字 *Shuōwén jiězì* the distinction between 文 *wén* and 字 *zì* is never presented as simple vs. compound. Due to space constraints, we shall not discuss the issue any further.

with the relationship between 老 *lǎo* 'old' and 考 *kǎo* 'aged, old age'

f. 假借 *jiǎjiè* 'loans', i.e. characters used to write a (near-)homphonous word without any implied semantic connection, as e.g. 被 *bèi* 'quilt' > 'passive marker'

The characters in Figure 3.1, which have a more or less evident iconic connection with their referents, are examples of the categories a. (pictograms), b. (indicatives), and c. (etymonic compounds). These are the categories of characters which are often used as typical examples of Chinese writing, especially in non-specialistic discourse: thus, they tend to give the false impression that the Chinese script is, in essence, non-phonetic (DeFrancis 1984: 142). However, these types of characters are but a relatively small subset of the total: indeed, the vast majority (estimates range between 80% and 95%: see Li Jie 1996: 1408; Coulmas 2003: 55) of Chinese characters belongs to the category of phonetic compounds, which do contain clues as to the sound shape of the word they represent. The very nature of phonetic compounds further confirms the status of the Chinese script as a tool for writing down *language* and not 'ideas'.

Given that phonetic compounds are by far the most common type of character in the Chinese script, let us now elaborate a bit on their structure. As already mentioned, 形聲 *xíngshēng* characters are made of a semantic component (the so-called 形旁 *xíngpáng* or 義符 *yìfú*), and a phonetic component, or 'phonophoric' (聲旁 *shēngpáng* or 音符 *yīnfú*): in the example discussed before, namely 粉 *fěn* 'powder, flour', 米 *mǐ* 'rice' is the 形旁 *xíngpáng* (often corresponding to the 'radical' of the character, or 部首 *bùshǒu*) and 分 *fēn* is the 聲旁 *shēngpáng*. In this example, we may already see that the reading of the phonetic component 分 *fēn* is not identical to that of the phonetic compound 粉 *fěn*: the distance is greater in some other characters which have 分 *fēn* as phonophoric, as e.g. 貧 *pín* 'poor' (with 貝 *bèi* 'shell, money') and 頒 *bān* 'issue' (with 頁 *yè* 'head').

There are two reasons for this seemingly irregular relationship between a phonetic constituent and the actual sound shapes of words in MSC. Firstly, phonophorics were never intended to necessarily stand for *exactly* the same sound of the word represented by the character they are found in: they only had to share the rhyme and the place and manner of articulation of the onset (Sagart 2006, among others).

Secondly, the (imperfect) correspondence between phonophoric and word did hold at the time of the creation of each character: except for the recent simplification (§3.2.3), the shape of characters has not undergone significant changes in the past two millennia, but the sound of the words they represent has obviously changed. Compare, for instance, the Old Chinese and the MSC reading of some characters containing the phonophoric 兌 *duì* 'joyful' (now 'exchange'; Sagart 2006; BSOL).

Table 3.1 Examples of characters containing 兌 *duì* in Old Chinese and in MSC

Character	Semantic component	OC	MSC
兌 'joyful'		*lˤot-s	duì
銳 'sharp'	金 *jīn* 'metal'	*lot-s	ruì
閱 'read'	門 *mén* 'door'	*lot	yuè
說 'speak'	言 *yán* 'word'	*l̥ot	shuō

As is apparent in Table 3.1, while the current MSC sound shape of those four words seem almost completely unrelated, their OC versions, while not identical, were similar enough to be associated with the phonophoric 兌 *duì*. Indeed, as we shall see in the next chapter (§4.1.1), the phonetic constituents of 形聲 *xíngshēng* characters are one of the main sources of evidence for the reconstruction of Old Chinese. Thus, if phonophorics could be considered as an 'imperfect syllabary' (Sagart 2006) at the time when they were first used to create phonetic compounds, their function as clues to the pronunciation of words has been partially lost in MSC (as well as in other Sinitic languages): estimates on the share of 形聲 *xíngshēng* characters which still provide reliable phonetic clues range between 18.5% and 66% (DeFrancis 1989: 111–12; Taylor and Taylor 2014: 78). At any rate, scholars generally agree on the point that in Chinese writing, phonetic constituents are not less relevant than semantic constituents (see Coulmas 2003: 57–8). Actually, the fact that phonetic compounds quickly became the dominant model for the creation of new characters, as we shall see later (§3.2.1), further attests to the importance of sounds, rather than meaning only, in the genesis of 漢字 *Hànzì*.[3]

---

[3] Interestingly, the 'ideographic myth' often leads to misunderstandings concerning the structure and origin of some characters, mainly due to the interpretation of phonophorics as semantic constituents. Hansell (2003: 162–3) cites the example of 星 *xīng* 'star', made of

The fifth category of characters in the 六書 *liùshū* classification, namely 專注 *zhuǎnzhù*, has given rise to endless controversies, as hinted at earlier. Qiu Xigui (2000: 156–61) lists as many as nine different definitions for this category which may be found in the literature, and he concludes that it may be dispensed with. Due to space constraints, we shall not discuss the issue further here. What is more interesting, in order to understand the historical evolution of Chinese writing, is the category of 假借 *jiǎjiè*, i.e. characters 'borrowed' for writing other (near-) homophonous words, following the well-known rebus principle (Coulmas 2003). We shall see later (§3.2.1) that the use of pictographs or indicatives as 假借 *jiǎjiè* was the first step in the process of the partial 'phonetization' of Chinese writing.

3.1.2 Quantitative data

Phonographic scripts, as e.g. the Latin alphabet, are generally made up of a very limited number of graphemes. While the time necessary to learn how to write may vary, depending on the characteristics of each orthography, the number of written symbols to be learned is anyway quite low, if compared to the Chinese script. Thus, mastering Chinese writing is often perceived to be a tremendous task, requiring considerable effort: indeed, the question of how many graphemes there are in the Chinese writing system often comes up in ordinary conversations about Chinese.

In order to obtain a rough idea of the size of the inventory of Chinese characters, let us first look at the data on the number of characters listed in some reference lexicographic works published between the second and the twentieth century AD (Table 3.2).

Besides these very impressive numbers, we may also cite the Taiwanese 'Chinese Character Analysis Group' estimate of 74,000 distinct characters attested in the history of Chinese writing (qtd. in Huang and Huang 1989: 49–51). It goes without saying that it is virtually impossible for any individual to learn all of them: a writing system with tens of thousands of graphemes in use would just be unfit for ordinary usage.

---

the components 日 *rì* 'sun' and 生 *shēng* 'be born', which has been wrongly interpreted as a 會意 *huìyì* character, in which stars are depicted as newborn suns. However, here 生 *shēng* (OC *sreŋ; BSOL) is but the phonophoric for 星 *xīng* (*s-tsʰˤeŋ). For similar examples drawn from the literature on Chinese writing, see Sagart (2006).

Table 3.2 Number of characters listed in a sample of lexicographic works (2nd–20th cent. AD)

Work	Year	Nr. of characters
說文解字 *Shuōwén jiězì*	Ca. 100	9,353
切韻 *Qièyùn*	601	16,917
廣韻 *Guǎngyùn*	1011	26,194
集韻 *Jíyùn*	1039	53,525
康熙字典 *Kāngxī zìdiǎnī*	1716	47,035
中華大字典 *Zhōnghuā dà zìdiǎn*	1916	49,905
漢語大字典 *Hànyǔ dà zìdiǎn*	1986–90	54,678

Adapted from Norman 1988: 73 and Abbiati 2012: 157.

Thus, how should we interpret these figures? First and foremost, we must stress the fact that large lexicographic works often record many variants, or 'allographs', for the same character (known as 異體字 *yìtǐzì* or 重文 *chóngwén* in Chinese). Thus, for instance, about a third of the 74,000 characters collected by the Chinese Character Analysis Group are actually variants. A dictionary of variants (異體字字典 *Yìtǐzì zìdiǎn*)[4] published in 2004 lists as many as 106,230 characters (Taylor and Taylor 2014: 48): for instance, for the character 丘 *qiū* 'mound' as many as fourteen allographs are listed. Secondly, Chinese lexicographers also record characters that are no longer in use, while adding newly coined characters or variants, leading to a progressive expansion of the inventory (Norman 1988: 71–2). Lastly, Chinese characters generally correspond to morphemes and not necessarily to words: from relatively early on, the Chinese lexicon began to grow by combining morphemes to build new words (see §5.1), rather than by creating new morphemes (and the related characters).

Hence, the astonishingly high number of characters recorded in dictionaries does not correspond to the number of characters in actual use at any specific time. The 'List of commonly used characters in Modern Chinese' (现代汉语通用字表 *Xiàndài Hànyǔ tōngyòngzì biǎo*), published in 1988 by the Ministry of Education of the P.R.C., contains 7,000

---

[4] The 異體字字典 *Yìtǐzì zìdiǎn*, sponsored by the Taiwanese Ministry of Education, is freely available online: <http://dict.variants.moe.edu.tw/variants/rbt/home.do> (last access: 13 November 2019).

items, but the 'List of Modern Chinese characters for everyday use' (现代汉语常用字表 *Xiàndài Hànyǔ chángyòngzì biǎo*), also from 1988, has only 3,500 items: besides, these characters are divided into a primary list, containing 2,500 items, and a secondary list with 1,000 characters (Abbiati 2012: 160; Taylor and Taylor 2014: 50).[5] Thus, for the purposes of ordinary writing in any Sinitic language, no more than 7–8,000 characters have ever been in current use at any single time (Norman 1988: 73; Abbiati 2012: 156–61; Taylor and Taylor 2014: 49).

Moreover, the frequency of use for characters varies considerably. According to the data quoted in Abbiati (2012: 158–60), 28 characters only represent about 20% of a text in Modern Chinese: with 243 characters, the coverage reaches 70%. The 1,000 most frequent characters reach 90% of all occurences in an average text, and the 2,400 most frequent items cover 99%. This entails that the remaining 4,200 commonly used characters represent only 1% of all occurrences. For instance, the five-volume 'Selected works of Mao Zedong' (毛泽东选集 *Máo Zèdōng xuǎnjí*) contain a little more than 3,000 distinct characters (out of 900,000 tokens; Abbiati 2012: 158).

Thus, how many characters do you *actually* need to know to read (and write) Chinese? While one may be expected to meet as many as 7,000 distinct graphemes, given that the majority of them have a quite low frequency, knowing the 3,500 most common characters is enough for functional literacy: at this level, a reader will use a dictionary only occasionally (Taylor and Taylor 2014: 50). Over the six years of primary school Chinese pupils learn about 2,800 characters (Taylor and Taylor 2014: 138), which is enough to cover for the vast majority of textual occurrences: indeed, knowing 1,500–2,000 characters may already be enough for basic literacy (Abbiati 2012: 161). Needless to say, specialists in language, literature, and/or philology often know many more characters than those needed for functional literacy, but even in that case the number rarely exceeds 6,000.

Lastly, we would like to point out that 'knowing' a character does not necessarily mean being able to read and write it with ease: generally

---

[5] Note that the number of commonly used characters is somewhat lower (6,500) in the 'List of standardized Chinese characters in current use' (通用规范汉字表 *Tōngyòng guīfàn Hànzì biǎo*), published in 2013 <http://www.gov.cn/gzdt/att/att/site1/20130819/tygfhzb.pdf> (last access: 13 November 2019). The list contains a total of 8,105 characters: besides the above-mentioned 6,500 items, the remaining 1,605 items include characters for personal names, place names, as well as some characters used to write scientific and technical terms which are not part of the 'core' list.

speaking, passive competence is greater than active competence, and anyway (Abbiati 2012: 161–2; our translation)

[l]earning to read and write in Chinese is a lifelong process, since the goal can never be reached, given the incredibly high number of graphemes. Even a very literate and well-educated Chinese may see a character for which s/he does not know the meaning or reading, and thus which s/he cannot understand or read.

However, it is important to stress the point that the number of characters one learned is not directly proportional to the number of *words* one can read and write, since every character/morpheme is normally used in many different words. Indeed, common characters often appear in tens of words (Abbiati 2012: 162; Taylor and Taylor 2014: 50; see §5.1.3).

3.2 A short history of Chinese writing

In the historical evolution of Chinese writing, there have been two opposite tendencies: on the one hand, the permanence of a writing system which has survived, in essence, unchanged for more than three millennia; on the other hand, the push towards innovation that led to several modifications, mostly aimed at increasing its efficiency. Specifically, the three main trends which we may see in the diachronic development of the Chinese script are: the reduction of iconicity, the simplification of character shapes and, as already mentioned, its partial phonetization (Yin Binyong 1994: 44). The most radically innovative proposal in the whole history of Chinese writing, namely the abandonment of logographic writing and its substitution with a phonographic script, while being an important point of debate for several decades in contemporary Chinese history (as we shall see later), has never really gained widespread acceptance: the role of 漢字 *Hànzì* as a key component of the linguistic and cultural identity of China remains virtually unchallenged to this day.

3.2.1 Early attestations of writing in China

The earliest written documents which are universally recognized to be attestations of the Chinese script are the oracle bone inscriptions, dating back to the fourteenth century, as mentioned in §2.2.1. However, the fact that the script was already mature at this stage suggests that writing had already undergone a long process of development before these

Shang period attestations (Abbiati 2012: 28–9). While Boltz (1994, 1999) believes that writing in China should not have appeared much earlier than the oracle bone documents, others, including Demattè (2010), believe it is unlikely that a writing system not based on an existing blue-print could develop so quickly. She also highlights that in the pre-Shang Erlitou culture (二里頭 *Èrlǐtóu*; 1900–1500 BC) there already was a complex societal organization which, arguably, required at least some system for recording information, if not fully-fledged writing. It also appears likely that, at that time, perishable writing supports (as e.g. bamboo strips; see §2.2.1) were in use, and hence the lack of attestations of writing for this stage is not surprising (Demattè 2010, among others).[6] Besides, there are artifacts connected with the so-called Dadiwan (大地灣 *Dàdìwān*) and Dawenkou (大汶口 *Dàwènkǒu*) cultures, obviously much older than oracle bone inscriptions, which do have some sort of graphic symbols on them: if we interpret these as forerunners of writing, then we would have to date the beginnings of the Chinese script to nearly seven millennia ago (Qiu Xigui 2000: 29–33).[7]

Actually, the symbols associated with the Dadiwan and Dawenkou cultures are fundamentally different, and they are usually analysed separately. The earliest type of symbols, dating back to the Neolithic period, are termed 'carved symbols' (刻劃符號 *kèhuà fúhào*; see Yin Binyong 1994: 2). They are simple, regular symbols, which do not appear to resemble any referent and are painted and carved on pottery (Boltz 1994: 35)—Qiu Xigui (2000: 30) calls them 'type A symbols'. Figure 3.2 shows

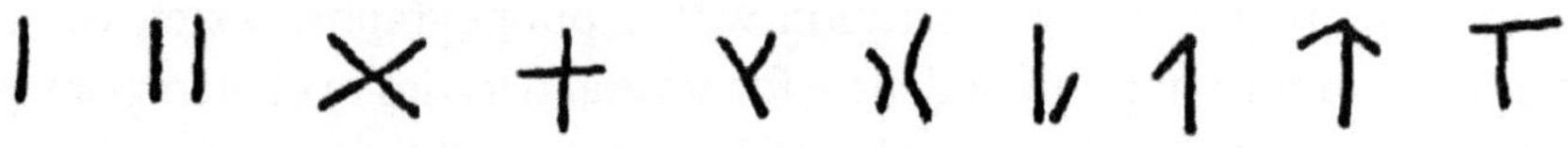

Figure 3.2 Examples of type A pottery marks

Source: Boltz, William G. (1994). *The Origin and Early Development of the Chinese Writing System*, p.36. Reproduced with permission.

[6] As pointed out e.g. by Demattè (2010: 226) and Abbiati (2012: 29), the archaic shapes of characters as 冊 *cè* 'book, volume' and 典 *diǎn* 'codex, document' (respectively, 冊 and 典 in oracle bone inscriptions) contain some depiction of an object made of wooden strips tied together: this might entail that that type of writing support already existed at the time of the earliest attestations of Chinese writing.

[7] The oldest archaeological finds are arguably those from the Jiahu (賈湖 *Jiǎhú*) site in Henan, namely fragments of (possible) oracle bones on which three 'characters' were carved. However, while the fragments have been dated to 5500 BC, it is likely that the symbols were carved on them much later (Demattè 2010: 213).

some examples of type A symbols, found on artifacts excavated from the Banpo (半坡 *Bànpō*) archaeological site in Shaanxi, which probably date back to the period between 4800 and 4200 BC.

Some (mostly Chinese) archaeologists and paleographers argue that type A symbols are actually a stage in the development of Chinese writing (see Yin Binyong 1994 and the references quoted in Boltz 1994 and Demattè 2010): for instance, it has been suggested that the symbol X is an archaic shape of the character 五 *wǔ* 'five' or that 丁 is connected to 示 *shì* 'show'. However, others (e.g. Boltz 1994, 1999; Qiu Xigui 2000; Demattè 2010) believe that it is not possible to prove that there is a direct relationship between these early signs and the Chinese script. There are three main arguments against seeing early carved symbols as forerunners of writing (Boltz 1994: 37–9; Qiu Xigui 2000: 31–2):

a. given that these signs have a very simple structure and that there is no clue as to their function and(/or) meaning, there is no compelling evidence for a connection with actual characters
b. between Banpo inscriptions and the earliest oracle bone inscriptions there is a 3,000-year gap, which is way too long for the development of writing
c. if type A symbols really were the ancestors of oracle bone characters, we would expect them to be *more* iconic (i.e. more pictographic), rather than *less* iconic than the latter, since the degree of iconicity of characters generally decreased with time (see §3.1.1)

However, these arguments do not apply to Dawenkou symbols. Termed 'type B symbols' by Qiu Xigui, Dawenkou symbols are also found on pottery, but they are much more recent (c. 2800–2500 BC), and they are clearly pictographic. See the examples in Figure 3.3.

Figure 3.3 Examples of type B pottery marks
Source: Qiu Xigui (2000), *Chinese Writing*, p.34. Reproduced with permission.

Those symbols are usually interpreted as markings of the creator or owner, possibly indicating also their clan or social status (Boltz 1994; Qiu

Xigui 2000; Abbiati 2012): they are always found in isolation, rather than in a text. Nevertheless, they possess some features which might suggest a possible connection with actual Chinese writing: first and foremost, the fact that they do look like the archaic shapes of some characters, as e.g. 旦 *dàn* 'dawn' (旦) or 斤 *jīn* 'axe' (斤). Moreover, similar symbols may be found on jade discs (璧 *bì*) associated with the Liangzhu (良渚 *Liángzhǔ*) culture: this may be interpreted as indicative of a shared system of graphic symbols between these cultures (Qiu Xigui 2000: 35–7; Demattè 2010: 222–3).

Nevertheless, several scholars (Boltz 1994; Qiu Xigui 2000; Demattè 2010; Abbiati 2012) believe that at this stage we are not yet looking at writing *stricto sensu*, i.e. a system of graphic representation of language, but rather at 'proto-writing': namely, a system of graphic symbols conveying limited information, rather than actual language. Indeed, the use of characters similar to type B symbols as clan emblems in bronze inscriptions from the Shang and Zhou periods, a time when the Chinese script was already developed, could be the direct continuation of this system of proto-writing (Boltz 1994: 46–52). Moreover, Dawenkou symbols might have provided a model for the earliest pictographic characters (Abbiati 2012: 27–8). New archaeological finds in the future might shed light on the development of writing in the transition period between the Late Neolithic and the Early Bronze Age.

Be it as may, oracle bone inscriptions are the earliest documents which are universally accepted as writing proper. For some oracle bone characters, the iconic relationship between the shape of the grapheme and its meaning is still clearly visible, as seen in Figure 3.1. The pictographic origins of some characters are still evident in the other two pre-Qin writing styles, namely the already mentioned bronze inscriptions and the so-called 'large seal script' (大篆 *dàzhuàn*):[8] for instance, the character 馬 *mǎ* 'horse' is written as 馬 in 甲骨文 *jiǎgǔwén* and as 馬 and 马 in the latter two series.

Although at this stage pictographic characters are still a majority (DeFrancis 1984: 84), the two 'phonographic' strategies introduced in §3.1.1, namely loans and phonetic compounds are already productively used to create new characters. As is often the case for writing systems which make use of pictograms (as e.g. Mesopotamian cuneiform or Egyptian hieroglyphs), creating pictographic characters for each word of the language (especially, for abstract notions) soon became impracti-

---

[8] Note that 'large seal script' is sometimes used to refer to all forms of pre-Qin writing, including 甲骨文 *jiǎgǔwén* and 金文 *jīnwén* (Qiu Xigui 2000: 77).

cal: the obvious solution was to use existing graphemes for their sound value, rather than for their meaning, following the above-mentioned principle of rebus writing (Coulmas 2003; see §3.1.1). Thus, for instance, the character 象 *xiàng* (OC *s.daŋ?; BSOL) 'elephant' was used also for 'image', and 來 *lái* (OC *mə.rˤək; BSOL) 'wheat' was used for the verb 'come'. A related strategy was to use a character to write a semantically related word, which however sounded very different, as e.g. 目 *mù* 'eye' (OC *C.m(r)uk) for *jiàn* (OC *kˤen-s; now written as 見) and *kàn* (OC *khˤar-s; BSOL; now 看), both meaning 'see' (Boltz 1994: 63).

While these strategies had the welcome effect of limiting the overall number of characters, they also increased ambiguity, since the very same grapheme could be used to write different words: phonetic compounds (see §3.1.1) were thus created to curb this ambiguity, by adding a semantic component. Going back to the examples of rebus writing seen earlier, the 'person' radical (亻) was added to 象 *xiàng* 'elephant' when used for 'image' (像); the 'grass' radical (艹) was added to 來 *lái* when used as 'wheat' (萊); the verbs *jiàn* and *kàn* 'see' were associated to the characters 見 (目 *mù* 'eye' + 人 *rén* 'person') and 看 (目 *mù* 'eye' + 手 *shǒu* 'hand'), respectively. Moreover, a phonophoric constituent could be added to an existing character to provide clues as to its pronunciation: for instance, the early shape of the pictogram 鳳 *fèng* 'phoenix', namely 鳳, was altered with the addition of the phonophoric 凡 *fán* 'ordinary' (in oracle bone inscriptions, 凡; Qiu Xigui 2000: 8–9). While not all of those additions date back to the Shang and Zhou periods, phonetic strategies were already developed at this stage, and they soon became virtually the only productive methods for character formation. Already in the second-century dictionary 說文解字 *Shuōwén jiězì* (see §3.1.1), 82% of the characters listed belong to the category of phonetic compounds (DeFrancis 1984: 84–5; Boltz 1994: 68–72).

3.2.2 Writing in imperial China

Chinese society changed significantly in the transition from the Spring and Autumn period to the Warring States period: one of the consequences was that writing no longer belonged only to the nobles, and its diffusion in all strata of society began. With the spread of writing, 'popular' variants of characters, which were easier to draw, made their appearance. Moreover, the political fragmentation of China led to the emergence of regional variation in writing: see, for instance, six variants of the characters 者 *zhě* 'one who' and 市 *shì* 'market, city', which were in use in different states before imperial unification (Figure 3.4).

| Qin | Chu | Qi | Yan | Han, Wei, & Zhao |

Figure 3.4 Six local variants for the characters 者 *zhě* 'one who' and 市 *shì* 'market, city'

Source: Qiu Xigui (2000), *Chinese Writing*, p. 87. Reproduced with permission.

Then, in order to support the actual unification of the country, under the first Qin emperor the units of measure, currencies, and laws of the pre-Qin Chinese states were harmonized: writing too was part of this process of standardization, and the characters in use in the state of Qin became the officially sanctioned form of writing in the whole empire. Since the Qin writing system was very conservative, its adoption guaranteed a strong continuity with the past. However, note that, just as for other territories, in the state of Qin there actually was a distinction between the 'canonical' shapes of characters and their popular variants: the former were the basis for the so-called 'small seal script' (小篆 *xiǎozhuàn*), while the latter were the basis for the 'clerical script' (隸書 *lìshū*; Qiu Xigui 2000: 105–7).

While small seal characters were the script in official use, the clerical script, simpler and faster to write, was commonly used for informal writing. Actually, even small seal characters already possessed the features of a mature writing system, to some extent: they are less iconic (if compared to oracle bones and bronze inscriptions), they have a stable shape, and they fit into a so-called 'ideal square'. Moreover, in the small seal script we see a marked increase in the number of phonetic compounds. With the clerical script, Chinese writing eventually detached itself from its pictographic origins: shapes become simpler, and strokes become regular, as is expected for a writing system for current use.

A related development is that alternative forms were introduced for some characters, when used as constituents for other characters, in order to be able to keep the whole character within the ideal square mentioned before. Thus, for instance, the character 水 *shuǐ* 'water' becomes 氵 when appearing as a lefthand constituent: compare e.g. 漿 *jiāng* 'syrup' and 江 *jiāng* 'river' (Yin Binyong 1994: 35–48). However, in the Qin and early

Han periods the clerical script was still developing: it reached its maturity between the Western and Eastern Han periods, when it became the standard form of writing for the Chinese empire (thus replacing the small seal script; Qiu Xigui 2000: 108–13).[9] Compare, for instance, the shapes of the characters 無 *wú* 'nothing', 香 *xiāng* 'perfume', and 莫 *mò* 'not' in the small seal and in the (mature) clerical script (Figure 3.5).

Figure 3.5 The characters 無 *wú*, 香 *xiāng*, and 莫 *mò* in 小篆 *xiǎozhuàn* and in 隸書 *lìshū*

The modern phase of the history of Chinese writing begins in the Han dynasty. Besides the maturation of the clerical script mentioned before, and the introduction of the cursive script (草書 *cǎoshū*, lit. 'hasty writing')[10] and of the running script (行書 *xíngshū*), towards the end of the Han period the so-called regular script (楷書 *kǎishū*) made its appearance: the latter is particularly important, as it is the canonical form of Chinese writing still in use today (Qiu Xigui 2000: 113).

The early, Han period form of the cursive script, known as 章草 *zhāngcǎo*, was characterized by the use of simplified forms of characters: for instance, a constituent as 灬 *huǒ* 'fire' (a variant of 火 used as a component in other characters) was written as a single horizontal stroke (一). On the whole, in the 章草 *zhāngcǎo* cursive the strokes are more 'fluid' and quicker to draw. Note that the cursive script was not invented from scratch: part of its conventions come from current popular forms of abbreviated writing (Qiu Xigui 2000: 131). This early cursive script first evolved into

[9] The terms 古隸 *gǔlì* (lit. 'old clerical') and 新隸題 *xīnlìtǐ* ('new clerical') are sometimes used to refer to the early form of the clerical script of the Qin period and to its late Han form, respectively.

[10] Sometimes the Chinese term 草書 *cǎoshū* is (mis)translated into English as 'grass script' (see Yin Binyong 1994: 41). This is because the usual meaning of 草 *cǎo* is actually 'grass', while it is found as 'hasty' only in some compound words (as e.g. 草稿 *cǎogǎo* '(rough) draft'; Qiu Xigui 2000: 130).

some sort of shorthand, termed 今草 *jīncǎo* (lit. 'modern cursive'), and later, in the Tang period, in a more artistic style of writing known as 狂草 *kuángcǎo* ('crazy cursive'): the latter was used for calligraphy and may be read only by specialists (Abbiati 2012: 63–7). Besides those forms of cursive writing, which involved major simplifications and restructuring of characters, between the third and the fourth century the above-mentioned runnning script emerged: this is the form still in use for handwriting. In the running script, strokes are often joined and simplified, but the structure of the character is well preserved, differently from the cursive script: it is thus both convenient and easily readable (Abbiati 2012: 67–9).

The next stage in the evolution of Chinese writing was the creation of the regular script, as mentioned earlier, between the Han period and the Three Kingdoms. The regular script was not fundamentally different from the clerical script: however, if compared to the latter, the regular script makes more use of curved strokes and is also further removed from the small seal script (Yin Binyong 1994: 38).

To conclude, let us compare the forms of the character 雲 *yún* 'cloud' from its early oracle bone shape up to the present day (Figure 3.6).

甲骨文	金文	小篆	隸書	草書	行書	楷書
jiǎgǔwén	*jīnwén*	*xiǎozhuàn*	*lìshū*	*cǎoshū*	*xíngshū*	*kǎishū*
'oracle bone script'	'bronze script'	'small seal script'	'clerical script'	'cursive script'	'running script'	'regular script'

Figure 3.6 The evolution of the character 雲 *yún* 'cloud'

The oldest attestations of the character 雲 *yún*, namely, those found in oracle bone and bronze inscriptions, are basically pictographic, somehow depicting a cloud. Later on, the character in its original form was borrowed (see §3.2.1) to write the word 云 *yún* 'say', and a new character for 'cloud' was created wth the addition of the semantic constituent 雨 *yǔ* 'rain'. If we look at the small seal version of 雲 *yún*, we may already see that the character has lost all of its (weak) iconic connection with its referent. In the clerical script, 雲 *yún* becomes more regular and easy to write: the shape of the character in the regular script has no evident connection with the small seal version. As for the running and cursive scripts, while in the former the character is easily recognizable despite some simplification of its strokes, in the latter it is much harder to identify the character as 雲 *yún*.

In the Tang period, the regular and running scripts became the dominant styles of writing in China (Norman 1988: 70): with the exception of changes aimed at the management of variants (Qiu Xigui 2000: 404; see §3.1.2) and of the already mentioned simplification of characters in the second half of the twentieth century, the shapes of characters have survived pretty much unchanged to the present day.

Another noteworthy event in the history of Chinese writing in the imperial age is the creation of the first phonographic writing system, namely the already mentioned 'Phags-pa alphabet (§2.2.3). 'Phags-pa writing is named after its creator, the lama 'Phags-pa 'excellent, glorious' (八思巴 *Bāsībā*), and was developed in the thirteenth century, as instructed by the Mongolian emperor Kublai Khan. It was primarily conceived as a script for the Mongolian language, but it was also meant to be used for other languages of the Yuan empire, including Chinese.

The 'Phags-pa alphabet is based on the Tibetan script, which follows the Indian model: it was written vertically, and it had variants designed for writing different languages. Thus, the variant of the 'Phags-pa script used to write Mongolian is not identical to that used for writing Chinese (Coblin 2007a: 1–5). From the structural point of view, the 'Phags-pa alphabet resembles (unsurprisingly) an Indian abugida: all consonant letters are associated with the vowel *a* ([a]) as a default, while other vowels must be explicitly marked (Figure 3.7).

o	*tha*	*tho*	*thwo*	*tham*

Figure 3.7 Examples of 'Phags-pa writing

As we may see in Figure 3.7, vowel sounds, except *a*, have their own grapheme, while the basic consonant letters were interpeted as having an implicit *a*. When (non-default) vowels were added to a consonant, they were written without the horizontal stroke and added below the consonant. Moreover, between a consonant and a vowel, a glide could be added, as in *thwo*, while at the end of the syllable either a semivowel or a consonant could be added, as in *tham*. Tones, however, were never marked (Coblin 2007a: 32–3).

Even though the 'Phags-pa script was fairly short-lived, as it fell almost completely out of use within less than a century (namely, at the end of the Yuan dynasty), the extant documents written in 'Phags-pa are indeed extremely valuable sources for the reconstruction of the historical phonology of Chinese languages (see §4.1.1, 4.1.4).

3.2.3 Writing in republican China: phonetization vs. simplification

As hinted at before (§2.2.4), between the end of the imperial age and the early Republican period, the reform of Chinese writing (and language) became one of the most debated issues in intellectual and political circles. The motto 言文合一 *yán wén héyì*, mentioned with reference to the currents of opinion in favour of the unification of the spoken and written language, was adopted not only by supporters of the use of the vernacular(s) in writing, but also by those who advocated the adoption of a phonographic script for Sinitic languages (Kaske 2008: 90–1).

Besides the 'Phags-pa alphabet, the idea of using phonographic writing for Chinese has its origins in the work of Catholic and Protestant missionaries, who created transcription systems for Sinitic languages. Catholic missionaries active between the sixteenth and the eighteenth century mostly used the Latin alphabet for transcriptions, conceived as aids for language learning: these constituted a model for contemporary romanization systems for Chinese. On the other hand, Protestant missionaries living in the southeastern coastal provinces of China in the nineteenth and early twentieth century created actual phonographic writing systems for Chinese dialects (known in Chinese as 教會羅馬字 *jiàohuì luómǎzì* 'romanized church script(s)'), often used in translations of Christian sacred texts. One such example is the *Pe̍h-ōe-jī* 白話字 system (lit. 'vernacular script'; henceforth, POJ), also known as *Church Romanization* or as *Xiamen Missionary Romanization* in English (see §3.3.1). The POJ system, based on the Latin alphabet, was created in the nineteenth century by Protestant missionaries in Southeast Asia as an orthography for Southern Min: it later spread to Fujian, the homeland of Min dialects, and it became widely used in missionary schools, reaching as many as 100,000 users in the first half of the twentieth century (Klöter 2005: 92). Actually, POJ is still in use today in Taiwan.[11]

---

[11] Interestingly, the articles in the Southern Min (閩南語 *Bân-lâm-gí*) Wikipedia are written either in POJ or in the *Taiwanese Romanization System*, but not in Chinese characters <https://zh-min-nan.wikipedia.org/wiki/Th%C3%A2u-ia%CC%8Dh> (last access: 28 November 2019).

It is important to stress the point that the POJ system was not meant to be an aid in learning Chinese characters: it was a fully-fledged independent script for Southern Min. In Figure 3.8, we may see an excerpt from an early Taiwanese publication in POJ, namely the journal *Taiwan Church*

Tâi-oân-hú-siân
Kàu-hōe-pò.

TĒ IT TIŪ
Kong-sū XI nî, 6 goéh:

Tâi-oân-hú-siâ° ê Kàu-su mn̄g Kàu-hōe-lāi ê hia°-tī chí-moāi° pêng-an : Goán Siōng-tè siú°-sù lín tāi-ke tōa in-tián.

Goán kòe--lâi chit-pêng sī in-ūi ài thôan Thian-kok ê tō-lí, hō͘ lâng bat Siōng-tè lâi tit-tiòh kiu. Só͘ thôan ê tō-lí lóng sī Sèng-chheh só͘ kà-sī--ê; nā° m̄-sī Sèng-chheh ê tō-lí, goán m̄-ká° kóng. Só͘-í goán taùh-taùh khó͘-khn̄g lín tiòh thàk-chheh lâi khòa° Sèng-keng, n̂g-bāng lín ná°-kú ná°-bat Siōng-tè ê tō-lí; iā m̄-bián tek-khak oá-khò Bòk-su á-sī Thôan-tō-lí ê lâng lâi kóng tō-lí hō͘ lín thia°; in-ūi lín pún-sin khòa° Sèng-chheh, siū Sèng-sîn ê kám-hòa, sui-jiân bô lâng lâi kà-sī, lín iáu kú ē chai Siōng-tè ê chí-ì. Khó͘-sioh lín pún-kok ê jī chin oh, chió chió lâng khòa° ē hiáu--tit. Só͘-í goán ū siat pát-mih ê hoat-tō͘, ēng pèh-oē-jī lâi ìn-chheh, hō͘ lín chèng-lâng khòa° khah khoài bat. Iā kīn-lâi tī chit-ê Hú-siâ° goán ū siat chit-ê ìn-chheh ê khì-khū, thang ìn-jī chhin-chhiū° chit hō ê khóan-sit. Ta° goán n̂g-bāng lín chèng-lâng beh chhut-làt òh chiah-ê pèh-oē-jī; aū-lâi goán nā ìn sím-mih chheh lín lóng ē hiáu--tit khòa°. Lâng m̄-thang phah-sǹg in-ūi i bat Khóng-chú-jī só͘-í m̄-bián òh chit-hō ê jī; iā m̄-thang khòa°-khin i, kóng sī gín-á só͘ thàk--ê. Nn̄g-iū° ê jī lóng ū lō͘-ēng; put-kò in-ūi chit-hō khah-khoài iā khah-bêng, só͘-í lâng tiòh tāi-seng thàk-i. Aū-lâi nā° beh sòa thàk Khóng-chú-jī sī chin hó; chóng-sī pèh-oē-jī tiòh khah tāi-seng, kia°-liáu nā° m̄-thàk, lín bē hiáu--tit khòa° goán pát-jit só͘ ìn-ê. Só͘-í goán khó͘-khn̄g lín chèng-lâng, jip-kàu í-kíp thia° tō-lí ê lâng, lâm-hū ló-iù, bat-jī, m̄-bat-jī ê lâng lóng-chóng tiòh kín-kín lâi òh. Chhin-chhiū° án-ní° lín chiū ē hiáu--tit thàk chit-hō ê Kàu-hōe-pò kap gōa-chheh kap Sèng-chheh: n̂g-bāng lín-ê tō-lí ná°-chhim, lín-ê tek-hēng ná°-chiâu-pī.

Figure 3.8 First page of the June 1885 issue of *Taiwan Church News*

News (*Tâi-oân-hú-siân Kàu-hōe-pò* 臺灣府城教會報), first printed in 1885 (Klöter 2005: 93).

These romanized church scripts were very influential among native Chinese language reformers, as they came to be seen as prime examples of how an alphabetic script could be effectively used to write any Chinese language (thus, not limited to the literary standard; DeFrancis 1984: 241; Chen Ping 1999: 164–5).

A major milestone in the history of writing reform in China is the publication of a phonographic script for the Min dialect of Xiamen in 1892. Its creator, Lu Zhuangzhang (盧戇章, 1854–1928), was a Chinese Christian convert who had witnessed the work of missionaries. Lu's idea, which was shared by many reformers of his time, was that the considerable effort required to learn Chinese writing was hindering the diffusion of literacy, as well as subtracting time to the study of hard sciences, seen as crucial for the development of China. Thus, the adoption of a phonographic script, which could be mastered with limited effort and in a short time, would help China to grow rapidly, following the model of the great Western powers (Chen Ping 1999: 165–6; Kaske 2008: 94–5). From the publication of Lu's orthography to the fall of the Qing, no less than twenty-nine different writing systems for Sinitic languages were proposed: they were either based on the Latin alphabet or on 'shorthand' conventional graphemes,[12] or, also, on parts of Chinese characters (Kaske 2008: 93 and the table on page 152–8). An orthography that met with some success, namely the syllabary 官話合聲字母 *Guānhuà héshēng zìmù* (lit. 'alphabet to put together the sounds of Mandarin') by Wang Zhao (王照, 1859–1933), made use of graphemes composed of parts of Chinese characters, just as Japanese *kana* syllabaries. Thus, for instance, the 'hand' radical (扌) was used for the syllable [p^{h}u], and the 'person' radical (亻) was used for the initial [n] (see the table in Chen Ping 1999: 179).

Initially, many of those phonographic orthographies were explicitly aimed at facilitating the spread of literacy, either as substitutes of characters or to support their study. However, towards the end of the imperial age, language reformers moved their focus to the creation of a system for the transcription of standard pronunciation, in order to promote the spread of the emerging national language (see §2.2.4). While

---

[12] The so-called 'shorthand' transcription systems made use of simple graphemes which resemble those of stenography devised for European languages (see Figure 5.2 in Abbiati 2012: 98).

reformers in the early days believed that orthographies based on local dialects, i.e. the mother tongues of the vast majority of the Chinese people at the time, would be more useful and effective than a writing system for Standard Mandarin, the prioritization of the national language led to a decline in the interest for dialect literacy (Chen Ping 1999: 119–20; Kaske 2008: 150–1).

One of the most prominent products of this period is the 注音字母 *Zhùyīn zìmǔ* 'phonetic alphabet', later known as 注音符號 *Zhùyīn fúhào* 'phonetic symbols', or also as *bopomofo* (i.e. its first four syllables). This script, also based on the shapes of Chinese characters, was the first officially sanctioned (in 1918) system for the transcription of Chinese characters, and it was conceived as a device for the diffusion of the 'correct' pronunciation of the national standard (Chen Ping 1999: 180–2). In Figure 3.9, we provide some graphemes (and combinations of graphemes) of the 注音符號 *Zhùyīn fúhào* system, with the corresponding *Pinyin* transcriptions.

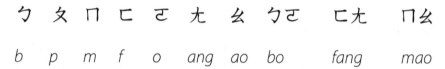

b   p   m   f   o   ang   ao   bo   fang   mao

Figure 3.9 Examples of 注音符號 *Zhùyīn fúhào*

Just as most phonographic scripts created for Sinitic languages, graphemes do not necessarily correspond to individual sounds but, rather, to syllable constituents (i.e. initials, medials, and finals); there are also diacritics for tones, just as in *Pinyin*. While the *bopomofo* is no longer used in Mainland China, in Taiwan it may still be seen in textbooks for primary education, and it is also used as an input method for electronic devices.

Note, however, that even at this stage the idea that characters should be eliminated was not yet dead. Even some of the supporters of the 注音字母 *Zhùyīn zìmǔ* believed that this system could eventually substitute characters (Chen Ping 1999: 181–2).[13] The first official transcription system for Chinese based on the Latin alphabet, the *Gwoyeu romatzyh* (國語羅馬字 *Guóyǔ luómǎzì*), was also regarded by many intellectuals of the time as a possible alternative to Chinese characters (Chen

---

[13] The change in the name from 注音字母 *Zhùyīn zìmǔ* to 注音符號 *Zhùyīn fúhào* in 1930 was motivated by the need to stress that this script was an auxiliary writing system, rather than an alternative to Chinese characters (DeFrancis 1984: 242).

Ping 1999: 182–3).[14] Actually, among the supporters of phonographic writing as a tool for promoting mass literacy we find some of the most influential figures in Chinese culture and politics of the first half of the twentieth century: the already mentioned Chen Duxiu and Lu Xun, and even Mao Zedong and Liu Shaoqi (劉少奇, 1898–1969), who would later become president of the P.R.C. (DeFrancis 1984: 246–51). These ideas were well represented in the *Latinxua Sin Wenzi* (拉丁化新文字 *Lādīnghuà xīn wénzì* 'new Latinized script'), which was explicitly designed as an alternative to characters. The *Latinxua Sin Wenzi* was created by a team of Chinese and Soviet experts and was published in 1929 in the USSR: it was first used among Chinese migrant communities in the Soviet Union and later spread to the areas of China controlled by the Communist forces. It was then adapted for writing several dialects (Cantonese, Hakka, Shanghai Wu, etc.), much in agreement with the spirit of the early reformers. However, this attracted harsh criticism: having different orthographies for each dialect was seen as a threat to the unity of the Chinese people (DeFrancis 1984: 246–7). Eventually, the diffuson of *Latinxua Sin Wenzi* came to a halt in the chaos of the Chinese Civil War (Abbiati 2012: 100). Moreover, at the beginning of the 1950s, Mao changed his mind and decided to promote the simplification of characters, rather than their abandonment (DeFrancis 1984: 257–9).

Despite its quick demise, the spirit of *Latinxua Sin Wenzi* survives in the *Pinyin* system (漢語拼音 *Hànyǔ Pīnyīn* 'phonetic writing for Chinese'). This romanization system, based on the Latin alphabet with the addition of four diacritics for tones, was approved in 1958 by the government of the P.R.C. as an auxiliary device for transcribing characters, especially for teaching, with the aim of spreading the standard pronunciation of 普通話 *Pǔtōnghuà* in the whole country (Abbiati 2012: 101). Hence, *Pinyin* was not meant to have dialectal variants. In fact, *Pinyin* was originally conceived by some also as a substitute for characters (Chen Ping 1999: 188), but this was never part of official Chinese language policy. In 1986, at the Second National Conference on Language and Script (全國語言文字會議 *Quánguó yǔyán wénzì huìyì*), the fact that *Pinyin* is meant only as a tool for the transcription for

---

[14] The *Gwoyeu romatzyh* romanization, which fell out of use long ago in Mainland China, is still used in scientific works by a small group of U.S. sinologists following in the tradition of Chao Yuen Ren (see Branner 2000: 2).

characters was emphasized once again, and the implementation of a true phonographic script for Chinese was postponed indefinitely (Rohsenow 2004: 30–1).

Currently, *Pinyin* is the only romanization system for MSC which is officially sanctioned not only in the P.R.C, but also in Taiwan and Singapore. However, Outside China proper, for quite some time *Pinyin* was competing with other transcriptions, the most popular of which was arguably the Wade-Giles system, created in the nineteenth century by Thomas Wade (see §2.2.3) and Herbert Allen Giles. This is the reason why we may find different versions of the same Chinese names in works written in European languages, as *Mao Tse-tung* (Wade-Giles) for *Mao Zedong* (*Pinyin*), or *I Ching* for the 易經 *Yìjīng* 'Book of Changes'.

Besides the introduction of *Pinyin*, the most important event in this phase of the history of Chinese writing is the simplification of characters. The use of simplified variants for very complex characters was common practice well before the twentieth century: these alternative characters, referred to as 俗(體)字 *sú(tǐ)zì* 'popular characters', were however never officially recognized in imperial China (Yin Binyong 1994: 103–5). In fact, many of the early supporters of the adoption of phonographic writing were also in favour of a 'regulation' of popular simplified variants: in 1935, the government of the Republic of China issued a list of 324 simplified characters, to be used in teaching and in publishing. This reform met with the opposition of conservative figures in the Republican administration and was cancelled shortly after (Chen Ping 1999: 153).

The project of the simplification of Chinese characters was resumed after the founding of the P.R.C.: indeed, the Chinese Script Reform Association (中國文字改革協會 *Zhōngguó wénzì gǎigé xiéhuì*) was reportedly established the very same day of the formal proclamation of the establishment of Communist China (Rohsenow 2004: 23). After the issue of a first list of 515 simplified characters (and fifty-four components) in 1956, the full list of 2,236 simplified shapes (簡化字總表 *Jiǎnhuàzì zǒngbiǎo* 'General list of simplified characters') was published in 1964. This list, with some changes introduced during the above-mentioned Second National Conference on Language and Script, is still in use today.

As hinted at before, since simplified characters were meant to be easily accepted by language users, very few among them were created from scratch: the vast majority of simplified characters are based either on existing popular or calligraphic variants or on simpler (near-)homophonous characters (Yin Binyong 1994: 111; Abbiati 2012: 94). The main strategies used for simplification are shown in Table 3.3.

Table 3.3 Main strategies for the simplification of characters

Strategy	Example
Adoption of popular variants	体 for 體 *tǐ* 'body'
Adoption of archaic variants	从 for 從 *cóng* 'follow'
Adoption of regularized cursive variants	发 for 發 *fā* 'emit'
Substitution of a character with one of its constituents	广 for 廣 *guǎng* 'wide'
Substitution of a constituent with a simpler one	丁 *dīng* for 登 *dēng* in 灯 *dēng* 'lamp' (vs. 燈)
Substitution with a (near-)homophonous character	后 both for 后 *hòu* 'queen' and for 後 *hòu* 'after'

Incidentally, the substitution of a character with a (near-)homophone also had the effect of reducing the number of distinct graphemes.

In December 1977, an additional list with 853 more simplified characters was issued. This list, known as the 'Draft for the Second Chinese Character Simplification Scheme' (第二次漢字簡化方案草案 *Dì-èr cì Hànzi jiǎnhuà fāng'àn cǎo'àn*), was widely criticized, and it was withdrawn within six months from its publication. Later on, at the above-mentioned 1986 Conference, the second simplification was officially cancelled, and it was also resolved that no further large scale simplification schemes would be considered in the future (Rohsenow 2004: 27–9). One of the main reasons behind the failure of the second simplification scheme was that the general public was not familiar with many of the chosen shapes. Besides, the reduction in the number of strokes, mostly applying to characters which already had relatively few strokes (no more than thirteen), together with the excessive use of homophonic characters, meant that characters became less differentiated and, hence, more difficult to recognize (Chen Ping 1999: 159–62). For instance, the characters 衩 *chǎ* (also *chà*) 'crotch (of trousers)', 扠 *chā* (also *chāi*) 'spear, beat', 杈 *chà* (also *chā*) 'branch, twig', and 汊 *chà* 'branch of a river' were all substituted by the character 叉 *chā* 'fork, intersection'. Nevertheless, some characters from this second simplification schema actually gained some acceptance and may still be seen in informal writing, as e.g. 歺 for 餐 *cān* 'meal'.

3.3 Writing other languages

Just as the Latin alphabet and many other writing systems, Chinese characters have been used to write different languages. Chinese characters have been used both for Sinitic languages, including non-standardized varieties (i.e. dialects), and for non-Sinitic languages in the Chinese sphere of cultural influence: these are the so-called 'Sino-Xenic' varieties, i.e. Japanese, Korean, and Vietnamese, as well as some minority languages of China.[15]

Needless to say, the use of Chinese characters for writing languages other than (standard/literary) Chinese necessarily requires some degree of adaptation. In order to write Chinese dialects, Japanese, and Korean, some new graphemes had to be created, and some characters are used just for their sound value, as syllabic graphemes. In the case of the Vietnamese *chữ Nôm* and Zhuang *Sawndip* scripts, the principles of character formation have been applied to create new graphemes to a much larger extent, resulting in what we may term 'Chinese-derived' scripts. Yet other systems, as the Tangut script, were not actually derived from Chinese characters but, rather, followed the Chinese model (Abbiati 2012: 207–8). For reasons of space and opportunity, here we shall focus on dialect writing, but we shall also discuss briefly the *chữ Nôm* and *Sawndip* scripts.[16]

3.3.1 Writing Chinese dialects

In the linguistic history of China, a standard written language based on spoken varieties gained official acceptance only relatively recently. As discussed earlier (§2.2.4), this is easily explained by the importance of the Classical language in Chinese culture and by the rigid separation of spoken and written language in the Chinese tradition. In this context, the fact that dialect writing was underdeveloped in premodern China, and continues to be marginal nowadays, is hardly surprising. Nevertheless, outside the domain of official usage, and in less prestigious literary genres, some Chinese dialects did enjoy limited popularity

---

[15] The term 'Sino-Xenic' was coined by Samuel Martin to refer to the systems for reading Chinese characters in Japan, Korea, and Vietnam (Norman 1988: 34).

[16] On Chinese writing in Japan and Korea see, respectively, Shibatani (1990), Miyake (2003), and Frellesvig (2010), and Sohn (1999) and Lee and Ramsey (2011; see also Taylor and Taylor 2014; Handel 2019).

also in writing, most often based on Chinese characters (Klöter 2005: 29–30). Besides, phonographic scripts based on the Latin alphabet for Chinese dialects were developed by Protestant missionaries, as mentioned in §3.2.3.

Before the beginning of the twentieth century, the status of dialect writing was comparable (but not equal) to that of 白話 *báihuà*, in some respects. Both dialects and 白話 *báihuà* were generally used only for low prestige literary genres and often for texts which were supposed to reflect the spoken language to some extent: for instance, 'prompt books' (話本 *huàběn*) for story-telling, operas, and theatre plays. These genres were all conceived for oral recitation (Snow 2004: 40–1), and even when dialects are used in novels, dialect words and expressions are found mostly in dialogues (Snow, Zhou, and Shen 2018). Starting from the Ming dynasty, we begin to see some dialect literature: for instance, the scripts for the 彈詞 *táncí* genre of story-telling accompanied by music (Zhou and You 1986: 185; Snow 2004: 33). The oldest document partly written in Southern Min is the theatre play 荔鏡記 *Lìjìngjì* 'Tale of the Lychee Mirror', dating back to 1566 (first edition), while the earliest representative work in a Wu dialect is the collection of Suzhounese songs 山歌 *Shān Gē* 'Mountain Songs', edited by Feng Menglong (馮夢龍, 1574–1646) and published in 1618 or 1619 (Snow, Zhou, and Shen 2018: 146–7). What is arguably most interesting about these early documents is that they suggest that their authors expected their audience to be able to read dialect words and, hence, that there was at least some degree of consensus on how to write them.

However, dialect literature was held in contempt by many educated Chinese, and it was even seen as immoral by imperial officials (Klöter 2005: 59): indeed, the worship of Classical Chinese was so entrenched that even just using vernacular expressions in 文言 *wényán*, or dialect words in 白話 *báihuà*, was frowned upon (Chen Ping 1999: 117). While the above-mentioned Feng Menglong was a member of the educated elite, he regarded his works in Classical Chinese as superior to his vernacular texts, and in the preface to the 'Mountain Songs' he tried to justify his use of Suzhounese, knowing that the collection would be criticized by other intellectuals (Snow, Zhou, and Shen 2018: 150). Also, it is important to point out that what we term 'dialect literature', in this context, was by no means written entirely in a Chinese dialect: they are literary works basically written in 白話 *báihuà* which contain a varying percentage of dialect words and expressions.

In the cultural climate of the late nineteenth century (see §2.2.4), dialects did manage to find some space even in some novels from Mandarin- and Wu-speaking regions (Zhou and You 1986: 183).[17] Nevertheless, in Wu dialect novels, obviously more distant from Mandarin-based 白話 *báihuà*, the use of dialect was limited to dialogues, in the mouths of characters of a low social status: often, prostitutes. A notable exception is Han Bangqing's (韓邦慶, 1856–94) novel 海上花列傳 *Hǎi shàng huā lièzhuàn* 'The Sing-song Girls of Shanghai' (1892; also known as 'Shanghai Flowers' in English), where all the dialogues are in the Suzhou dialect. Interestingly, despite the extensive use of Suzhounese, the novel had some degree of commercial success (Snow, Zhou, and Shen 2018: 158). However, the fact that Wu dialects were not readily understandable for every Chinese, the morally shady settings of most dialect novels, and the highest prestige of Northern 白話 *báihuà* led to a rapid decline of this (sub-)genre (Snow 2004: 33–4).

Nevertheless, the use of dialect in Chinese literature never really disappeared completely: for instance, the dialogues in Zhou Libo's (周立波, 1908–79) 山鄉巨變 *Shānxiāng jùbiàn* 'Great Changes in a Mountain Village' (1958; Sec. Ed. 1979) are mostly written in the Yiyang (益陽) Xiang dialect (see the analysis in Wu Yunji 2005: 58–64). A recent notable example is Jin Yucheng's (金宇澄, b. 1952) novel 繁花 *Fánhuā* 'Magnificent Flowers' (2013) which, while being written mostly in Standard Mandarin, contains a significant amount of Shanghainese vocabulary: as pointed out by Snow, Shen, and Zhou (2018: 218), 'Magnificent Flowers' is the first novel partly written in a non-Mandarin dialect which enjoyed critical and commercial success since the founding of the P.R.C. Indeed, the use of written Shanghainese has seen an increase in the past ten years, and there have even been publications *entirely* or mostly in the Shanghai dialect (as e.g. 濃濃滬語海上情 *Nóngnóng Hùyǔ Hǎishàng Qíng* 'Rich Shanghainese Feeling'; Snow, Shen, and Zhou 2018: 232). These, however, are but sparse occurrences in mainstream Chinese literature, and the case of Shanghainese is a recent development (on the future prospects for Wu dialect literature, see Snow, Shen, and Zhou 2018). On the other hand, the use of dialect writing has enjoyed, and still enjoys, some popularity in Hong Kong and, to a much lesser extent, in Taiwan, as we shall see later.

---

[17] Actually, words and expressions in Suzhounese may be already found also in novels from the late Ming period: once again, Suzhounese is typically used in dialogue lines of lower-class characters, for comedic effect (Snow, Zhou, and Shen 2018).

Generally speaking, the use of Chinese characters for dialect writing poses some practical problems. The ideal solution to write a dialect word/morpheme is using a character with the same etymon, as e.g. 三 *sān* 'three' for Cant. *sāam* 'three'. However, this is not always possible, since characters were obviously not created to write just *any* Sinitic language (see §3.1.1). Thus, in many cases one has to find an alternative grapheme, and this choice has consequences for the readability of texts, The main strategies used in the choice of graphemes for dialect writing are summarized in Table 3.4 (You Rujie 1992: 177–85; Snow 2004: 52–7; Klöter 2005: 30–4; Wu Yunji 2005: 45–7; Matthews and Yip 2011: 9–10; Bauer 2018).

Table 3.4 Main strategies for the choice of graphemes for dialect writing

Strategy	Example
Use of an obsolete character, which is claimed to represent the word/morpheme at issue (a procedure known in Chinese as 本字考 *běnzì kǎo* 'study of original characters')	搇 for Ningbo Wu [tɕhiŋ⁴⁴] 'squeeze and hold'
Use of a (near-)homophone with no obvious semantic connection with the dialect word/morpheme	朽 'rotten' for [ɕiəu⁴¹] 'arrogant' in Changsha Xiang
Use of a character with the same meaning as the dialect/word morpheme, but with a different reading (known as 訓讀 *xùndú*, lit. 'learned reading')	柴 *chái* 'firewood' for Meixian Hakka [tʃʰiau⁴⁴] (which shares an etymon with 樵 *qiáo*)
Coining a new character	㑷 for the Taiwanese pronoun *in* 'they', a phonetic compound made up by the radical 亻 *rén* 'person' and the phonophoric 因 *in* 'cause'
Use of the Latin alphabet	'D' for Cantonese 啲 *dī* 'a bit'
Use of a small square shape	□ for Cantonese *lyūt* (an onomatopoeic syllable) in 滑 □□ *waaht-lyūt-lyūt* 'smooth as a baby's bottom'

Not all of the strategies listed in Table 3.4 are equally common and accepted. The procedure of 本字考 *běnzì kǎo* involves significant effort in locating the possible original character in ancient lexicographic words, and specialists sometimes disagree on what is the correct 本字 *běnzì* for a word/morpheme. Moreover, language users often do not accept the 'correct' character because it may be very unfamiliar to the average person: thus, for instance, in the Cantonese expression 擔高個頭 *dāam gōu go tàuh* 'lift up one's head', the etymologically correct character for the verb *dāam* is 㩒, but it is rarely used (Matthews and Yip 2011: 9). New characters created specifically for dialect writing are also not really easy to recognize (one must not forget that only characters for writing Standard Chinese are taught in schools in almost all of the Chinese-speaking world): hence, this strategy is seldom used (Snow 2004: 53, 55). In some cases, characters coined by individual authors are used only by their own creators (for some examples, see Klöter 2005: 204–5). However, a pattern for coining characters which is fairly common, particularly for Cantonese writing, is the addition of the 'mouth' radical (口) to an existing character to indicate that the grapheme is used only for its sound value: see e.g. Cant. 哋 *deih* 'plural suffix', from 口 *háu* 'mouth' and 地 *deih* 'place', or 嘢 *yéh* 'thing', from 口 *háu* 'mouth' and 野 *yéh* 'wild' (Bauer 2018: 129).

The use of the Latin alphabet is not rare even in informal written registers of the standard language, as in computer-mediated communication (CMC). Alphabetic writing for vulgar words, as *B* 'female genitalia' (MSC 屄 *bī*), and (pseudo-)acronyms, as *GCD* '(Chinese) Communist Party' (共產黨 *Gòngchǎndǎng*), is quite common in the language of Chinese netizens. Indeed, even written Cantonese for CMC makes use of the Latin alphabet more often, also for words which are associated with a common character (Snow 2004: 54). In Taiwanese writing, the Latin alphabet is sometimes used together with Chinese characters, to write function words, words with an obscure etymon, or words associated with an uncommon character. This produces a 'mixed' system, comparable to that of Japanese (which combines Chinese logograms and native syllabaries), as we may see in the following example (adapted from Klöter 2005: 302–3):

(1) *Ah lín tang* 時 *beh* 對看?
     ah   lín   tang-sî   beh   tuì-khuànn
     Ah   2SG   when   want   introduce
     'Ah, and when will you be introduced to each other?'

Arguably, the most common strategy in dialect writing is the use of (near-)homophonous characters. Actually, even when characters are created, graphemes which contain at least a constituent suggesting their reading are preferred (Snow 2004: 56–7). When loan characters are used, since almost every grapheme conveys a meaning, the reader is faced with the problem of recognizing whether a character is used for its sound only or also for its meaning (Chen Ping 1999: 116). However, since the use of characters for their phonetic value is very common, when users read an unfamiliar character they tend to interpret it as a loan (Snow 2004: 57).

Because of the use of different strategies for the choice of graphemes, with a low level of standardization, dialect writing tends to be 'polyorthographic': namely, the same word/morpheme may be associated with more than one character, with much interuser variation. Even a common word as the Cantonese verb *jūngyi* 'like' has two frequently used variant graphic forms, namely 鍾意 and 中意. In his analysis of the graphemes used to write 100 Taiwanese expressions in a sample of seven texts of the twentieth and early twenty-first centuries, Klöter (2005: 267–80) shows that only fifteen of those expressions are written with the same graphemes in all the texts considered: the remaning eighty-five have at least one variant (Klöter 2005: 217). For instance, in Klöter's sample, the following graphemes are used for the Taiwanese verb *tuè* 'follow': 隨 'follow' (MSC *suí*), 隶 'catch' (*dài*),[18] 綴 'sew, stitch' (*zhuì*), and three phonetic compounds coined *ad hoc*, namely 亻豕 (with the 'person' radical'), 迖 and 遾 (with the 辶 *chuò* 'go' radical). Interestingly, 綴 is currently the most commonly used character for *tuè* 'follow', possibly because the verb 綴 *zhuì* seems to be etymologically related to *tuè* (Klöter 2005: 217).

Besides the already mentioned low prestige, and the problems with the choice of graphemes, among the reasons behind the underdevelopment of dialect writing in China we must point out the hostility of much of the *intelligentsia*, and of the Chinese government: dialect writing was, and often still is, seen as a threat to the unity of the Chinese nation, while the written (literary) language has always been a strong element of cohesion (Chen Ping 1999: 117–21; see §2.1). This is tightly connected with the debate on the adoption of a phonographic script: as discussed in §3.2.3, while the earliest phonographic writing systems of modern China were conceived as orthographies for dialect writing and were meant to promote mass literacy, in the twentieth century the focus shifted towards the use of phonographic writing to help the diffusion of the standard pronunciation of the national language (i.e. MSC). It is no coincidence that

---

[18] The character 隶 is currently associated with the morpheme *lì* 'slave'. However, this character was originally used to write the word *dài* 'catch', currently written as 逮.

dialect writing has gained more acceptance in two regions of the Chinese-speaking world which are culturally and politically quite distant from (present-day) Mainland China: namely, Hong Kong and Taiwan.

What is now the Hong Kong Special Administrative Region of the P.R.C. has been under British rule from 1841 to 1997 (excluding the period of Japanese occupation during the Second World War): under the principle known as 'One country, two systems' (一國兩制 *yī guó liǎng zhì*), Hong Kong still enjoys some degree of autonomy from the Beijing government. While MSC has an increasingly important role in Hong Kong, and its use as a medium of instruction in schools has grown in the past fifteen years (Bauer 2018: 103–4), Cantonese is still by far the dominant language in the former British colony. According to the 2016 Population By-Census, Cantonese is the 'usual spoken language' for 88.9% of the population aged five and over in Hong Kong, while MSC has the same function for only 1.9% of the population (although almost half of Hongkongers speak it as a second language; see also Bauer 2018).[19] The language policy of the Hong Kong government is often summarized with the Cantonese phrase 兩文三語 *léuhng màhn sāam yúh*: namely, the promotion of two written languages (文 *màhn*), English and (standard) Chinese, and three spoken languages (語 *yúh*; see §2.2.4), English, 普通話 *Pǔtōnghuà*, and Cantonese. Thus, *written* Cantonese has no official recognition, and the only written language taught in schools and used in formal texts is Modern Standard Chinese.

Despite the lack of official support, written Cantonese is commonly used in colloquial texts, as e.g. popular novels, comic books, advertisements, and in (informal) CMC. Interestingly, while written Cantonese is often used for a faithful transcription of dialogues in texts mostly written in standard Chinese (e.g. in newspaper articles), there are also texts written entirely or mostly in Cantonese. This entails that written Cantonese has achieved, to some extent, independence from the national standard, differently e.g. from the Suzhounese literature discussed before (see Snow, Zhou, and Shen 2018: 161–4). See, for instance, the poster in Figure 3.10.

[19] <https://www.bycensus2016.gov.hk/data/16bc-main-results.pdf> (last access: 5 December 2019). Interestingly, according to the By-Census data, in the period between 2006 and 2016, the total number of speakers of MSC in Hong Kong increased from 44.7% to 53.2%, while speakers of Cantonese decreased from 96.5% to 94.6%. Hence, while the growth in the number of speakers of the national standard is indeed significant, the decline of Cantonese is not too prononunced.

Figure 3.10 Poster in Cantonese in the Hong Kong Mass Transit Railway

Photo: authors' own, June 2018

In this poster, meant to remind the passengers of the underground trains that pushchairs are allowed only in lifts (not on escalators), the main message is written *entirely* in Cantonese:

(2)　推BB車要搭䡓。
　　tēui   bìhbī-chē   yiu   daap   līp
　　push   baby-car   have.to   take   lift
　　'When you are pushing a pushchair, you must take the lift.'

Here we see some of the strategies presented in Table 3.4: the Latin letters *BB* are used to write the English loanword 'baby' (*bìhbī* in Cantonese), and 䡓 is an original Cantonese character specifically coined to write the word *līp*, a loanword from English 'lift'. Note that the character 䡓 is a typical phonetic compound, with 車 *chē* 'car' as the semantic component (a lift is a kind of vehicle), and 立 *lahp* 'stand' as phonophoric. And this is by no means an exception: the use of Cantonese in this type of advertising is quite common in Hong Kong (Bauer 2018: 105–6), and the works of popular literature known as 'pocketbooks', some of which were written in Cantonese only, indeed met with commercial success (at least, until the early 1990s; Snow 2004).

Thus, if written Cantonese may be used to convey a message which is meant to reach the largest possible audience, it is because it is widely understood by literate Hongkongers (but, very often, not by speakers of Sinitic languages other than Cantonese). What is interesting is that, as said before, this is true despite the fact that, just as the Chinese from other regions of China, students in Hong Kong are never formally taught how to write in Cantonese. Nevertheless, as pointed out by Bauer (2018: 116),

[...] Cantonese-speaking schoolchildren have still been able to pick them [the conventions for writing Cantonese] up informally and so learn to read and write Cantonese through their contact with and exposure to its texts that pervade the domains in which written language is used

According to Snow (2004: 175–211), the success of Cantonese in Hong Kong may be explained, first and foremost, by the attitude of local governments: although the authorities of the territory never actively encouraged the use of written Cantonese, they also never opposed it, somehow 'sheltering' it from the pro-普通話 *Pǔtōnghuà* policies of the P.R.C.[20] Other relevant factors are the prestige associated with the

---

[20] Needless to say, the situation of written Cantonese is very different in Guangzhou, the other major centre of the Cantonese-speaking world. Since the P.R.C. laws on language and

Cantonese-speaking community, among the most prosperous and culturally active in the Chinese-speaking world, the role of local media, which have promoted the use of the language, and the role of Cantonese as a symbol of Hong Kong identity (on the symbolic function of local literature in Cantonese, see Snow 2004: 204–6). Moreover, the widespread use of loan characters makes written Cantonese easy to learn and use, helping its diffusion despite the above-mentioned lack of formal instruction: in fact, it might even be argued that, in a sense, it is easier to learn than the written national standard, given that Cantonese is the mother tongue of the vast majority of Hongkongers. On the other hand, it is important to stress the point that written Cantonese, just as virtually any other written form of a Chinese dialect, is generally associated with low prestige genres: as pointed out by Snow, Shen, and Zhou (2018: 241), '[…] publications that wish to be taken seriously generally use little or no Cantonese. To the extent that written Cantonese appears in books, these are generally what would be considered popular literature, rather than books with greater aspirations to literary merit'.

The relationship between language and writing, and between language and local identity, is more complex in another region of the Chinese-speaking world in which dialects have a somewhat different role from the P.R.C.: namely, Taiwan. Just as Hong Kong, Taiwan has been politically separated from the mainland for more than a century: between 1895 and 1945 as a Japanese colony, and from 1949 to the present day as a territory governed by the Republic of China (see §2.1). The largest regional group among the ethnic Chinese population is that of the Fujianese immigrants, known as *Hoklo* or *Holo* (福佬, Taiw. *hok-ló*, lit. 'Fujianese', or 河洛 *hô-lók*; see Wang Fu-chang 2014), associated with Southern Min dialects. Also, the island has a sizeable Hakka minority, and more than half a million residents classified as 'indigenous',[21] belonging to Austronesian-speaking ethnic groups. However, the Taiwanese people first saw the imposition of Japanese, and then of MSC, the language of the 'Mainlanders' (known in Taiwan as 外省人 *wàishěngrén* 'people from other provinces'), while the use of Chinese

---

script do apply there, the use of written Cantonese is very restricted, and relatively uncommon (Bauer 2018: 105). On the current status of Cantonese in the Chinese mainland, see Gao Xuesong (2012). On some recent initiatives for the preservation of dialects, also in their written form, see Li Jia (2019).

[21] According to the 2010 Population and Housing Census <https://census.dgbas.gov.tw/PHC2010/english/rehome.htm> (last access: 6 December 2019).

dialects and indigenous languages was severely restricted until 1987 (the year of the lifting of martial law). The use of the 'native' languages of the Taiwanese was forbidden in schools, and students could be punished just for speaking Taiwanese or Hakka. These languages were reintroduced in the school curriculum only in the 1990s, and even then they were, and still are, clearly subordinate to MSC, by far the dominant language in education (Tsao Feng-fu 2008; Wu Ming-Hsuan 2009).

In this context, the use of languages is loaded with ideological significance: Min and Hakka dialects may become the symbols of a new Taiwanese identity, separated from the 'Chinese' identity of the Mainlanders. Indeed, already in the 1930s writers experimented with writing in Southern Min with the aim of 'claiming' a Taiwanese identity. While the Taiwanese dialect literature of the 1970s did not seem to be politicized at the beginning, it became associated with the opposition to the Kuomintang government and to the ties with the Chinese mainland (Hsiau A-chin 2000: 38–46; Snow 2004: 35–9; Klöter 2005: 157–8, 188–91). Thus, writing has played an important role in the quest for a Taiwanese identity: between the end of the 1980s and the mid 1990s, at least twelve associations for the revitalization of local languages have been established, and these associations actively tried to promote the standardization of written Taiwanese, as well as the diffusion of Taiwanese literature. The possibility to write in Taiwanese, rather than in 國語 *Guóyǔ*, came to be seen by many as crucial for the construction of a local identity independent from mainland China (Hsiau A-Chin 2000: 136–9).

However, the situation of Taiwan is actually quite different from that of Hong Kong. First and foremost, while Cantonese is clearly the language of Hong Kong identity, treating the Southern Min dialects spoken by the *Hoklo* population as *the* Taiwanese language, entails discriminating against the Hakkas and the indigenous people, resulting again in linguistic injustice (Hsiau A-Chin 2000: 139–44; Wang Fu-chang 2014).[22] Besides, differently from Hong Kong, MSC is slightly more common than Taiwanese as a home language in Taiwan, and the preference for the national standard is much more prononunced in the younger generation.[23] This is probably one of the main reasons why

---

[22] Actually, while the term 台語 *Táiyǔ* 'Taiwanese' is commonly used in Taiwan to refer to the local Southern Min variety, in official documents the more neutral term (台灣) 閩南語 (*Táiwān*) *Mǐnnányǔ* '(Taiwan) Southern Min' is preferred.

[23] See the data on language use of the 2010 Population and Housing Census <http://eng.stat.gov.tw/public/data/dgbas04/bc6/census022e%28final%29.html> (last access: 6 December

language does not seem to be crucial in the construction of Taiwanese identity (Tsao Feng-fu 2000: 99–100; Snow 2004: 39). Moreover, while written Cantonese, despite the lack of standardization, is however conventionalized enough to be easy to read, Taiwanese publishers typically accept the orthographic choices of each author, thus leading to a rather unstable situation, as seen before: as Klöter (2005: 249) puts it, '[f]or the time being, the reader of Taiwanese texts will have to come to terms with chaos'. While mixed scripts (ex. 1) seem to be preferred by many Taiwanese authors, there are no shared conventions for the choice of characters to write Taiwanese words and for when (and how) to use the Latin alphabet (Klöter 2005: 225). Besides, there are as many as fifty writing systems entirely based on the Latin alphabet, as well as many different conventions for the choice of Chinese characters, even in lexicographic works (see Klöter 2005: 205–7, 220). And things are not looking better in the context of formal education: while local languages have been accepted in the school curriculum for more than twenty years now, the issue of the standardization of writing is far from being resolved (Klöter 2005: 244–8; Wu Ming-Hsuan 2009: 109–10; Klöter 2017).

As mentioned before, the teaching of local languages in schools has been allowed since the 1990s: starting from 2001, the study of Taiwanese, Hakka, or of an indigenous language has become compulsory in primary education for at least one hour a week. However, because of the lack of a standard, editors are not eager to publish textbooks for those languages, and many instructors just gave up teaching the written language, focussing rather on oral skills (Tsao Feng-fu 2008). In 2012, the Ministry of Education of the R.O.C. did publish a series of textbooks to learn Hakka with Chinese characters and romanization, but since no single variety has the role of the 'standard' for Taiwanese Hakka, as many as six different versions had to be published.[24] Taiwanese (Southern Min), on the other hand, does have some sort of 'national' variety, termed 通行 *tōngxíng* 'common' (Klöter 2005: 4), on which teaching materials may be based. Moreover, in 2010 the Ministry of Education published a list of 700 officially sanctioned characters for writing

2019): MSC is a home language for 96% of the population aged 6–14, while Taiwanese is below 70%.

[24] These textbooks may be freely downloaded from <https://cirn.moe.edu.tw/WebFile/index.aspx?sid=1107&mid=5648> (last access: 6 December 2019).

Taiwanese (revised in 2014),[25] a decision which could help the process of standardization of the written language.

However, the standardization of the orthography alone may not be enough for the promotion of written Taiwanese, in the absence of policies for status planning aimed at extending the domains of use of this variety, which is under intense pressure from MSC and even from English (Klöter 2005: 247–8; see also Klöter 2009). Besides, it is unclear whether the measures for the standardization of Taiwanese had any significant impact outside the educational system. For instance, in the academic publication *Journal of Taiwanese Vernacular* (Taiw. 台語研究 *Tâi-gí gián-kiù*), published since 2009 by the Department of Taiwanese Literature of Cheng Kung University in Tainan, many articles still make use of mixed writing: for instance, the Taiwanese function words *kap(/kah)* 'and' and *ê* 'of' are normally romanized, despite the fact that they are associated with the characters 佮 and 的, respectively, in the above-mentioned list. Also, it is far from uncommon for articles in this journal to be written entirely in the POJ script.[26]

Lastly, we must point out that on 25 December 2018 the Taiwanese parliament approved a law, the 'National Languages Development Act' (國家語言發展法 *Guójiā Yǔyán Fāzhǎn Fǎ*), granting equal protection to all 'national' languages, including Taiwanese (Southern Min), Hakka, and indigenous languages. According to the official news release of the Ministry of Culture,[27] the Act is meant to 'protect the rights of all ethnic groups to education, communication, and public services in their mother tongues'. As for the written language, we read that:

[...] the Act stipulates that the government should develop standardized orthographies for the purpose of properly recording and preserving national languages. The government shall thus work with civic groups to develop each orthographic reference standard, including both Sinitic and romanized orthographies, digital input methods, and other methods of expression.

It does not, however, place restrictions on how people may write, allowing for the coexistence of multiple varying forms of writing. In the future, central government agencies will cooperate closely with the Ministry of Education to ensure the preservation of all national languages.

---

[25] <https://ws.moe.edu.tw/001/Upload/userfiles/file/iongji/700iongji_1031222.pdf> (last access: 6 December 2019).

[26] <http://ctlt.twl.ncku.edu.tw/jotv.html> (last access: 6 December 2019).

[27] https://www.moc.gov.tw/en/information_196_96138.html (last access: 6 December 2019).

Thus, while setting out a plan for the standardization of orthographies for languages other than MSC, the Act explicitly allows for the existence of a plurality of orthographies. The possible impact of the Act on the use and status of Taiwanese and other languages of Taiwan remains to be seen.

3.3.2 *The* Chữ Nôm *and* Sawndip *writing systems*

While Vietnamese and Zhuang do not appear to have any genetic relationship with Chinese (see §2.3.1), there is little doubt that they have been in contact with Sinitic languages and, also, that Chinese culture has been very influential in the history of the Vietnamese- and Zhuang-speaking communities.

The regions corresponding to present-day northern and central Vietnam have been under Chinese rule between the second and the tenth century AD, and there is a longstanding history of Chinese immigration to that area. Even after Vietnam became independent from the Chinese Empire, the political and philosophical framework of the country was still based on the Chinese tradition, and Classical Chinese was the language of formal writing and higher education until the beginning of the twentieth century. Words of Chinese origin, which often entered the Vietnamese lexicon through the written language, probably represent about 70% of the lexicon of Modern Vietnamese (Nguyen 1997; Bisang 2001b; Alves 2001, 2009).

The Zhuang people (壮族 *Zhuàngzú*) are one of the officially recognized ethnic minorities of the P.R.C.: there are about eighteen million ethnic Zhuang in China, and they mostly reside in the Guangxi Zhuang Autonomous Region. There is no single Zhuang language, but rather a fairly homogeneous cluster of Tai-Kadai varieties which are collectively referred to as 'Zhuang' (Luo Yongxian 2008: 317–18). The Zhuang were part of the 'hundred Yue' (see §2.2.2), the historical inhabitants of Southern China, and their first contacts with the Han Chinese probably date back to the conquest of present-day Guangxi by the first Qin emperor, in 219 BC (Holm 2008: 415). While during the Yuan and Ming periods Zhuang people enjoyed some degree of autonomy from the central government, due to the Chinese custom of choosing locals for the administration of non-Han areas, starting from the Qing dynasty the Zhuang-speaking region became integrated in the imperial administration: ethnic Han replaced local officials, and Han Chinese migrated *en masse* to the region. The influx of Chinese-speaking people at different times in the history of the Zhuang had a very significant impact on local culture and language(s) (Luo Yongxian 2008: 319–20).

Hence, it is perhaps unsurprising that both Vietnamese and Zhuang people developed writing systems derived from Chinese characters. Many of the principles for adapting the Chinese script to Vietnamese and Zhuang are analogous to those seen in the preceding section for Chinese dialect orthographies: characters could be used for their meaning only, for their sound only, and they could also be created, following the same strategies for building new characters in the Chinese script (see §3.1.1). Moreover, when writing words of Chinese origin, characters could be used both for their meaning and for their sound. However, the fact that Vietnamese and Zhuang, differently from Chinese dialects, are unrelated to Sinitic, meant that the task of adapting the Chinese script was much more complicated, and many more characters had to be coined. Besides, due to the important differences in the sound systems of Sinitic, Vietnamese, and Zhuang, the use of loan (rebus) characters often involves a high degree of approximation in matching sounds (Hannas 1997: 83; Holm 2008: 416). Lastly, as we shall see later, some strategies for character formation of the Zhuang *Sawndip* script are not normally used in Chinese dialect writing.

The oldest documents in the Vietnamese *chữ Nôm* system (𡨸喃, lit. 'popular/vernacular writing') date back to the fourteenth century (although it is likely that the system was already in use well before), and *chữ Nôm* was in use until the nineteenth century, primarily for Vietnamese literature (as opposed to writing in Classical Chinese; see Thompson 1987 [1965]: 53–4; Nguyen 1997: 6–7). At the beginning of the twentieth century, under French colonial administration, Chinese writing in every form was substituted by the romanized script *chữ quốc ngữ* (lit. 'national language writing'), based on a writing system created by Catholic missionaries in the seventeenth century. The *chữ quốc ngữ* is still in use today, while the *chữ Nôm* is known only by a limited number of specialists (Thompson 1987 [1965]: 54). Some examples of how Chinese characters were adapted in the *Nôm* system for the purpose of writing Vietnamese (see Hannas 1997: 80–2) are shown in Table 3.5.

Just as the dialect orthographies discussed in the preceding section, the *chữ Nôm* script had limited prestige, if compared to Classical Chinese, and its level of standardization was quite low. The same character could be associated with different words, and the same word could be written with different characters, similarly to Japanese (Shibatani 1990:

Table 3.5 Examples of the use of the Chinese script in Vietnamese *chữ Nôm* writing

Strategy	Example
Use of a (near-)homophone with no obvious semantic connection	固 *gù* 'solid' for *có* 'have'
Use of a character with the same meaning as the Vietnamese word	役 *yì* for *việc* 'work, task, matter'
Coining of a new 會意 *huìyì* character (see §3.1.1)	𡗶 *giời* 'sky', from 天 *tiān* 'sky' and 上 *shàng* 'above'
Coining of a new phonetic compound	𠀧 *ba* 'three', from 巴 *bā* 'hope, cling' (phonophoric) and 三 *sān* 'three'
Use of a component of a character	⺶ *làm* 'do, make', from 為 *wéi* 'do, act'
Use of a character to write the corresponding word of Chinese origin	頭 *tóu* 'head' for *đầu* 'head'

130; Frellesvig 2010: 268): even the first word in the name of this Vietnamese script, *chữ* 'character, writing', was written with two different characters, namely 𡨸 and 𡦂 (both coined in Vietnam). Besides, the very same components were sometimes used in complex characters as phonophorics, and sometimes for their meaning (see the examples in Hannas 1997: 83). The complexity of the *chữ Nôm* system, and the fact that it enjoyed limited consideration among educated Vietnamese, are the main reasons why this script could not really challenge the status of Chinese writing in Vietnam. Nevertheless, just as seen before for Taiwanese writing, there were times when the *chữ Nôm* script was also a 'vehicle for social protest' (Hannas 1997: 83).

The traditional Zhuang *Sawndip* script (散姓, lit. 'uncooked script'; MSC 古壯字 *gǔ zhuàngzì* 'old Zhuang characters')[28] was used at least from the Tang period for the transcription of folk stories, legends, songs, and theatre scripts, but also for more mundane uses, as e.g. family genealogies and contracts. Moreover, Daoists used *Sawndip* to write down religious texts (Bauer 2000; Holm 2008). The story and the structural features of *Sawndip* have much in common with the Vietnamese *chữ Nôm* system: indeed, different hypotheses have been put forth as to the relationship between the Vietnamese and Zhuang scripts (see Holm 2013: 763–9). Just

---

[28] The Zhuang script is called *ndip* 'uncooked, raw' because it is not standardized, and because 'graphic renderings of Zhuang words are made in a "raw", that is, unmediated and improptu fashion' (Holm 2008: 415).

as *chữ Nôm*, the *Sawndip* system has a very low degree of standardization (see Fn. 28): in *Sawndip* texts the practices of using different characters to write the same word, or the same character to write different words, are quite common. For instance, the Chinese character 而 *ér* 'and, you' is used in Zhuang to write as many as ten different words(/morphemes), as e.g. *rox* 'know', *ra* 'look for', *rwz* 'ear', etc. This reduces the readability of *Sawndip* texts, and, indeed, the earliest Zhuang documents may even be unintelligible without the help of the keepers of the original manuscript. In some cases, *Sawndip* may be defined as some sort of 'private' writing, which was not meant to be understood by outsiders (Holm 2008: 415–7).

The process of adaptation of Chinese characters for writing Zhuang languages is even more complex than in the case of the *Nôm* script. We cannot discuss this here in detail due to space constraints (the reader is referred to Holm 2013: 49–60, 68–74): here we shall just illustrate a few particularly interesting examples of how *Sawndip* characters are created. Besides the strategies seen for *chữ Nôm* (Table 3.5), the Zhuang script also

Table 3.6 Examples of strategies for the formation of *Sawndip* characters

Strategy	Example
Graphemes made of two Chinese characters, in which the first one is a phonophoric for the initial of the Zhuang word, and the second is a phonophoric for the rhyme	竺 *raet* 'mushroom', from 竹 *ruk* (MSC *zhǔ*) 'bamboo' and 失 *saet* (MSC *shī*) 'lose'
Graphemes which look like Chinese characters but do not correspond to any actual character	且 *ningq* 'penis', resembling 且 *qiě* 'moreover'
Characters made of two semantic components	目看 *gaeuj* 'look', from 目 *mù* 'eye' and 看 *kàn* 'look'
Characters made of two phonophoric components	山三 *san* 'white rice', from 山 *shān* 'mountain' and 三 *sān* 'three'
Original creations based on the reinterpretation of the graphic structure of Chinese characters	正 正正 *canz* 'drying platform', made of three Chinese 正 *zhèng* 'right': the *Sawndip* grapheme iconically represents stacked firewood under a drying platform in a traditional Zhuang farmhouse
Graphemes completely unrelated to Chinese characters	3• *aemq* 'carry on one's back'

makes use, among others, of the types of graphemes listed in Table 3.6 (Bauer 2000: 230–44; Holm 2008: 426, 2013: 49–60, 68–74).

Note that the original Zhuang graphemes with no relation to Chinese characters are but a small fraction of the total of *Sawndip* graphemes (for further examples, see Osterkamp 2017: 123). In some cases, they could derive from other historical scripts in the same area (Bauer 2000: 233–4). An interesting aspect of phonetic compounds in *Sawndip* is that, in some characters, semantic components are not used as radicals, i.e. as costituents indicating the (broad) semantic area of the word represented by the character (see §3.1.1), but rather to convey the exact meaning of a Zhuang word. This is the case, for instance, of 鴾 *roeg* 'bird', made up of the phonophoric 六 *roek* 'six' and 鳥 (MSC *niǎo*) 'bird' (Holm 2013: 73). Also, just as seen for Cantonese in §3.3.1, the 'mouth' (口 *kǒu*) radical is sometimes used to indicate that the other constituent of the character is used for its sound value only (Bauer 2000: 237–8; Holm 2013: 69).[29]

Just as seen before for Vietnamese, starting from the 1950s the *Sawndip* system was substituted by an officially sanctioned Latin-based alphabetic script, known in Chinese as 莊文 *Zhuàngwén* 'Zhuang writing': this is also the orthography we use here for the transcription of Zhuang words. However, differently from *chữ Nôm*, the traditional *Sawndip* script is still used by many educated people in Zhuang-speaking territories (Holm 2008: 415). The official alphabetic writing, on the other hand, had limited success among Zhuang people: this is because the orthography is based on the Northern Zhuang variety of Wuming (武鳴) and is thus hard to master for speakers of Southern Zhuang languages (Bauer 2000: 228).

---

[29] On a possible relationship between *Sawndip* and Cantonese writing, see Bauer (2000: 244–8).

4

The sounds of Chinese

4.1 Historical phonology

Historical phonology is arguably the most impenetrable branch of Chinese linguistics, not only for historical linguists with no background in Chinese, but also for scholars specializing in other domains of Chinese studies. This is both because the methodology for the reconstruction of earlier stages of Chinese is mostly very different from the usual tools of Indo-European historical linguistics and because of the use of traditional Chinese terminology, obviously inaccessible to outsiders. Needless to say, in an introductory book as the present one we cannot provide an exhaustive presentation of such a complex and dynamic field of Chinese linguistics: here, we will just propose a concise overview, with a focus on some fundamental methodological issues and on the main results of this research domain (as well as some controversies).

4.1.1 The reconstruction of earlier stages of Chinese

In historical linguistics, the term 'reconstruction' is normally used to indicate a hypothesis concerning an unattested stage of a language or an unattested proto-language (Hock 1991; Campbell 2004, among others): for instance, Proto-Germanic (or Common Germanic), the reconstructed ancestor of all Germanic languages, or Proto-Slavic. Reconstruction as a scientific enterprise began with ninteeenth-century

Chinese Linguistics: An Introduction. Giorgio Francesco Arcodia and Bianca Basciano, Oxford University Press.
© Giorgio Arcodia and Bianca Basciano 2021. DOI: 10.1093/oso/9780198847830.003.0004

research on Indo-European, the hypothetical ancestor of a very large number of languages spread over Europe and Asia: the cornerstone of Indo-European reconstruction is the comparative method, 'arguably the most stable and successful of all linguistic metodologies' (Rankin 2003: 208). The comparative method is based on the comparison of attested sister languages; when no sister languages are available, the alternative is internal reconstruction, obviously less reliable than reconstruction based on comparison of actual language data (Ringe 2003: 244). Note, however, that the internal reconstruction of the morphology of a language can be used as a complement to the comparative method (Branner 2000: 23).[1]

However, 'reconstruction' has a somewhat different meaning in the Chinese context. This is because of a notorious paradox: while Chinese has one of the longest uninterrupted written traditions in the world (starting from the second millennium BC), because of the nature of the Chinese script (and of its stability over time), written sources do not provide us with enough information on the spoken language at different historical stages. As said earlier (§3.2.1), the presence of phonophoric constituents in Chinese characters does tell us that some characters were associated to words with a similar (though, crucially, not necessarily identical) sound structure at the time when Chinese writing was codified and standardized: see e.g. 路 *lù* 'road' and 客 *kè* 'guest', which share the phonophoric 各 *gè*. However, this leaves us with no direct indication as to how these words were actually realized in speech (Handel 2014: 576–7). Thus, in the case of Chinese, we have to reconstruct the phonology (as well as the morphology; see §5.1.2) of stages of the language for which we have a huge number of written documents. This is in fact the case also for languages with a phonographic writing system, as Sanskrit or Latin: we must anyway, in a sense, 'reconstruct' the phonetic values of graphemes. However, since phonographic writing systems are generally meant to reflect in a more direct way the sounds of language, the task of matching script with phonemes or syllables is much simpler. Moreover, this type of 'reconstruction' is normally regarded as 'interpretation of written sources', rather than as reconstruction *senso strictu*: thus, for instance, Classical Latin

---

[1] On the comparative methods (and its limits), see Rankin (2003), Harrison (2003), and Campbell (2004).

pronunciation is not normally 'starred', while reconstructed Indo-European and Old Chinese forms are (Coblin 2002c; Campbell 2004).

How is reconstruction done for the historically attested stages of Chinese, then? The traditional method is associated, as mentioned in §2.2.5, with the Swedish sinologist Bernhard Karlgren, who fruitfully combined the findings of native Qing period philologists with the techniques of Indo-European comparative linguistics (Baxter and Sagart 2014: 2–3).[2] Karlgren believed that it is possible to reconstruct two distinct stages for Chinese, namely Middle Chinese (in his terminology, 'Old Chinese') and Old Chinese (in his terminology, 'Archaic Chinese'), following a very different procedure. The basis for the reconstruction of Old Chinese is actually the reconstruction of Middle Chinese; moreover, reconstructed Middle Chinese provides the framework for the study of the phonology of Modern Sinitic languages, as we shall see later (§4.2).

Let us then start from the reconstruction of Middle Chinese. This is based on three main sets of data:

a. rime dictionaries, especially the 切韻 *Qièyùn* (see §2.2.3), in its more recent edition, the 廣韻 *Guǎngyùn*[3]
b. rime tables
c. the readings of characters in Sinitic and Sino-Xenic varieties

Additional 'clues' for the reconstruction of the phonology of Middle Chinese may be gathered from transcriptions of Chinese words in phonographic scripts (Tibetan, *brāhmī*, and Uyghur), from transcriptions of foreign words in Chinese characters, from rhyming in poetry, and from glosses in commentaries of classical literary works (as e.g. the 經典釋文 *Jīngdiǎn Shìwén*, sixth century AD), which sometimes offered information on the pronunciation of Chinese characters (Baxter 1992: 12–14).

---

[2] The most important reference work on the reconstruction of Old and Middle Chinese by Karlgren is *Grammata Serica Recensa* (Karlgren 1957; see Schuessler 2009).

[3] The 廣韻 *Guǎngyùn* is an expanded edition of the 切韻 *Qièyùn* published in 1007. The (almost complete) manuscript of the 切韻 *Qièyùn* was found only in 1947, and philologists and historical linguists have relied much on the 廣韻 *Guǎngyùn* (Baxter 1992: 38–40).

Each of those sets of data has a different role in the process of reconstruction. Rime dictionaries present in a systematic way the rhymes of characters, which are arranged by tone, rhyme, and, within each rhyme, by homophone group. Thus, for instance, the first volume of the 廣韻 *Guǎngyùn* begins with the 平 *píng* (level; see §4.1.3) tone and the 東 *dōng* 'East' rhyme. The first homophone group, thus, contains all the characters which have the same initial, final, and tone as 東 *dōng*; homophone groups are separated by a small circle (○), known as 紐 *niǔ* 'button'. The reading of each group is then represented by means of the 反切 *fǎnqiè* notation: the standard formula is character 1 (上字 *shàngzì* 'first character') + character 2 (下字 *xiàzì* 'second character') + 切 *qiè*' (or 反 *fǎn*, in the oldest books), in which the first character indicates the initial, while the second indicates the final and the tone. So, the 反切 *fǎnqiè* for the above-mentioned homophone group 東 *dōng* is 德紅切 *dé hóng qiè*: the character 東 *dōng* must have had the same initial of 德 *dé* 'virtue' and the same final and tone of 紅 *hóng* 'red'. The fact that this is no longer true for MSC (東 *dōng* is a first tone word, whereas 紅 *hóng* has a different tone) shows us that the 反切 *fǎnqiè* notation works only for a specific variety at a specific time (Handel 2014: 582). This entails that the 反切 *fǎnqiè* notation does tell us which characters had the same initial or the same final(/tone) at some time in the past,[4] but it does not tell us much about the actual phonetic values for them (Baxter 1992; Jacques 2017b).

Rime tables, on the other hand, offer a systematic presentation of initials, besides finals. In the already mentioned 韻鏡 *Yùnjìng* (§2.2.3, 2.2.5), initials are arranged according to their articulatory features (Jacques 2017b). Tables are designed as grids: each column corresponds to a place of articulation (labial, dental, etc.), while rows are arranged in groups of four, sharing the same final and tone; each row represents a 'division' or 'degree' (等 *děng*), a notion we will introduce later. A reproduction of a small portion of the first table (轉 *zhuǎn*) of the 韻鏡 *Yùnjìng* is shown in Figure 4.1.

---

[4] Note, also, that each initial and each final were associated with at least *two* characters (often, more than three) for 反切 *fǎnqiè* notation. Through the association of the different characters used to represent the same initial or final (a method known in Chinese as 系聯法 *xìliánfǎ*), it is possible to establish the number of distinct finals and initials in the 廣韻 *Guǎngyùn* system (Jacques 2017b).

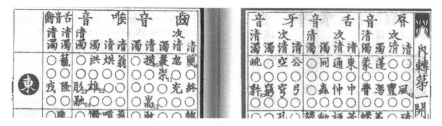

Figure 4.1 Excerpt from the first table of the 韻鏡 *Yùnjìng*

Source: From the 覆宋永祿 *Fù Sòng Yǒnglù* (1564) edition of the 韻鏡 *Yùnjìng*, available on Wikimedia <https://commons.wikimedia.org/wiki/File:Yunjing.jpg> (last access: 29 July 2019).

In this excerpt we see that the characters rhyming with 東 *dōng* (the same opening rhyme of the 切韻 *Qièyùn*) are divided according to their place of articulation: 'lip sounds' (脣音 *chún yīn*, i.e. labial consonants), 'tongue sounds' (舌音 *shé yīn*, i.e. dental and retroflex stops), 'back-tooth sounds' (牙音 *yá yīn*, i.e. velar stops and nasals), 'front-tooth sounds' (齒音 *chǐ yīn*, i.e. dental and retroflex affricates and fricatives), 'throat sounds' (喉音 *hóu yīn*, i.e. velar fricatives and the glottal stop), and 'linguo-dental sounds' (舌音齒 *shè yīn chǐ*); the latter category includes the lateral *l-* (also known as 半舌 *bànshé* 'half-tongue') and the palatal nasal *ny-* (also known as 半齒 *bànchǐ* 'half-front-tooth'; see Pulleyblank 1984: 64; Baxter 1992: 46–59; Jacques 2017b). These classes of initials are further divided into four groups: 清 *qīng* 'clear', i.e. voiceless unaspirated, 次清 *cìqīng* 'secondary clear', i.e. voiceless aspirated, 濁 *zhuó* (or 全濁 *quánzhuó*) 'muddy', i.e. voiced obstruents, and 清濁 *qīngzhuó* (or 次濁 *cìzhuó*) 'clear-muddy', i.e. sonorants.[5]

While rime tables provide many articulatory details for initials, finals are not classified according to their internal makeup: rather, they are presented as a whole, disregarding the characteristics of the single segments. It is worth remarking here that, in the native Chinese tradition of linguistic analysis, the syllable was the fundamental unit of phonology: the idea that syllables can be decomposed in constituent parts (which, however, do not necessarily correspond to single phonemes) was 'imported' from the Indian tradition (Baxter 1992: 33). Given that

---

[5] In Zhang Linzhi's (張麟之 *Zhāng Línzhī*) preface to the 韻鏡 *Yùnjìng* we find more distinctions within the categories discussed here. The reader is referred to Pulleyblank (1984: 64–7) for an overview. Also, a (partial) English translation of Zhang's preface, with a comment, may be found in Coblin (2006).

Middle Chinese did not have initial consonant clusters, the articulatory details provided in the rime tables for initials actually concern individual sounds. This, however, does not apply to the finals, which often include more than one segment.

As mentioned before, in the 韻鏡 *Yùnjìng* rhymes are arranged into four 'divisions' (等 *děng*). There is much disagreement as to what is the nature of this partition and as to what are the phonetic features of each division. The four divisions have been associated with the presence of specific medials and/or to features of nuclear vowels; we will return to this in §4.1.4.

Moreover, each table in the 韻鏡 *Yùnjìng* is marked as 內 *nèi* 'inner' or 外 *wài* 'outer', and as 開口 *kāikǒu* 'open mouth' or 合口 *hékǒu* 'closed mouth'. The meaning of the 內 *nèi*/外 *wài* opposition is, again, controversial: an interpretation which is often found in the literature is that 'inner' tables are associated with high/closed vowels, while 'outer' tables are associated with low/open vowels (Coblin 2006: 126–7, 147–8). As for the distinction between 開口 *kāikǒu* and 合口 *hékǒu*, it has been suggested that it is related to the presence ('closed mouth') or absence ('open mouth') of a medial approximant (-*w*-) or a rounded vowel (Branner 2006b: 18; Jacques 2017b).[6] Lastly, the distribution of empty slots (see Fig. 4.1) tells us which combinations of initial and final were not attested.

To sum up, through the analysis of rime books and rime tables we can reconstruct a system of phonemic contrasts; in the latter, we also find some hints as to the articulatory features on which these contrasts are based. Nevertheless, as mentioned before, if we want to translate this phonological system into actual sounds, we need to rely on the comparison between modern Sinitic languages and Sino-Japanese, Sino-Korean, and Sino-Vietnamese readings of Chinese characters. Note, however, that the term 'comparison' does not imply that the comparative method is applied: rather, dialect and Sino-Xenic forms are used to add 'meat' to a phonological system which has been reconstructed independently from modern varieties (Coblin 2002c: 205). Thus, for instance, we associate Middle Chinese (全)濁 (*quán*)*zhuó*

---

[6] Moreover, in a rime table published after the 韻鏡 *Yùnjìng*, the 四聲等子 *Sìshēng děngzǐ*, rhymes are divided into sixteen 攝 *shè* 'groups'. Each 攝 *shè* includes all the 'inner' or 'outer' rhymes having the same final consonant or approximant (Norman 1988: 32). The term 攝 *shè* is often found in the literature on Chinese historical phonology, also in English and other European languages.

sounds to voiced obstruents because there are voiced initial stops in modern Wu and Xiang dialects (see §4.2.3, 4.2.4). Two lexemes as 頭 *tóu* 'head' and 偷 *tōu* 'steal' both have a voiceless aspirated dental stop initial in MSC, but in the 韻鏡 *Yùnjìng* the former is in the 濁 *zhuó* 'muddy' column, while the latter is in the 次清 *cìqīng* 'secondary clear' column: in Wenzhounese, a Wu dialect, we have [dəu³¹] for 'head' (Zhengzhang Shangfang 2008: 290), and its cognate in the Shuangfeng (雙峰 *Shuāngfēng*; Yuan *et al.* 2001: 110) Xiang dialect has a voiced initial too. Thus, the starting point for this process of 'reconstruction' is not the comparison of attested forms, but the phonological system of rime books and tables: Middle Chinese has been reconstructed by applying this method, although with some controversies concerning the details of its phonology (see also §4.1.3).

Several aspects of the Karlgrenian method have come under criticism in the recent literature. We already mentioned (§2.3.2) Norman and Coblin's (1995) alternative view of the nature of Middle Chinese, according to whom rime books and tables are based on the 'literary' readings of characters and do not directly represent any spoken variety. This entails that any attempt at reconstruction based only on the 切韻 *Qièyùn* system does not tell much about the actual evolution of the spoken Sinitic languages (see Handel 2014: 595–6). As an alternative approach, Norman (2006) proposes a 'Common Dialectal Chinese' which reconciles the 切韻 *Qièyùn* system with modern dialect phonology, thus eliminating categories and constrasts which have no reflex in modern Sinitic languages. Moreover, as hinted at in §2.2.3 and 2.2.5, Pulleyblank (1984, 1991, 1998) believes that rime tables are not based on the same system as the 切韻 *Qièyùn*: the difference is not merely a matter of chronological distance, but is rather motivated by the fact that the earlier and later sources were based on different 'standards'. This is the reason why Pulleyblank does not offer a reconstruction of Middle Chinese as such, but rather of two distinct stages: Early Middle Chinese (the rime books 'language') and Late Middle Chinese (the rime tables 'language'). Yet other scholars, while proposing their reconstruction of a unitary Middle Chinese language, use the 切韻 *Qièyùn* as their basis, while rime tables are taken into account only as an auxiliary source. Indeed, if the reconstruction of Middle Chinese is to be used as the foundation for the reconstruction of Old Chinese, the earlier sources are obviously more valuable (Baxter 1992; Baxter and Sagart 2014).

The principles and methods applied in the reconstruction of Old Chinese are quite different from those seen before for Middle Chinese. Old Chinese is, in a sense, a second-level abstraction, since it is based on another reconstructed system (Norman 1988: 45; Sagart 1999b: 10): thus, the foundations for the reconstruction of Old Chinese are inevitably less solid, and there are indeed significant differences in different proposed reconstructions, as we shall see in the next section. Traditionally, the reconstruction of the phonology of Old Chinese is based on three main sets of data:

    a. Rhymes in ancient poetry (especially in the *Classic of Poetry*)
    b. Phonophoric constituents in characters (see §3.1.1)
    c. The phonological system of the 切韻 *Qièyùn*

Besides, early works on philology, as e.g. the Eastern Han period commentaries on classical texts analysed by Coblin (1983; see Baxter and Sagart 2014: 37), do provide some indications as to the readings of characters, and are hence used as auxiliary sources for the reconstruction of Old Chinese.

The starting point for the reconstruction of the phonology of Old Chinese is identifying the rhymes. For instance, since 采 *cǎi* 'pick' and 有 *yǒu* 'there be, have' do rhyme in the *Classic of Poetry*, we may infer that they most likely had the same rhyme (OC *s.r̥ˤəʔ vs. *Gʷəʔ; BSOL). Words rhyming with each other in Old Chinese are assigned to a group, known as 韻部 *yùnbù* (lit. 'rhyme section/group'): the phonetic interpretation of these rhyme groups is then based on the 廣韻 *Guǎngyùn* rhymes. Thus, the names for Middle Chinese rhymes were used, and are still used, also as labels for Old Chinese rhyme groups (Baxter and Sagart 2014: 22).

However, by using this method we can analyse only the rhymes of words which were actually used in rhyming in classical poetry. A major innovation, introduced by the Qing philologist Duan Yucai (段玉裁 *Duàn Yùcái*; 1735–1815), was to take into consideration the phonophoric constituents of characters, which allows us to find out the connections between words which were never used in rhyming (Norman 1988: 43–4). The method laid out by Duan Yucai is relatively simple: assuming that characters with the same phonophoric could rhyme, they can be grouped into 'phonetic series' (諧聲系列 *xiéshēng xìliè*). For instance, 波 *bō* 'wave' (OC *pˤaj), 疲 *pí* 'tired' (*b(r)aj), and 被 *bèi* 'quilt' (*m-p(h)raj?), which share the constituent 皮 *pí* 'skin' (*m-p(r)aj; BSOL), are part of the same phonetic series. This method is applied also to words which were written with homophone characters (i.e. the 假借 *jiǎjiè* 'phonetic loans' discussed in §3.2.1), and which were then distinguished by adding a semantic constituent. For instance, in archaic texts 奴 *nú* 'slave' (OC *nˤa), 汝 *rǔ* 'you' (*na?), and 如 *rú* 'like' (*na) could all be written with the character 女 *nǚ* 'woman' (*nra?; BSOL), which is still retained as a phonophoric (Sagart 2006: 35). Moreover, as mentioned earlier (§3.1.1), characters in the same 諧聲 *xiéshēng* series also had initial consonants which shared the same place of articulation:[7] this realization provided a basis for Karlgren's first reconstruction of Old Chinese initials (but see Norman 1988: 44–5 on initial consonant clusters).[8]

However, just as seen before for Middle Chinese, this procedure gives us only a phonological 'skeleton', a system of oppositions of initials and finals without any phonetic value. Thus, the Middle Chinese system is used in order to reconstruct Old Chinese word forms. While the reconstruction of Middle Chinese is not uncontroversial, there are several aspects of Old Chinese phonology on which broad agreement has been reached; we will get back to this in the next section. For instance, in an Old Chinese phonetic series we may find initials which correspond both to alveolar and to retroflex consonants of Middle Chinese, as e.g. 豬 *zhū* 'pig' (MC *trjo*), 都 *dū* 'capital' (MC *tu*), and 著 *zhù* 'visible' (MC *trjoH*; BSOL). Through a comparison of 切韻 *Qièyùn* and 廣韻 *Guǎngyùn* phonology, and modern dialect reflexes (see §4.2.5, 4.2.8), it has been suggested that Old Chinese had only alveolar consonants, and that retroflex initials developed by the Middle Chinese stage (Handel 2014: 594; Dong Hongyuan 2014: 34–5; see §3.1.2). It has been proposed that the evolution of alveolars into retroflex consonants was caused by the presence of an initial or medial *r (Baxter and Sagart 2014: 80, among others): thus, the three words mentioned here have been reconstructed as *tra, *tˤa, and *t<r>ak-s (BSOL).

---

[7] In the case of phonetic series based on 假借 *jiǎjiè* homophone writing, it may be assumed that the relationship between members must have been at least close to homophony (see Pan Wuyun 2017).

[8] Since the current shape of Chinese characters was set during the Qin and Han periods (except for the simplification of the twentieth century; see §3.2.2), but the Old Chinese period began much earlier, there are cases in which the phonophorics may actually be misleading. In order to avoid this, one must look a pre-Qin writing, which reflects an earlier stage of Chinese phonology (Baxter and Sagart 2014: 28–9).

As for the stage following Middle Chinese, which we termed Old Mandarin, the most important source is the fourteenth-century rime book 中原音韻 *Zhōngyuán yīnyùn* ('Rhymes of the Central Plain'), as mentioned earlier (§2.2.3). The 中原音韻 *Zhōngyuán yīnyùn* is very different from other Chinese works on phonology, since it is much closer to spoken varieties, if compared to the archaic model of earlier rime books (Norman 1988: 48–9). However, there is no agreement as to what dialect was represented in it. The procedure applied for the reconstruction of the phonology of the 中原音韻 *Zhōngyuán yīnyùn* is partly different from what we discussed earlier for Middle Chinese rime books and dictionaries. This is because the 中原音韻 *Zhōngyuán yīnyùn* does not make use of the 反切 *fǎnqiè* notation, and no other clues as to the articulatory features of initials are provided: for the sake of conciseness, we shall not illustrate the procedure here (the reader is referred to Dong Hongyuan 2014: 72–4). Methodological differences notwithstanding, the reconstruction of 中原音韻 *Zhōngyuán yīnyùn* phonology involves adding phonetic 'meat' to a system of phonological opposition, just as for Old and Middle Chinese. One major difference is that, for Old Mandarin, texts written in phonographic scripts are also used, namely the corpus of writings in the Mongolian 'Phags-pa alphabet (especially the rime dictionary 蒙古字韻 *Měnggǔ zìyùn*, 'Rhymes in Mongol Script'; Pulleyblank 1991: 3–4; compare Coblin 1999; 2007a: 72–3). Although it is very likely that the variety represented in the 中原音韻 *Zhōngyuán yīnyùn* is not the same as that of the 'Phags-pa literature, as mentioned earlier (§2.2.3), they are both very valuable sources for understanding the linguistic history of their time.

After the Old Mandarin stage, the task of reconstructing the sounds of Chinese becomes, in a sense, more manageable. This is because in the Ming and Qing periods we have at our disposal several works compiled by and for foreigners, written in phonographic scripts, which provide explicit information about the sound system of the (perceived) 'standard' language. The sources available for this period, in fact, do not reflect a single variety, but rather two: namely, 'southern/Nanjing' phonology (南音 *nányīn*) and 'northern/Beijing' phonology (北音 *běiyīn*; see §2.2.3, 2.2.5). Besides, sometimes details on diastratic variation are also provided (Coblin 2007a: 74–6).

The earliest phonographic sources for Chinese from this period are the works of the Korean sinologist Sin Sukju (1417–75): particularly, his transcription in the Korean *hangeul* script of the rime dictionary

洪武正韻 *Hóngwǔ Zhèngyùn* ('Correct Rhymes of the Hongwu Period', 1375). The 洪武正韻 *Hóngwǔ Zhèngyùn* includes both literary readings (正音 *zhèngyīn*, lit. 'correct pronunciation'; see §2.2.3) and 'vulgar' readings 俗音 (*súyīn*) of characters in southern 官話 *Guānhuà*, elicited from several informants (Coblin 2007d: 7-10). Another Korean author, Choe Sejin (1467-1542), provides us with the earliest transcription of the 'standard' northern Chinese pronunciation of his time (Sagart 2007: 5). As for the period between the sixteenth and the eighteenth century, we already mentioned (§3.2.3) the transcriptions into the Latin alphabet of southern Mandarin by Catholic missionaries. Starting from the eighteenth century, we see the first transcriptions into the Manchu script, based on northern Mandarin phonology, followed by the romanization systems devised by English-speaking missionaries in the ninteenth century (as the already mentioned Edkins and Wade).

Despited the peculiar nature of the methodology for phonetic reconstruction in Chinese historical linguistics, the 'conventional' comparative method has also been used for this purpose. Starting from the end of the twentieth century, a number of scholars have called into question the traditional approach to reconstruction in Chinese linguistics, stressing the importance of comparing attested modern Sinitic languages to improve our understanding of previous stages of Chinese (see Norman and Coblin 1995; Branner 2000; Coblin 2002c). This new approach has been applied in the very recent reconstruction of Old Chinese by William Baxter and Laurent Sagart (Baxter and Sagart 2014), discussed in the next section, which takes into account also data from the most conservative modern dialects (Min, Hakka, and Waxiang), as well as very old Chinese loanwords in Mon-Khmer, Hmong-Mien, and Tai-Kadai languages. Some well-known examples of the application of the comparative method to Sinitic languages are Jerry Norman's reconstruction of 'Proto-Min' (1973, 1974, 1981), based on the comparison of modern Min diaelcts[9], Baxter's sketch of 'Proto-Macro-Mandarin' (2006; see §2.3.2), and the 'Proto-Central Jiang-Huai' proposed by Coblin (2000c), based on five varieties of the Nanjing area (for other examples of reconstructed 'micro-systems', see Coblin 1994 2007d, 2011).

---

[9] Norman's reconstruction of Proto-Min met with much criticism. The reader is referred to Handel (2010) and Baxter and Sagart (2014).

4.1.2 Old Chinese

As mentioned earlier, there are many controversial aspects in the reconstruction of Old Chinese. This may be explained both by the fact that Old Chinese phonological distinctions which did not survive into modern Sinitic languages may have different interpretations and by open issues in the reconstruction of Middle Chinese, the foundation for Old Chinese reconstruction.

For instance, we may compare the shape of three words in five different reconstructions for Old Chinese: namely, Karlgren's (1957), Li Fang-Kuei's (1980 [1971]),[10] Pan Wuyun's (2000), Zhengzhang Shangfang's (2003), and Baxter and Sagart's (2014; BSOL).

Table 4.1 Examples of Old Chinese words in five different reconstructions

Word	Karlgren	Li F.-K.	Pan W.	Zh. S.	B. & S.
罪 zuì 'crime'	dz'wəd	dzədx	sblul	zuulʔ	dzˤuiʔ
念 niàn 'think of'	niəm	niəmh	mqlɯms	nɯɯms	nˤim-s
俗 sú 'vulgar'	dzi̯uk	sgjuk	sɢlŏk	ljog	s-ɢok

The five reconstructions compared in Table 4.1 are quite different from one another, even at a first glance. Firstly, Pan Wuyun's system stands out as being the most diverse from the others: we see consonant clusters as *sbl- and *mql-. If the three word forms in Li Fang-Kuei's system seem to be compatible with Karlgren's original reconstruction, they do have tones, absent from other reconstructed systems. Also, the initial for 俗 *sú* is quite different from Karlgren's own version, but consistent with Pan Wuyun's and Baxter and Sagart's reconstruction. Baxter and Sagart's Old Chinese is also compatible with Karlgren's to some extent, but there are important differences between them too: for instance, the different treatment of finals and the presence of pharyngealized initials (noted as superscript <ˤ>). Zhengshang Shangfang's reconstructions resemble Baxter and Sagart's, but, in the former system, the interpretation of the initial for 俗 *sú* is completely different, and,

---

[10] In Li Fang-Kuei's notation, final '-x' stands for an ascending tone, while '-h' stands for a (possible) falling tone. However, tones should not be phonemic at this stage (Li Fang-Kuei 1980: 34).

also, vowel length is distinctive in Zhengzhang's system. Note that major divergences between competing reconstructions as those shown in Table 4.1 are not rare. As a further example, we may cite the different forms for 水 *shuǐ* 'water' in Karlgren's, Li Fang-Kuei's, and Baxter's (1992) reconstructions: respectively, *śi̯wər, *hwrjidx, and *h(l)juj? (Handel 2003a: 543, Fn. 1; compare BSOL *s.tur?).

One of the most debated aspects of the reconstruction of Old Chinese is the type of initial consonant clusters. As pointed out before, Middle Chinese did not have consonant clusters: they were reconstructed for Old Chinese on the basis of the observation that, in the very same 諧聲 *xiéshēng* series (see §4.1.1), we find words which have initials with different places of articulation in Middle Chinese; for instance, MC 監 *kaemH* 'mirror' (MSC *jiān*) and 藍 *lam* 'indigo' (*lán*; BSOL). In order to explain these seemingly inconsistent patterns, it was proposed[11] that Old Chinese words could have initial consonant clusters, one of which had a place of articulation consistent with the phonetic series: the simplification of those clusters led to the unexpected reflex in Middle Chinese. For instance, the above-mentioned MC words 監 *kaemH* and 藍 *lam* are reconstructed as OC *kram e *g-ram (with *g-r- > *l*; compare Thai *khraam* 'indigo') in Baxter (1992: 23, 199–201). However, other scholars have come up with very different solutions (see Table A.9.1.2 in Handel 2003a: 562, and Sagart 1999b: 121–30): there is thus no general agreement on the interpretation of these MC alternations. Note that the issue of consonant clusters is of the utmost significance for the reconstruction of Old Chinese morphosyntax, since reconstructed (largely prefixal) Old Chinese morphology (see §5.1.2), is based on specific hypotheses on which initial consonants and consonant clusters were allowed in Old Chinese words (Sagart 1999b: 11).

Another topic in Old Chinese phonology which has generated much controversy is the distinction between syllable types. As mentioned before (§4.1.1), Middle Chinese syllables are arranged into four divisions: traditionally, Middle Chinese syllables belonging to divisions I, II, and IV are termed 'type A', while division III syllables are termed 'type B'. In Baxter and Sagart's (2014: 68) notation for Middle Chinese, type-B (i.e. division III) syllables may contain -*i*-, prevocalic -*j*-, or both, or have an initial -*y*-; type-A syllables, on the other hand, have none of these. The Old Chinese origin for this distinction is debated: while there

---

[11] At least starting from Maspero (1920; see Sagart 1999b: 2).

seems to be general agreement on the point that the distinction itself is relevant also for Old Chinese phonology, its actual nature is controversial. Karlgren (1940) suggests that type-B syllables had a medial yod (-i̯-) before the nuclear vowel; Pulleyblank first proposed (1962a-b) that type-B syllables contained a long vowel, and then (1973) that the distinction between the two types had to do with stress position. Norman's (1994) hypothesis is that type-A syllables have a pharyngealized initial, while non-pharyngealized initials later underwent palatalization (Baxter and Sagart 2014: 68–70).

Given the introductory nature of the present volume, we shall not discuss further the differences among competing reconstructions of Old Chinese (the reader is referred to Handel 2003a). In what follows, we shall rather propose an overview of some features of Old Chinese phonology for which there is broad agreement among scholars; to this end, we use Baxter and Sagart's reconstruction as a default (2014).[12]

Reconstructed Old Chinese appears as very distant, typologically, from Middle Chinese, and even more distant from modern Sinitic and, generally speaking, East and Southeast Asian languages (see §2.3.1). On the other hand, the phonology of Old Chinese does look closer to that of many Tibeto-Burman languages. Firstly, Old Chinese was probably neither a tonal nor a monosyllabic language: as we shall see in the next section, phonemic tone arguably developed in the transition from Old to Middle Chinese, following the loss of some final consonants. Syllable structure allowed for 'presyllables' or 'minor syllables' (what we referred to as 'sesquisyllabism'; see §2.3.1; Michaud 2012), consisting of a consonant or a consonant and a schwa (*ə),[13] similarly to Khmer. It has been suggested that these minor syllables are the outcome of the reduction of a constituent in old disyllabic words (Baxter and Sagart 2014: 50–3, 318–19). On the whole, Old Chinese syllable structure appears to be way more complex than that of Modern Sinitic languages (see §4.2.1), as shown in Figure 4.2.

---

[12] See also Schuessler's (2009) 'Minimal Old Chinese', a simplified notation (rather than a reconstruction *senso strictu*) of those features of Old Chinese which gained broad acceptance among specialists.

[13] In Baxter & Sagart's model (2014: 42), pre-initial consonants which were not followed by a neutral vowel, and hence had a closer relation with the syllable initial, gave rise to the consonant clusters discussed earlier.

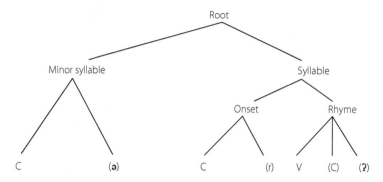

Figure 4.2 Old Chinese syllable structure according to Baxter and Sagart (2014).

Source: Adapted from Baxter and Sagart (2014: 53)

All the constituents included in brackets are optional: thus, in this reconstruction, the minimal syllables were CV (e.g. 卑 *pe 'humble', MSC *bēi*; BSOL), whereas the most complex syllable type (with a pre-syllable) was Cǝ.CrVCʔ, to which a suffix *–s could be added (e.g. 灑 *Cǝ-s<r>erʔ-s 'sprinkle', MSC *sǎ*; BSOL).[14] However, possible syllable structures vary considerably depending on the individual reconstruction: for instance, Baxter and Sagart's minor syllables mostly correspond to consonant clusters in other reconstructions. One aspect that is shared by virtually all reconstructions is that the inventory of final consonants was larger, and the complexity of syllable codas was higher, in Old Chinese, if compared to Middle Chinese and to modern Sinitic languages.

As to the sound inventory of Old Chinese, here is a list of features that are generally accepted by specialists in historical phonology (Handel 2014: 593):

a. a contrast between voiced and voiceless sonorant consonants
b. the absence of palatal and retroflex initial consonants
c. a series of labiovelar initials
d. a relatively simple vowel inventory (typically, between two and six vowels)[15]

---

[14] In Baxter and Sagart's notation, 'C' stands for a consonants which they have not been able to reconstruct with reasonable certainty.

[15] The most notable exceptions are Karlgren's Archaic Chinese, with fourteen distinct vowels, and Tung T'ung-ho's system (1944), with as many as twenty.

Voiceless sonorant initials are reconstructed in Old Chinese to account for those cases in which, in the same phonetic series, we find words that in Middle Chinese have both sonorant and voiceless obstruent initials. For instance, MC 難 *nan* 'difficult' (MSC *nán*) and 灘 *than* 'beach' (*tān*), on the basis of which the OC forms *nˁar and *n̥ˁar have been proposed (Baxter and Sagart 2014: 111). We already discussed before (§4.1.1) the role of medial -*r*- in the evolution of alveolar initials into retroflex consonants. As to the relationship between Old Chinese alveolar stops and nasals and Middle Chinese palatals, Baxter and Sagart's hypothesis is that non-pharyngealized initials, associated with type-B syllables, palatalized in Middle Chinese: for instance, 真 *tin 'true' > MC *tsyin* (MSC *zhēn*). This enhanced the contrast between type-A and type-B syllables, and reduced the reliance on pharyngealization as a distinctive feature (Baxter and Sagart 2014: 76).

4.1.3 Middle Chinese

The time between the Old Chinese and the Middle Chinese stage is arguably the most important period in the history of the Chinese language. As pointed out before, at this time Chinese underwent a major typological shift, from a more 'Tibeto-Burman-style' phonology (and morphology) towards the Mainland Southeast Asian type, with phonemic tones, a simple syllable structure, and no consonant clusters.

Even though, as mentioned earlier, the foundations for the reconstruction of Middle Chinese are more solid than those for Old Chinese, there is still no agreement on some aspects of Middle Chinese phonology, and no universally agreed upon reconstruction (Baxter 1992: 27; Handel 2014: 586). Besides, not all scholars accept Pulleyblank's (1984) division of the Middle Chinese period into Early and Late Middle Chinese: specifically, the nature of the system represented in the 韻鏡 *Yùnjìng* and its use as the main source for Late Middle Chinese is controversial (see e.g. Miyake 2003: 96–8; see §2.2.3). The use of rime table categories as a key to the interpretation of the 切韻 *Qièyùn*, a hallmark of the Karlgrenian approach, is also very controversial (see Norman 1988: 40–1; Baxter and Sagart 2014: 9).

On the whole, the different proposed versions of Middle Chinese are mostly structurally equivalent. The use of traditional Chinese terminology, as e.g. '東 *dōng* rhyme' or '日 *rì* initials' (see §4.1.1), without overtly stating a phonetic interpretation, obscures the differences among competing reconstructions: however, the variation in the interpretation of each class of sounds becomes relevant, above all, when Middle Chinese is used as the basis for reconstructing Old Chinese (Handel 2014: 586–7). Generally speaking, the reconstruction of Middle Chinese finals (especially vowels and approximants) is much more controversial than that of initials (Norman 1988: 36–40; see Tables 22.2 and 22.3 in Handel 2014). This is easily explained by the different treatment of initials and finals in rime books and tables: as mentioned in §4.1.1, finals are classified as a whole, rather than on the basis of individual sounds. Besides, the interpretation of the divisions (等 děng), the most arcane categories in Middle Chinese phonology, is still an unsolved issue.[16]

Moreover, as discussed in §2.2.3, many scholars believe that the 切韻 Qièyùn system does not reflect an individual language, but rather a collection of literary readings of characters from different prestige varieties. Therefore, rather than a reconstruction senso strictu, several scholars proposed 'transcriptions' or 'notations' for Middle Chinese phonological categories, without necessarily committing to a specific phonetic interpretation (Coblin 2002c: 206; Branner 2006a: 265). This is the case also for Baxter and Sagart's (2014) system, which we use as a default in the present volume (for a comparison of some notations for Middle Chinese, see Branner 2006a).

There are several characteristics of Middle Chinese (understood here as the 切韻 Qièyùn 'language') on which there appears to be universal agreement among specialists. For instance (Handel 2014: 587):

a. a three-way distinction among voiced, unvoiced, and aspirated unvoiced obstruent initials (see §4.1.1)
b. six different consonantal codas (-p, -t, -k, -m, -n, -ng)
c. the absence of consonant clusters
d. four tone categories (平 píng, 上 shǎng, 去 qù, 入 rù)
e. a relatively complex system of vowels and glides

Towards the end of the Tang period, i.e. at the Late Middle Chinese stage, following Pulleyblank's (1984) definition, we see some significant

---

[16] For an extensive treatment of Middle Chinese divisions, see Branner (2006b: 18–32), Chan Abraham (2006), and Ferlus (2009). For an overview of the interpretation of divisions in Baxter and Sagart's reconstruction, see Baxter and Sagart (2014: 17).

changes in the language, compared to the 切韻 *Qièyùn* stage. These include:

a. the genesis of labiodental initials, through spirantization of bila-bials (when occurring before the glide *-j-* or a back vowel; Baxter 1992: 46–7), as e.g. EMC 風 *puwŋ* 'wind' > LMC *fuwŋ* (MSC *fēng*; Pulleyblank 1991: 95)

b. the fusion of palatal and retroflex initials in a single series, in complementary distribution (e.g. [ʂ,] [ɕ] > [ʂ])

c. The (partial) devoicing of voiced obstruents, probably realized as murmured sounds (Pulleyblank 1984: 68; Ferlus 2009: 194).[17]

More generally, in the evolution from Old to Middle Chinese, two changes are particularly relevant for the typological shift we men-tioned earlier: the loss of consonant clusters, which led to the devel-opment of palatal and retroflex initials; and the simplification of syllable codas, which was instrumental in the genesis of phonemic tones. Middle Chinese syllable structure appears as much simpler than that of Old Chinese, and it is compatible with the syllable struc-ture of conservative Southern Sinitic languages, as e.g. Yue and Hakka (see §4.2.6, 4.2.7): on the other hand, Modern Standard Chinese and most northern and central dialects retained only nasal codas, as we shall see later.

The hypothesis that Middle Chinese tones are connected with Old Chinese final consonants was first proposed by Haudricourt (1954b), who suggested a similar pathway of evolution for tonogenesis in Vietnamese and Chinese (See Sagart 1999a; Michaud 2012). Specifically, the departing (去 *qù*) tone should derive from a *-s coda (probably >*-h > Ø), the use of which as a suffix has been already mentioned (§2.3.1). Mei Tsulin (1970) then proposed that the ascending (上 *shǎng*) tone derives from a glottal stop ([ʔ]), just as Haudricourt (1954a) hypothe-sized for the Vietnamese *sắc-nặng* tone category. In a nutshell, these coda consonants had micromelodic effects on syllables: with the loss of the codas, these differences became distinctive (see Baxter 1992: 308–39 and Sagart 1999a for a critique of this theory and for some alternative

---

[17] For more examples of Late Middle Chinese innovations, see the table in Pulleyblank (1984, Appendix A).

hypotheses).[18] The other two tone categories, namely, 'level' (平 píng) and 'entering' (入 rù) correspond, respectively, to syllables ending in a vowel or sonorant and to syllables ending in a stop consonant. However, note that, for 入 rù tone syllables, coda stops are still retained in Middle Chinese: hence, this is not always seen as a 'tone' category *stricto sensu* (Norman 1988: 54; Ferlus 2009: 193). As to the pitch contour of the four tones of Middle Chinese, while it seems very likely that the four labels attached to them were meant as a description ('level', 'rising', etc.; Baxter 1992: 304; Ting Pang-hsin 1996: 152; Ferlus 2009: 193, among others), we have as yet no way of knowing for sure.

Due to the influence of voicedness distinctions in syllable onsets on tone realization, the four Middle Chinese tone categories underwent a split into two registers: a higher register (陰 yīn 'dark'), with voiceless initials, and a lower register (陽 yáng 'light'), with voiced initials. While we do not have direct evidence for dating this split, it is mentioned as a feature of some Chinese dialects (including the prestige Chang'an variety) in the 'Siddham Treasury' (悉曇藏 Shittan Zō), a work by the Japanese monk Annen written in 880 AD (de Boer 2005: 373–5, 2008: 73–5). This distinction between 陰 yīn and 陽 yáng tones became phonemic following the loss of the voicedness contrast for syllable onsets: the tone systems of modern Sinitic languages may all be derived from this eight-way model. Also, note that the evolutionary pathways for tonogenesis sketched here is not limited to Sinitic, but is rather shared by many East and Southeast Asian languages (Ferlus 2009; Michaud 2012).

4.1.4 Early Mandarin

As mentioned earlier (§4.1.1), the quantity and quality of the data available for the reconstruction of the evolution of the 'standard' languages of China in the last three major dynasties, i.e. Yuan, Ming, and Qing—enables us to gain a much better understanding of the genesis of Modern Chinese, if compared to what we know about Old and Middle Chinese. However, precisely because of the wealth of information on the languages in use during this time at our disposal, in this section we shall provide a less detailed picture, due to space constraints: hence, we shall

---

[18] We may mention here two proposals: Pulleyblank (1978, 1984) believed that glottalization (-ʔ) and aspiration (-ʰ) were still part of the 切韻 Qièyùn system and survived even beyond that; Ting Pang-hsin (1996: 143–5), on the other hand, suggested that tone distinctions were already present in Old Chinese.

discuss only some of the most important aspects of the linguistic history of this long period. It is important to stress the fact that, more often than not, we shall be dealing with 'languages' which are based on different regional varieties and, thus, did not evolve out of a single genetic lineage.

The first stage which is commonly recognized after the (Late) Middle Chinese period is termed 'Old Mandarin': this is the variety represented in the fourteenth-century rime book 中原音韻 *Zhōngyuán Yīnyùn* (see §2.2.3). Old Mandarin has many innovations which survived in modern Mandarin dialects (see §4.2.1, 4.2.2), including (Pulleyblank 1991; Coblin 2000a; Dong Hongyuan 2014):

a. the loss of voiced obstruent initials, which became unvoiced aspirated in the level tone, and unaspirated in all other tone categories
b. a reduction in the distinctions among labiodental fricative initials ([f] and [ʋ] or [v])
c. the loss of the 入 *rù* tone category, together with the coda stops associated with it (*-p, -t, -k*)[19]
d. a tone system with three categories and a register distinction, resulting in four tones: 陽平 *yáng píng*, 陰平 *yīn píng*, 上 *shǎng*, and 去 *qù*

More generally, Old Mandarin has a simpler sound inventory than Middle Chinese: for intstance, there are only twenty-one distinct initials, whereas Middle Chinese has thirty-six (Ye Baokui 2001: 64–5). Among the conservative features of Old Mandarin, we may include the same three-way distinction for nasal codas (*-m, -n*, and *-ŋ*) as Middle Chinese and the retention of velar and alveolar initials before high front vowels, which have become palatalized in Modern Standard Chinese: compare OM 劍 kjɛm 'sword' and 箭 tsjɛn 'arrow'[20] with MSC *jiàn* for both (Pulleyblank 1991; we will get back to this later).

While the loss of voiced obstruents is a fundamental defining feature of the Mandarin group, and of most modern dialects (see §4.2), this category of initials seems to be preserved not only in the corpus of 'Phags-pa writings but also in Sin Sukju's 'standard readings', literary

---

[19] Although the conclusion that coda stops were entirely lost at this stage is not universally accepted (see Dong Hongyuan 2014: 77).
[20] For ease of presentation, we omit tone markers for Old Mandarin.

readings collected in the mid-fifteenth century, i.e. much later than the 中原音韻 *Zhōngyuán Yīnyùn*.[21] This apparent inconsistency is easily explained by the different underlying dialect for the 中原音韻 *Zhōngyuán Yīnyùn*, for the 'Phags-pa texts, and for the standard readings: the former, as hinted at earlier (§2.2.3), might reflect either a dialect of the Luoyang-Kaifeng area or even a northeastern dialect, while the latter two might reflect a northern and a southern variety of a possible Central Plains standard pronunciation (Coblin 1999, 2001, 2007a). Furthermore, in the so-called 'right readings' collected by Choe Sejin in Beijing and in the Liaodong region, which most likely represent the sixteenth-century northern Chinese *koinè* (the 北音 *běiyīn*; see §4.1.1), Sin Sukju's voiced obstruents correspond to unvoiced initials (Coblin 2007c), consistently with the (much older) 中原音韻 *Zhōngyuán Yīnyùn* sound system.

Generally speaking, Southern Mandarin dialects appear to be more conservative, while Northern Mandarin dialects tend to be more innovative. For instance, in the already mentioned nineteenth-century grammar of 'Beijing Mandarin' by Joseph Edkins (see §2.2.3), the author compares the Beijing and Nanjing versions of words as 腳 *jiǎo* 'foot' or 恰 *qià* 'appropriate': while in the Nanijng variety these words still had a velar initial (romanized as *kioh* and *k'iah*, respectively), in Beijing Mandarin they were already palatalized (Coblin 1997: 534; compare OM kjaw, k^{h}ja; Pulleyblank 1991). As pointed out by Coblin, by comparing the descriptions of Nanjing Mandarin between the second half of the nineteenth century and the beginning of the twentieth century, we may reconstruct the palatalization of this class of sounds: initially, palatalized onsets were found in the speech of the educated class, but they later spread to the whole community (Coblin 1997: 536–7). However, in the northern *koinè* described in Manchu sources, the palatalization of velars before high front vowels is already attested in the mid-eighteenth century (Coblin 2007c: 53–5).

The next stage in the history of Mandarin is usually termed just 'Ming-Qing Mandarin' (明清官話 *Míng-Qīng Guānhuà*; Coblin 2000a; Ye Baokui 2001): however, this period actually saw the coexistence of *at least* two distinct traditions (i.e. Southern and Northern Mandarin; see §2.2.3). The phonology of the northern *koinè*, i.e. the basis for

---

[21] However, note that 'voiced' obstruents in Sin Sukju's standard readings might in fact be murmured, rather than actually voiced (Coblin 2000b: 273).

present-day 普通話 *Pǔtōnghuà*, was influenced not only by southern 官話 *Guānhuà* but also, in all likelihood, by the northeastern dialects brought to the capital by the Manchu conquerors. Moreover, during this period, Chinese *koinai* underwent some important changes. As to Northern Mandarin, besides the already mentioned palatalization of velars, some major innovations are (Coblin 2007b-c; Sagart 2007):

a. the change from *j-* to *r-* of the initial consonant of 容 *róng* 'contain' syllables (MC *yowng*, OM juŋ; BSOL; Pulleyblank 1991)
b. the loss of the distinction between finals in syllables like 半 *bàn* 'half' and 班 *bān* 'class', which were still different in the above-mentioned right readings (respectively, *-ɔn* and *-an*)
c. the change from *-y* to *-u* of nucleus vowels in syllables like 主 *zhǔ* 'main', 處 *chù* 'place', 書 *shū* 'book', and 如 *rú* 'like' (OM tʂy, tʂʰy, ʂy, ry; Pulleyblank 1991)
d. the unrounding of *-ɔ* in syllables as 歌 *gē* 'song', 可 *kě* 'can', 河 *hé* 'river', and 鵝 *é* 'goose'

For a more extensive description of the phonology of Ming-Qing Mandarin, see Ye Baokui (2001: 292–313). Needless to say, the developments discussed in this section shaped the sound system of Modern Standard Chinese, as we shall see later.

4.2 The phonology of modern Sinitic languages

A basic feature of the phonology of modern Sinitic languages, which is apparent also to a casual observer, is the crucial role of the syllable and of its constituents, rather than individual sounds. As seen earlier, in the Chinese linguistic tradition, the syllable is the basic unit of phonological analysis: even in contemporary works on Sinitic languages, the phonology of any variety is normally described in terms of a list of initials and finals (besides tones), i.e. the immediate constituents of the syllable (Lin Hua 2001: 29).

The relevance of the syllable for the analysis of Chinese is partly motivated by the near perfect correspondence of syllables with graphemes (i.e. characters), on the one hand, and with morphemes, on the other hand, making the syllable particularly salient as a unit of speech. A further reason for this is the rigidity of syllable structure in Sinitic languages (Norman 1988: 138). Modern Standard Chinese has about 400 distinct syllables, which rise to more than 1,200 if we consider also tones: this is a relatively low figure, if compared e.g. to the 8,000 distinct syllables of English (although it is much higher than the 113 syllables of Standard Japanese; DeFrancis 1984: 42). What is most relevant here, though, is the impossibility of altering syllable constituents to create new syllables. The fixity of syllable structure and the relatively low number of syllable types mean, among other things, that foreign names have to be 'twisted' in order to fit into the Chinese syllable inventory. Thus, for instance, the name of Russian author Vladimir V. Majakovskij is 'translated' into Chinese as:

(1)　弗拉基米爾　·　馬雅可夫斯基
　　　fúlājīmǐ'ěr　　　*mǎyǎkěfūsījī*

As shown in (1), the only way to render consonant clusters in Chinese is to split each consonant and turn it into a syllable, as for *Vla-* > *fúlā*, and *-vskij* > *fūsījī*. Note, also, that the relevance of the syllable for the processing of Chinese seems to be confirmed also by experimental research: speakers of Chinese which never learned alphabetic writing (including *Pinyin*) experience difficulties in identifying the individual sounds which make up a syllable final (Lin Hua 2001: 29). Lastly, we may remark that most phonological processes in Chinese involve the syllable as a whole, rather than its constituents (Norman 1988: 138; see Zhu Xiaonong 2006: 5 for some examples, and Leong Che Kan 2006 for a psycholinguistic analysis).

Before moving on to the description of the phonology of modern Sinitic languages, a brief digression on the notation and terminology used for tones is necessary. The standard practice in Chinese linguistics is to follow Chao Yuen Ren's convention for tone notation (1968: 25–6): Tone height is represented with numbers from 1 to 5, 1 being the lowest pitch and 5 being the highest pitch. By using two or more of these numbers, we may represent the tone contour of any Chinese variety.[22] However, in the description of modern Sinitic languages, this system is normally associated with the Middle Chinese tone categories discussed

---

[22] For ease of presentation, we use Chao's tone numbers also in phonetic transcriptions, despite the fact that International Phonetic Alphabet has its own tone markers. However, in Chinese dialectology tones are sometimes marked by means of Chao's 'tone letters' (Chao Yuen Ren 1930), which make use of a vertical bar to indicate pitch height: for instance, ˥ (55), ˥˩ (51), ˧˥ (35), etc. Chao's tone letters have also been accepted in the IPA.

in §4.1.3: in a sense, we may say that Chinese dialectology is essentially based on the framework of the rime books (particularly, that of the 切韻 Qièyùn and of Song dynasty rime tables; see §4.1.1). Modern Sinitic languages are thus described by means of Middle Chinese phonological categories, both for initials and finals and for tones.[23] Thus, for instance, in the Mandarin dialects of Shenyang, Jinan, and Hankou, respectively, the tone contours 213, 55, and 42 are all presented as belonging to the 上 shǎng tone category (Yuan et al. 2001: 28), despite the fact that they have nothing in common, in terms of phonetics.

Because of this traditional approach, Chinese dialectology may seem to be a rather arcane subfield for linguists lacking a specific training in traditional Chinese phonology. Further problems arise when there is no regular correspondence between the tone categories of Middle Chinese and those of a modern dialect (Jacques 2017b). Hence, in keeping with the aims of this volume, we shall use Chao's numeric notation as a default, and we shall make reference to Middle Chinese categories only when necessary. Note also that, due to space constraints, we present each syllable in its basic (unmarked) tone, i.e. the tone they have when uttered in isolation: however, rather complex tone sandhi (變調 biàndiào) phenomena are quite common in Sinitic, and they add to the complexity of the phonology of many varieties (see Yip Moira 2002: 173 ff.).

4.2.1 Modern Standard Chinese

As pointed out by Norman (1988: 138), phonology is arguably the only aspect of the standard language which is strictly codified. We said before (§2.2.3, 2.2.4) that the phonology of 普通話 Pǔtōnghuà is based on the Beijing dialect. However, we want to stress the point that based on does not equal identical to: for instance, the realization of /w/ as [v] or [ʋ] in some syllables (e.g. 萬 wàn '10,000' [van⁵¹], 為 wèi 'for' [vei⁵¹]), found in the speech of many Beijing natives, is not an accepted variant in MSC (Chen Ping 1999: 38; Chirkova and Chen 2017). Moreover, the syllable inventory of the Beijing dialect is slightly larger than that of 普通話 Pǔtōnghuà (Duanmu San 2007: 5).

---

[23] The use of the categories of traditional Chinese phonology in the study of modern Sinitic has been criticized by VanNess Simmons (2006) and Jacques (2017b), among others.

A characteristic feature of modern Sinitic languages is the very simple syllable structure: the maximal syllable template is CGVV or CGVC, where G stands for 'glide', and VV may represent a long vowel or a diphthong (Duanmu San 2011, 2014). In MSC, the only coda consonants are [n] and [ŋ], to which we may add the rhotacized vowel [ɚ], sometimes intepreted as a vowel followed by [r] or [ɻ] (-兒 *-r* in *Pinyin*), which may have a morphological function (see §5.1.3.2; Duanmu San 2007: 71). The minimal syllable is made up of a single vowel, as e.g. MSC 餓 *è* 'hungry' or 五 *wǔ* ([u²¹⁴]) 'five' (but cf. Duanmu San 2014: 425). Even though southern dialects typically have a larger inventory e.g. of syllable finals (see §4.2.6, 4.2.7, 4.2.8), no modern Sinitic language has a syllable structure of the same complexity of Old Chinese, or even of Middle Chinese for many varieties.

The analysis of initials in modern Sinitic languages is particularly relevant for the partition of the family since, as said in §2.3.2, the evolution of Middle Chinese voiced obstruents is the most important criterion for the classification of dialect groups, in the traditional approach.[24] Being a standardized Mandarin dialect, MSC shows the typical profile of Northern Sinitic (§4.2.2): Middle Chinese voiced obstruents became unaspirated unvoiced consonants (compare MC 定 *dengX* and MSC *dìng* [tiŋ⁵¹] 'to set') or aspirated unvoiced consonants (MC 庭 *deng*, MSC *tíng* [tʰiŋ³⁵] 'court'), depending on their tone (Yan Margaret Mian 2006: 70; see §4.1.2), with the loss of voicedness as a distinctive feature. Typically, in descriptions of 普通話 *Pǔtōnghuà* as many as twenty-one initial consonants are listed, as shown in Table 4.2.

In some older descriptions (Chao Yuen Ren 1968; Norman 1988), the list of initials includes also the so-called 'zero initial' (零聲母 *língshēngmǔ*). This zero initial may be realized phonetically as a weak velar ([ɣ]) or uvular ([ʁ]) fricative, or even as a glottal stop ([ʔ]) or as a nasal velar ([ŋ]; Chao Yuen Ren 1968: 20; Duanmu San 2007: 72): it is found in many syllables without a consonant onset, as e.g. 案 *àn* 'case, file'. The presence of this 'hidden' initial is the reason why, in complex words as 翻案 *fān'àn* 'reverse a verdict', there is no liaison between the

---

[24] The use of the term 'evolution' entails that there is a direct genetic connection between Middle Chinese and modern Sinitic. However, as said earlier (§2.3.2), this conception of Chinese linguistic history has come under intense criticism by some specialists. Even though we believe that the criticism of the traditional view is fundamentally correct (as argued in Norman and Coblin's 1995 seminal paper cited earlier), in this volume we stick to inaccurate terms like 'evolution'. We nevertheless maintain that it is highly unlikely that all modern (non-Min) dialects may be derived from the 切韻 *Qièyùn* language.

Table 4.2 Modern Standard Chinese initials

Place of articulation	Pinyin	IPA	Example
Labials	b	[p]	八 bā 'eight'
	p	[pʰ]	胖 pàng 'fat'
	m	[m]	馬 mǎ 'horse'
	f	[f]	飛 fēi 'fly'
Alveolars	d	[t]	滴 dī 'drop'
	t	[tʰ]	踢 tī 'kick'
	n	[n]	難 nán 'hard'
Dentals	z	[ts]	賊 zéi 'thief'
	c	[tsʰ]	次 cì 'time'
	s	[s]	三 sān 'three'
	l	[l]	龍 lóng 'dragon'
Retroflexes	zh	[tʂ]	住 zhù 'dwell'
	ch	[tʂʰ]	醜 chǒu 'ugly'
	sh	[ʂ]	樹 shù 'tree'
	r	[ʐ]	柔 róu 'soft'
Palatals	j	[tɕ]	街 jiē 'street'
	q	[tɕʰ]	七 qī 'seven'
	x	[ɕ]	西 xī 'west'
Velars	g	[k]	歌 gē 'song'
	k	[kʰ]	開 kāi 'open'
	h	[x]	好 hǎo 'good'

Adapted from Sun Chaofen 2006: 36.

[n] coda of the first syllable and the vowel of the second syllable (Norman 1988: 140; see Duanmu San 2007: 72–9 for more details).

Note, however, that the initials listed in Table 4.2 are not all phonemic. The palatal consonants *j* ([tɕ]), *q* ([tɕʰ]), and *x* ([ɕ]) are in complementary distribution with the velars *g* ([k]), *k* ([kʰ]), *h* ([x]), with the dentals *z* ([ts]), *c* ([tsʰ]), *s* ([s]), and with the retroflexes *zh* ([tʂ]), *ch* ([tʂʰ]), and *sh* ([ʂ]): palatal sounds are found only before high front vowels or before the prenuclear glides [j] and [ɥ], whereas the other three series of initial cannot occur in this context.[25] This distribution is easily explained if we look at the history of palatals in MSC: as said earlier (§4.1.4), they evolved from velars and dentals before a high front vowel.[26]

[25] There are different positions in the literature on the relationship among these series of initials. For an overview, see Duanmu San (2007: 31).

[26] Incidentally, this is the reason why, for instance, the name 北京 *Běijīng* used to be transcribed as *Peking* in English or *Pékin* in French: these romanizations preserve the velar consonant in the onset of the second syllable.

Moreover, there is no universal agreement on the actual phonetic value of some initials: descriptions sometimes differ in this respect. For instance, the unvoiced stops *b* [p], *d* [t], and *g* [k] are interpeted by some (e.g. Chao Yuen Ren 1968; Norman 1988) as lenis (i.e. [b̥], [d̥], and [g̊]), rather than actually unvoiced: in point of fact, these sounds may be articulated as voiced in some contexts, as e.g. in unstressed syllables. However, this is not directly relevant for a phonemic analysis: the only pertinent feature is aspiration (i.e. aspirated vs. unaspirated).

As for the finals, besides the lack of the stop codas -*p*, -*t*, -*k* (already lost at the Old Mandarin stage; see §4.1.4), the nasal codas -*m* got merged with -*n* in MSC: compare MC 三 *sam* 'three' and MSC *sān* (Yan Margaret Mian 2006: 81–2). Many descriptions of MSC list thirty-five finals, but some include as many as thirty-nine distinct finals (see Huang and Liao 2002: 58): the gap is due to different interpretations of the status of some sounds (and combinations of sounds). Table 4.3 is based on Norman (1988: 141) and Dong Hongyuan (2014: 137–8), with some modifications: specifically, finals are grouped following the categories of traditional Chinese phonology, in order to help the reader to get acquainted with the terminology in use in this branch of Chinese linguistics. In this traditional terminology, grouping is based on the nature of the medial, i.e. the glide which comes before the syllable nucleus (see §4.1.1).[27] Due to space constraints, we shall provide but a few examples for each type of final (for the full list of finals, the reader is referred to the sources quoted here).

Table 4.3 Some examples of MSC finals

Type	Pinyin	IPA	Example
Rhymes without a medial (開口呼 *kāikǒuhū*, lit. 'open-mouth')	*a* *e* *ü*	[a] [ɤ] [y]	茶 *chá* 'tea' 喝 *hē* 'drink' 綠 *lǜ* 'green'
Rhymes with a medial [i] (齊齒呼 *qíchǐhū*, lit. 'even-teeth')	*iong* *iang* *ie*	[iʊŋ] [iaŋ] [iɛ]	窮 *qióng* 'poor' 強 *qiáng* 'strong' 鐵 *tiě* 'iron'

(Continued)

[27] Some readers may be puzzled by the use of the IPA symbols for vowels in the transcription of medials, rather than the symbols for glides. This is in fact the choice of most descriptions of Chinese phonology: see e.g. Chao Yuen Ren (1968); Norman (1988); Dong Hongyuan (2014). While some recent works (e.g. Duanmu San 2007; De Dominicis 2013) do transcribe medials as glides, here we chose to be consistent with the dominant trend in the literature.

Table 4.3 Continued

Type	Pinyin	IPA	Example
Rhymes with a medial [u]	uo	[uo]	國 guó 'country'
(合口呼 hékǒuhū, lit.	uan	[uan]	寬 kuān 'broad'
'closed-mouth')	un	[uən]	睏 kùn 'sleepy'
Rhymes with a medial [y]	ün	[yn]	群 qún 'crowd'
(撮口呼 cuōkǒuhū, lit.	üan	[yan]	院 yuàn 'yard'
'pursed mouth')	üe	[yɛ]	虐 nüè 'cruel'

In the list of finals in Table 4.3, we did not include the above-mentioned 'rhotacized' final -兒 -r, which deletes the nasal coda, if present (e.g. 乾 gān [kan⁵⁵] > 乾兒 gānr [kaɚ⁵⁵] 'dry food'). Moreover, [ɚ] is used also as a stand-alone syllable (e.g. 耳 ěr [ɚ²¹⁴] 'ear'; Duanmu San 2007: 40).

The IPA transcriptions provided in Table 4.3 should not obscure the fact that each vowel may have different allophones, depending on the context (see Norman 1988: 142–3; Yip Po-Ching 2000: 22–3, and De Dominicis 2013: 309). A particularly controversial case is that of the vowel written as *i* in *Pinyin*, which we did not include in Table 4.3 for the sake of simplicity. This /i/ actually corresponds to at least three concrete sounds: besides [i] (as e.g. in 力 lì 'strength', [li⁵¹]), the other two allophones are understood by some (e.g. Duanmu San 2007, 2008) as syllabic consonants (i.e. [z̩] and [ʐ̩]), while (arguably) most Chinese scholars (e.g. Zee and Lee 2007) believe that they are apical vowels (i.e. [ɯ] and [ɨ]).[28] Besides the controversies related to the phonetic nature of individual sounds, opinions differ also as for how many vowel phonemes there actually are in MSC: the reader is referred to De Dominicis (2013: 326–8) for an overview.

Note, also, that the analysis of medials is not the same for all scholars: some believe that glides are part of the onset, rather than the final; some others believe that glides are part of the nucleus; yet others believe that prenuclear glides have their own slot in the structure of the syllable. Needless to say, there may be different interpretations of syllable structure, depending on the proposed collocation of the medial: we cannot enter into the debate here due to space constraints, and we refer the reader to Duanmu San (2008: 76–8) for an overview. We shall just point

---

[28] The apical vowels [ɯ] and [ɨ] are often transcribed in the Chinese linguistic literature with the non-standard IPA symbols [ɿ] and [ʅ] (e.g. in Zee and Lee 2007; Dong Hongyuan 2014).

out that, strictly speaking, 'final' and 'rhyme' are not synonymous, since medials are not part of the rhyme: thus, for instance, 慢 *màn* [mæn⁵¹] 'slow' rhymes with 麵 [mjæn⁵¹] 'noodles' (Duanmu San 2008: 77).

Lastly, the tone system of MSC is relatively simple. There are four tones, with only one register, to which we must add the neutral tone (輕聲 *qīngshēng*): some grammatical morphemes (e.g. the perfective aspect marker 了 -*le*)[29] and the righthand constituents of some complex words (e.g. 學生 *xuésheng* 'student') are in the neutral tone. In Table 4.4 we present the four tones of MSC, in terms of the traditional categories and of their actual tonal contour.

Table 4.4 The four tones of MSC

Tone category	Contour	Tone marker	Example
陰平 *yīnpíng*	55	ā	天 *tiān* 'sky'
陽平 *yángpíng*	35	á	魚 *yú* 'fish'
上 *shǎng*	214	ǎ	水 *shuǐ* 'water'
去 *qù*	51	à	辣 *là* 'spicy'

As mentioned in §4.2, the correspondence of tone categories between Middle Chinese and modern Sinitic languages is not as neat as it may appear in Table 4.4. For instance, the fourth tone of MSC is associated with the departing tone category because *most* MSC syllables in this category were in the 去 *qù* tone in Middle Chinese: however, some syllables in the 上 *shǎng* tone, as e.g. MC 道 *dawX* 'way', are in the fourth tone as well in MSC (*dào*; Jacques 2017b). Some irregularities in the evolution of tone may be (partly) explained by contact with other dialects (Sagart 1999a).

If tone is a prominent feature of modern Sinitic languages, the role of stress is less evident: even native speakers may feel it hard to identify word stress, and some even suggest that MSC does not have contrastive stress (see the overview in Duanmu San 2007: 129, 155). In fact, stress and tone are not entirely independent in Chinese: neutral tone syllables are by definition unstressed, and in stressed syllables the width of the

---

[29] Following Li and Thompson (1981), we add a dash before the *Pinyin* transcription of the perfective aspect marker 了 -*le*, in order to distinguish it from the homophonous sentence-final particle 了 *le*. On the relation between 了 -*le* and 了 *le*, see Soh Hooi Ling (2014).

tone contour is greater. Intensity is secondary, unless stress is used contrastively (Chao Yuen Ren 1968: 35). Besides, neutral tone syllables, also defined as 'weak' or 'light' syllables, are shorter than stressed (or 'full') syllables, and their rhymes may undergo segmental reduction (see Duanmu San 2007: 130). Compare:

(2) 媽媽
    māma [ma:^{55}.mə]
    'mum'

(3) 肉丸
    ròuwán [ʐəu^{51}.wan^{35}]
    'meatball'

In the word in (2), the second syllable is in the neutral tone, is shorter than the first syllable, and has undergone segmental reduction ([ma] > [mə]). There is thus no doubt that stress occurs on the first syllable in this case. However, the word in (3) is made of two full syllables, with their own tone and no reduction: hence, it is hard(er) to say which syllable is stressed, as is often the case for compounds also in other languages (e.g. Eng. *Red Cross*). Some believe that there is no difference in stress between the two syllables, whereas others believe that the second syllable has higher intensity (a position supported by phonetic studies; see Duanmu San 2014: 431 and the references cited therein).

Due to space constraints, here we cannot enter into the debate on the nature of stress in Chinese: the reader is referred to Duanmu San (2007: 129ff.) for an overview. We shall just point out that, usually, loss of tone and segmental reduction occurs on righthand constituents, both in complex words and in some phrases, based on a trochaic (strong-weak) foot (Yip Po-Ching 2000: 28; Ansaldo and Lim 2004: 359). This is the reason why reduced grammatical morphemes are generally located in the suffix position, as we shall see later (§5.1.3.5; see Arcodia 2013, 2015).

The presentation of the phonology of MSC in this section is based on the standard, 'textbook' norm. However, needless to say, regional varieties of 普通話 *Pǔtōnghuà* may differ significantly from this model (see §2.1). Some very common features of non-standard varieties of MSC are (Chen Ping 1999: 44):

    a. merging of the dental initials [ts], [tsʰ], and [s] with the retroflexes [tʂ], [tʂʰ], and [ʂ]

b. merging of the nasal codas [n] and [ŋ]
c. deviations of pitch contours of the four tones

See Chen Ping (1999: 42–3) for some examples of features of 普通話 *Pǔtōnghuà* as spoken in the Wu dialect area, Li *et al.* (2005) for varieties in the Southern Min area, and Wu Yunji (2005: 28–32) for an extensive description of the variety of MSC spoken in Changsha, known as 塑料 普通話 *sùliào Pǔtōnghuà* 'plastic *Pǔtōnghuà*'.

4.2.2 Mandarin and Jin

Mandarin dialects have by far the largest population in the Chinese-speaking world and are also those spread over the largest area. A prominent feature of the Mandarin group is the presence of many innovations, particularly in the lexicon, but also in the phonology: the sound system of Northern dialects is much simpler than that of Middle Chinese and, also, of Southern Chinese dialects, as hinted at before (Ho Dah-an 2003; Norman 2003; Yan Margaret Mian 2006).

While the Mandarin group as a whole is generally considered to be quite homogeneous (but cf. Szeto, Ansaldo, and Matthews 2018), there appears to be no agreement as to its internal structure. The main controversy concerns the position of Jin dialects, as mentioned earlier (§2.3.2). Until the mid-eighties, Jin dialects were normally seen as part of Mandarin, but then Li Rong (1985) proposed that these dialects constitute a separate, independent branch of Sinitic (on the same taxonomical level as Mandarin, Wu, Yue, etc.). The definition of Jin as a group is essentially based on the retention of the entering tone of Middle Chinese; this is expressed phonetically with the presence of a glottal stop in the syllable coda, which is the outcome of the evolution of Middle Chinese stop finals -*p*, -*t*, and -*k*. Thus, for instance, MSC 力 *lì* 'strength' (MC *lik*) corresponds to [lieʔ] in Taiyuan Jin (Yan Margaret Mian 2006: 82). The weak point of this proposal is that the basic defining criterion for Jin stands out as not being based on the evolution of aspirated voiced obstruents, as is the case for all other first-level branches of Sinitic (i.e. 方言 *fāngyán* or [大]區 [*dà*]*qū*; see §2.3.2). In fact, Li Rong (1985, 1987, 1989) also proposes a subdivision of Mandarin (excluding Jin, obviously) based on the evolution of the Middle Chinese entering tone (see Li Xiaofan 2005; Yan Margaret Mian 2006; Kurpaska 2010): the main defining feature of the Jiang-Huai subgroup of Mandarin would be the retention of the entering tone, a criterion which clearly overlaps with that for the individuation of Jin.

A number of scholars (e.g. Ting Pang-hsin 1991: 192) have thus suggested that this is not a valid criterion for the separation of Jin from Mandarin. On the other hand, Wen Duanzheng (1997) and Hou Jingyi (1999) do accept Li Rong's proposal for the definition of Jin and added further phonological, morphological, and lexical criteria according to which Jin may be separated from Mandarin. As to phonology, we may cite as an example the evolution into fricatives of part of Middle Chinese 崇 *chóng* initials (*dzr-* in Baxter and Sagart 2014) in the 平 *píng* tone. Li Rulong (2001: 42–3) offers an analysis of a very long list of distinctive features of Jin and highlights that a fundamental criterion for the definition of Mandarin, viz. the evolution of voiced obstruent initials in the 平 *píng* tone into voiceless aspirated consonants, does not apply to Jin, in which this class of sounds is normally unaspirated. Furthermore, the fusion of the *-m* and *-n* finals, another important feature of Mandarin, is not always found in Jin (for a more detailed overview of the differences between Mandarin and Jin, see Qiao Quansheng 2008: 273–319).

Thus, to sum up, while there appears to be general agreement on the fact that Jin dialects constitute a group, there is no agreement on whether they should be seen as a primary branch of Sinitic or as a subgroup within Mandarin. Due to space constraints, we shall not discuss this issue any further here.

We have already mentioned before that the main defining feature of Mandarin is the evolution of voiced obstruent initials into voiceless aspirated consonants for the 平 *píng* tone and into voiceless unaspirated consonants for all other tone categories. Another common trait of Mandarin dialects which we mentioned is the evolution of 陽上 *yángshǎng* tone syllables into departing (去 *qù*) tone syllables; moreover, most Mandarin varieties (including MSC; see Table 4.4) do not have the 陰陽 *yīn-yáng* register distinction in the 去 *qù* category (Norman 2003: 77). Some more peculiar features of Mandarin dialects are the limited number of distinct tones and the already mentioned (§2.3.2, 4.2.1) palatalization of velar consonants before high front vowels. The latter, however, is not universal in Mandarin: for instance, in MSC 酒 *jiǔ* 'alcoholic beverage' and 九 *jiǔ* 'nine' both have [tɕ] as their initial, but their Zhengzhou cognates have [ts] and [tɕ], respectively (Yuan *et al.* 2001: 30). Lastly, as pointed out in §2.3.2, there are lexical items which are considered to be distinctive for Mandarin dialects, including e.g. 穿 *chuān* for 'wear', 兒 *ěr* for 'son', or 下 *xià* 'descend' as the verb in the expression 'to rain' (MSC 下雨 *xià-yǔ*; Norman 2003: 78).

As mentioned before, Li Rong (1985, 1987, 1989; see also Yan Margaret Mian 2006: 61) proposes a partition of the Mandarin group into eight branches, mainly based on the evolution of the Middle Chinese entering tone. In his proposal, Jiang-Huai dialects are those which retained the entering tone (as mentioned earlier), expressed phonetically as a short tone (e.g. in Nanjing) and/or with a glottal stop (e.g. in Hefei), just as in Jin dialects. In the Central Plains (中原 *Zhōngyuán*) subgroup, entering tone syllables became either 陰平 *yīn píng* or 陽平 *yáng píng*, depending on the initial, while in Southwestern Mandarin they evolved into a low register level tone. Also, according to Li Rong's classification scheme, all entering tone syllables with a voiced obstruent initial are now in the 陽平 *yáng píng* tone in all Mandarin dialects.

A more 'traditional' partition has been proposed by Yuan *et al.* (2001: 24). In their scheme, there are only four subgroups of Mandarin, namely: Northern dialects 'in the narrow sense' (狹義的北方方言 *xiáyì de běifāng fāngyán*), including the Beijing dialect, Northwestern Mandarin, Southwestern Mandarin, and Jiang-Huai Mandarin. However, the defining criteria for each branch are not fully explicit: we may mention the lack of the distinction between retroflex and dental(/alveolar) sibilants and the levelling of the contrast between [n] and [l] as initials in most Southwestern and Jiang-Huai dialects (Yuan *et al.* 2001: 29, 31; Norman 1988: 193). A different scheme was proposed by Ting Pang-hsin (1991: 191), who posits five branches for Mandarin: Northern, Jin, Eastern (Jiang-Huai), Southwestern, and Chu. Ting's proposal is based on a combination of criteria, including: the evolution of the entering tone, the distinction between [n] and [l] initials, the weakening of nasal finals, the presence of the labio-palatal approximant [ɥ] in a set of syllables. Ho Dah-an (2017), on the other hand, proposes that Mandarin be divided into three major 'regions' only (namely, Northern, Southwestern, and Jiang-Huai), which are defined on the basis of phonological features partly overlapping with those suggested by Ting Pang-hsin (1991).

To sum up, while there are many differences among the classification schemes proposed in the literature for Mandarin(/Jin), there appears to be general agreement on a number of aspects: namely, the specificity of Jin varieties, as well as of the Jiang-Huai and Southwestern subgroups of Mandarin. The Northern Mandarin branch, on the other hand, is mentioned in all the schemes discussed here, but its definition varies: for instance, Li Rong does not include Beijing Mandarin in Northern Mandarin, but both the varieties of Southern Hebei and Northern Shandong are considered part of this group.[30]

4.2.3 Wu

If compared to Mandarin, Wu dialects are notably more conservative. For instance, they retain the Middle Chinese velar nasal initial *ng*: compare e.g. MSC 魚 *yú* 'fish', MC *ngjo*, and Wenzhou [ŋøy³¹] (see Norman 1988: 200). Nevertheless, they also possess some innovative features, as the reduction of many diphthongs. Wu dialects are characterized by a very high degree of internal differentiation, which often results in a relatively low level of mutual intelligibility within the group (Pan Wuyun 1991: 29). While a partition of Wu into as many as six subgroups has been proposed in the literature (Li Rong 1987; Wang and Cao 2012), these dialects are often simply seen as divided into a Northern (Jiangsu) and a Southern (Zhejiang) type. Southern Wu dialects are deemed as representative of the 'original' Wu dialect type, despite Min influence,[31] while Northern Wu dialects have been influenced to a greater extent by Mandarin, as hinted at before (§2.2.2, 2.3.2; for a list of the phonological features of Northern and Southern Wu, see Pan Wuyun 1991: 286–7).

The basic defining feature of the Wu group is the retention of the distinction between voiced, voiceless, and aspirated voiceless initial obstruents (Chao Yuen Ren 1967), as hinted at in §2.3.2. While in some Wu dialects this distinction is retained as a true voiced vs. voiceless contrast, in other (especially, Northern Wu) varieties Middle Chinese voiced obstruents correspond to murmured (rather than voiced) initials: compare e.g. MC 白 *baek* 'white' (BSOL), MSC *bái* [pai³⁵], Wenzhou [ba²¹²] (Zhengzhang Shangfang 2008: 254), and Shanghai *baq* [b̥aʔ²⁴]

---

[30] In point of fact, in Li Rong (1989) the label 北方官話 *Běifāng Guānhuà* 'Northern Mandarin' is replaced by 冀魯官話 *Jì-lǔ Guānhuà*, lit. 'Hebei (冀 *Jì*) and Shandong (魯 *Lǔ*) Mandarin'.

[31] The presence of shared archaisms between Min and some Wu varieties of Southern Zhejiang, as e.g. the correspondence between 澄 *chéng* initials and [t], is interpreted by You Rujie (1992: 99) as evidence of the common origin of these two groups (see §2.3.2), rather than as the product of the influence of Min on Wu. On this issue, see Chappell (2001: 12–13).

(Zhu Xiaonong 2006: 9).[32] However, this does not happen only in Wu and is attested also in some varieties classified as Xiang (VanNess Simmons 1999a: 4). Moreover, the three-way distinction of initials is not preserved in its entirety in some varieties at the periphery of the Wu-speaking area in which, due to the influence of Mandarin, Gan, and Min, voiced obstruents are often just devoiced (Pan Wuyun 1991: 253, 260–1). Given the limitations discussed here, some specialists proposed alternative models for the definition of the Wu group.

For instance, Norman (2003) stresses the fact that the tone system of Wu appears to be rather unique within Sinitic: Wu dialects typically have a two-register distinction in all tone categories, which often results into 7–8 distinct tones. The Wenzhou dialect, for instance, has an eight-tone system (Zhengzhang Shangfang 2008: 92). This feature of the tone system may be used to distinguish Wu dialects from those Xiang varieties which, as said before, have a three-way distinciton of initials, but e.g. no register distinction in the entering tone (Norman 2003: 78). Yu Zhiqiang (1999) proposes eleven fundamental features which define Wu, but he also stresses that there are two of them which have the highest predictive value ('highly valued features'), namely the typical Wu vowel system (see Yu Zhiqiang 1999: 249–54) and the use of a morpheme with a labiodental initial consonant ([f] or [v]/[f̬]) as the simple negator (compare SMC 不 bù and Shanghai 勿 veq [feʔ²⁴]; Zhu Xiaonong 2006).

VanNess Simmons (1999a) proposes a more elaborate classification scheme. In essence, through dialect comparison, he identifies a number of features which define 'Common Wu', the basis on which the affiliation of each variety may be assessed. Among Common Wu features, we may mention here:

a. the presence of nasals as initials for the 日 rì 'day' (MC nyit) and 微 wēi 'tiny' (MC mjj; BSOL) categories
b. velar initials in words for which Mandarin has a palatal initial
c. the (already mentioned) labiodental (rather than bilabial) initial consonant in the morpheme for simple negation
d. a single phonemic nasal as syllable coda, in contexts for which other Chinese dialects do make a distinction (as e.g. MSC 金 jīn

---

[32] Note that the murmured initials of Wu dialects may surface as voiced in word-internal position: see e.g. Shanghai 雪白 sijqbaq [ɕɪ⁴⁴baʔ²⁴] 'snow-white' (Zhu Xiaonong 2006: 9).

'gold' vs. 京 *jīng* 'capital'; VanNess Simmons 1999a: 80–1; Yan Margaret Mian 2006: 98)

However, these features should not be understood as having the same value: in fact, they are presented by VanNess Simmons as being of greater or smaller importance in the definition of the Wu prototype. Moreover, he admits that there may be 'transitional' varieties, e.g. between Wu and Mandarin (see VanNess Simmons 1999a for the details); the existence of hybrid dialects is expected, given the already mentioned background of language contact between Wu and Mandarin, as well as other dialects (see Pan Wuyun 1991).

4.2.4 Xiang

Xiang dialects are a typical instance of the Central transitional zone of Sinitic. The hybrid nature of Xiang varieties is clearly visible not only in their phonology, but also in their lexicon, morphology, and syntax (Wu Yunji 2005).

One prominent feature of the Xiang group is that it can be divided into two major subgroups, the so-called 'new' Xiang dialects (新湘語 *xīn Xiāngyǔ*), as e.g. the Changsha variety, and 'old' Xiang dialects (老湘語 *lǎo Xiāngyǔ*), as e.g. Shuangfeng (see §4.1.1; Yuan et al. 2001: 101). Old Xiang dialects, located in Southern Hunan, retain some archaic features, while New Xiang, found in Hubei and Northern Hunan, developed in close contact with the dialects spoken by Northern immigrants[33] and, as a consequence, absorbed many Mandarin traits (Yan Margaret Mian 2006: 105), as mentioned earlier (§2.3.2).

Old Xiang dialects typically retain the contrast between voiced and voiceless initials, just as Wu (§4.2.3), while in New Xiang varieties Middle Chinese voiced initials mostly correspond to unaspirated consonants (Yuan et al. 2001: 101; Wu Yunji 2005: 21; Yan Margaret Mian 2006: 109). The loss of voiced obstruents, an archaic feature, in the main urban areas of Hunan (Yuan et al. 2001: 101), may be seen as the product of contact with other non-Xiang dialects, especially Mandarin. In this connection, while the distinction between New and Old Xiang generally holds, the level of 'mandarinization' varies for each

---

[33] Specifically, Northern immigrants from the Central Plains area, which moved towards Xiang-speaking areas at the time of the An Lushan rebellion (755–63), during the Tang period (Yan Margaret Mian 2006: 105).

dialect. More conservative varieties, as e.g. the Chengbu (城步 *Chéngbù*) dialect in the far southwest of Hunan, retain voiced stop initials in all tone categories, while innovative varieties, as the above-mentioned Changsha dialect, have only voiceless obstruent initials; however, we find also dialects in which some initials are voiced, and some others became voiceless, as the Shaoyang variety (邵陽 *Shàoyáng*; Norman 1988: 207).

While a subset of Xiang dialects shares with Wu the retention of voiced obstruents, as pointed out before, a distinctive feature of Xiang dialects is that they completely lost final stops in entering tone syllables; these finals often correspond to glottal stops in Wu (Norman 1988: 208). As to the tone system, Xiang dialects typically have five to seven distinct tones and, as mentioned earlier (§4.2.3), lack the register distinction for the entering tone, differently from Wu dialects. An archaic feature of Old Xiang varieties is the retention of Middle Chinese bilabial stops; in some Xiang dialects, both Old and New, these sounds evolved into velar fricatives, rather than into bilabial fricatives as most other Northern and Central dialects (Yan Margaret Mian 2006: 109; but see §4.2.5, 4.2.6). Compare, for instance, MC 封 *pjowng* (BSOL) 'seal', MSC *fēng*, and Changsha [xoŋ³³] (Yuan *et al.* 2001: 103). This is understood by Norman (1988: 211) as a defining feature of Southern Chinese dialects, and hence its presence in Xiang is rather remarkable. Lastly, as to the finals, Xiang shares with Southwestern Mandarin the [n] reflex for Middle Chinese -*m* and -*ŋ* (Yan Margaret Mian 2006: 114).

4.2.5 Gan

Among the seven commonly accepted branches of Sinitic, Gan and Hakka are arguably those whose status is most controversial. In Li Fang-Kuei's often-quoted seminal paper (1973 [1937]), Gan and Hakka are seens as part of the same branch, namely Gan-Hakka (贛客家 *Gàn-Kèjiā*): while these are now most often presented as two separate major groups (See Kurpaska 2010: 50–7), even in the recent literature (e.g. Li Xiaofan 2005) they are occasionally seen as a single branch.

The basic feature for the identification of a dialect as Gan is the correspondence between Middle Chinese voiced obstruents and aspirated voiceless initials in all tone categories. However, Hakka dialects (with a few exceptions), as well as some Mandarin and Min varieties, share the same pattern (Norman 1988: 204). Moreover, in some varieties which are usually classified as Gan, as e.g. the Xiushui (修水 *Xiūshuǐ*) and the Duchang (都昌 *Dūchāng*) dialects, there actually are voiced initials, sometimes even aspirated (Yan Margaret Mian 2006: 151–2): compare MSC 破 *pò* 'broken', MC *phaH* (BSOL), Xiushui [b'ɔ], and Duchang [bɔ] (Li and Zhang 1992: 20; tones omitted here). Hence, the usual criterion of the evolution of voiced obstruents cannot be used to clearly separate Gan from Hakka. Among the other features which set Gan apart from Hakka which have been proposed in the literature, we may cite here the typical Northern and Central evolution of bilabial stop initials into labiodental fricatives for Gan, while Hakka retains the Middle Chinese bilabials; also, while many Hakka varieties fully retain Middle Chinese stop finals, in Gan these sounds have different reflexes (see Li and Zhang 1992: 193–4 for an extensive list of shared and divergent features between Gan and Hakka; see also Sagart 1988). Note, however, that fricative reflexes for Middle Chinese bilabial stops are actually not universal in Gan dialects, and some varieties actually do retain bilabials (Sagart 2002: 133–4). As pointed out before (see §2.3.2), the border between dialect groups may sometimes be 'blurred', and even basic defining criteria may not apply in some cases.

A remarkable feature of Gan dialects is the wide range of variation in tone systems, from a minimum of five to a maximum of ten distinct tones (as in the already mentioned Duchang variety; Yan Margaret Mian 2006: 162). As to the initials, some Gan dialects apparently retained the Old Chinese alveolar stops *t-, *tʰ-, *d-: see e.g. Xiushui 豬 [ty] 'pig' vs. MSC *zhū*, MC *trjo*, OC *tra (Yan Margaret Mian 2006: 153, tones omitted; BSOL); interestingly, this archaic feature is shared with Min and, also, with some Old Xiang varieties. Just as Wu, Gan dialects may also be divided into a Northern and a Southern group; in the case of Gan, however, the Northern group is actually the more conservative one, while Southern Gan appears to be more innovative (Sagart 1993: 27). An alternative proposal (Yan and Bao 1987; Xie Liuwen 2012) sees Gan as divided into nine subgroups, mostly defined on the basis of their tone system and/or on segmental features.

4.2.6 Hakka

As said in the preceding section, the definition of the Hakka group has been an object of controversy among specialists in Chinese dialectology.

For instance, while Sagart (1988, 1993, 2002) proposes that Gan and Hakka have a common origin, Norman (1988, 2003) believes that the features shared by Gan and Hakka have limited significance and that Hakka has a common origin with Yue and Min (see §2.3.2). The Southern origin of Hakka, according to Norman (1988: 211–13), may be argued on the basis of some important features shared with Yue and Min:

a. the retention of (Early Middle Chinese) bilabial stop initials
b. strong resistance to the palatalization of velars
c. the shared treatment for diphthongs belonging to the 歌 gē group (*-aj / *-oj; BSOL; see §4.2.8)
d. a similar syllable structure, with few initials, no voicing distinction, and the retention of the full set of Middle Chinese syllable codas (although this does not hold for all Hakka dialects, as we shall see)

In Hakka dialects, as said earlier, Middle Chinese voiced obstruents generally correspond to aspirated voiceless consonants, just as in Gan; however, some exceptions to this pattern are attested. A feature of Hakka is the evolution of many lower rising tone syllables into the upper 平 píng tone: this is attested in Gan for syllables with obstruent initials, but in Hakka this happens also for syllables with sonorant initials (Norman 2003: 80). In fact, Norman (1989) suggests that a dialect may be defined as Hakka if the syllables in the rising tone with sonorant initials are divided into two tones, 陰平 yīnpíng and 陰上 yīnshǎng, depending on the lexical item. However, others (Sagart 1998; Lau Chun-fat 2002) stress the fact that those patterns of evolution may be found also in some dialects classified as Gan and Yue: Sagart (1998) actually believes that there is no criterion which may be applied to define a dialect as unequivocally Hakka, a position which is shared also by Branner (2000: 82; see Yan Margaret Mian 2006: 168).

Among the typical features of Hakka dialects, we already mentioned the retention of bilabial stop initials, at least for many (but not all) varieties. Another Hakka trait in the system of initial consonants is the labiodental reflex for Middle Chinese velar fricatives, found in the majority of Hakka dialects: compare MC 紅 huwng 'red', MSC hóng, Meixian (梅縣 Měixiàn) [fuŋ¹¹] (Yuan et al. 2001: 169; Yan Margaret Mian 2006: 180–1). In the inventory of finals, while many Hakka varieties retain the full set of Middle Chinese stops, as well as the three nasal consonants ([n], [ŋ], and [m]), there are other dialects, as e.g. Changting (長汀 *Chángtīng*), in which stop codas have been lost, and which retain only one nasal final ([ŋ]; Yan Margaret Mian 2006: 185; Xie and Huang 2012). Lastly, tones range from five to seven, and most Hakka dialects have six distinct tones.

4.2.7 Yue

The Yue (or Cantonese; see §2.3.2) branch of Sinitic developed in a situation of intense contact with non-Chinese peoples in Southern China, including speakers of Tai, Hmong-Mien, and Austroasiatic languages (Chappell 2004b: 16; §2.2.2). This is the reason why modern Yue dialects possess several Tai and Hmong-Mien features in their lexicon and, as we shall see, in their phonology (Yue Anne Oi-Kan 1991: 304–7; Bauer 1996: 1812–14).

The evolution of Middle Chinese voiced obstruents does not follow a unitary pattern in Yue. Most varieties have aspirated voiceless reflexes for voiced obstruents in 平 *píng* tone syllables (as well as in some 上 *shǎng* tone syllables), and unaspirated voiceless reflexes for all other cases. However, in some varieties traditionally classified as Yue, as the Bobai (博白 *bóbái*) dialect, we find only aspirated voiceless reflexes in all tone categories, just as in Gan and Hakka; in yet other varieties, as the Tengxian (藤縣 *Téngxiàn*) dialect, we find only unaspirated voiceless reflexes, just as in Xiang (Yue Anne Oi-Kan 1991: 301–2). However, since, on the whole, even varieties as Bobai and Tengxian have more shared features with the rest of Yue than with Gan, Hakka, or Xiang, additional criteria have been proposed in the literature to define the Yue group. Norman (1988, 2003) believes that a feature found only in Yue is the partition of the upper entering tone into two subtypes, depending on the length of the nucleus vowel: for instance, in Guangzhou the tone values for the 陰入 *yīnrù* tone category are 5(5) (上陰入 *shàng yīnrù*) and 33 (下陰入 *xià yīnrù*; Yan Margaret Mian 2006: 217). This peculiar development is attested also in some Tai languages, and may be understood as the possible outcome of contact between Yue and Tai (Bauer 1996).

Yue dialects have a conservative system of finals: they mostly retain the full set of six coda consonants of Middle Chinese, even more consistently than Min and Hakka (Norman 1988: 217; Yue Anne Oi-Kan

1991: 304): as mentioned in the preceding section, this may be seen as a defining feature of Southern dialects. Generally speaking, Yue phonology is quite close to Late Middle Chinese (Chappell 2001: 16; Dong Hongyuan 2014: 166). Another feature of Yue phonology not generally found in other dialect groups which could be of Tai origin is the distinctiveness of vowel length: e.g. Cant. 新 *sān* 'new' vs. 山 *sāan* 'mountain'[34] (Bauer 1996: 1813; ex. from Matthews and Yip 2011: 24). Yue dialects are also characterized by complex tone inventories, ranging from six to ten distinct tones (Yan Margaret Mian 2006: 216): however, note that these phonetic distinctions are not necessarily also phonemic. For instance, (Hong Kong) Cantonese is usually described as having nine tones, but only six of those are relevant (distinctive) on the phonemic level: entering tones, i.e. syllables with a stop final, may be seen as the short variants of the tones 陰平 *yīnpíng* (55), 陰去 *yīnqù* (33), and 陽去 *yángqù* (22; Matthews and Yip 2011: 27–9).

4.2.8 Min

As pointed out before (§2.3.2), Min dialects stand out for their retention of phonological distinctions which are not found in Middle Chinese (understood here as the 切韻 *Qièyùn* language).[35] This is the reason why Min dialects are often claimed to have split from the rest of Sinitic before the Middle Chinese stage, either from Old Chinese or, anyway, from an ancestor language which split from Old Chinese before the Middle Chinese stage. Specifically, as mentioned earlier (§4.1.3), Min is the only group which has not undergone the 'first palatalization of velars':[36] compare OC 支 (also 枝) *ke, MC *tsye*, MSC *zhī* 'branch', and proto-Min *ki (Baxter and Sagart 2014: 33, 77–9), Taiw. *ki*. Since this change in the system of initials probably dates back to the time between the second century BC and the beginning of the first millennium, the ancestor of modern Min dialects should have split from the rest of Sinitic before this period (on the relationship between Min and Old Chinese, see Handel 2010).

---

[34] Note that here the difference in length has an effect on vowel quality too ([ɐ] vs. [aː]).

[35] Note that, in fact, Hakka dialects (see §4.2.6), as well as Waxiang (瓦鄉 *Wǎxiāng*, a cluster of unclassified Southern Hunan Sinitic varieties) do have some phonological features which cannot be derived from Middle Chinese (Baxter and Sagart 2014: 32–4): however, this has not received much attention in the literature as in the case of Min.

[36] The use of 'first' is meant to distinguish it from the palatalization of velar which occurred much later in Mandarin (see §4.2.2).

As to the modern reflexes of Middle Chinese voiced obstruents, in Min dialects we mostly find unaspirated voiceless initials or, in a limited number of cases, aspirated consonants. Specifically, among low register syllables we find both aspirated and unaspirated obstruents, depending on the lexical item: compare e.g. MSC 步 *bù* 'step' and 鼻 *bí* 'nose' with Fuzhou [puo] and [pʰei], Xiamen [pɔ] and [pʰĩ] (Norman 2003: 81; tones omitted). In other dialect groups, as seen earlier, the reflexes for this class of sounds are more regular. As to tone inventories, Min dialects typically have six to eight distinct tones (Yan Margaret Mian 2006: 141).

Some very conservative traits of Min have already been mentioned before, including the retention of alveolar stops (compare Xiamen 竹 [tiɔk³²] 'bamboo', OC *truk with MC *trjuwk*, MSC *zhú*; BSOL; Yuan *et al.* 2001: 261), the retention of Middle Chinese bilabial stops (compare Taiw. 飛 *pue* 'fly', MC *pjɨj*, with MSC *fēi*; BSOL), which in this dialect is more pervasive than in the rest of Southern Sinitic, and the fact that Min dialects have not undergone the first palatalization of velars. However, while the conservativeness of Min has been higlighted time and again in the literature, in Min dialects we actually find many unique innovations; incidentally, these innovations are evidence of the validity of Min as a separate branch of Sinitic (Baxter and Sagart 2014: 33). Besides many innovations in the lexicon, as an example of an innovative phonological feature we may cite here the Proto-Min reflex *-d-[37] for OC *r: compare OC 鯉 *mə-rəʔ 'carp', MC *liX*, MSC *lǐ*, and Jian'ou (建甌 *Jiàn'ōu*) [ti] (Norman 2005: 1, tone omitted; Baxter and Sagart 2014: 179). Moreover, Northern Min dialects have an [s] reflex for Middle Chinese 來 *lái* initials: compare MSC 李 *lǐ* 'plum', MC *liX*, with Jian'ou [sɛ] (Norman 2005: 2; tones omitted).

We already said that Min is a very diverse and fragmented group, with a relatively low degree of mutual intelligibility (§2.3.2). We also mentioned the main partitions which have been proposed for this group: namely, Central and Northern Min, also known as 'Inland Min', and Eastern, Southern, and Puxian Min, also known as 'Coastal Min'.[38] These subdivisions are based on phonological and/or lexical features: for instance, Southern Min dialects have the voiced initials *b-, l-,* and *g-,*

---

[37] The hyphen before the 'd' indicates that it is a 'softened' (弱化 *ruòhuà*) consonant. This is a class of initials specific to Proto-Min, proposed by Jerry Norman (see Handel 2003b, 2010).

[38] Different classification schemes may be found e.g. in Yan Margaret Mian (2006), Kurpaska (2010), and Zhou Changji (2012).

while Puxian dialects lack the fricative initials [s] and [ʃ], generally 'substituted' by [ɬ] (Zhang Zhenxing 1987; Kurpaska 2010; Zhou Changji 2012). Generally speaking, the most conservative varieties are those in the Southern part of the Min-speaking region(s) (Yan Margaret Mian 2006: 138). However, even in Southern Min dialects we find innovations not attested in other Min dialects: for instance, a set of nasal vowels, the product of the contraction of a vowel-nasal consonant sequence (compare MSC 安 *ān* and Xiamen [ũã⁵⁵]; Yan Margaret Mian 2006: 136). Moreover, the distance between literary and colloquial readings (see §2.2.2) is particularly notable in Southern Min dialects: for instance, in Xiamen, the lexeme 媒 'matchmaker' (MSC *méi*) has the literary reading [mui] and the colloquial reading [hm̩] (Yan Margaret Mian 2006: 139; tones omitted).

4.2.9 Hui, Pinghua, and unclassified patois

Just as Jin dialects, both Hui and Pinghua have been separated only recently from other dialect groups, and there is yet no agreement on their status (Kurpaska 2010: 75–6; Zhao Rixin 2012). Specifically, Hui dialects have been usually seen as either Mandarin or Wu, while Pinghua dialects are still often classified as Yue.

The hybrid nature of Hui dialects was already pointed out in the 1930s by Chao Yuen Ren, who remarked that Anhui dialects possess an important Wu feature, namely the register split in departing tone syllables; however, unlike Wu, Middle Chinese voiced obstruents do not have voiced reflexes in Hui (Li Rong 1989: 248; Kurpaska 2010: 75). But, on the other hand, the development of voiced obstruents in Hui does not follow the Mandarin pattern either. While in Mandarin, as mentioned in §4.2.2, the modern reflexes may be aspirated or unaspirated, depending on the tone category of the syllable, Hui dialects are not always predictable in this respect: while most Hui dialects have aspirated obstruent initials, not all varieties follow a regular pattern of evolution (Zhengzhang Shangfang 1987; Zhao Rixin 2012). The composite nature of Hui dialects may be explained by their historical background: Hui is the product of the overlap of several layers, probably on a Southern Sinitic base, which include Northern Mandarin (from the Northern and Southern dynasties and the Tang and Song periods), Jiang-Huai Mandarin (Ming and Qing periods), and Wu (Chappell 2004b: 17).

Some other phonological features of Hui are:

a. the loss of most nasal codas (which have sometimes become rhotacized)
b. the loss of the distinction between 泥 *ní* and 來 *lái* initials (compare MSC 腦 *nǎo* 'brain' and 老 *lǎo* 'old' with Tunxi [屯溪 *Túnxī*] [lɤ²⁴] for both)
c. a register split in the 平 *píng* and 去 *qù* tone categories (see this section; Zhengzhang Shangfang 1987; Kurpaska 2010; Zhao Rixin 2012).

Interestingly, despite the limited geographical extension of Hui dialects, they have a rather high degree of internal differentiation, and five distinct subgroups have been proposed for these varieties (Zhao Rixin 2012).

The basis for the separation of Pinghua dialects from the Yue group are arguably even more debatable. In Pinghua we typically find voiceless unaspirated reflexes for Middle Chinese voiced initial obstruents in all tone categories: however, this is true also for the Goulou (勾漏 *Gōulòu*) subgroup of Yue (Li Rong 1989: 249; Kurpaska 2010: 76; Wu Wei 2012: 127). Moreover, there are important differences between the Northern (桂北 *Guīběi*) and Southern (桂南 *Guīnán*) subgroups of Pinghua dialects. Firstly, the unaspirated reflexes mentioned here are not without exceptions in the Northern Pinghua dialects; they are found most consistently only in 桂南 *Guīnán* Pinghua dialects (Tan Yuanxiong 2012: 153). While Southern dialects retain the full set of nasal and stop codas, just as in Yue, in northern Pinghua these are generally lost: compare e.g. MSC 男 *nán* 'male' and Sanjie (三街 *Sānjiē*) [nuo⁴²]. Moreover, some 桂南 *Guīnán* dialects do have a height distinction within the 陰入 *yīnrù* and 陽入 *yángrù* tone categories, similarly to Yue, while northern Pinghua lacks this distinction. Lastly, 桂北 *Guīběi* dialects sometimes have dental stops instead of the expected retroflex consonants, just as in Min and in some Gan and Xiang dialects: see e.g. Sanjie 豬 [ty⁴²] (Liu Cunhan 1987; Tan Yuanxiong 2012). Thus, in a sense, Southern Pinghua dialects look much more Yue than northern Pinghua: for instance, Sagart believes that southern Pinghua is in fact part of Yue, while northern Pinghua might have a shared ancestor with Xiang (Chappell 2004b: 18; Kurpaska 2010: 76).

Recently, it has been highlighted that some unclassified *patois* (土話 *tŭhuà*) of Guangdong, Hunan, and Guangxi (as the Shaozhou *patois*; see §2.3.2) show some shared features with Pinghua in their phonology, as e.g. the same reflex for 微 *wēi* and 母 *mŭ* initials: compare MSC 尾 *wěi* 'tail', Nanning Pinghua [mi²⁴], and the Jiangyong (江永 *Jiāngyŏng*) *patois* form [mø¹³] (Tan Yuanxiong 2012: 155). These features, how ever, are not exclusive of these dialects and may be found also in Yue (compare Cantonese *méih* 'tail'). More shared features are attested between the local *patois* and the 桂北 *Guĭběi* subgroup: for instance, while 桂南 *Guīnán* dialects retain the -*p*, -*t*, and -*k* coda stops, as said earlier, Middle Chinese entering tone syllables developed into open syllables not only in northern Pinghua dialects but also in the *patois* (Tan Yuanxiong 2012: 156). This has been understood by some as indicative of a close relationship between Pinghua dialects (especially, northern Pinghua varieties) and these unclassified vernaculars (see Tan Yuanxiong 2012: 154 and the references cited therein).[39]

---

[39] For a brief overview of the different positions expressed in the recent literature on the relationship between Pinghua and Yue, and between Pinghua and the local *patois*, see de Sousa (2015: 161–2).

5

Morphology and the lexicon

5.1 The morphology of Chinese

Chinese is generally seen as a textbook example of an isolating language, with little or no inflectional morphology and few affixes, the origin of which is often transparent (Sagart 2004: 123). Moreover, Chinese is characterized by a fairly straightforward relation between meaning and form: morpheme borders are generally stable, there is no cumulative exponence, there is neither allomorphy nor suppletion. Thus, morphemes generally have only one phonological form (Packard 2006).

However, this does not entail that Chinese has little in the way of morphology. First and foremost, the lexicon of most modern Sinitic languages contains a high number of complex words, i.e. words composed of more than one morpheme (typically, two). Moreover, we do find lexical items which have turned into affixes, sometimes also with some phonological (suprasegmental and/or segmental) reduction, as the MSC aspect markers 了 *-le* (perfective, < 了 *liǎo* 'to finish') and 過 *-guo* (experiential, < 過 *guò* 'to pass through'). Also, Sinitic languages make extensive use of reduplication, as we shall see in §5.1.3.3. In addition to that, despite the isolating nature of Sinitic, in some modern Chinese varieties we find phenomena such as root modification, tone change, and 'rhotacization' used for derivational or grammatical(/inflectional) exponence, especially in the dialects of Shanxi,

Chinese Linguistics: An Introduction. Giorgio Francesco Arcodia and Bianca Basciano, Oxford University Press.
© Giorgio Arcodia and Bianca Basciano 2021. DOI: 10.1093/oso/9780198847830.003.0005

Shaanxi, Henan, and Shandong (Arcodia 2013, 2015), as we shall see in §5.1.3.5.

5.1.1 Morphemes and words

Chinese morphemes are overwhelmingly monosyllabic; Chinese is thus characterized by a strong correspondence between morpheme and syllable. As hinted at earlier (§3.1), DeFrancis (1984) uses the term 'morphosyllabic' to define Chinese writing because in this system (almost) each character represents a syllable, which in turn most often also corresponds to a morpheme, as e.g. 鳥 *niǎo* 'bird' or 吃 *chī* 'to eat'. There are, however, a fairly small set of multisyllabic morphemes, mostly phonetic adaptations of foreign words, as e.g. 玻璃 *bōli* 'glass' (< Sanskrit *sphatika* 'quartz crystal'), 葡萄 *pútao* 'grapes' (< Elamite *būdawa; Wiebusch 2009; see §5.2), or 咖啡 *kāfēi* 'coffee'; the syllables in these words have no meaning of their own (i.e. they are not morphemes) and form disyllabic morphemes.

Perhaps because of this near perfect correspondence between syllable and morpheme, in the Chinese lexicon a syllable forming a multisyllabic morpheme can sometimes be reanalysed as a morpheme by itself, within complex words (Basciano and Ceccagno 2009: 109–12). Take, for instance, the syllable 咖 *kā* in the above-mentioned disyllabic morpheme 咖啡 *kāfēi* 'coffee': while 咖 *kā* has no meaning of its own, it stands for 'coffee' in some compound words, as e.g. 奶咖 *nǎi-kā* 'milk-coffee, latte', 清咖 *qīng-kā* 'pure-coffee, black sugarless coffee', 冰咖 *bīng-kā* 'ice-coffee, iced coffee', 熱咖 *rè-kā* 'hot coffee, hot coffee'. An analogous case is that of the syllable 啤 *pí*, a meaningless constituent in the hybrid form 啤酒 *píjiǔ* 'beer' (see §5.2.1), in which 啤 *pí* is the phonetic rendering of English *beer*, while 酒 *jiǔ* 'wine, alcohol' places the word in the category of alcoholic beverages. Just as in the case of 咖 *kā*, the syllable 啤 *pí* stands for 'beer' in complex words as 生啤 *shēng-pí* 'raw-beer, draught beer' or 淡啤 *dàn-pí* 'light-beer, light beer' (see Packard 2000: 268–83; Basciano and Ceccagno 2009: 112). In this connection, an interesting case is that of 吧 *bā*, a phonetic adaptation for English *bar* within the word 酒吧 *jiǔ-bā* 'alcohol-bar, bar' (see §5.2.1): 吧 *bā* is nowadays used also in complex words with the meaning 'bar', as e.g. 吧女 *bā-nǚ* 'bar-woman, barmaid', 網吧 *wǎng-bā* 'net-bar, internet café'. Having acquired morphemic status, 吧 *bā* underwent further meaning extension, and it has been used to indicate a fairly broad range of entertainment and meeting places, also virtual, as e.g. 考吧 *kǎo-bā* 'roast-bar, barbecue bar', 球吧 *qiú-bā* 'ball-bar, a website offering information on ball games', 陶吧 *táo-bā* 'pottery-bar, a pottery workshop where customers may create their own products', 貼吧 *tiē-bā* 'post-bar, internet forum' (Arcodia 2011).

Moreover, new morphemes may also be created by a meaning shift in which an existing morpheme stands for a whole complex word, similarly to what we saw before for meaningless word constituents (Packard 2000: 275–80). For instance, 麵 *miàn* 'flour, noodles' is used with the meaning 'van' in words as 麵的 *miàn-dí* 'van-taxi' (compare 的士 *díshì* 'taxi'), taxi van, or 微麵 *wēi-miàn* 'tiny-van, minivan'. The new meaning for 麵 *miàn* comes from its use in the compound 麵包車 *miànbāo-chē* 'bread-vehicle, van' (compare 麵包 *miàn-bāo* 'flour-wrap, bread') and may be understood as an abbreviation of this word (Packard 2000: 275–8; see also §5.1.3.4).

Both grammatical and lexical morphemes in Chinese may be free or bound. A free grammatical morpheme is the question particle 嗎 *ma*, while a bound grammatical morpheme is the plural/collective suffix -*men* 們. However, since the majority of morphemes in Chinese are lexical, corresponding to roots, the most important distinction is that between free and bound roots (see e.g. Packard 2000; Yang Xipeng 2003; Basciano and Ceccagno 2009; Ceccagno and Basciano 2009). A root is free if it can occupy a syntactic slot by itself, thus corresponding to a syntactic word, as e.g. 樹 *shù* 'tree', or 說 *shuō* 'to speak'. Bound roots are also lexical in nature, but they are not autonomous in syntax: in order to be used in a sentence, they must be combined with another root, a word, or an affix, thus forming a complex word. For instance, the bound root 衣 *yī* 'garment' cannot be used as it is in a sentence; it is rather found as part of complex words like 大衣 *dà-yī* 'big-garment, coat', 雨衣 *yǔ-yī* 'rain-garment, raincoat', or 衣櫃 *yī-guì* 'garment-cabinet, wardrobe'.

According to Packard (2000), roughly 70% of the roots in the Modern Chinese lexicon are bound; the vast majority of them were used as free roots in Old Chinese (see also Dai John Xiang-ling 1990; Shi Yuzhi 2002). However, the distinction between bound and free roots is not always clear-cut, also because there are no differences in the shape of the two types of roots. Firstly, some bound roots may actually be used as free words, depending on the context and on the register (see e.g. Yang Xipeng 2003; Basciano and Ceccagno 2009; Ceccagno and

Basciano 2009). Bound roots often appear in a syntactic word slot in (formal) written Chinese, a register of the language which still retains some stylistic features of Classical Chinese, as e.g. the tendency to use monosyllabic words instead of multisyllabic, multimorphemic words. For instance, the bound root 殴 *ōu* 'to hit, beat' is not normally used by itself as a verb; it is rather found in compounds as 殴打 *ōu-dǎ* 'hit-hit, to hit'. However, in written Chinese 殴 *ōu* is sometimes used as a free root, i.e. in a syntactic slot for a word, as in the following example from a newspaper article (qtd. in Yang Xipeng 2003: 205):

(1) 中国一男子在东京机场被殴。
    Zhōngguó yī nánzǐ zài Dōngjīng jīchǎng bèi ōu
    China   one man at Tokyo   airport PASS hit
    'A Chinese man was assaulted at Tokyo airport.'

Note, also, that words made of (quasi-)synonymous constituents, as the above-mentioned 殴打 *ōu-dǎ*, are quite common in MSC. According to Feng Shengli (1998), the historical development of the Chinese language, characterized by a gradual increase in disyllabic words,[1] led to the creation of a considerable number of coordinating constructions, often formed by two (quasi-)synonymous, or anyway tightly related, constituents. This tendency is explained by the fact that coordinating constructions are, in a sense, easier to build to satisfy prosodic constraints, as one can combine (quasi-)synonymous morphemes without any significant change in meaning, in the absence of the pragmatic need to create a new label. However, disyllabification did not occur in the same way in all modern Sinitic languages: in fact, many disyllabic words of MSC correspond to monosyllabic words in some other dialects, especially Southern Sinitic (see Table 2.1; see also Yang Xipeng 2003: 207).

Some scholars (e.g. Packard 1998, 2000; Pirani 2008) note that Chinese bound roots do resemble the so-called 'neoclassical constituents' of Standard Average European languages: these are bound roots of Greek or Latin origin with a lexical (rather than grammatical) meaning, which however cannot be used by themselves in a sentence, i.e. they are not (syntactic) words. Thus, for instance, Eng. *anthropo-* 'pertaining to

---

[1] On the motivations for the disyllabification of the Chinese lexicon, see Packard (1998: 6–7, 2000: 266–7) and Feng Shengli (1998), among others.

human beings' (< Greek *anthropos* 'human being') may combine with other neoclassical constituents (*anthropology*), with a derivational suffix (*anthropic*), but it is not normally used as such (*anthropo). Neoclassical constituents are widely used in European languages to build new words, especially (but not exclusively) technical and scientific terms. Chinese bound roots have much in common with neoclassical constituents: they are bound forms deriving from words of a prestige 'classical' language (Classical Chinese, in this case), they have lexical content and may take part in word formation processes just as any other root; also, they are not syntactic words. However, there are some significant differences between Chinese bound roots and neoclassical constituents: first of all, bound roots in Chinese represent the rule, rather than the exception, given that they represent the majority of lexical roots, as said before. Second, Chinese bound roots are not dominantly used to build technical and scientific terms: they are rather readily available and used to build just any type of word. Lastly, not all bound roots come from Old/Classical Chinese: in fact, as we have shown, new bound roots may be created through a process of reanalysis (Packard 2000: 280–3; Basciano and Ceccagno 2009: 116). Furthermore, Basciano and Ceccagno (2009: 116–17; see also Packard 2000: 77) note that Chinese bound roots are actually closer to lexical roots in inflectional languages like Italian. Unlike English, in which lexical morphemes are generally free, i.e. they are also syntactic words (e.g. *ball*, *dog*, *glass*), in Italian most roots are bound, and hence they must combine (at least) with an inflectional suffix to be used in a sentence: see e.g. the word *bella* 'pretty', formed by the bound lexical root *bell-* and the inflectional morpheme *-a* ('F.SG'). Since Chinese has virtually no inflectional morphology, bound roots must combine with other (bound or free) roots, or with derivational morphemes, in order to build words.

However, according to Ceccagno and Basciano (2009) and Basciano and Ceccagno (2009: 117–20), in Modern Chinese we may actually find a group of bound roots which are fairly similar to neoclassical constituents: these are roots with a specialized meaning which, in combination with other (free/bound) roots, form complex words belonging to a specialized register of the language, or anyway to a formal register. For instance, the root 學 *xué*, a free verb root ('to study'), is also used as a bound root with the meaning 'study, branch of science', as e.g. in 語言學 *yǔyán-xué* 'language-study, linguistics', 社會學 *shèhuì-xué* 'society-study, sociology', or 哲學 *zhé-xué* 'wise-study, philosophy'. A similar case is that of 家 *jiā* 'specialist, professional', as used in words like 藝術

家 *yìshù-jiā* 'art-specialist, artist', 畫家 *huà-jiā* 'paint-specialist, painter', 政治家 *zhèngzhì-jiā* 'politics-specialist, politician'. These bound roots tend to form nouns and normally combine with items belonging to a specific word class (mostly, nouns); moreover, they occupy a fixed position in complex words. Hence, they are more similar to (derivational) affixes than other, 'ordinary' bound roots (see §5.1.3.2).

Moreover, there is another set of bound roots which may be regarded, in a sense, as quite similar to neoclassical constituents. In Chinese (or, better, in MSC), there are pairs of synonymic morphemes, one of which is bound and reflects classical usage, while the other is free and has a more modern flavour, so to say: this is the case e.g. for 食 *shí* vs. 吃 *chī* 'to eat', 飲 *yǐn* vs. 喝 *hē* 'to drink', 函 *hán* vs. 信 *xìn* 'letter'. The first terms in these pairs, i.e. 食 *shí*, 飲 *yǐn*, and 函 *hán*, are used as free forms in Old/Classical Chinese, and they are sometimes still used as such in the (formal) written language (see Ex. 1 and the related discussion). For instance, the root 食 *shí* 'to eat' may be used as a free form only in the written language, which anyway constitutes marked usage, while it is ordinarily treated as a bound root meaning 'food, related to food', found in complex words like 食品 *shí-pǐn* 'food-product, food', 食堂 *shí-táng* 'food-hall, canteen', 豬食 *zhū-shí* 'pig-food, pig feed'. These bound roots come from the Classical language, have a corresponding free root, do not have a fixed position in complex words, and may combine among them, as in 飲食 *yǐn-shí* 'drink-food, food and drink, diet'; lastly, they are used to form ordinary words and not only specialized terminology (Arcodia and Basciano 2014 [2012]).

Another much debated aspect of the Modern Chinese lexicon, which is crucial for our presentation, is the definition of the 'word'. While in many languages the word is a very intuitive notion, albeit one difficult to define in a rigorous way, this is not the case for Chinese (see Packard 2000). Note that the modern Chinese term for (syntactic) word, 詞 *cí*, began to be used in this sense only in the twentieth century, following the translation of Western grammatical works: it is thus somehow an imported notion, alien to the Chinese tradition of linguistic analysis. In the mid-twentieth century, within the 文字改革運動 *Wénzì gǎigé yùndòng* 'Movement for Script Reform' (see §2.2.3, 3.2.3), attempts were made to define the word for Chinese; however, no agreement could be reached. The elusiveness of the notion of word for Chinese led some to believe that, perhaps, it was not necessary. As Chao Yuen Ren famously put it (1968: 138):

Whatever conception of the syntactic word we shall find scientifically justifiable to define, it plays no part in the Chinaman of the street's conception of the subunits of the Chinese language. Thus, if one whishes to ask what the syntactic word *shianntzay* 'now' means, one would say: '現在' 这两个字是什么意思？ *Shianntzay jey leanngg tzyh sh sherm yihsy?* 'What is the meaning of these two *tzyh* '*shianntzay*'?'[2]

Thus, Chao claimed that the 'character' (字 *zì*), rather than the word (詞 *cí*), is perceived to be the most salient basic unit of the Chinese lexicon (see also Lü Shuxiang 1981), despite the fact that, as already mentioned, Modern Chinese words are most often made of more than one character/syllable (/morpheme). The term 詞 *cí* in Chinese mostly belongs to the technical vocabulary of linguistics; sentences are often seen by the laypeople as sequences of characters. As proposed by Chao Yuen Ren, in Chinese the character is the 'sociological word', the most salient unit of speech. This popular conception of the 字 *zì* seems to be confirmed by some metalinguistic statements in ordinary speech. For instance, in Feng Xiaogang's 2010 film 唐山大地震 *Tángshān Dà Dìzhèn* (known in the West as *Aftershock*), the female protagonist, Fang Deng, utters the following sentence:

(2) 我媽說，'救弟弟'。　　這三個字就寫在我耳朵邊上。
　　wǒ mā　　　shuō　'jiù　dìdi'　　　　zhè　sān
　　1SG mother　say　save　younger.brother　this　three
　　ge　zì　　　　jiù　xiě　zài　wǒ　ěrduo　biānshàng
　　CLF　character　just　write　on　1SG　ear　side
　　'My mother said: save the younger brother. These words are engraved in my ears.'

In the sentence in (2), the expression which we translated as 'these words' literally means 'these three characters'. The phrase 救弟弟 *jiù dìdi* is made of the verb 救 *jiù* 'to rescue' and the noun 弟弟 *dìdi* 'younger brother', i.e. two words: however, Fang Deng describes it as consisting of three characters. This is expected if the character, rather than the word, is perceived as the basic unit of speech.

How can we define, then, the 'word' (in the sense of 詞 *cí*) for Chinese? In the general linguistic literature, the word may be defined according to different criteria: syntactic, semantic, phonologic, and orthographic (see e.g. Packard 2000; Dixon and Aikhenvald 2002; Ceccagno and Basciano 2009). For the sake of simplicity, here we stick to a syntactic

---

[2] We kept the *Gwoyeu romatzyh* transcription (see §3.2.3) of the original.

definition of the word: a 詞 *cí* is a unit of language which may occupy by itself a syntactic slot, i.e. a minimal free form. There are three basic types of words, in this sense, in Chinese:

a. monosyllabic and monomorphemic words, i.e. words formed by a single morpheme/syllable, as e.g. 花 *huā* 'flower', 腳 *jiǎo* 'foot', 買 *mǎi* 'to buy'
b. multisyllabic and monomorphemic words, as e.g. 檸檬 *níngméng* 'lemon', 巧克力 *qiǎokèlì* 'chocolate'
c. multisyllabic and multimorphemic words, i.e. words made of more than one syllable/morpheme, as e.g. 書店 *shū-diàn* 'book-shop, bookshop', 籃球 *lán-qiú* 'basket-ball, basketball', 洗碗機 *xǐ-wǎn-jī* 'wash-bowl-machine, dishwasher'.

Since, as said earlier, the majority of roots in Chinese appear to be bound, the multimorphemic word is the most common model for the MSC lexicon; disyllabic/bimorphemic words are especially common, as a consequence of the process of disyllabification briefly described above.

5.1.2 Word formation in Old and Middle Chinese

As said in the preceding chapter (§4.1.2), according to some reconstructions, Old Chinese was typologically quite different from modern Sinitic languages and made use of morphological processes based on non-syllabic exponents. Among the non-syllabic affixes of Old Chinese we find, for instance, the already mentioned (§2.3.1, Ex. 6) prefix *s-, which had among its functions that of causativization (Baxter and Sagart 1998; Sagart 1999b; Xu Dan 2006; Schuessler 2007, among others; ex. from Baxter and Sagart 2014: 142):

(3) 視 *gijʔ > *dzyijX* > *shì* 'to look; see'
     示 *s-gijʔ-s > *zyijH* > *shì* 'to show'

Another non-syllabic affix is the prefix *N-, which formed intransitive verbs, later leading to the sonorization of the following (stop or affricate) consonant (Baxter and Sagart 2014: 54):

(4) 折 *tet > *tsyet* > *zhé* 'to bend; break'
     折 *N-tet > *dzyet* > *shé* 'to bend (intransitive)'

The infix *-r- has been reconstructed as a marker of distributed action (for verbs) or distributed object (for nouns); it could also act as an intensifier for stative verbs. See the following example (Baxter and Sagart 2014: 57):

(5)　洗 *sˤərʔ > sejX > xǐ 'to wash'
　　　灑 *Cə.s<r>ərʔ > sreajX > sǎ 'to sprinkle'

The suffix *-s (see §2.3.1, Ex. 8) is said to have many functions, the most common of which is probably nominalization for verbs (Baxter and Sagart 2014: 58):

(6)　內 / 納 *nˤup >nop >nà 'to bring/send in'
　　　內 *nˤup-s >*nut-s >nwojH > nèi 'inside'

Another type of monosyllabic complex words in Old Chinese are the so-called 'fusion words' (Pulleyblank 1995a; Packard 1998). Fusion words are the contracted form of two syllables, one of which is generally a pronoun or a demonstrative (Norman 1988: 85–6). Since the outcome is a single syllable, following the general principles of Chinese writing outlined before, fusion words were written with one character, as e.g. 耳 *nzi 'that's all' (而 nzi 'and' + 已 i 'end') and 盍 *gˤap 'how not' (何 *gˤa 'how' + 不 *pu 'not'; Packard 1998: 5).

Old Chinese also made use of conversion, i.e. derivation without exponents, as in the case of lexical causatives: intransitive verbs, nouns, and adjectives could be used also as transitive/causative verbs, without any formal change (Pulleyblank 1995a: 25; Xu Dan 2006: 119):

(7)　王請大之。(Mencius)
　　　wáng qǐng　　dà　　zhī
　　　king please　great　3SG
　　　'I beg your majesty to make it great.'

Differently from the contemporary lexicon in which, as already mentioned, disyllabic items are the most common word type, the lexicon of Old Chinese was prevalently made of monosyllabic words. However, in Old Chinese as well we do find complex words built by combining syllabic morphemes: according to the data in Shi Yuzhi (2002: 72), disyllabic words already made up about 20% of the Chinese lexicon before the third century BC.

Some often quoted examples of syllabic derivational affixes used in Old Chinese are the prefix 有 yǒu-, which could be added to toponyms, ethnonyms, and even to some other common nouns (and, as we shall see later, had other functions);[3] 阿 *ā*-, originally a question particle, and later used as a prefix for kinship terms, personal pronouns, and nick-names; the suffix 子 *-zǐ* 'son', used as a diminutive (also expressing endearment), which later became a 'dummy' noun-forming suffix (Wang Li 1980 [1958]: 217–28).

(8)   有苗   阿誰   阿你   奴子

      yǒu-miáo   *ā-shéi*   *ā-nǐ*   *nú-zǐ*

      PREF-Hmong   PREF-who   PREF-you servant-SUFF

      'the Hmong tribe' 'who'   'you'   'servant'

As highlighted by Packard (1998), 'dummy', meaningless prefixes as 有 *yǒu-* mostly disappeared in the Warring States period. Packard (1998: 11) also mentions some verbal prefixes, i.e. 爰 *yuán-*, 曰 *yuē-*, and 言 *yán-*, which have been claimed to be allomorphs of a single verbalizing prefix (Wang Li 1980 [1958]: 299–300; Cheng Xiangqing 1992). Some other examples of Old Chinese syllabic verbal prefixes are 載 *zài-*, 有 *yǒu-*, and 式 *shì-*, which indicate the continuation of the action described by the verb, as in (Hong Bo 2005: 181; our glosses and translation):

(9)   既見復關, 載笑載言。 (*Classic of Poetry*)

      jì   *jiàn*   *Fùguān* *zài-xiào*   *zài-yán*

      already see   Fuguan   PREF-laugh   PREF-talk

      'When I saw [you coming from] Fuguan, I laughed and spoke inces-santly.'

Verbs could also bear suffixes, as e.g. 止 *-zhǐ*, indicating past/com-pleted action, and 得 *-dé*, indicating attainment of a result (Wang Li 1980 [1958]: 301–2; Packard 1998: 12). There were also affixes which turned adjectives into adverbial modifiers, as the prefixes 斯 *sī-*, 思 *sī-*, and (again) 有 *yǒu-*, and the suffixes 斯 *-sī*, 其 *-qí*, 如 *-rú*, and 然 *-rán* (Cheng Xiangqing 1992; Packard 1998: 12). Hong Bo (2005: 182) men-tions also adjectival prefixes with an intensifying function, like 有 *yǒu-*, 其 *qí-*, and 載 *zài-* (e.g. 有忡 *yǒu-chōng* 'PREF-sad, very sad'; ex. from the *Classic of Poetry*). As we shall see later, meanings as continuation of an action and intensification for adjectives could be conveyed also by reduplication in Old Chinese.

---

[3] Hong Bo (2005: 178) remarks that 有*yǒu-* derives from a noun meaning 'region' (域 *yù*), 'country' (國 *guó*).

While not as widespread as in modern Sinitic languages, compounding was attested also in Old Chinese. See the following examples (Baxter and Sagart 1998: 67–8):

(10) a. 邦君

   *proŋ-k-lju[r, n] > *pæwng-kjun* > *bāng-jūn* 'country-ruler, ruler of a country'

   b. 木瓜

   *mok-kʷra > *muwk-kwæ* > *mù-guā* 'tree-melon, quince (*Cydonia oblonga*)'

   c. 司馬

   *sji-mraʔ > *si-mæX* > *sī-mǎ* 'manage-horse, official in charge of a royal or feudal household'

The words in (10) all involve a relation of subordination or modification between the constituents; these are the most common types in the early stages of the development of compounding in Chinese (the Spring and Autumn Period). However, at this time we also find instances of coordinating compounds, in which the constituents are in a symmetrical relation, as e.g. 尺寸 *chǐ-cùn* '⅓.of.a.metre-inch, measure', 忖度 *cǔn-duó* 'think.over-estimate, speculate' (Feng Shengli 1998: 208–9). After the Warring States Period, coordinating compounds grew in number (see §5.1.1), while other (asymmetric) compound types became less prominent; Feng Shengli (1998) remarks that compounds with a verb-object, verb-result, and subject-predicate structure (see §5.1.3.1) were especially rare in Old Chinese.

Lastly, as already mentioned, Old Chinese made use of several distinct reduplication constructions (Sagart 1999b; Sun Jingtao 1999). Sagart (1999b: 137) identifies four patterns of reduplication:

   a. total reduplication, e.g. 關關 *[a]kron-kron > *kwæn-kwæn* > *guān-guān* 'the cry of the ospreys'
   b. reduplication with *e/o or *i/u vowel alternation, e.g. 邂逅 *[a]greʔ-groʔ > *heaïX-huwX* > *xièhòu* 'carefree and happy', 蟋蟀 *[b]srit-srut > *s(r)it-srwit* > *xīshuài* 'cricket'
   c. partial reduplication involving rhymes only, known as 疊韻 *diéyùn* in Chinese, e.g. 窈窕 *[a]ʔiwʔ-liwʔ > *ewX-dewX* > *yǎotiǎo* 'elegant, beautiful'

d. partial reduplication involving onsets only, known as 雙聲 *shuāngshēng* in Chinese, e.g. 參差 *ᵇsr-hlim-sr-hlaj > *cēncī* 'uneven, irregular'

Besides those, another pattern is the so-called 'fission reduplication', attested not only in Old and Middle Chinese but also in some modern Sinitic languages (Sun Jingtao 1999). In this construction, a syllable is split into two parts, i.e. onset and rhyme: the onset is retained in the first syllable of the reduplicated form, while the rhyme is retained in the second syllable, with a liquid (*l-) or (*r-) onset. See the following example (Sun Jingtao 1999: 141):

(11) 頭 *dáɥ > *dəw* > *tóu* 'head'
 → 髑髏 *dák⁴ ráɥ > *dəwk ləw* > *dúlóu* 'skull' (*Zhuangzi*)

As to the functions of reduplication, it is generally believed that total reduplication was used to obtain a vivid description of some state or process. As a matter of fact, reduplicated words in Old Chinese were most often used as if they were adjectives(/adverbs) (Sun Jingtao 1999: 166; examples from the *Classic of Poetry*):

(12) 霏霏 *fēi~fēi* '(of rain or snow) fall thick and fast'
 明明 *míng~míng* 'brightly'
 楚楚 *chǔ~chǔ* 'luxuriant'

There was also another reduplication construction, still in use in MSC and several other modern Sinitic languages, which follows an 'ABB' pattern: a base item (A) is followed by a reduplicated form (B), as e.g. 分總總 *fēn-zǒng~zǒng* 'numerous and confused', 芳菲菲 *fāng-fēi~fei* 'fragrant'. The reduplicated forms (BB) are added, again, to convey vividness (Sun Jingtao 1999: 172).

Sun Jingtao (1999) remarks that total reduplication of nouns and verbs was not yet fully developed in Old Chinese. Noun reduplication had a distributive value, as e.g. in 人人 *rén~rén* 'person-person, every person', or 朝朝 *cháo~cháo* 'morning-morning, every morning'. As to verbs, Sun Jingtao (1999) argues that reduplicated verbs indicating repetition or continuation of the action appeared towards the end of the Eastern Han Period. In the *Nineteen Old Poems* (古詩十九首 *Gǔ shī shíjiǔ shǒu*, ca. 520 AD), we find the following sentence (Sun Jingtao 1999: 183):

(13) 行行重行行，與君生別離。

     xíng~xíng   chóng   xíng~xíng   yǔ   jūn   shēng   biélí
     go~go   again   go~go   with 2SG life   leave
     'I will keep going on a long journey, and I am apart forever from
     my darling.'

In this example, the verb 行 *xíng* 'to go, walk' is reduplicated, indicating repetition, continuation. However, Sun Jingtao (1999) believes that this pattern of total reduplication was not fully developed yet, as it often involved other items indicating repetition, like 重 *chóng* 'again' in (13). According to Sun Jingtao, in Old Chinese the dominant pattern to indicate repetition was 'retrogressive' reduplication, in which the reduplicant comes before the base (as Eng. *crisscross*). In retrogressive reduplication, the initials of the base and the reduplicant do not change, while the final of the reduplicant undergoes some phonological change, as in 輾轉 *trànʔ trwànʔ > trianʔtrwianʔ > zhǎnzhuǎn* 'toss and turn endlessly (in bed)' (example from the *Classic of Poetry*; Sun Jingtao 1999: 99).

Partial reduplication, on the other hand, was apparently used to indicate small referents, or anyway with a diminutive meaning (Sun Jingtao 1999: 51):

(14) 蜉蝣 *bɔ̀w lɔ̀w > buw juw > fúyóu* 'larval mayfly' (*Classic of Poetry*)
     螳螂 *dàŋ ràŋ > daŋ laŋ > tángláng* 'mantis' (*Zhuangzi*)
     蒲盧 *báɣ ráɣ > bɔ lɔ > púlú* 'solitary wasp' (*Book of Rites* – 禮記 *Lǐji*)

Moreover, partial reduplication, just as total reduplication, could also convey vividness, as e.g. in 豐融 *pʰèŋʷ lèŋʷ > pʰwŋ juwŋ > fēngróng* 'luxuriant, flourishing' (*Book of Han* - 漢書 *Hànshū*), 卓犖 *t(r)ákʷ rákʷ > traɨwk laɨwk > zuōluò* 'unique, superb extraordinary' (典引 *Diǎnyǐn*; Sun Jingtao 1999: 66). Fission reduplication, in Sun's words, leads to a 'specialization' of meaning (see Ex. 11). Here we cannot discuss the topic of reduplication any further due to space constraints: for a detailed treatment, see Sun Jingtao (1999).

In the diachronic evolution of Chinese, some morphological processes disappeared: first and foremost, non-syllabic affixation (see Exx. 3–6). As to causative exponents, Mei Tsu-lin (1991) remarked that Old Chinese morphological and lexical (labile) causatives gradually disappeared from the language. Note that, in the evolution towards the Middle Chinese stage, Chinese developed contrastive tones: as said earlier (§2.3.1, 4.1.3), it is believed that tones developed from Old Chinese affixes. The loss of those affixes, then, led to the creation of new morphological processes, as tonal contrast. Schuessler (2007: 40) highlighted that in Middle Chinese the 'departing' tone (去聲 qùshēng, corresponding to the fourth tone of MSC; see Table 4.4) was used as a marker of causativization:

(15) 飲 yǐn < ʔɨm (上聲 shǎngshēng) 'to drink'
      飲 yìn < ʔɨm (去聲 qùshēng) 'to give to drink'

Vestiges of this derivational pattern may still be found in MSC, as e.g. 涼 liáng 'cold'/liàng 'to cool'; 聞 wén 'to hear'/問 wèn 'to ask'.

Another device to express causativity in Middle Chinese was the alternance between voiced and voiceless initials, known in Chinese as 清濁別義 qīng-zhuó bié yì (see Mei Tsu-lin 1991; Pulleyblank 2004, among others); for each pair, the causative verb had a voiceless initial (Pulleyblank 2004: 1732):

(16) 見 jiàn < kɛn^h 'to see'
      見 / 現 xiàn < ɣɛn^h 'to appear'

However, Mei Tsu-lin (1991) noted that these non-syllabic, nonconcatenative exponents of causativity fell gradually out of use as well, and completely disappeared by the Late Middle Chinese stage. According to Mei, this is the time when Chinese underwent a major typological shift towards greater analiticity. The expression of causativity is a domain in which the effects of this shift are clearly visible: following the loss of synthetic strategies, new analytic constructions for the expression of causativity were developed, as e.g. the separable resultative construction (Shi Yuzhi 2002) and, later, resultative compounds (see §5.1.3.1).

Resultative compounds are formed by two verb roots in an 'action-result' relation, as e.g. 壓死 yā-sǐ 'push-die, crush to death', 擊敗 jī-bài 'hit-be.defeated, defeat', 搖醒 yáo-xǐng 'shake-wake.up, shake awake'. Ōta (1987) believes that resultative compounds appeared in the Tang period, at the latest. The emergence of resultative compounds seems to be connected to the loss of other strategies for the expression of causativity (Mei Tsu-lin 1991); another hypothesis is that resultative compounds developed from the separable resultative construction, also because of the above-mentioned tendency towards disyllabification in the Chinese lexicon.

It is indeed true that, as seen earlier, compounding became more and more productive in the historical evolution of Chinese. The stronger tendency towards disyllabism also led to the diffusion of other morphological processes involving the agglutination of syllables: as highlighted by Wang Yunlu (2005: 290 ff.), in Middle Chinese we find several 'dummy', meaningless word constituents, just as those in Ex. 8, the main function of which was prosodic, i.e. turning a monosyllabic word into a disyllabic one. For instance, the suffix 手 -shǒu, originally 'hand', could be added to adjectives or time adverbs to form disyllabic lexical items, without adding any relevant meaning to the base word (e.g. 急手 jí-shǒu 'urgent-SUFF, urgent, anxious').

A parallel development which began in the evolution from Old to Middle Chinese, and continued in the Middle Chinese phase, is the emergence of evaluative affixes, as the already mentioned 阿 ā-, which stabilized as an endearment prefix for (monosyllabic) personal names and surnames (e.g. 阿寶 Ā-Bǎo 'Bao'), and 子 -zi (see Ex. 8), which developed from a diminutive into a noun-forming suffix (Wang Li 1989: 9), the basic function of which is to turn a monosyllabic root into a disyllabic word. During the Tang era, 子 -zi became a generic noun suffix, as e.g. in 車子 chē-zi 'vehicle-SUFF, vehicle' or 船子 chuán-zi 'boat-SUFF, boat' (Ōta 1987: 86); in the same period, 子 -zi also developed a nominalizing function, as in 刷子 shuā-zi 'brush-NMLZ, brush', 倚子 yǐ-zi 'lean-NMLZ, chair' (currently written 椅子; Ōta 1987: 86). Another noun-forming suffix is 頭 -tou (< tóu 'head'), which also became widely used in the Tang period: it was combined with roots indicating concrete objects, as e.g. 石頭 shí-tou 'stone-SUFF, stone', 枕頭 zhěn-tou 'pillow-SUFF, pillow'. A similar suffix is 兒 -r (< ér 'child'), which however emerged later than 子 -zi and 頭 -tou. In the Tang period, we find a few examples of 兒 -(é)r combined with nouns, with a diminutive/endearing function: during the Song period, the number of 兒 -r-suffixed nouns grew considerably, but even at this stage 兒 -r still (partly) retained an evaluative meaning, which is preserved also in some MSC words (compare e.g. 老頭兒 lǎotóur 'old chap' vs. 老頭子 lǎotóuzi 'old fogey, codger'). However, in Song times the diminutive meaning became gradually more 'bleached', and we begin to see 兒 –r used as a dummy noun suffix; this became even more evident in the Yuan period (Ōta 1987: 89).

Other affixes that developed from the Han period on, and are still in use nowadays, are 可 *kě-* (< 可 *kě* 'can, to be able'), an adjective-forming prefix, roughly comparable to Eng. *-able* (e.g. 可吃 *kě-chī* 'PREF-eat, edible)', and 第 *dì-*, a prefix for ordinal numbers (e.g. 第七 *dì-qī* 'PREF-seven, seventh').

Another prefix mentioned by Ōta (1987: 172) is 打 *dǎ-*, whose original meaning is 'to hit'. Starting from the Tang period, the verb 打 *dǎ* gradually underwent meaning extension and developed a more generic meaning: when combined with nouns, it could indicate various types of actions, as e.g. in 打球 *dǎ-qiú* 'hit-ball, play ball games', 打漁 *dǎ-yú* 'hit-fish, to fish', 打水 *dǎ-shuǐ* 'hit-water, to draw water' (Zhu Jianjun 2003: 471). During Song and Yuan times, 打 *dǎ* underwent further abstraction of meaning and began to be used also in combination with abstract nouns, as e.g. 打話 *dǎ-huà* 'hit-word, to discuss'. The verb 打 *dǎ*, thus, acquired a generic meaning, becoming roughly equivalent to 'to cause' (Zhu Jianjun 2003): this usage is still found in MSC, in constructions as e.g. 打噴嚏 *dǎ-pēntì* 'hit-sneeze, to sneeze', 打電話 *dǎ-diànhuà* 'hit-telephone, to make a phone call'. Moreover, 打 *dǎ* further broadened its distribution and began to be used also with adjectives, meaning 'cause to become ADJ', as e.g. in 打硬 *dǎ-yìng* 'hit-hard, to harden' (Zhu Jianjun 2003: 472); while this usage of 打 *dǎ* is no longer productive in MSC (some exceptions are discussed in Basciano 2013), it is still possible in other Sinitic languages, as e.g. Taiwanese Hakka (Basciano 2010). During the Song and Yuan periods and up until the Ming Dynasty, 打 *dǎ*, in its abstract sense, began to be used also with verbs, both transitive and intransitive, as e.g. 打招 *dǎ-zhāo* 'hit-recruit, to recruit', 打折 *dǎ-zhé* 'hit-break, to snap, break' (Zhu Jianjun 2003: 472), thus becoming a (pseudo-)affix (Chiu Hsiang-Yun 2008). Some of these complex verbs are still in use in MSC, as 打掃 *dǎ-sǎo* 'hit-sweep, to sweep, clean up', 打攪 *dǎ-jiǎo* 'hit-disturb, to disturb' (see Basciano 2010, 2013).

As to reduplication, the patterns found in Middle Chinese are pretty close to those still in use in MSC. For both monosyllabic and disyllabic nouns, reduplication had a distributive meaning, just as in Old Chinese: starting from the Tang period, we find reduplication of nouns indicating time periods, meaning 'gradual progress', as in 日日 *rì~rì* 'day~day, day after day' or 年年 *nián~nián* 'year~year, year after year' (Ōta 1987: 80). Moreover, during the same period we begin to see reduplication of nouns for family members, as e.g. 家家 *jiā~jiā* 'aunt (father's sister)' (compare MSC 姑姑 *gū~gu*), 兄兄 *xiōng~xiōng* 'elder brother' (Ōta 1987: 81).

As for adjectives, in Middle Chinese we see a greater diffusion of monosyllabic adjectival reduplication with an intensive value, expressing vividness (Ōta 1987: 157). The 'AABB' pattern of reduplication (as e.g. 高興 *gāoxìng* 'happy' > 高高興興 *gāo~gāo-xìng~xìng* 'very happy'), on the other hand, appeared relatively late (Ōta 1987: 158). During the Tang period, there was also a notable development of the 'ABB' pattern for adjectives, which is especially frequent in Yuan theatre (Ōta 1987: 158).

Verbal reduplication also underwent major developments in the Middle Chinese period. We said that the 'AA' verbal reduplication pattern was used in Old Chinese to convey repetition or continuation of the action: this construction gradually declined in use, and by the Song Dynasty it had become quite uncommon (Ōta 1987: 175). On the other hand, starting from the Song period, the pattern 'A 一*yi* A' emerged, with the insertion of 一*yi* (< *yī* 'one') between the base and the reduplicant, as e.g. in 看一看 *kàn yi kàn* 'look one look, to have a look' (朱子語類 *Zhūzǐ yǔlèi*); this construction had a very different function from the Old Chinese 'AA' pattern, as it indicates short duration of an action, just as in MSC (Ōta 1987: 176). Ōta (1987: 176) believes that the 'AA' pattern indicating short duration of an action, without the insertion of 一*yi*, probably appeared during the Yuan period: see e.g. 坐坐 *zuò~zuo* 'sit~sit, have a seat' (竹塢聽琴 *Zhú wù tīng qín*), 開開 *kāi~kai* 'open~open, briefly open' (碟砂擔 *Zhūshā dān*). Ōta also highlights that verbs reduplicated with the 'A 一*yi* A' pattern were often followed by the abovementioned suffix 兒 *-r*, as in Yuan drama: see e.g. 告一告兒 *gào yī gào-r* 'say one say-SUFF, say a bit' (金線池 *Jīnxiànchí*), 睡一睡兒 *shuì yī shuì-r* 'sleep one sleep-SUFF, sleep a bit, have a nap' (馮玉米 *Féng Yùmǐ*). In these examples, the reduplicant followed by 兒 *-r* seems to behave similarly to a noun or a classifier. Note that in the Yuan period, the 'AA' verb reduplication construction, without the insertion of 一*yi*, could not be followed by 兒 *-r*; this usage is found in Ming and Qing period texts (see §5.1.3.3).

Another construction which emerged during the Yuan Dynasty is the 'ABAB' pattern for disyllabic verbs, which, again, indicates short duration of action; this is still found in MSC.

5.1.3 Word formation in Premodern and Modern Chinese

In this section, we shall deal with the morphology of Premodern and Modern Chinese. Since these two stages, differently from Old and

Middle Chinese, have very much in common in the domain of word formation (and beyond), for the sake of conciseness we shall focus on the modern language: characteristic morphological phenomena of the premodern stage will be mentioned when appropriate.

5.1.3.1 Compounding

We said before that compounding had a strong growth in the diachronic evolution of Chinese, and currently it is by far the single most important word formation process in the language: according to the figures in Xing Janet Zhiqun (2006: 117), compounds make up about 80% of the MSC lexicon. Masini (1993: 123) highlighted that, up until the nineteenth century, between 70% and 80% of compounds in the Chinese lexicon were made of (quasi-)synonymous constituents (see §5.1.1, 5.1.2). Later, starting from the seventeenth century, and more evidently from the nineteenth century on, newly coined disyllabic compounds typically had a modifier/argument-head structure (Masini 1993: 123; see §5.2.1): generally speaking, right-headed compounds became the dominant pattern of (nominal) compounding in MSC (see the data in Ceccagno and Basciano 2007).

However, a huge *caveat* is in order here: there is, in fact, no consensus on the definition of 'compound' in Chinese. Needless to say, the relative weight of this phenomenon in the Chinese lexicon depends entirely on how compounding itself is defined. Some scholars (e.g. Chao Yuen Ren 1968; Li and Thompson 1981) regard all words made of free and/or bound roots (see §5.1.1) as compounds, while others argue that only those complex words made of other words, but not bound roots, are *bona fide* compounds (e.g. Dai John Xiang-ling 1992; Packard 2000). Dai (1992) believes that the only productive pattern of compounding in MSC involves the combination of words, i.e. free forms; complex words formed by (at least one) bound root, according to Dai, are rather stored as such in the lexicon, and they are not true compounds. Thus, a word as 水鳥 *shuǐ-niǎo* 'water-bird, aquatic bird' is to be understood as a compound because it is formed by two free roots (i.e. two words), while a word like 筆友 *bǐ-yǒu* 'pen-friend, pen pal' is not a compound, since 友 *yǒu* 'friend' is a bound root. In the same spirit, Packard (2000: 80–1) makes a distinction between compound words, made of two free roots (in his terminology, 'root words'), as e.g. 冰山 *bīng-shān* 'ice-mountain, iceberg', and 'bound root words', i.e. words made of bound roots, as e.g. 橡皮 *xiàng-pí* 'rubber.tree-skin, eraser'.

However, we may remark that, in fact, Chinese bound roots are not only formally undistinguishable from free roots but, also, they are productively used in word formation in the same way. Sproat and Shih (1996) note that compounds containing at least one bound root are in fact productive (*contra* Dai 1992); Dong Xiufang (2004) regards the combination of bound roots (詞根復合 *cígēn fùhé*) as the most common word formation pattern of MSC. Thus, there appear to be no strong arguments to treat complex words made of bound roots as different from those made of free roots: although this might be (and, indeed, has been) used as a criterion for compoundhood, e.g. in English, there appears to be substantial agreement in the literature on the fact that the exact nature of compound constituents may vary, depending on the morphological profile of the language at issue (see e.g. Bauer 2006: 719; Lieber and Štekauer 2009: 4–8; Scalise and Vogel 2010: 5–6).

We thus believe it is safe to conclude that the label 'compound', for Chinese, may be applied to any word made of two or more roots, be they free or bound. In an even broader sense, we may include also words containing other complex words, as e.g. 獅子頭 *shīzi-tóu* 'lion-head, stewed pork meatballs', in which the constituent 獅子 *shīzi* 'lion' is in turn a complex word containing the bound root 獅 *shī* 'lion' and the noun suffix 子 *-zi* (see §5.1.2). Moreover, compounds may also have a phrasal constituent as a modifier (crucially, not as the head), just as Eng. *pipe-and-slipper husband* (Plag 2003; Lieber and Scalise 2006; ex. from He Yuanjian 2004: 2):

(17)   盜竊國寶犯
      dàoqiè-guó-bǎo-fàn
      steal-state-treasure-criminal
      'thief of state treasures'

In the word in (17), the head constituent 犯 *fàn* 'criminal' is a bound root, while the modifier 盜竊國寶 *dàoqiè guóbǎo* 'steal state treasures' is obviously a phrase.

In this connection, another much debated topic in the literature on Chinese morphology is the distinction between words and phrases, i.e. between morphological and syntactic items. Several diagnostics have been proposed to assess wordhood for Chinese, as e.g. lexical integrity, conjunction deletion between coordinate items, freedom of the constituents, semantic compositionality, the number of syllables, exocentricity, productivity, and more (see Chao Yuen Ren 1968; Huang C.-T. James 1984; Duanmu San 1998, among others). Within this domain, the status of verb-object construction is particularly controversial. Again, many criteria to distinguish verb-object compounds from verb-object phrases have been proposed in the literature (Chao Yuen Ren 1968; Li and Thompson 1981; Huang C.-T. James 1984; Chi Telee 1985; Packard 2000): lexicalization or specialization of meaning, inseparability of the constituents, having at least one bound constituent, exocentricity of the construction, possibility of taking an object argument. However, the proposed tests sometimes yield contradicting results: for instance, a verb-object construction like 擔心 *dān-xīn* 'carry.on. shoulder-heart, to worry' is often separable (18a), and thus lacks lexical integrity, despite its opaque, lexicalized meaning and the fact that it can be followed by an object argument (18b; exx. adapted from Huang C.-T. James 1984: 64):

(18)   a. 他擔了三年的心 。
       tā   *dān-le*   *sān*   *nián*   *de*   *xīn*
       3SG.M   carry-PFV   three   year   MOD   heart
       'He worried for three years.'

       b. 我很擔心這件事 。
       wǒ   *hěn*   *dān-xīn*   *zhè*   *jiàn*   *shì*
       1SG   very   carry-heart   this   CLF   matter
       'I'm very worried about this matter.'

According to Dai John Xiang-ling (1992: 81–2), a verb-object construction like 擔心 *dān-xīn* is a phrase; however, in sentence (18b), it can be analysed as a word. Thus, it appears that at least some verb-object constructions have a 'hybrid' nature, showing features both of compound words and of phrases.

Chinese compounds may be classified according to different (sets of) criteria (see e.g. Packard 2000; Pan, Yip, and Han 2004). A classification scheme which is often found in the literature is based on the syntactic relation between the constituents (see Chao Yuen Ren 1968; Li and Thompson 1981; Yip Po-Ching 2000). Chao Yuen Ren (1968) identified the following compound types:

a. Subject-predicate compounds: e.g. 頭疼 *tóu-téng* 'head-hurt, headache'

b. Coordinate compounds: e.g. 書報 *shū-bào* 'book-newspaper, books and newspapers'. This group also includes (quasi-)synonymic compounds, as e.g. 打擊 *dǎ-jī* 'hit-hit, to hit', and compounds made of antonyms, as e.g. 大小 *dà-xiǎo* 'large-small, size', 吸呼 *hū-xī* 'inhale-exhale, to breathe'

c. Subordinative compounds, i.e. words in which there is a modifier-head relation between the constituents, as e.g. 牛肉 *niú-ròu* 'cow-meat, beef'

d. Verb-object compounds (both nouns and verbs), as e.g. 動身 *dòng-shēn* 'move-body, to set off, leave', 司機 *sī-jī* 'manage-vehicle, driver'

e. Verb-complement compounds, as e.g. 改良 *gǎi-liáng* 'change-good, to improve'; this also includes the above-mentioned (§5.1.2) resultative compounds

More recently, some proposed other types of verb-verb compounds, as the following ones (Hong Miao 2004; Chen Zhong 2007; Yi Dan 2007; for an overview, see Steffen Chung 2006):

f. Serial verb compounds (連動型 *liándòngxíng*), in which there is a sequential relation between the verbs, as e.g. 拆洗 *chāi-xǐ* 'take.apart-wash, to strip and clean'

g. 'Double complement' compounds (兼語型 *jiānyǔxíng*), in which normally the object of the first verb is the subject of the second verb, as e.g. 勸退 *quàn-tuì* 'advise-retire, to persuade someone to retire'

However, Ceccagno and Scalise (2006) highlight several shortcomings of these schemes for classification (see the source for the details) and suggest that, for a comprehensive analysis of compounds, one should take into consideration categorial, functional, and semantic aspects. In the same spirit, Ceccagno and Basciano (2007) propose an alternative classification of Chinese compounds based on Bisetto and Scalise's (2005) framework. Put very briefly, this scheme first divides compounds into three macro-types, basing on the relation between the constituents: subordinate (i.e. having a head-argument relation), attributive (i.e. having a modifier-head relation), and coordinate. Each macro type is further divided into two subtypes, depending on whether there is (at least) one constituent which may be understood as the head: endocentric (headed) and exocentric compounds (on headedness in Chinese compounds, see Packard 2000; Ceccagno and Basciano 2007). An example for each of the six categories is provided in Table 5.1.

Table 5.1 The classification of Chinese compounds according to Ceccagno and Basciano's (2007) taxonomy

Compound type	Headedness	Example
Subordinate	Endocentric	雞毛 *jī-máo* 'chicken-feather, chicken feather'
	Exocentric	鎮紙 *zhèn-zhǐ* 'press-paper, paperweight'
Attributive	Endocentric	斑馬魚 *bānmǎ-yú* 'zebra-fish, zebrafish'
	Exocentric	花心 *huā-xīn* 'false-heart, unfaithful'
Coordinate	Endocentric	酸辣 *suān-là* 'hot-sour, hot and sour'
	Exocentric	長短 *cháng-duǎn* 'long-short, length'

From Arcodia and Basciano 2018: 229.

Each category in turn includes different subtypes, depending on the word class of the constituents and on the exact semantic relation between the constituents (for a concise overview, see Arcodia and Basciano 2018).

Compounding is generally very productive, as said before, and nominal compounding has the highest degree of productivity and creativity (Li and Thompson 1981; Basciano, Kula, and Melloni 2011): new compounds may be created quite freely, and the semantic relation between the constituents is open, as for English and other Germanic languages. Li and Thompson (1981: 49–53) propose a list of the most common semantic relations between the constituent of Chinese nominal compounds, which includes e.g. 'N$_2$ is used for N$_1$' (衣架 *yī-jià* 'clothes-rack, clothes rack'), 'N$_2$ is caused by N$_1$' (水痕 *shuǐhén* 'water-mark, water stains'), or 'N$_2$ is a metaphorical description of N$_1$' (龍船 *lóng-chuán* 'dragon-boat, dragon boat'), among many others. However, they stress the fact that their list is open: it appears that the only restriction which applies to nominal compounding in Chinese is pragmatic, i.e. whether the compound is appropriate in context or not; in fact, the interpretation of a (novel) compound may be dependent on the speech context, again just like in English (Li and Thompson 1981: 48).

Resultative compounds too are very productive in Chinese, and there is a huge variety of possible combinations between their constituents (Chen Jidong 2008; Basciano 2010). Thus, the same V_1 may combine with different V_2s:[4] see e.g. 踢破 *tī-pò* 'kick-break, break by kicking', 踢累 *tī-lèi* 'kick-tired, kick until one gets tired, get tired by kicking', 踢開 *tī-kāi* 'kick-open, open by kicking'; moreover, the same V_2 may combine with different V_1s, as e.g. 寫累 *xiě-lèi* 'write-tired, write until one gets tired', 看累 *kàn-lèi* 'look/read-tired, look/read until one gets tired', 騎累 *qí-lèi* 'ride-tired, ride until one gets tired' (see Cheng and Huang 1994: 192).

As to the choice of V_1, there appear to be few restrictions: almost all transitive and unergative verbs, and even some stative verbs (particularly, verbs of 'spatial configuration' like 坐 *zuò* 'to sit, be seated' or 站 *zhàn* 'to stand', which have both stative and dynamic properties), may appear as the first constituent in resultative compounds (see Chen Jidong 2008). Even some intransitive change of state verbs may be used as V_1s, as e.g. 破 *pò* 'to break' in 破碎 *pò-suì* 'break, smash, smash to pieces', in which V_2 further specifies the change of state expressed by V_1.

On the other hand, only a limited number of roots may appear as V_2 in resultative compounds: adjectives (see Fn. 4) like 乾 *gān* 'dry', 乾淨 *gānjìng* 'clean', 累 *lèi* 'tired'; verbs of change of state or position, like 斷 *duàn* 'to break', 醒 *xǐng* 'to wake up', 跑 *pǎo* 'to flee'; 哭 *kū* 'to cry' and 笑 *xiào* 'to laugh', which are the only two unergative verbs allowed in this construction;[5] lastly, some stative verbs, which allow also for an eventive reading (Sybesma 1992: 17), like 懂 *dǒng* 'understand', 會 *huì* 'to know'.[6]

---

[4] Note that the second constituent in a resultative compound can also be an adjectival root, as 累 *lèi* 'tired' in the examples shown here. However, since adjectival items which appear in resultative compounds may also be used by themselves as intransitive change of state verbs, we believe it is safe to assume that all constituents of resultative compounds are in fact verbs (see Basciano 2010).

[5] These verbs may be allowed in resultative compounds as they can be conceived as externally caused in some instances (see Basciano 2010, 2017c).

[6] On semantic categories which are allowed in resultative compounds, see Chen Jidong (2008: 39).

Another interesting feature of MSC resultative compounds is that one may combine constituents expressing different, or even (seemingly) contradictory, semantic relations between the causing event and its result (Talmy 2000; Chen Jidong 2008; Basciano 2010). For instance, a verb like 洗 *xǐ* 'to wash' may appear in an 'ordinary' resultative, like 洗乾淨 *xǐ-gānjìng* 'wash-clean', in which what is washed becomes clean, as expected; however, it may also be associated with other result states, as e.g. 洗髒 *xǐ-zāng* 'wash-dirty', 洗破 *xǐ-pò* 'wash-broken', or 洗皺 *xǐ-zhòu* 'wash-creased'. A resultative compound as 洗髒 *xǐ-zāng* 'wash-dirty' may be found, for instance, in a context in which a shirt is washed in filthy water and, as a result, it become dirty, rather than clean, after washing (compare Eng. **I washed my shirt dirty*).

While the examples we used in this section are all of MSC, compounding is fairly homogeneous throughout Sinitic: variation in this domain of word formation is relatively modest. For instance, as to the position of the head in nominal compounds, the overwhelmingly dominant order is modifier-head, while only subordinate verbal compounds (i.e. verb-object, resultative, and verb-complement compounds) are left-headed (Ceccagno and Basciano 2007). Nevertheless, in some dialects we may find a few examples of left-headed (head-modifier) nominal compounds, as in Cantonese (see §2.3) and Teochew (潮州 *Cháozhōu*): see e.g. Teochew *hou*[35-21]-*mui*[55] 'rain-minute/small, drizzle' (compare MSC 小雨 *xiǎo-yǔ* 'small-rain'; Xu Hui Ling 2007: 66). Also, resultative compounds may behave differently from MSC in some dialects (see Basciano 2017c). For instance, in Cantonese RVCs are much more constrained than in MSC: one restriction is that the choice of V_2 is mostly limited to result states which are unique to a particular action (described by V_1). Thus, a V_2 as e.g. 攰 *guih* 'tired', which could be associated with many different V_1s, is not generally used in resultatives (compare the examples with MSC 累 *lèi* 'tired' seen before; Lau and Lee 2015: 236).

5.1.3.2 Derivation

If the definition of compounding for Chinese is far from uncontroversial, as seen in the preceding section, the status of derivation is perhaps one of the most debated issues in the research on Chinese word formation, generating even bigger controversies. In point of fact, there is as yet no general consensus on what constitutes a derivational affix in Chinese and even on whether productive derivation exists at all (for an overview, see Pan, Yip, and Han 2004; Arcodia 2011, 2012). There are two essential reasons behind this. Firstly, as said earlier, lexical morphemes in MSC are most often bound, just like derivational affixes, but they have full lexical meaning, just as words. Secondly, there is a considerable number of lexical morphemes which appear in a fixed position and have a fixed meaning in complex words, again just as affixes, but which are also formally identical to free or bound lexical roots.

An exception to this is represented by a very small number of items which are generally described as affixes in the literature. They are mostly former compound constituents which, in time, lost their tone and much of their lexical content: these are the already mentioned 子 -zi (< zǐ 'child'; yǐ-zi 椅子 'chair-SUFF, chair'), 兒 -r (< ér 'child'; huà-r 畫兒 'paint-SUFF, painting'), and 頭 -tou (< tóu 'head'; see §5.1.2). As hinted at before, 子 -zi and 兒 -r originally had an evalutative meaning, which was mostly lost; their basic function, just as for 頭 -tou, is to indicate nominal word class: compare e.g. 擦 cā 'to rub, wipe' and 擦子 cāzi 'eraser'. These three suffixes were quite productive in Premodern Chinese (on 兒 -r and 頭 -tou, see the figures in Arcodia and Basciano 2012) but became almost unproductive in MSC.

Two more formants which are often -included among affixes in the literature, despite having undergone no formal reduction, are: 化 -huà (< huà 化 'to change'), roughly corresponding to Eng. '-ize, -ify', as in 現代化 xiàndài-huà 'modern-SUFF, modernize, modernization', and 性 -xìng (< xìng 性 'inherent nature'), roughly corresponding to Eng. -ity, -ness, -hood, as in 爆發性 bàofā-xìng 'explode-SUFF, explosiveness'. Both became productive at the beginning of the twentieth century, arguably under the influence of Japanese, as they were used in that language to render the corresponding suffixes of English and other European languages (see Wang Li 1980 [1958]; Masini 1993; Arcodia 2012); the close functional correspondence with European suffixes probably led scholars to analyse them as derivational suffixes (Pan, Yip, and Han 2004: 67). However, note that, for instance, 化 -huà-derived verbs may be found also in Early Mandarin (Arcodia 2012; Arcodia and Basciano 2012): generally speaking, the development of 化 -huà seems to be, in essence, independent from the European model (Steffen Chung 2006).

An interesting case is that of another often-quoted instance of derivational suffix, namely 者 -zhě, mostly forming agentive nouns ('one who Vs'), as in 讀者 dú-zhě 'read-SUFF, reader', 愛國者 ài-guó-zhě 'love-country-SUFF, patriot', 共產主義者 gòngchǎn-zhǔyì-zhě 'communist-doctrine-SUFF, communist'. In Classical Chinese, the morpheme 者 *zhě* was mostly used as a demonstrative ('the one who...'); in MSC, it combines with nouns, verbs, or adjectives, always yielding a noun. However, the peculiarity of this item is that it can combine also with phrases, as e.g. in (Dong Xiufang 2004: 85):

(19) 破坏社会治安者
      pòhuài   shèhuì   zhì'ān-zhě
      destroy   society   order-SUFF
      'disturber of public order'

Thus, it appears that 者 *-zhě* is not yet fully grammaticalized, as it can still sometimes combine with phrases: there has been, hence, no scope reduction (Lehmann 2015). However, an alternative analysis could be that examples as (19) are vestiges of the Classical Chinese usage of 者 *zhě* as a particle: as already mentioned (§5.1.1), formal written Chinese is characterized by the use of some Classical stylistic conventions (see also Arcodia 2012).

Besides the small set of items we discussed here, there is a huge number of morphemes with some derivation-like features which have, as mentioned before, an ambiguous status. Take, for instance, the root 學 *xué* 'to study', which was discussed before (§5.1.1) in connection with neoclassical constituents. We may note that, as a constituent in complex words with the meaning 'branch of learning', 學 *xué* is always found to the right: the pattern which we exemplified with 語言學 *yǔyánxué* 'linguistics' is fully productive, and 學 *xué* may be used to create just any word indicating a branch of learning, as e.g. 生物學 *shēng-wù-xué* 'living-thing-study, biology', 人類學 *rén-lèi-xué* 'human-species-study, anthropology', etc. For these reasons, some define constituents like 學 (-) *xué* as 'affixes' (詞綴 *cízhuì*) or 'affixoids' (類詞綴 *lèicízhuì* or 準詞綴 *zhǔncízhuì*): however, there is again no agreement on the criteria to identify affixes and/or affixoids, and, hence, the items included in these sets vary considerably (Pan, Yip, and Han 2004; Arcodia 2012). The issue is not only met in the literature on MSC: for instance, in Matthews and Yip's grammar of Cantonese (2011: 45), they propose a list of 'noun suffixes' which includes items like 度 *douh* 'degree' (高度 *gōu-douh* 'high-degree, height') and 法 *faat* 'way, method' (講法 *góng-faat* 'speak-way, way of speaking'), the use of which is not different from that of the corresponding MSC morphemes. However, apart from their productivity, there appears to be no reason to treat them as fundamentally different from any other compound constituent. Take, for instance, the following two MSC examples:

(20) a. 我喜歡那個人。
      wǒ xǐhuan nà   ge   rén
      1SG like   that   CLF   person
      'I like that person.'

    b. 俄羅斯人
      Éluósī-rén
      Russia-person
      'Russian'

In (20a), the root 人 *rén* 'person' is free and occupies a syntactic slot: it is indeed a word. In (20b), the very same root is bound and is used as the head of a complex word. The pattern exemplified by (20b) may be used in MSC to create just any word indicating a person from a certain country, city, etc., as e.g. 比羅比詹人 *Bǐluóbǐzhānrén* 'Birobidžaner'. Because of its 'versatility' (≈ productivity; see Chao Yuen Ren 1968) in complex words, Yip Po-ching (2000: 59–60) treats 人 *rén* as a noun suffix. However, the number of words created following a certain word formation pattern is not normally used as a diagnostic test for affixhood, given that a compounding pattern may be very productive as well. Moreover, we wish to stress once again the point that there is virtually no difference in meaning between the free (20a) and bound (20b) usages of 人 *rén*.

Thus, in short, there appears to be no agreement on how to define and identify derivational affixes (and affixoids) in Chinese, with the exception of a small number of items, many of which are no longer productive. As to the many items with derivation-like features (i.e. fixed position and a stable meaning), the jury is still out.

5.1.3.3 Reduplication

In modern Sinitic languages, both partial and total reduplication are generally very productive; a broad variety of reduplication patterns are attested. Total reduplication consists in the repetition of a root or word, as e.g. 胖胖 *pàng~pàng* 'fat~fat, quite fat', 考慮考慮 *kǎolǜ~kǎolǜ* 'ponder~ponder, to think over a bit'. Partial reduplication, on the other hand, consists in the repetition of phonological units (mostly, syllables), as e.g. 冷冰冰 *lěng-bīng~bīng* 'cold-ice~ice, ice-cold', the intensified form of 冰冷 *bīng-lěng* 'ice-cold' ('AB' > 'BAA'): in this case, the reduplicated element is both a phonological and a morphological unit, i.e. both a syllable and a morpheme. Since reduplication in modern Sinitic mostly involves syllables, rather than syllable constituents or single phonemes, it inevitably involves morphemes, given that most Chinese syllables correspond to morphemes (see §5.1.1).

In MSC, reduplication can have both iconic and anti-iconic meanings. Iconic patterns of reduplication, i.e. expressing intensification, emphasis, plurality, etc., are mainly those for adjectives and, marginally, classifiers and nouns; anti-iconic patterns of reduplication, i.e. expressing diminution, short duration, etc., are limited to verbs and, very marginally, nouns. However, as we shall see later, these associations do not hold for all modern Sinitic languages.

Noun reduplication in MSC has very limited productivity: nouns just cannot freely reduplicate (see Xu Dan 2012: 3). Reduplication of nouns conveys a meaning labelled as 'collective plural' or 'distributive' (Paris 2007; Xu Dan 2012), as e.g. 事事 *shì~shì* 'matter~matter, everything', 人人 *rén~rén* 'person~person, everyone'. Nouns which may reduplicate are mainly monosyllabic; however, there are also some reduplicated disyllabic coordinate nouns, sometimes fully lexicalized (Xu Dan 2012), as e.g. 子子孫孫 *zǐ~zǐ-sūn~sūn* 'child~child-grandchild~grandchild, heirs, offspring' (compare 子孫 *zǐ-sūn* 'child-grandchild, children and grandchildren, descendants'), 家家戶戶 *jiā~jiā-hù~hù* 'family~household-family~household, each and every family/household' (家戶 *jiā-hù* 'family-household, family, household; see Melloni & Basciano 2018).

A different pattern of noun reduplication, now fully lexicalized (note the loss of tone on the second syllable) is represented by nouns for family members (see §5.1.2), as e.g. 哥哥 *gēge* 'older brother', 妹妹 *mèimei* 'younger sister'; they very likely come from child language and/or child-directed speech (Ōta 1987). In point of fact, sometimes the personal names of children are used by their parents in a reduplicated form, as e.g. 亮亮 *Liàng~liang* (from 亮 *Liàng*), again with loss of tone on the second constituent (Lin Hua 2001: 72). Reduplication of nouns and other items is commonly found also in Cantonese baby talk, as e.g. 去街街 *heui gāai~gāai* 'go street~street, go out' (Matthews and Yip 2011: 42). Interestingly, in Shanghainese the reduplication of nouns may be used both for universal quantification (家家 *kà~ka* 'family~family, every family') and to express a diminutive meaning (花花 *hò~ho* 'flower~flower, small flower'; Zhu Xiaonong 2006: 58).

The reduplication of classifiers, just as for nouns, yields a distributive meaning in MSC (and many other Chinese dialects): see e.g. 本本 *běn~běn* 'CLF(BOOKS)~CLF(BOOKS), each and every (book)' (see Xu Dan 2012: 3). According to Paris (2007), when reduplicated classifiers appear before the verb they actually have a distributive meaning, while when they appear after the verb they have a collective meaning; Zhang Niina Ning (2014), on the other hand, believes that the reduplication of classifiers in MSC may be used productively to express 'abundant plurality' (adapted from Zhang Niina Ning 2014: 6):

(21) 河裡漂著 (一) 朵朵蓮花。
      hé-lǐ   piāo-zhe   (yī)   duǒ~duǒ lián-huā
      river-LOC float-DUR one   CLF~CLF lotus-flower
      'There are many lotuses floating in the river.'

According to Zhang, the reduplicated classifier 朵 *duǒ* indicates 'plurality of units', rather than 'plurality of individuals', and it is incompatible with a singular reading; moreover, its meaning of 'abundant plurality' entails that a sentence like (21) is unacceptable 'if there are only two or three lotuses in the river' (Zhang Niina Ning 2014: 6).

Verb reduplication is very common and productive in MSC, in which it is used to convey the so-called 'tentative' or 'delimitative' aspect (see Chao Yuen Ren 1968; Li and Thompson 1981; Tsao Feng-fu 2004; see §5.1.2): do something 'a little bit' (Li and Thompson 1981: 29), for a short time, quickly, in an informal, relaxed way. Moreover, it has also the function of 'relaxing' the tone of the utterance, to mitigate a request (Xiao and McEnery 2004).

Both monosyllabic and disyllabic verbs may reduplicate in MSC. See the following examples:

(22) a. 看 *kàn* 'look'('A') >
         看看 *kàn~kan* ('AA') 'look~look, have a look'
      b. 休息 *xiūxi* 'rest' ('AB') >
         休息休息 ('ABAB') *xiūxi~xiūxi* 'rest~rest, rest a little'

In the reduplication of monosyllabic verbs (22a), the reduplicant loses its tone; moreover, only for monosyllabic reduplicated verbs the numeral *yi* 一 (again, with tone neutralization) may be inserted between the base and the reduplicant (看一看 *kàn yi kàn*), apparently with no change in meaning. If the base is a separable verb-object compound ('AB'), the reduplication pattern is 'AAB', i.e. only the verb is reduplicated: 跳舞 *tiào-wǔ* 'jump-dance, to dance' > 跳跳舞 *tiào~tiao-wǔ* 'dance a little'. If the base verb is disyllabic (22b), the reduplicant retains the original tone; moreover, as already mentioned (§5.1.2), the numeral *yi* 一 cannot appear between the base and the reduplicant.

As hinted at in §5.1.2, during Ming and Qing times, differently from earlier stages of the language, we do find instances of monosyllabic reduplicated verbs followed by the suffix 兒 *-(é)r*: see e.g. 侯侯兒 *hóu~hóu-r* 'wait~wait-SUFF' (*The Plum in the Golden Vase*), and 等等兒 *děng~děng-r* 'wait~wait-SUFF' (*The Dream of the Red Chamber*; Ōta 1987: 176–7). Ōta remarks that these reduplicated verbs could not be followed by an object and generally appeared at the end of a sentence; however, an object (generally, a personal pronoun or a proper noun) could appear between the base and the 兒 *-(é)r*-suffixed reduplicant, as in the following example:

(23)　大官人......不進裡面看他看兒? (*The Plum in the Golden Vase*)
　　　dàguānrén ...... *bù　jìn　lǐmiàn　kàn　tā　kàn-r*
　　　Your.honour　not　enter　inside　look　3SG.M　look-SUFF
　　　'Your honour ... won't you go inside and have a look?'

In MSC, the 兒-*(é)r* suffix cannot be added to the reduplicant, and the direct object cannot be inserted between the verb and the reduplicant; it can only follow it.

Note that while, as already mentioned, verb reduplication is generally productive, there are indeed verbs which cannot reduplicate in MSC. Delimitative reduplication is in fact restricted to verbs which express dynamic events controlled by the subject/agent (see Tsao Feng-fu 2004; Xiao and McEnery 2004; Paris 2007); thus, telic verbs (including resultative compounds) and statives do not reduplicate. In fact, verb reduplication seems to add a time boundary to the event described by the verb (Xiao and McEnery 2004): this is proven by the incompatibility of reduplicated verbs with the durative (著 *-zhe*) and progressive (正在 *zhèngzài*) aspect markers, while, on the other hand, they are compatible with the perfective aspect marker 了 *-le*, indicating a completed or terminated action (Basciano and Melloni 2017).

However, in MSC and many other Chinese dialects (see Arcodia, Basciano, and Melloni 2015) there is also another pattern of verb reduplication which has an iconic, 'augmentative' function: it expresses pluractionality or action in progress (Hu Xiaobin 2006). This pattern of reduplication does not overlap with the delimitative pattern, as it requires disyllabic ('AB') bases in which A and B are two verbs in a relation of coordination, including synonymy and antonymy: for instance, 進進出出 *jìn~jìn-chū~chū* 'enter~enter-exit~exit, shuttle in and out' (進出 *jìn-chū* 'enter and exit'), which describes two related actions performed alternatedly and repeatedly. In some cases, this pattern of reduplication conveys a semantic nuance of vividness: 跑跑跳跳 *pǎo~pǎo-tiào~tiào* 'run~run-jump~jump, skip and jump, skip along' (跑跳 *pǎo-tiào* 'run and jump'). Differently from delimitative verb reduplication, this construction has no particular aspectual restrictions on its base verbs, and, in fact, it allows telic verbs as 進 *jìn* 'enter' and 出 *chū* 'exit'.

Adjectival reduplication, already attested well before the Modern Chinese period (see §5.1.2), is widely used in MSC, and it always conveys a sense of intensity and vividness. Both monosyllabic and disyllabic adjectives may reduplicate; in the latter case, each syllable is reduplicated independently ('AB' > 'AABB'):

(24) a. 高 *gāo* ('A') 'tall' > 高高 *gāo~gāo* ('AA') 'very tall'

b. 高興 *gāo-xìng* ('AB') 'happy' > 高高興興 *gāo~gāo-xìng~xìng* ('AABB') 'quite/very happy'

Perhaps unsurprisingly, only gradable/scalar adjectives may reduplicate; absolute adjectives are not allowed in this construction (Zhu Jingsong 2003; Paul 2010: 139, Fn. 19): note the ungrammaticality of *方方 *fāng~fāng* (< 方 *fāng* 'square').[7] The reduplicated adjective, differently from the base adjective, is not gradable (hence the ungrammaticality of *很高高興興 * *hěn gāo~gāo-xìng~xìng*, lit. 'very quite/very happy'): thus, adjectival reduplication turns a gradable adjective into a non-gradable one (see Melloni and Basciano 2018). Moreover, only disyllabic *and* bimorphemic items are allowed in this construction: monomorphemic (native and borrowed) adjectives cannot reduplicate following the 'AABB' pattern, as e.g. 摩登 *módēng* 'modern'

---

[7] Although the reduplication of 方 *fāng* is acceptable in the case of a coerced reading, as e.g. 方方的臉 *fāng~fāng de liǎn* 'square~square MOD face, (very) square face' (Tang 1988: 283).

(< Eng. *modern*) > *摩摩登登 **mó~mó-dēng~dēng* (Paul 2010: 137). Lastly, both morphemes must be lexical, while derivation-like items, as the prefix(oid) 好 *hǎo-* 'easy/pleasant to V' cannot (see Zhu Jingsong 2003): see e.g. 好看 *hǎo-kàn* 'pleasant-look, pretty, easy on the eye' > *好好看看 **hǎo~hǎo-kàn~kàn*.

There are some disyllabic adjectives which, besides the above-mentioned 'AABB' reduplication pattern, can also reduplicate following the 'ABAB' pattern (Paris 2007): 高興 *gāo-xìng* (AB) 'happy' > 高興高興 *gāoxìng~gāoxìng* (ABAB) 'have some fun' (compare Ex. 22b). This is allowed only for adjectives which may describe a process, just as verbs; in this case, the meaning conveyed by reduplication is akin to delimitative aspect (compare 高高興興 *gāo~gāo-xìng~xìng* 'very happy'). See the following example:

(25)   讓他們高興高興吧。
     ràng   *tā-men*   *gāoxìng~gāoxìng*   *ba*
     CAUS   3M-PL   happy~happy   EXH
     'Let them have some fun.'

Lastly, there is yet another pattern of reduplication for disyllabic adjectives, in which the adjectival base is reduplicated as a whole ('ABAB'), just as for verbs, but which apparently has an augmentative/intensifying value, just as for the 'AABB' pattern. This is limited to compound adjectives with a modifier-head structure, as e.g. 冰涼 *bīng-liáng* 'ice-cold' > 冰涼冰涼 *bīng-liáng~bīng-liáng*. We may remark that, while adjectives which reduplicate following the 'AABB' pattern must be gradable, adjectives which follow the 'ABAB' pattern are not gradable, as the modifier turns the head into a nongradable item. Thus, despite having roughly the same meaning, the two patterns of reduplication for adjectives, i.e. 'AABB' and 'ABAB', seem to be the result of different processes (see Melloni and Basciano 2018).

As mentioned at the beginning of this section, there is considerable variation among Sinitic languages in the domain of reduplication (on verb reduplication, see Arcodia, Basciano, and Melloni 2015); for instance, in some Mandarin dialects spoken in Yunnan, verbal reduplication is never used in the delimitative function; it rather indicates repetition/continuation of the action, similarly to verb reduplication in Old Chinese (Shi Yuzhi 2007: 60–1; see §5.1.2). Also, while reduplication of resultative compounds is not allowed in MSC (e.g. 吃飽 *chī-bǎo* 'eat-full' > *吃吃飽 **chī~chī-bǎo*), in some other dialects, as e.g. Taiwanese, V_1 does reduplicate (Tsao Feng-fu 2004; Shi Yuzhi 2007).

Patterns of reduplication differ also for adjectives. For instance, in Taiwanese the reduplication of monosyllabic adjectives actually has a diminishing function, as e.g. 紅紅 *âng~âng* 'red~red, reddish'; in order to obtain intensifying semantics, the base adjectives must be repeated three times, as e.g. 紅紅紅 *âng~âng~âng* 'red~red~red, very red'. Taiwanese disyllabic adjectives reduplicate according both to the 'ABAB' pattern, with diminishing semantics, as e.g. 老實老實 *láusit~láusit* 'honest~honest, kind of honest', and with the 'AABB' pattern, with intensifying semantics, as 老老實實 *láu~láu-sit~sit* 'honest~honest, very honest' (Tsao Feng-fu 2004: 297; Lin Philip T. 2015: 167–9).[8]

Interestingly, despite the fairly broad range of variation we see within Sinitic in the domain of verbal reduplication, the 'AABB' pattern is in fact very homogeneous: Sinitic languages in which 'AABB' reduplication of verbs is possible generally behave like MSC (Arcodia, Basciano, and Melloni 2015). For instance, in Cantonese a coordinate verb as上落 *séuhng-lohk* 'rise-fall, go up or down' may reduplicate as 上上落落 *séuhng~séuhng-lohk~lohk* 'rise~rise-fall~fall, rise and fall, go up and down': the reduplicated verb expresses two coordinate actions performed alternatedly and repeatedly (Matthews and Yip 2011: 40), just as in MSC. Generally speaking, while the reduplication of monosyllabic verbs and adjectives shows considerable variation among Sinitic languages, there appears to be an interesting form-function correlation for disyllabic verbs and adjectives: the 'AABB' pattern is strongly associated with (broadly defined) augmentative semantics, while the 'ABAB' pattern is strongly associated with diminishing semantics.

Besides total reduplication, in modern Sinitic languages there are also a few patterns of partial reduplication. See the following MSC examples:

[8] Interestingly, Tsao Feng-fu (2004: 296–7) and Lin Philip T. (2015: 167–9) gave two radically different accounts of how reduplication works for disyllabic adjectives in Taiwanese. According to Tsao, the 'ABAB' diminishing pattern is the authentically Taiwanese pattern, whereas the 'AABB' intensifying pattern is but a calque from the corresponding MSC construction, and is quite rare. Lin, on the other hand, believes that the 'AABB' pattern is the dominant one, whereas the 'ABAB' pattern is not fully productive, and anyway has intensifying semantics. We suggest that this may be interpreted as a sign of the growing influence of MSC on Taiwanese, which turned a possibly 'imported' pattern into the dominant one, at the expense of the original, native construction.

(26)   a. 通紅 *tōnghóng* ('AB') 'red through and through' > 紅通通
       hóng-tōng~tōng (BAA) 'bright red'

   b. 糊塗 *hútu* ('AB') 'confused' > 糊裡糊塗 *hū-li-hū-tu* (A-裡 *li*-
       AB) 'confused'.

   c. 黑咕隆咚 *hēi-gu-lōng~dōng* 'pitch dark'

   d. 黑 *hēi* 'black/dark' > 黑糊糊 *hēi-hū-hū* 'black-SUFF-SUFF,
       black/dark'

The pattern exemplified in (26a), based on the reduplication of a single syllable of a disyllabic item, is quite widespread in Sinitic; it is found
also with the 'ABB' order (Wang Fang 2011). For instance, in Taiwanese
some verbs may reduplicate according to the 'ABB' pattern, with delimitative semantics, as e.g. 修理 *siu-lí* 'fix-fix, to fix' > 修理理咧 *siu-lí~lí*
leh 'fix-fix~fix EMPH, fix a little' (Chuang Hui-ju 2007: 33). Often, verbs
which reduplicate as 'ABB' in Taiwanese are fully lexicalized synonymic
compounds, as in the example just mentioned.

The pattern in (26b) is also fairly common in Sinitic, and it generally
has a pejorative meaning, although it can also act as an intensifier
(Wang Fang 2011). In Wenzhounese, pejorative meaning is conveyed
by the pattern 'AB-巴-B' (Wang Fang 2011; no transcription is provided
for 巴 in the source). Note that unproductive patterns as those in (26c)
and (26d) seem to involve the reduplication of subsyllabic units: in
(26c) the syllable final (*-ōng*) is repeated, while in (26d) the initial (*h-*)
is repeated.

5.1.3.4 Abbreviation

Another very productive word formation pattern in Chinese is abbreviation (縮略 *suōlüè*). Given the general preference of MSC for disyllabic lexical items, and the tendency to avoid very long words, it comes
as no surprise that words and expressions of more than three syllables
are often shortened to two.

According to Packard (2000: 268), '[a] new word is considered an
abbreviated form if (a) there is a clear preexisting word or phrase that
contains all the constituents of the abbreviation, and (b) the abbreviation is considered to be derived directly from that longer word or
phrase'. Thus, following Packard's definition, the input of abbreviation
can be both a compound word (27a) and a phrase (27b; Exx. adapted
from Packard 2000: 271):

(27) a. 勞動保險   → 勞保
     láo-dòng   *bǎo-xiǎn*   *láo-bǎo*
     work-move   protect-risk   work-protect
     'work, labour'   'insurance'   'labour insurance'

    b. 環境與發展   →
     huán-jìng   *yǔ*   *fā-zhǎn*
     surround-border   and   emit-expand
     'environment'   'and'   'development'
     環發
     huán-fā
     surround-emit
     'environment and development'

Since, as said earlier, virtually all Chinese characters correspond to a syllable (with the exception of the suffix *-r* 兒), there is no way to represent in written form only the initial segments of words, as in acronyms (Eng. *radar* < *radio detecting and ranging*) and initialism (Eng. *BBC*). Hence, Chinese abbreviations are made of a selection of syllables of the words which make up the word or phrase (Lin Hua 2001: 78–9), as shown in (27). Moreover, since, as seen before, most Chinese syllables correspond to morphemes, the constituents of abbreviation are generally meaningful units, rather than mere sound strings (Yang Xipeng 2003: 138).

Lin Hua (2001: 79) suggests that abbreviations in MSC are generally formed with the first syllable of each constituent of the word or phrase, even though there are instances of abbreviations which use syllables other than the first one(s): see e.g. 外長 *wàizhǎng* 'Minister of Foreign Affairs', from 外交部長 *wài-jiāo bù-zhǎng*, lit. 'outside-relation ministry-head'. According to Lin, the choice is motivated by the pragmatic need to avoid ambiguity: if one chose the first syllable of each word, the result would be 外部 *wàibù*, which however is an existing word, meaning 'outside'. Nevertheless, homonymy avoidance does not seem to be the rule for abbreviations in MSC: for instance, 人工流產 *réngōng liúchǎn* 'induced abortion' is abbreviated as 人流 *rénliú*, despite the fact that 人流 *rénliú* is an existing word, meaning 'stream of people'. There are also instances in which two items are abbreviated with the same form: 人大 *Rén-Dà* is both the abbreviation of (全國)人民代表大會

(*Quánguó*) *Rénmín Dàibiǎo Dàhuì* '(National) People's Congress' and of 人民大學 *Rénmín Dàxué* 'Renmin University'. Thus, ambiguous abbreviations do exist in MSC. On the other hand, there are also cases in which the same item may have two different abbreviations: for instance, 郵政編碼 *yóuzhèng biānmǎ* 'post code' is abbreviated both as 郵編 *yóubiān* and as 郵碼 *yóumǎ* (Yuan Hui 2002: 7–8).

According to Yuan Hui (2002: 7), a commonly used criterion for the choice of syllables/morphemes in abbreviation is their semantic relevance; that is, the most salient morphemes in the word or phrase are chosen, independently from their position, as e.g.:

(28) 歷史資料   > 史料
  lì-shǐ   *zī-liào*   *shǐ-liào*
  experience-**history**   resource-**material**   **history-material**
  'history'   'material'   'historical materials/
                                          data'

In Ex. (28), the abbreviation is made of the characters 史 *shǐ* and 料 *liào*, rather than 歷 *lì* and 資 *zī*, supposedly because they are more salient, as they mean by themselves 'history' and 'material', respectively. On the other hand, the basic meanings of 歷 *lì* are 'experience' and 'age', while 資 *zī* means 'resource' and 'money', among others (Ceccagno and Basciano 2009: 117).

Thus, Chinese abbreviations look much like 'blends', as Eng. *smog* (< *smoke* and *fog*), or like 'clippings', i.e. words made of the initial parts of the constituents of a compound, as Eng. *sitcom* (< *situation comedy*); however, the constituents of Chinese abbreviations are nearly always morphemes, rather than mere sound strings. Ceccagno and Basciano (2007: 225) coined the label 'metacompounds' to describe Chinese abbreviations which contain at least one constituent taken from an underlying compound word, as Exx. (27a) and (28). A metacompound is often semantically and structurally opaque: its meaning and makeup may be understood only by making reference to the underlying constituents. Thus, for instance, the compound 衛視 *wèishì* 'satellite TV', formed by the constituents 衛 *wèi* 'to defend' and 視 *shì* 'to look', might at first sight seem like an exocentric and semantically opaque verb-verb compound; however, its constituents are actually clipped forms of the compounds 衛星 *wèixīng* 'satellite' and 電視 *diànshì* 'television'. If we refer to the underlying compounds, the meaning and (modifier-head) structure of the word become clear (Ceccagno and Basciano 2007: 226). Note that, as mentioned before (§5.1.1), a morpheme which is chosen as part of an abbreviation may then acquire the meaning of a whole compound or phrase (Packard 2000: 275). For instance, the morpheme 幾 *jī* 'machine' acquired the meaning 'airplane' following its use as the abbreviated form of 飛機 *fēi-jī* 'fly-machine, airplane' in words like 機場 *jīchǎng* 'airport' (Myers 2006: 173): see e.g. 機票 *jī-piào* 'plane-ticket, plane ticket' and 登機 *dēng-jī* 'step.on-plane, board a plane'.

There are also instances of abbreviations in which the order of constituents is different from that of the original compounds or phrases: see e.g. 上鋼五廠 *Shànggāngwǔchǎng* 'Shanghai N. 5 Steel Mill', the abbreviation of 上海第五鋼鐵廠 **Shànghǎi dìwǔ gāngtiěchǎng** (Yuan Hui 2002: 4). As already mentioned, there appears to be a strong preference for disyllabic abbreviations, independently from the number of syllables of the abbreviated items (Yuan Hui 2002), very likely because the two-syllable unit is the most common word form and the minimal free-standing prosodic unit in MSC (Feng Shengli 2001). However, there are also many abbreviations made of more than two syllables, as e.g. 北師大 *Běi Shī Dà* 'Beijing Normal University', from 北京師範大學 **Běijīng Shīfàn Dàxué**, or 環委會 *huánwěihuì* 'Committee for Environmental Protection', from 環境保護委員會 **huánjìng bǎohù wěiyuánhuì**.

Besides the abbreviations formed by a selection of syllables from words or phrases, there are also other patterns of abbreviations in Chinese. For instance, words or phrases which have a shared element (mostly, the head) can be abbreviated by deleting the repeated occurrences of the shared constituent:

(29)	房產	地產	>	房地產
	fáng-chǎn	*dì-chǎn*		*fáng-dì-chǎn*
	house-property	land-property		house-land-property
	'house (property)'	'landed estate'		'real estate'

Another pattern according to which words or phrases with a shared constituent are abbreviated in Chinese consists in a number plus the shared item:

(30) 舊思想、   舊文化、   舊風俗、   舊習慣   >
       jiù sīxiǎng *jiù wénhuà* *jiù fēngsú* *jiù xíguàn*
       old idea   old culture old custom   old habit
       'old ideas,   old culture, old customs, old habits'
       四舊
       sì-jiù
       four-old
       'the four olds'[9]

Lastly, we may remark that there is some variation in abbreviations used in different regions of the Chinese-speaking world. Thus, for instance, 公車 *gōng-chē* 'public-vehicle' is the abbreviation of 公共汽車 *gōnggòng qìchē* 'bus' in Taiwan, whereas in the P.R.C. it stands for 公家 的車 *gōngjiā de chē* 'public vehicle' (Lin Hua 2001: 81).

5.1.3.5 Nonconcatenative morphology

Despite claims to the contrary in the literature (see e.g. Bisang 1996, 2004, 2008), some phenomena of phonological reduction of morphemes, with blurring of morpheme boundaries and fusion between root and affix, as well as allomorphy, are indeed attested in Sinitic. Particularly, they appear to be more frequent in Mandarin and Jin dialects (Arcodia 2015). For instance, in Huojia (獲嘉 *Huòjiā*), a Jin dialect of Henan province, perfective aspect and other grammatical values are expressed by means of 'rhyme change' (變韻 *biànyùn*), i.e. ablaut (in the sense of Bickel and Nichols 2007). Compare Exx. (31a) and (31b), quoted from He Wei (1989: 58):

(31) a. 我買葱。
         ua? mai^{53} ts'uŋ^{33}
         1SG buy   scallion
         'I am buying scallion.'

      b. 我買葱。
         ua? mɛ^{53} ts'uŋ^{33}
         1SG buy.PFV   scallion
         'I bought scallion.'

---

[9] The label 'four olds' was used during the Cultural Revolution (1966–76) in the P.R.C. to indicate those aspects of traditional Chinese culture which had to be eradicated in order to make China move foward.

The pattern of rhyme change (ablaut) exemplified in (30a-b) is termed 'D rhyme change' (D 變韻 *dì biànyùn*) in Chinese linguistics: it is generally used to convey grammatical (mostly, aspectual) meaning. It has been often claimed that patterns of rhyme change arise from the fusion of erstwhile affixes (suffixes) with lexical roots (see Xin Yongfen 2006; Lamarre 2009): in the case of (31b), the most obvious candidate would be a suffix with the same etymon as the perfective aspect marker 了 *-le* of MSC.

The diachronic process which, presumably, led to the genesis of rhyme change is still somehow visible, for instance, in Boshan (博山 *Bóshān*), a Mandarin dialect of Shandong province. In this variety, many suffixes and particles, as e.g. perfective 了 *-liɔ* (again, cognate to MSC 了 *-le*) and progressive 著 *-tʂuə*, can be substituted by the so-called '-ə suffix'. The actual shape of the '-ə suffix' depends on the shape of the rhyme of the verb it attaches too, thus showing allomorphy: e.g. [ɤ] after [i]; [ʌ] after [a], [ia], and [ua]; [ʌ] after [aŋ], [iaŋ], and [uaŋ], etc. (Qian Cengyi 1993: 24–5). According to Chen Ning's description of Boshan (2006: 320), the '-ə suffix' may be substituted by the lengthening of the nucleus vowel in the root, together with tone change:

(32)　換　　　　>　換
　　　xuã³¹　　　*xuã:²¹⁴*
　　　change　　　change.PFV
　　　'change'　　　'changed'

While older speakers mostly use the -ə suffix, younger speakers tend to use vowel/tone change: this may be interpreted as evidence of a transition in progress from a more analytic towards a more synthetic strategy to mark perfectivity (Chen Ning 2006: 318, 321), which goes against the general tendency of modern Sinitic languages towards greater analyticity discussed earlier (§5.1.2).

In some Mandarin dialects of Shandong and Hebei, the so-called 'rhotacization' (兒化 *érhuà*) may be used to mark, for instance, perfective aspect and attainment of a goal. See the following example of the Qixia dialect (棲霞 *Qīxiá*, Shandong; adapted from Zhang and Li 2007: 98):

(33)　問了　　　　　　　　>　問
　　　uən⁴¹-lə　　　　　　　*uər⁴¹*
　　　ask-PFV　　　　　　　ask.PFV
　　　'(I, you, she, etc.) asked'

Rhyme change may also be used for derivation, as in the Xun (潯 *Xùn*) County dialect (Henan; Xin Yongfen 2006: 51):

(34) 籃 > 籃
     lan⁴²   *læ⁴²*
     'basket'

This type of ablaut is termed 'Z rhyme change' (子變韻 *zi biànyùn*), because it probably originates from the fusion of a morpheme with the same etymon as the MSC suffix 子 -*zi* with a lexical root, with which it shares its basic function, i.e. that of indicating noun class (compare MSC 籃子 *lánzi* 'basket'). Z rhyme change may involve the suprasegmental level only, as in Yuanqu (垣曲 *Yuánqǔ*), a Jin dialect of Shanxi (Hou and Wen 1993: 94):

(35) 脖 > 脖
     p'o¹³   *p'o:⁴⁴²*
     'neck'

Tonal morphology is not limited to Northern China. For instance, a well-known pattern of tone change with derivational functions is the so-called 'sound change' or *pinjam* (Cant. 變音 *binyàm*) of Yue dialects. *Pinjam* may be used to express a fairly broad range of functions and meanings (see Bauer and Benedict 1997), among which are the nominalization of verbs (36) and marking diminutive (37), as in the following Cantonese examples (Yu Alan Ji-Leun 2007: 192):

(36) 掃 > 掃
     sou   *sóu*
     'to sweep'   'broom'

(37) 臺 > 臺 /檯
     tòih   *tói*
     'stage, terrace'   'table'

Furthermore, the Cantonese perfective marker 咗 -*jó* may be omitted, causing tone change in the verb root (Matthews and Yip 2011: 31):

(38) 食咗飯未呀?   >   食飯未呀?
     sihk-jó-faahn meih a   *sík-faahn*   *meih a*
     eat-PFV-food NEG Q   eat.PFV-food   NEG Q
     'Have you eaten?'

In Xinyi (信宜 *Xìnyí*), another Yue dialect, the 'diminutive' (for lack of a better term) form of nouns (39), verbs (40), adjectives, and adverbs is built by adding a nasal coda to the root and raising the pitch towards the end of the tonal contour (Luo Kangning 1987: 200–3; changed tone values are not provided in the source):

(39) 猪   >   猪
         tsy^{53} *tsyn*
         'pig'   'piglet'

(40) 食飯   >   食飯
         sek^{22}*-fan*^{11} *seŋ-fan*^{11}
         eat-food   eat.ATT-food
         'to eat'   'eat a little'

Just as for D and Z rhyme change, it is generally believed that these 'tonal morphemes' are the byproduct of a former process of fusion between root and exponent: thus, tone change may be understood as 'the morphologisation of a sandhi pattern in the immediate past' (Yu Alan Ji-Leun 2007: 203).

Lastly, vestigial subsyllabic infixation may still be found in some Jin, Min, Yue, and Hakka dialects. These patterns normally have limited productivity; they are probably what remains of Old Chinese *-r- infixation, which was found in nouns indicating distributed objects and verbs indicating distributed action (see §2.3.1, 5.1.2). For instance, the Yimeng (伊盟 *Yīméng*) Jin dialect of Inner Mongolia makes use of an infix -l-, preceded by a short central vowel (Sagart 2004: 134–5; [ʔ] is hardly ever realized in ordinary speech, hence the brackets):

(41) 擺   >   擺
         pai^{3} *pə(ʔ)lai*^{3}
         'to agitate'   'to swing, oscillate'

(42) 兜   >   兜
         tau^{1} *tə(ʔ)lau*^{1}
         'hood, hanging pouch'   'cluster(s) of fruit hanging
                                          from branches'

The infixes which supposedly derive from OC *-r- have also other functions in modern Sinitic languages: for an overview, see Sagart (2004).

5.2 Foreign words in the Chinese lexicon

The lexicon of modern Sinitic languages is the product of a long and complex process of historical development and stratification, in which contact with other languages had, and still has, a key role. As expected, the oldest layer of the Chinese lexicon contains the core shared Sino-Tibetan vocabulary (see §2.3.1). In the preceding section, we already discussed the general trends in Chinese word formation at different historical stages: besides 'autochtonous' lexemes, loans and calques from other languages have been a very important part of the Chinese lexicon.

Arguably, the oldest loanwords in Chinese came from Austroasiatic and Hmong-Mien languages, spoken in (what we now call) Southern China at least until the Han Dynasty (see §2.2.2, 2.3.1): these include some basic lexical items as e.g. 虎 *hǔ* 'tiger' (OC *qʰˤra; Proto-Austroasiatic *kalaʔ), 舟 *zhōu* 'boat' (OC *tu; Proto-Viet-Muong *doːk), 狗 *gǒu* 'dog' (OC *Cə.kˤroʔ; Proto-Hmong-Mien *klu2 < Proto-Mon *clur; Wiebusch and Tadmor 2009: 578; Schuessler 2007; BSOL). Norman (1988: 16–17) suggests that the Chinese lexicon might have acquired more loanwords before the time of the earliest written records, given the relatively small number of Sino-Tibetan lexemes in the language; however, the identification of those very early loanwords, some of which could come from languages long extinct, is an extraordinarily difficult task (Wiebusch and Tadmor 2009: 595).

Later, following the opening of the Silk Road (during the Han Dynasty), a small number of lexemes from languages of Western and Central Asia entered the Chinese lexicon; they are mostly loanwords which have been adapted to Chinese phonology, indicating plants, animals, and other items typically found in the territories where these languages were spoken: see e.g. 駱駝 *luòtuo* 'camel' (< Xiongnu *dada*), or the already mentioned (§5.1.1) 玻璃 *bōli* 'glass' (< Sanskrit *sphatika*), 葡萄 *pútao* 'grapes' (< Elamite *būdawa). Quite often, the words coming from West and South Asia reached Chinese through the mediation of other languages, as e.g. Uyghur (Wiebusch and Tadmor 2009).

Moreover, a strong impulse to the introduction of foreign words in Chinese came from the translation of Buddhist scriptures, especially from Sanskrit; this enterprise, which began in the first century AD and lasted over a thousand years (Lock and Linebarger 2018: 2), not only had a tremendous impact on Chinese philosophical and religious thought, but also contributed in a significant way to the evolution of the Chinese lexicon. Many terms used in Buddhist texts simply did not have an exact match in Chinese back then, and words had to be either chosen or coined to translate them; large numbers of those are still in use. For instance, Common MSC words as 真理 *zhēnlǐ* 'truth', 智慧 *zhìhuì* 'wisdom', 未來 *wèilái* 'future', or 理論 *lǐlùn* 'theory' were all introduced through their use in Buddhist texts (Yip Po-ching 2000: 329; Wiebusch and Tadmor 2009: 579). In some cases, the original Buddhist terms survived but underwent a shift in meaning, as e.g. 方便 *fāngbiàn* 'convenient', originally a rendering of Sanskrit *upaya* 'expedient means (in teaching)' (Lock and Linebarger 2018: 9). Sometimes, when no suitable Chinese term could be found, the solution was phonetic rendering, as for 菩提薩埵 *pútísàduǒ* 'bodhisattva'; however, again, the aversion of Chinese for very long words often led to their shortening, as MSC 菩薩 *púsà* for 'bodhisattva'.

Later, during the Yuan and Qing dynasties, China was ruled, respectively, by Mongols and by Manchus: this is a time when loanwords from those languages were introduced in the Chinese lexicon. However, very few of them survived until the present day: one such example is 胡同 *hútòng* 'lane, alley' (< Mongolian *khôtagh* 'water well'), a word indicating the characteristic alleys of old Beijing (Bulfoni 2009: 218; Wiebusch and Tadmor 2009: 580).

In the seventeenth century, between the end of the Ming Dynasty and the beginning of the Qing Dynasty, European missionaries and traders became regular visitors to China. Those missionaries were often involved in translations of Western works, and through these translations many words were introduced in the Chinese lexicon (Chen Ping 1999: 101; Bulfoni 2009: 219): for instance, both 幾何 *jǐhé* 'geometry' and 地球 *dìqiú* 'Earth' were introduced by the Italian Jesuit Matteo Ricci (Masini 1993).

5.2.1 The evolution of the lexicon after the Opium Wars

With the exception of the times when Buddhism was being introduced to China, the Chinese people were not particularly interested in foreign cultures. Even the above-mentioned translations of Western works by missionaries did not arouse much interest, except for those which presented historical and geographical information. Things changed dramatically following China's defeat in the First Opium War (1840–2): the sudden realization of the military and technological superiority of foreign powers gave rise to a desire for modernization, which then meant opening up to Western science and ideas. Thus, several works written in European languages were translated into Chinese, and in 1862 the first modern school of foreign languages, the 同文館 *Tóngwénguǎn* of Beijing, was founded in China. The 同文館 *Tóngwénguǎn* and the so-called Jiangnan Arsenal (江南機器製造總局 *Jiāngnán jīqì zhìzào zǒngjú*) in Shanghai gave an important contribution to the 'modernization' of the Chinese lexicon, thanks to their translations: a considerable number of new words were created to translate foreign terms which did not have a direct Chinese equivalent (Masini 1993: 41–5). Following the presentation (and terminology) in Masini (1993: 128), in what follows we illustrate the main strategies for rendering foreign words, which are still in use today.

One of the strategies used to introduce foreign words into the Chinese lexicon is the phonetic loan, as e.g. 沙發 *shāfā* 'sofa', 鴉片 *yāpiàn* 'opium'. Here, the foreign word is divided into syllables, and then the closest match for the syllable is chosen from the Chinese inventory. As to the written form of the loanword, generally characters with a 'neutral' (for lack of a better word) meaning are chosen: for instance, the above-mentioned 沙發 *shāfā* 'sofa' is made of the characters 沙 *shā* 'sand' and 發 *fā* 'to emit'. Characters with negative meanings are generally avoided; sometimes, characters with a meaning related to that of the loanwords are chosen (this is sometimes done also in the translation of brand names in the contemporary language; see Basciano 2017a), as e.g. for the above-mentioned 幾何 *jǐhé* 'geometry', which supposedly renders the sound of *geo* and means 'how much', thus having a (broad) semantic connection with the word (Masini 1993: 139, Fn. 25). On occasion, characters have been created on purpose to render a foreign word, as e.g. 咖 *kā / gā* in 咖啡 *kāfēi* 'coffee' and 咖喱 *gālí* 'curry', which have no meaning of their own: this was obtained by adding the radical 口 *kǒu* 'mouth' to the character 加 *jiā* 'to add' (the phonetic component). The same goes for 啡 *fēi* (compare 非 *fēi* 'no, not') and 喱 *lí* (compare 厘 *lí*, a Chinese unit of measure). Two examples of phonetic loans introduced in the mid-nineteenth century are 得力風 *délìfēng* 'telephone', later substituted by 電話 *diànhuà*, and 巴厘滿 *bālǐmǎn* 'parliament', later substituted by 議會 *yìhuì*.

Another strategy used to translate foreign words is the creation of 'hybrids', i.e. phonetic loans to which a semantic element, indicating the broad category the word belongs to, is added. See, for instance, 漢堡包 *hànbǎo-bāo* 'hamburger-bun, hamburger' or 啤酒 *pí-jiǔ* 'beer-alcohol, beer'. Sometimes, hybrids may be formed by the phonetic rendering of part of the foreign word and by the direct translation of one of its constituents, as e.g. 迷你裙 *mínǐ-qún* 'mini-skirt', 因特網 *yīntè-wǎng* 'internet, internet'. As said before (§5.1.1), sometimes the phonetic part of these hybrid forms may acquire the meaning of the whole word, as a constituent in other compound words.

Graphic loans are words written in regular Chinese characters taken from Japanese usage and read as if they were Chinese. For instance, the Japanese word 政策 *seisaku* 'political measures, policy' was introduced in the mid-nineteenth century into the Chinese lexicon, and has been 'naturalized' with the pronunciation *zhèngcè*. This was the most commonly used strategy to introduce foreign words into Chinese in the second half of the nineteenth century: because of the shared logographic writing system, these words could be readily adopted by Chinese users. This entails that Japanese had a crucial role in the modernization of the Chinese lexicon: many Western notions were first introduced to Japan and then adopted in China. Moreover, besides 'original' graphic loans, i.e. words coined in Japan and introduced to China, there were also 'return' graphic loans, i.e. obsolete Chinese terms which came back in use with a new meaning, again following Japanese usage. For instance, 世界 *shìjiè*, originally a Chinese Buddhist term for 'cosmos, time and space' (< Sanskrit *lokodhatu*), was reintroduced as the word for 'world', following Japanese 世界 *sekai* (Masini 1993: 197). A similar case is 民主 *mínzhǔ* (Jap. *minshu*), originally meaning 'ruler of the people', which acquired the meaning 'democracy', reflecting current Japanese usage.

Contact with Japanese, and the introduction of a large number of graphic loans, also led to the development of word formation patterns involving (pseudo-)affixes. For instance, take the above-mentioned (§5.1.3.2) root 學 *-xué* 'study, branch of learning', which could be (and has sometimes been) analysed as a pseudo-suffix. We may remark that many trisyllabic words with this constituent to the right were imported from Japan to China in the nineteenth century (Masini 1993: 149–51): while 學 *-xué* was already commonly attested in disyllabic words, it is only at this crucial juncture in the history of Chinese that we find it in trisyllabic words as e.g. 動物學 *dòngwù-xué* 'animal-study, zoology' (Jap. *dōbutsugaku*), 地理學 *dìlǐ-xué* 'geography-study, geography'

(Jap. *chirigaku*). A similar case is that of 主義 *zhǔyì* 'doctrine' (Jap. *shugi*), which, following its development in the Japanese lexicon, has turned into a pseudo-suffix in MSC, pretty close to Eng. *-ism*, as in 社會主義 *shèhuì-zhǔyì* 'society-ism, socialism', 資本主義 *zīběn-zhǔyì* 'capital-ism, capitalism'. The diffusion of a large number of those (pseudo-) affixes (mostly, suffixes) was arguably favoured by contact with Japanese, especially in the twentieth century, when even more trisyllabic graphic loans entered the Chinese lexicon: this facilitated the diffusion of (pseudo-)suffixes as 家 *-jiā* and 者 *-zhě*, both (broadly) agentive (Arcodia 2012).

Interestingly, despite the fact that graphic loans are very convenient and easy to accept for speakers of Chinese, there are also some phonetic loans from Japanese in modern Sinitic languages. For instance, in Chinese advertisements you may run across the word 卡哇伊(/依) *kǎwayī*, a rendering of Japanese 可愛い *kawaii* 'cute, lovely', notwithstanding the fact that a direct MSC equivalent exists (i.e. 可愛 *kěài*). In Hong Kong Cantonese, one may also find so-called 'Sino-Japanese' words (Leung Chi Hong 2010: 424): for instance, the Japanese morpheme 激 *geki* 'much, excessive, super', used in Japanese to form words as 激似 *gekini* 'very similar', or 激安 *gekiyasu* 'very cheap', is employed in Cantonese (where it is pronounced *gīk*) as a (pseudo-)prefix in Sino-Japanese words like 激突 *gīkdaht* 'very prominent' or 激新 *gīksān* 'very new' (Leung Chi Hong 2010: 424).

A yet different technique for rendering foreign words in Chinese is the semantic loan, i.e. assigning a new meaning to an existing word. One of the earliest semantic loans of the nineteenth century is 新聞 *xīnwén* (lit. 'new-hear'): this word originally meant 'recently heard facts', but then developed the meaning 'news' (Masini 1993: 143), which is still current in MSC. Sometimes, existing words acquire a new meaning because they are used to render foreign words which sound similar: for instance, the expression 托福 *tuōfú* 'thanks to you' has been used as the translation of the well-known test of English proficiency TOEFL (*Test of English as a Foreign Language*; see Ceccagno and Basciano 2009). Assigning a new meaning to an existing word, or extending its current meaning, is not only a way to render foreign words: it is, more generally, a technique to create neologisms (Ceccagno and Basciano 2009: 149–55). For instance, 老總 *lǎozǒng* was, in origin, a term of address for policemen or soldiers; it was then extended and is now used to address e.g. a boss, a manager, etc.

Foreign words may also be introduced as loan translations, which reproduce both the meaning and the morphological structure of the foreign word. For instance, 鐵路 *tiě-lù* 'iron-road, railway' was introduced in the mid-nineteenth century as a calque (probably) from German *Eisenbahn* (Masini 1993: 200).

Masini (1993: 142–3) notes that semantic loans were quite common in the nineteenth century, but, starting from the beginning of the twentieth century, loan translations seem to become more common than the former. Masini also remarks that assigning new meanings to monosyllabic words (or morphemes) had a crucial role in the development of the Chinese lexicon: those monosyllabic words were productively used, with their new meaning, in loan translations. For instance, the morpheme 電 *diàn*, originally 'flash', acquired the meaning 'electricity', and was used as such to build loan translations and other types of neologisms, as e.g. 電池 *diànchí* 'battery', 電車 *diànchē* 'tram', 電燈 *diàndēng* 'electric lamp'.

Lastly, sometimes foreign words were translated by autochtonous neologisms, i.e. newly coined Chinese words which were not based on a foreign model: for instance, 飛機 *fēi-jī* 'fly-machine, airplane', 聲學 *shēng-xué* 'sound-study, acoustics'.

Generally speaking, semantic loans and loan translations have always been more common than phonetic loans (Masini 1993; Liu Lydia He 1995). However, Kim (2012) highlights that phonetic loans are actually growing in number in MSC. According to Kim, this increased use comes, first and foremost, from the exposure of the Chinese public to new technologies and to foreign brand and company names, which became more common in China starting from the late Seventies. Kim notes that semantic loans and loan translations are not effective for the translation of proper names, and hence phonetic rendering is generally preferred (see also Fetscherin *et al.* 2012). Moreover, English is enjoying ever-growing popularity in the Chinese-speaking world, and hence more and more Chinese acquire some degree of familiarity with English, which makes the acceptance of phonetic loans more likely.

Note, also, that in some cases the rendering of foreign words may not be the same in different Chinese-speaking territories (Bulfoni 2009: 226). For instance, *mouse* (the pointing device) has been translated with the hybrid form 鼠標 *shǔ-biāo* 'mouse-pointer' in the P.R.C., while in Taiwan the form 滑鼠 *huá-shǔ* 'slide-mouse' is generally preferred.

5.3 Recent trends in Chinese word formation

The lexicon of every language is inevitably influenced by historical, cultural, and societal developments: Chinese is no exception to this. For instance, after the establishment of the P.R.C. in 1949, a number of lexical items reflecting the new political situation of China were introduced in the language. Since the USSR was arguably the most important international partner of the P.R.C. in its early years, some of those neologisms are of Russian origin (Wang Fusheng 1998: 148–51; Yip Po-ching 2000: 332 ff.): see, for instance, phonetic loans as 蘇維埃 *súwéi'āi* 'soviet' or 布拉吉 *bùlājí* 'woman's dress' (< Russian *plat'e*), or loan translations as 集體農莊 *jítǐ nóngzhuāng* 'collective farm, kolkhoz' (< Russian *kollektivnoe chozjaistvo*). Other 'political' words which were created in the time between 1949 and the Cultural Revolution (1966–9) include, among others, 右派份子 *yòupài fènzǐ* 'right-wing element', 反革命 *fǎngémìng* 'counter-revolutionary' (arguably a loan translation of French *contre-révolutionnaire*), and 平反 *píngfǎn* 'rehabilitate'.

Following the implementation of the so-called 'one-child policy' in the P.R.C., neologisms as 超生 *chāo-shēng* 'surpass-bear, have more children than allowed' were introduced. Interestingly, 超生 *chāoshēng* was already an existing word, meaning 'to reincarnate' (in Buddhism) and 'be tolerant'. According to Ceccagno and Basciano's analysis (2009: 154), meaning extension was made possible by the polysemy of the constituents of this word: 超 *chāo* means both 'to transcend' and 'to surpass', while 生 *shēng* means both 'to be born' and 'to give birth, to bear'. The Buddhist term 'to reincarnate' is based on the meanings 'transcend' and 'be born' of its constituents, whereas its newly acquired meaning 'have more children than allowed' is based on the meanings 'surpass' and 'bear'.

In the twentieth century and in the early twenty-first century, the need to create a large number of words for new referents, often related to new technologies, arose as well. Among those neologisms we find phonetic loans as 雷達 *léidá* 'radar' and quite many loan translations (and hybrid forms): for instance, 軟件 *ruǎn-jiàn* 'soft-item, software', 下載 *xià-zǎi* 'down-load, download', 在線 *zài-xiàn* 'at/on-line, online', 電子郵件 *diànzǐ-yóujiàn* 'electronic-mail, e-mail' (compare 伊妹兒 *yīmèir* 'e-mail', a phonetic loan; Bulfoni 2009: 223). During the same period, some (pseudo-)affixal items developed too: for instance, 族 *zú* 'clan, tribe', is nowadays productively used to indicate a social group sharing some salient feature(s). See e.g. 低頭族 *dī-tóu-zú* 'low-head-clan, people who are crazy about their smartphone'; 上班族 *shàng-bān-zú* 'go-work-clan, employees', 追星族 *zhuī-xīng-zú* 'chase-star-clan, groupie/fan'. A similar case is that of the root 迷 *mí* 'fan, enthusiast', as used in words like 足球迷 *zúqiú-mí* 'football-fan, football fan', 电影迷 *diànyǐng-mí* 'film-fan, cinema lover' (see Bulfoni 2009; see also the discussion of 客 *-kè* in §5.3.2). Moreover, the growing presence of English led to the acceptance in the Chinese lexicon of acronyms and other words containing letters from the Latin alphabet (Bulfoni 2009: 225–6), as e.g. CD (also known in MSC as 光盤 *guāng-pán*, lit. 'light-dish'), WTO (also 世界貿易組織 *shìjiè màoyì zǔzhī* 'World Trade Organization'), AA制 *zhì* 'go Dutch', ABC孩子 *háizi* '(lit.) ABC child', in which 'ABC' stands for 'American Born Child'.

Another major factor in the evolution of the Chinese lexicon was (and still is) the spread of the internet. As in many other regions, the growth of internet users had a major impact in the Chinese-speaking world; it is sometimes ironically claimed that the typical Chinese greeting 吃飯了嗎? *chīfàn le ma?* 'have you eaten?' is being substituted by 上網了沒有? *shàngwǎng le méiyǒu?* 'have you surfed the net?'. The rapid development of the internet and computer-mediated communication in China has given rise to a new variety of written Chinese, i.e. the so-called 'Chinese Internet Language' ([漢語]網絡語言 [*Hànyǔ*] *wǎngluò yǔyán*; see Wu Chuanfei 2003; Bulfoni 2010; Gao Liwei 2012).

As far as the lexicon is concerned, Gao Liwei (2012: 12–14) mentions three (macro-)categories of internet neologisms: words made of Chinese characters only; words written in *Pinyin*, Latin letters, numbers, or other symbols; words written with a combination of the above. Words made of Chinese characters may in turn be divided into several subcategories (Wu Chuanfei 2003; Yang Chunsheng 2007; Zhang Yunhui 2007; Bulfoni 2010; Gao Liwei 2012):

a. Meaning extensions, as e.g. 貓 *māo* 'cat', which has acquired the meaning 'modem' (arguably also because of the phonetic similarity); 灌水 *guàn-shuǐ* 'pour-water, to pour water', which is used on the internet to mean 'meaningless reply on a forum'; 山寨 *shānzhài* 'mountain stronghold', used to mean 'counterfeit product'. We may also include in this category cases of metaphors and personification (比拟 *bǐnǐ*; Gao Liwei 2012: 13), as e.g. 大蝦 *dàxiā* 'shrimp', which is used online to mean 'expert': the metaphor underlying this is that an expert (on computer matters) is someone who spends a long time bent in front of a monitor, just like a shrimp (Wu Chuangei 2003: 103). In this category we also find words which originally had a positive meaning, used in an opposite negative sense (Bulfoni 2010: 100): for instance, 偶像 *ǒuxiàng* 'idol', used to mean 'disgusting person'. We may also mention those cases in which a word acquires a new meaning in internet usage because of its (near-)homophony with another word, as e.g. 斑竹 *bānzhú* 'mottled bamboo' for 版主 *bǎnzhǔ* 'forum moderator'. Lastly, an existing word may be assigned a new meaning, which derives from the abbreviation of longer expressions, as e.g. 蛋白質 *dàn-bái-zhì* 'egg-white-substance, protein', which is used as short for 笨蛋＋白痴＋神經質 *bèndàn + báichī + shénjīngzhì* 'stupid + idiot + nervousness' (Zhang Yunhui 2007: 533).

b. Compound words, as e.g. 點對點 *diǎn-duì-diǎn* 'point-to-point, peer-to-peer', or 給力 *gěi-lì* 'give-power, great, fantastic'.

c. Analogy, as e.g. 釣蝦 *diào-xiā* 'fish-shrimp, woman chasing men', coined by analogy with 釣魚 *diào-yú* 'fish$_v$-fish$_n$, man chasing women'.

d. Phonetic loans, as the above-mentioned 酷 *kù* 'cool' or 粉絲 *fěnsī* 'fan' (lit. 'bean starch vermicelli').

e. Homophones, i.e. the choice of a (near-)homophonous word to stand for another word: for instance, 美眉 *měi-méi* 'beautiful-eyebrow, pretty girl' is used for 妹妹 *mèimei* 'younger sister'. Note that the word 美眉 *měi-méi* not only is a near-homophone of 妹妹 *mèimei*, but it has also a related meaning, i.e. 'pretty girl'.

f. Fusion forms (音變 *yīnbiàn*), as e.g. 醬紫 *jiàng-zǐ* 'sauce-purple' for 這樣子 *zhè yàngzi* 'this way', or 錶 *biǎo* 'watch' for 不要 *bùyào* 'do not (negative imperative)'.

g. Reduplication of morphemes, as an intentional imitation of child language (Wu Chuanfei 2003: 103), as 漂漂 *piào-piào* 'pretty-pretty' instead of 漂亮 *piàoliang*.

h. Decomposition of one or more characters, i.e. the 'extraction' of parts of characters to form a new disyllabic word: e.g. 走召

zǒu-zhào 'walk-summon, super' (the decomposition of 超 *chāo* 'surpass, super'), or 監介 *jiān-jiè* 'supervise-introduce, awkward' (the decomposition of 尷尬 *gāngà* 'awkward').

Words which are formed only by letters of the Latin alphabet include acronyms based on the *Pinyin* transcription of a word, as e.g. JS 'unscrupulous merchant, profiteer' (< 奸商 *jiānshāng*), GG 'elder brother' (< 哥哥 *gēge*), LG 'husband' (< 老公 *lǎogōng*). Some other acronyms and abbreviations are rather based on English expressions, as e.g. IAE (< in any event), ICQ (< I seek you), THX (< thanks); note that some English words are used in their full form, as *cookies* or *banner*. Beside Latin letters, sequences of numbers may also stand for words or even phrases: the numbers are chosen because of their sound, which has to be similar enough to the words they stand for. For instance, 88 *bā-bā* for 'bye-bye', 668 *liù-liù-bā* for 聊聊吧 *liáo liáo ba* 'let's chat'. Lastly, besides 'ordinary' emoticons, speakers of Chinese also make use of some characters as emoticons: this is the case e.g. for 囧 *jiǒng*, an obsolete character meaning 'window', 'shiny' (Yang Ji 2013), which is nowadays used in Internet Chinese to indicate a sad face (the component 八 *bā* represents the eyes and eyebrows, while 口 *kǒu* represents a mouth).

Lastly, there are 'mixed' words, made of a combination of Latin letters and other symbols or numbers, as e.g. ^B 'to part while crying' ('B' here stands for English *bye*), f2f (< Eng. *face to face*), or b2b (< Eng. *business to business*).

5.3.1 Chinese 'buzzwords' (流行語 liúxíngyǔ)

Among recent trends in the Chinese lexicon, a phenomenon which has attracted much attention is that of the so-called 'buzzwords' or 流行語 *liúxíngyǔ* (lit. 'fashionable words/expressions'). These are words or phrases which become very popular in a given period, but are generally short-lived (see e.g. Xu Zhaohui 2013): 流行語 *liúxíngyǔ* typically last a few years or decades at most, although some of them become entrenched in the lexicon and survive, as the above-mentioned neologism 酷 *kù* 'cool'. 流行語 *liúxíngyǔ* may be single words, as e.g. 裸婚 *luǒ-hūn* 'naked-marriage', indicating a marriage without material basis (i.e. no house, no car, no honeymoon), or 剩女 *shèng-nǚ* 'left.over-woman', indicating a woman with a career who has remained single; a 流行語 *liúxíngyǔ* may also be a phrase, or even a whole sentence.

These fashionable expressions may be connected to specific events, or may become popular thanks to their use in mass and social media. Many 流行語 *liúxíngyǔ* actually achieved popularity because of their extensive use on the web (see §5.3; see also Yu and Chen 2013), as e.g. 雷人 *léi-rén* 'thunder-person, shocking, horrible', or 土豪 *tǔháo*, originally indicating a local tyrant, which developed the meaning 'rich person who loves to show off her/his own wealth', typically used in reference to Chinese *nouveaux riches*. Other similar examples inclued the 流行語 *liúxíngyǔ* 你太有才了 *nǐ tài yǒu cái le* 'you really have got talent', antiphrastically used to indicate the opposite meaning, which originates from a comedy sketch by Zhao Benshan and Song Dandan for a 2007 Chinese New Year show. One of the 流行語 *liúxíngyǔ* of 2008, 打醬油 *dǎ jiàngyóu* 'buy soy sauce', originates from a news story: a Chinese citizen interviewed by a journalist on his opinion concerning the sex scandal in which Hong Kong singer-actor Edison Chen was involved, replied just 我出来打醬油的 *wǒ chūlái dǎ jiàngyóu de* 'I went out just to buy soy sauce', in order to dodge the question. Following this incident, the phrase 打醬油 *dǎ jiàngyóu* was used on the net to express one's lack of interest or knowledge on an issue, or to express unwillingness to make public one's opinion on sensitive topics.

Interestingly, some 流行語 *liúxíngyǔ* give rise to a whole family of constructions by analogy. This is the case, for instance, of an expression which became incredibly popular thanks to its diffusion on the Chinese web, i.e. 賈君鵬, 你媽媽喊你回家吃飯 *Jiǎ Jūnpéng, nǐ māma hǎn nǐ huíjiā chīfàn* 'Jia Junpeng, your mother wants you to get back home to eat': this is the title of a post which appeared in 2009 in a forum for the online role-playing game *World of Warcraft*. This apparently meaningless post was seen by an incredible number of users, and many replied by using 'Jia Junpeng's mother', or 'Jia Junpeng's grandfather', etc., as a nickname. This expression gained instant popularity, and was a model to create similar expressions by analogy, as e.g. 台灣, 祖國 喊你回家吃飯 *Táiwān, zǔguó hǎn nǐ huíjiā chīfàn* 'Taiwan, the Motherland wants you to get back home to eat', or 易中天, 老師喊你回 學校聽課 *Yì Zhōngtiān, lǎoshī hǎn nǐ huí xuéxiào tīngkè* 'Yi Zhongtian, your teacher wants you to get back to school to attend classes'.

This expression was even used as a model for advertising slogans, as e.g. 賈君鵬, 你媽媽叫你把榮威５５０开回家 *Jiǎ Jūnpéng, nǐ māma jiào nǐ bǎ Róngwēi 550 kāi huíjiā* 'Jia Junpeng, your mother wants you to drive back home a Rongwei 550', a slogan used by a car retailer.[10] Similarly, in 2013, a commercial of the cosmetics retailer 聚美優品 *Jùměi yōupǐn* became wildly popular among young netizens, especially for its closing sentence, spoken by the company ADO Chen Ou: 我是陳歐, 我為自己代言 *wǒ shì Chén Oū, wǒ wèi zìjǐ dàiyán* 'I am Chen Ou, I am my own spokesperson'. This led to the creation of many other sentences by analogy in which the name of Chen Ou could be substituted by any name: it became a way to express young people's desire for independence.

5.3.2 A case study: Chinese 客 -kè neologisms

As mentioned before (§5.3), in recent years, some lexical morphemes seemingly developed into (pseudo-)affixal elements, with a shift of their original meaning, through their use in a relatively high number of neologisms. An interesting case is that of the morpheme 客 *kè* 'guest' which, as the righthand constituent in complex words, has developed a meaning close to 'a person doing a certain activity', or 'a person with certain characteristics'. The following presentation is based on Arcodia and Basciano (2018), with some modifications.

客 *kè* is a bound root whose core meaning in MSC is 'guest'; other meanings of 客 *kè* include 'passenger', 'traveller', 'client', and 'person who goes from place to place in pursuit of something'. In Classical Chinese, 客 *kè* was also used to indicate 'person specializing in a certain activity', and we find it with this meaning in complex words at least since the first century AD: see e.g. 俠客 *xiá-kè* 'chivalrous-guest, knight errant', 劍客 *jiàn-kè* 'sword-guest, swordsman'. Later examples seem to have a more bleached meaning, generally indicating a person with certain characteristics: 瘦客 *shòu-kè* 'thin-guest, emaciated', 醉客 *zuì-kè* 'drunk-guest, drunkard', 說客 *shuō-kè* 'speak-guest, persuasive talker'. It could be argued that the pseudo-affixal use of the morpheme 客 *kè* is the result of the generalization of this meaning; however, in its current usage, (pseudo-)affixal 客 *-kè* has some differences in terms of semantic nuances and stylistic connotations, as we shall see.

---

[10] <http://media.people.com.cn/GB/22114/52789/177638/10783724.html> (last access: 21 June 2018).

How did (pseudo-)affixal 客 -*kè* develop in MSC, then? Probably the most popular 客 -*kè* word to appear in recent times is 黑客 *hēi-kè* 'black-guest, hacker', which entered the Chinese lexicon in the late '90s as a phonetic-semantic adaptation of English *hacker*: the word approximately recalls the pronunciation of the source word and, at the same time, the modifier 黑 *hēi* 'black, shady, illegal' conveys the negative meaning of the term (compare 黑車 *hēi-chē* 'black-vehicle, unlicensed taxi'). It is thus, in a sense, a hybrid form, although here all the characters function both as semantic and as phonetic elements. Starting from the beginning of the twenty-first century, under the influence of foreign languages and Netspeak, many more words containing this morpheme have been coined. The 新世纪新词语大詞典 *Xīn Shìjì Xīncíyǔ Dà Cídiǎn* 'New Century Comprehensive Dictionary of Neologisms' (Kang and Liu 2015, henceforth: *Xinciyu*), which collects neologisms coined in the period 2000–15, lists twenty-four new words formed with 客 *kè* as the righthand constituent, indicating specific types of persons; in the *Buzzwords* section of the *Shanghai Daily* (henceforth: SD)[11] we found thirty words of this type. In total we singled out forty-seven neologisms.[12] Along with words indicating different kinds of 'hackers' (43), we found neologisms indicating persons engaged in different kinds of activities (44):

(43)   a. 白客
          bái-kè
          white-guest
          'online security guard; hacker-fighter'

       b. 紅客
          hóng-kè
          red-guest
          'patriotic hacker, defending the security of domestic networks and fending off attacks'

       c. 灰客
          huī-kè
          grey-guest
          'unskilled hacker'

[11] <http://buzzword.shanghaidaily.com> (last access: 6 February 2017).
[12] We excluded words in which 客 *kè* bears the meaning 'guest' or 'client', as e.g. 顧客 *gùkè* 'customer', and compounds in which the righthand constituents is a 客 *kè* word, as 心理 黑客 *xīnlǐ-hēikè* 'psychology-hacker, a person who helps others solve psychological issues'.

(44)   a. 換客

huàn-kè

exchange-guest

'one who sells/exchanges goods online'

   b. 切客

qiē-kè

cut-guest

'fan of location-based services who regularly checks in to keep friends and relatives posted on her/his whereabouts' (cf. Eng. *check in*)

   c. 粉飛客

fěn-fēi-kè

fan[13]-fly-guest

'fanfictioner, fan who likes to write sequels or change plots of TV series to express her/his ideas, passions, etc.' (cf. Eng. *fanfic*)

Of the forty-seven words analysed, twenty-seven belong to the domains of technology and the web; this means that the internet has had an important role in the development of this word-formation pattern. According to Zhang and Xu (2008), this word-formation pattern is typical of Netspeak and was then extended to the media in general and to everyday language too (mainly used by young people). Some of these 客 -kè words are phonetic adaptations from English, as in the case of 'hacker', or 極客 jí-kè 'extremely-guest, geek';[14] nevertheless, for most of them the derivational meaning of the morpheme 客 kè emerges clearly. Take, for instance, 切客 qiē-kè (44b): it is a (partial) phonetic adaptation of English *check-in*, but the Chinese word indicates a 'person', and this meaning is borne by the morpheme 客 kè. The same can be said of 粉飛客 fěn-fēi-kè (44c), which, as already mentioned, is a phonetic adaptation of *fanfic*; 客 kè, besides rendering the pronunciation of the last part of the word, contributes the meaning of 'person' (compare *fanfictioner*). Sometimes, we find calques or hybrid forms to render English words, as e.g. in the case of 創客 chuàng-kè 'create-guest,

---

[13] 粉 fěn (literally, 'powder') here stands for 粉絲 fěnsī, the above-mentioned phonetic adaptation of Eng. *fan*.

[14] The Chinese term refers to a person who does not dress fashionably but is addicted to and good at computers.

maker':[15] 創 *chuàng* translates *make*, while 客 *kè* is the equivalent of the suffix *-er*, recalling the pronunciation of the last part of the word *maker* as well. A similar example is 追客 *zhuī-kè* 'follow-guest', which refers to those who regularly refresh web pages to follow the latest updates of online series, TV series, bloggers, or podcasts: this seems to be a calque from Eng. *follower.*

Neologisms with 客 *-kè* are not limited to loans and words connected to the internet and new technologies. Among new coinages we find 'persons' involved in all sorts of different activities or having certain characteristics, as e.g.:

(45)   a. 必剩客
       bì-shèng-kè
       certainly-remain-guest
       'person above the typical marriage age but still single; considered to be doomed to remain unmarried'

     b. 代掃客
       dài-sǎo-kè
       take.the.place.of-sweep-guest
       'those who offer a service consisting in visiting tombs (sweeping and offering sacrifices) during the Qingming festival (or Tomb-Sweeping Day)'

     c. 排客
       pái-kè
       line.up-guest
       'people paid to stand in a queue for others'

Thus, the morpheme 客 *kè* (to the right of the word) has apparently acquired a more general meaning, appearing in a fixed position, becoming an affixoid in a family of words indicating various kinds of persons, with a function comparable to that of English *-er*. However, this should not apply to the various 'hackers' mentioned here (43): they are best analysed, in our opinion, as analogical formations (see Booij 2010) from 黑客 *hēi-kè*, in which the modifier is invariably a colour term. A feature of this family of words, which is also acquired by analogy, is that the colour term is always understood in a metaphorical rather than literal

---

[15] It refers to the so-called *maker culture*, a technology-based extension of the DIY (do-it-yourself) culture.

sense. Also, neologisms where the whole 客 -kè word is a phonetic adaptation of an English word not indicating a person (see Exx. 44b-c) pose some problems, as they do not fit well in the generic definition provided here: in this case, the whole word is a phonetic adaptation, like *check-in* in (44b), but it indicates a person involved in an activity connected to the semantic of the phonetic adaptation as a whole (X-kè); thus, the role of 客 -kè is not only phonetic, as it contributes the meaning of 'person' too. Hence, we believe that they may be understood as special cases of the 客 -kè construction.

As said earlier, the basic meaning of 客 kè is 'guest, visitor', and this meaning is commonly found in compound words, as e.g. 旅客 lǚ-kè 'travel-guest, hotel guest/traveller', 船客 chuán-kè 'ship-guest, passenger of a ship', 請客 qǐng-kè 'invite-guest, invite/entertain guests'. However, it has been used for at least two millennia as the rightmost constituent in complex words indicating, at first, a 'person specializing in a certain activity', and later just a person with certain characteristics or involved in some activity. It appears that the influence of English and Netspeak gave an impulse to the development of an already existing pattern, rather than leading to the creation of a new one.

5.4 On lexical differences among Sinitic languages

Besides the phonology, the most obvious differences among Sinitic languages may be found in the lexicon. An extensive discussion of lexical differences within Sinitic would require more space than we may reasonably allot here: hence, we shall just provide an overview of the range of variation for representative items of basic vocabulary, taken from the Swadesh-100 list,[16] presented in Table 5.2. The different forms for each item come from the *Linguistic Atlas of Chinese Dialects* (Cao *et al.* 2008); for the sake of simplicity, we include only the MSC pronunciation of each lexeme(/etymon).

---

[16] The version of the Swadesh-100 list we used was retrieved from <http://www.web. pdx.edu/~connjc/Swadesh.doc> (last access: 22 June 2018). Note that 'he' is not part of this list; however, we decided to include this lexeme because it is quite important in the areal classification of Chinese dialects. Note, also, that the third person singular pronoun ('he/she/it/him/her') is included in the Leipzig-Jakarta list of basic vocabulary (Tadmor 2009).

Table 5.2 Examples of variation in the basic vocabulary of Sinitic languages

Meaning	MSC	Examples of dialect forms (and provinces where they are found)
'I'	我 wǒ	俺 ǎn (Hebei, Shandong, Henan, Anhui) 咱 zá (Liaoning)
'thou'	你 nǐ	尔 ěr (Anhui, Jiangxi, Hubei, Hunan, Zhejiang) 汝 rǔ (Fujian, Taiwan, Guangdong, Hainan) 您 nín (Shandong, Henan)
'he'	他 tā	渠 / 佢 qú (Jiangxi, Guangdong, Zhejiang, Fujian, Guangxi, Taiwan) 伊 yī (Fujian, Hainan, Guangdong,Taiwan)
'walk'	走 zǒu	行 xíng (Fujian, Guangdong, Guangxi, Hunan, Jiangxi, Hainan, Taiwan) 跑 pǎo (Jiangsu, the Shanghai area, Zhejiang)
'eat'	吃 chī	食 shí (Fujian, Guangdong, Hainan, Taiwan) 喫 chī (Guangxi, Guangdong, Hunan, Jiangxi, Anhui, Hubei)
'drink'	喝 hē	飲 yǐn (Guangdong, Guangxi) 食 shí (Fujian, Jiangxi, Guangdong) 喫 chī (Hunan, Jiangxi, Zhejiang, the Shanghai area, Jiangsu) 吃 chī (Yunnan, Guizhou) 林 / 啉 lín (Taiwan)
'say'	說 shuō	講 jiǎng (Zhejiang, Fujian, Guangdong, Guangxi, Hainan, Taiwan, Hunan, Anhui, Jiangsu, Chongqing) 話 huà (Fujian, Hunan)
'small'	小 xiǎo	細 xì (Guangdong, Guangxi, Fujian, Hunan, Zhejiang, Jiangxi) 嫩 nèn (Fujian) 瑣 suǒ (Zhejiang) 泥 ní (Guangxi) 娘 niáng (Anhui)
'black'	黑 hēi	烏 wū (Fujian, Hainan, Taiwan, Guangdong, Jiangxi)
'person'	人 rén	農 / 儂 nóng (Zhejiang, Fujian, Hainan, Taiwan, Guangdong)

Firstly, we may remark that the first person pronoun 我 *wǒ* is found virtually everywhere in China, apart from some localities in Shandong, Anhui, and Hebei. Other forms include 俺 *ǎn*, found mainly in southern Hebei, Shandong, western Henan, and in some areas of northwestern Anhui (sometimes as an alternative to 我 *wǒ*), and 咱 *zá*, attested in some localities of Lianoning (again, sometimes just as an alternative to 我 *wǒ*). Note that 我 *wǒ* is one of the items which is used as a diagnostic for 'Sino-Tibetanhood', as said earlier (§2.3).

The lexeme 你 *nǐ* for the second person pronoun is also found everywhere in China. Besides, one finds also 尔 *ěr*, particularly in southern Anhui, northern Jiangxi, eastern Hubei (mostly at the border with Anhui and Jiangxi), and in parts of Hunan and Zhejiang. 尔 *ěr* is also attested in scattered localities of Jiangsu, Fujian, Guangdong, and Guangxi. Another second person pronoun is 汝 rǔ, attested mostly in coastal Fujian, in Taiwan, in some coastal areas of Guangdong and in Hainan. The form 您 nín, on the other hand, is found mostly in Shandong and Henan, but also in some scattered areas of Hebei, Jiangsu, Anhui, Hunan, and Jiangxi.

The MSC third person pronoun 他 tā, as said earlier (§2.3.2), is taken by Norman (2003) as a defining feature of Northern Sinitic: it is in fact found in all of the country, except for Zhejiang, Fujian, Guangdong, Jiangxi, Hainan, and Taiwan. In Jiangxi, Guangdong, Zhejiang, Fujian, Guangxi, and northwestern Taiwan we find the pronoun 渠 / 佢 qú (e.g. Cantonese 佢 kéuih). The form 伊 yī is instead found in coastal Fujian, Hainan, in some coastal areas of Guangdong, and in Taiwan (Taiwanese 伊 i).

The verb 走 zǒu 'to walk' is not attested in the dialects of Fujian, Guangdong, Hainan, and Taiwan, while it is found only in some localities of Guangxi. The form 行 xíng is instead found in those regions, as well as in Hunan, Jiangxi, and in some scattered areas of Zhejiang and Anhui. In some localities of southeastern Jiangsu, the Shanghai area, and northern Zhejiang, the form 跑 pǎo is used.

The verb 吃 chī 'to eat', similarly to 走 zǒu 'to walk', is not found in the dialects of Fujian, Guangdong, Jiangxi, Hunan, Hainan, and Taiwan, and is attested only in some areas of Guangxi, Zhejiang, Hubei, Anhui, and Jiangsu. In Fujian, as well as in most of Guangdong, Hainan, Taiwan, in some areas of Zhejiang, Jiangxi, and Guangxi, the form 食 shí (§5.1.1) is used. The form 喫 chī is found in Guangxi, in some localities of western Guangdong, in Hunan, Jiangxi, Anhui, Hubei, and in scattered areas of Guizhou.

The 'northern' form 喝 hē for the verb 'to drink' is generally not found in Fujian, Guangdong, Hainan, Taiwan, and the Shanghai area; it is only marginally attested in Zhejiang, Guangxi, Jiangxi, Hunan, and Guizhou. In Guangdong and part of Guangxi the (more conservative) form 飲 yǐn (see §5.1.1) is rather used; 食 shí may be found in Fujian, southern Jiangxi, eastern Guangdong, and in some scattered localities in Guangxi, Taiwan, Hainan, and Zhejiang. The form 喫 chī is attested in Hunan, Jiangxi, Zhejiang, in the Shanghai area, in the Southern part of Jiangsu, and in some localities in Anhui, Guangxi, Guizhou, and Hainan. The form 吃 chī (same etymon as MSC 吃 chī 'to eat') is scattered here and there in Yunnan and Guizhou; it is less frequently found in Guangxi,

Anhui, and Zhejiang. Thus, there are Chinese dialects, e.g. in Fujian, in which 'eat' and 'drink' may be expressed by the same lexical item. An entirely unrelated verb for 'to drink' is Taiwanese 啉 *lim*, marginally attested also in Fujian and Guangdong.

The verb 說 *shuō* 'to say, speak' is not generally attested in Zhejiang (except for Hangzhou, whose dialect has been argued to belong to the Mandarin group; see §2.2.2, 2.3.2), Guangdong, Guangxi, Hunan, and Jiangxi. The most common form for 'say' in Central and Southern China is 講 *jiǎng*, found in Zhejiang, coastal Fujian, Guangxi, Hainan, Taiwan, Hunan, Anhui, Jiangsu, and in Chongqing; it is also attested in some localities of Jiangxi, Sichuan, and Yunnan. The form 話 *huà* is instead found in inland Fujian, in some localities of Hunan, and in a few more scattered areas.

The adjective 小 *xiǎo* for 'small' is again generally not in use in Guangdong, Taiwan, and Hainan, and it is only marginally attested in Guangxi, Jiangxi, and Fujian. The form 細 *xì* is used instead in Guangdong, part of Guangxi, Fujian, Hunan, and Zhejiang; 細 *xì* is quite common also in Jiangxi, and it is occasionally found in Hainan, southern Jiangsu, southern Hubei, and Anhui. 'Small' is actually a vocabulary item for which there are several competing forms throughout Sinitic: besides 小 *xiǎo* and 細 *xì*, we have 嫩 *nèn*, in northeastern coastal Fujian; 瑣 *suǒ*, in southeastern coastal Zhejiang; 泥 *ní*, mainly in some areas of Guangxi; and 娘 *niáng*, attested in some localities of Anhui.

The form 黑 *hēi* for 'black' is never found in Taiwan, and it is only marginally attested in Fujian and Hainan (i.e. the two other main Min-speaking province); here, the alternative form 烏 *wū* is used (e.g. Taiwanese 烏 *oo*), which is also occasionally found in Guangdong, Guangxi, Jiangxi, and Zhejiang.

Lastly, while the etymon 人 *rén* for 'person' is overwhelmingly dominant throughout China, we also find the form 農 / 儂 *nóng*, used in most of Zhejiang, in coastal Fujian, Hainan, Taiwan, and in some coastal areas of Guangdong.

Generally speaking, we may note that, often, Southern Sinitic languages prefer more 'archaic' etyma, in line with their conservative trends, while northern dialects often prefer more innovative forms: for instance, as mentioned before, in Southern dialects 食 *shí* and 飲 *yǐn* seem to be preferred to 吃 *chī* and 喝 *hē* for 'to eat' and 'to drink', respectively.

This, however, is to be taken as a (strong) tendency, rather than a firm rule: for instance, the form 啉 *lín* for 'to drink' dates back to the Tang period (Schuessler 2007: 343), and 儂 *nóng* for 'person' (< 農 *nóng* 'peasant'; Schuessler 2007: 403)[17] seems to be a lexical innovation of Southeastern coastal dialects. Note, also, that this is not the only case in which Southeastern coastal dialects (particularly, Min) pattern differently from other Southern dialects: we pointed out that third person pronoun forms cognate to 伊 *yī* (< 'this'), second person forms related to 汝 *rǔ*, and the form 烏 *wū* for 'black' are all mostly found in Southeastern coastal dialects. Hence, the differences in the basic lexicon of Chinese dialects are not necessarily always the expression of the North/South divide. Interestingly, for instance, a conservative Southern dialect as Cantonese uses 你 *néih* for the second person pronoun, which is likely a Northwestern Chinese dialect form (Norman 1988: 118; Schuessler 2007: 399).

In short, once again, even by looking at the few examples discussed here, it clearly appears that the lexicon of each and every Sinitic language is the product of a long and articulated process of historical stratification; while some general tendencies may be found, the time depth involved and the rich history of contact among dialects (and, indeed, among Sinitic and other non-Sinitic languages) make the picture extremely complex.

---

[17] Note, however, that an alternative hypothesis sees 儂 *nóng* as an early Tai borrowing (Schuessler 2007: 404).

6

Topics in Chinese syntax

6.1 Word order

The research on syntactic change in Chinese has developed significantly since the 1980s, when new studies on historical syntax began to be published again in China, after a few quiet decades (Peryaube 1996). In this context, the issue of word order change attracted much attention, starting from Li and Thompson's (1974) proposal that Pre-Archaic (i.e. oracle bone) Chinese was a SOV language, which then switched to SVO between the tenth and the third century BC, and is now going back to SOV. This hypothesis was accepted by several scholars (Wang Li 1958; La Polla 1994; Feng Shengli 1996; Xu Dan 2006), but was also strongly criticized by many others: for instance, by specialists who argue that Chinese is a VO language at present, while OV is a marked word order in MSC (see e.g. Light 1979; Sun and Givón 1985; Peyraube 1996; Aldridge 2013a; Djamouri, Paul, and Whitman 2013; Paul 2015). Moreover, there is a body of research showing that Chinese has been a VO language all along, since the earliest attestations (Guan Xiechu 1953; Chen Mengjia 1956; Djamouri 1988).

In what follows, we shall first discuss the evolution of word order in (mainstream) Chinese, focussing on the verb phrase, and on constituent

Chinese Linguistics: An Introduction. Giorgio Francesco Arcodia and Bianca Basciano, Oxford University Press.
© Giorgio Arcodia and Bianca Basciano 2021. DOI: 10.1093/oso/9780198847830.003.0006

orders which correlate with VO and OV (§6.1.1, 6.1.2); we shall then provide some remarks on word order in Chinese dialects (§6.1.3). We defer the discussion of the role of the subject in shaping word order to §6.2, since the notion of 'subject' is very controversial for Chinese (see also §6.2.1).

6.1.1 Word order in Old Chinese

As highlighted by Paul (2015), Li and Thompson's (1974) hypothesis on the SOV nature of Old Chinese briefly introduced in the preceding section is fundamentally flawed, as Li and Thompson apparently do not take into consideration the corpus of oracle bone inscriptions (§2.2.1). In Djamouri's (1988) analysis of the corpus of Shang dynasty oracle bone texts, we read that only about 6% of the 26,000 sentences considered has SOV order. Besides, this order is attested only in two constructions: namely, when the object is focussed and in negative sentences, when the object is a personal pronoun. (1) is an example of the object focus construction (Paul 2015: 17; glosses adapted):

(1)　王勿唯望乘比。
　　　wáng　wù　　　wéi　Wàng　Chéng　bǐ
　　　king　NEG.IMP　COP　Wang　Cheng　follow
　　　'It must not be Wang Cheng that the king will follow.'

Djamouri (1988, 2004) believes that all the occurrences of an argument noun phrase or prepositional phrase in preverbal position are but focus constructions: specifically, cleft sentences (Djamouri, Paul, and Whitman 2013), since the focussed constituent must follow a matrix copula (唯 *wéi* or 惠 *huì*; see also Djamouri 2004), similarly to the MSC 是······的 *shì...de* construction (Paul and Whitman 2008). As pointed out by Aldridge (2013a), this type of focus construction is found also in Archaic Chinese (i.e. starting from the tenth century BC), albeit with two differences: the copula became optional, and the preverbal object must be followed by 之 *zhī* or 是 *shì* (S-O-之 *zhī*/是 *shì*-V), understood either as resumptive pronouns or as markers of embedded nominalization (see Meisterernst 2010; Aldridge 2013a: 48). Thus, to sum up, it is clear that OV is not the canonical word order in Pre-Archaic Chinese, and the OV constructions seen here should not be taken as evidence of an OV stage in the history of the language.

The other structure with OV order in oracle bone inscriptions is shown in (2a), where an object personal pronoun is used in a negative sentence (Aldridge 2013a: 50; glosses adapted):

(2) a. 祖辛不我害？
     zǔ   Xīn   bù   wǒ   hài
     ancestor   Xin   NEG   1PL   harm
     'Does ancestor Xin not harm us?'

    b. 祖辛害我？
     zǔ   Xīn   hài   wǒ
     ancestor   Xin   harm   1PL
     'Does ancestor Xin harm us?'

As shown in (2b), in the affirmative counterpart of (2a) the object is placed after the verb, yielding the (canonical) VO order.

Another case of surface OV order in Old Chinese is that of interrogative constructions as (3), in which the object interrogative pronoun is found before the verb (from the *Discourses of the States*; Meisterernst 2010: 76; glosses adapted):

(3) 吾誰使先?
    wú   shéi   shǐ   xiān
    1SG   who   CAUS   precede
    'Who should I let precede?'

Examples like that in (3) have been used by Li and Thompson as arguments in favour of a SOV analysis for Pre-Archaic Chinese. However, as highlighted by Paul (2015), the example cited in Li and Thompson (1974: 208) comes from Confucius' *Analects*, composed nearly a thousand years later than the oracle bones texts discussed here: the *Discourses of the States* (3) also belong to the Late Archaic period. Aldridge (2010) suggests that sentences as (3) involve *wh*-movement of the pronoun below the subject (rather than above, as in English). Thus, interrogative sentences should not be seen as evidence for an OV analysis for Old Chinese. Moreover, as highlighted in Meisterernst (2010), these structures with surface OV order were frequent in classical texts, but they ceased to be productive in the Han period.

To sum up, the proposed 'exceptions' to VO order in Old Chinese (here, including the Pre-Archaic, Early Archaic, and Late Archaic stages; see §2.2.5) cannot be understood as evidence for a word order change from OV to VO in Chinese: preverbal objects are found only in specific constructions, rather than in simple transitive declarative sentences (see Meisterernst 2010: 77). Indeed, Pre-Archaic Chinese behaved as a rather consistent VO language: all arguments subcategorized for by the verb, including noun phrases and prepositional phrases, were normally placed in the postverbal position. See the following examples (Paul 2015: 9–10; glosses adapted):

(4) a. 王伐 舌方。
      wáng fá   gōng   fāng
      king fight   Gong   tribe
      'The king will fight the Gong tribe.'

     b. 娩唯女。
      miǎn   wéi   nǚ
      childbirth   COP   girl
      'The childbirth is a girl.'

     c. 王往于田。
      wáng   wǎng   yú   tián
      king   go   to   field
      'The King will go to the fields.'

     d. 帝受我年。
      dì   shòu   wǒ   nián
      Di   give   1PL   harvest
      '[The ancestor] Di will give us a harvest.'

Moreover, negators and auxiliaries were placed before the verb, again consistently with the basic VO order (Paul 2015: 10–11; glosses adapted):

(5) a. 雨不唯囝。
      yǔ   bù   wéi   huò
      rain   NEG   COP   misfortune
      '[This] rain is not harmful.'

     b. 王其擁羌。
      wáng   qí   yōng   Qiāng
      king   FUT   use.in.sacrifice   Qiang
      'The king will use in sacrifice [some] Qiang tribesmen.'

Paul (2015: 11) also remarks that non-phrasal adverbs like 亦 yì 'also' and 允 yǔn 'indeed' occur in preverbal position, to the right of the subject:

(6) 屮伐于黃尹亦屮于蔑。

yòu	fá	yú	Huángyǐn	yì	yòu	yú	Miè
offer	victim	to	Huangyin	also	offer	to	Mie

'We will offer victims [as sacrifice] to Huangyin, and also to Mie.'

Paul further adds that these adverbs were located to the left of the extended verbal projection, preceding negators and auxiliaries (see the examples in Paul 2015: 11).

On the other hand, adjuncts (noun or verb phrases) could occur in three different positions: before the subject (7a), between subject and verb (7b), or after the verb (and after the object, if present), as is often the case for VO languages (7c; Paul 2015: 12–13):

(7)   a. 于辛巳王圍召方。

yú	Xīnsì	wáng	wéi	Shào	fāng
at	Xinsi	king	surround	Shao	tribe

'On the Xinsi day, the king will surround the Shao tribe.'

b. 王在十二月在襄卜。

wáng	zài	shí'èr	yuè	zài	xiāng	bǔ
king	at	12	month	at	Xiang	divine

'The king in the twelfth month at the place Xiang made the divination.'

c. 乞令吳以多馬亞省在南。

Qǐ	lǐng	Wú	yǐ	duō	mǎyǎ	xǐng
Qi	order	Wu	lead	numerous	military.officer	inspect

zài	nán
at	south

'Officer Qi will order Wu to lead the numerous military officers to carry out an inspection in the south.'

Note that more than one adjunct was allowed in the preverbal position (7b), while in the postverbal position only one adjunct was allowed: starting from the third century AD (the Early Medieval Chinese stage), no adjuncts may be found after the verb.

6.1.2 Word order in Modern Chinese

As mentioned earlier, the canonical word order in MSC is still VO. Both the direct and the indirect object are placed after the verb, including in copular sentences:

(8)　a.　他看電視。

　　　　tā　　　kàn　　　diànshì
　　　　3SG.M　watch　TV
　　　　'He is watching TV.'

　　b.　張老師教我們語法。

　　　　Zhāng　lǎoshī　jiāo　　wǒ-men　　yǔfǎ
　　　　Zhang　teacher　teach　1-PL　　　grammar
　　　　'Teacher Zhang teaches us grammar'

Moreover, durative and frequency phrases also occur after the verb:

(9)　a.　我等了一個小時。

　　　　wǒ　　děng-le　　yī　　ge　　xiǎoshí
　　　　1SG　wait-PFV　one　CLF　hour
　　　　'I waited for an hour.'

　　b.　我已經去了三次了。

　　　　wǒ　　yǐjīng　　qù-le　　sān　　cì　　le
　　　　1SG　already　go-PFV　three　time　CRS
　　　　'I have already been [there] three times.'

Sometimes, the object appears in the preverbal position, introduced by 把 *bǎ* (Li Audrey Yen-hui 2006: 377):

(10)　a.　我忘了鑰匙了。

　　　　wǒ　　wàng-le　　yàoshi　　le
　　　　1SG　forget-PFV　key　　　CRS

　　b.　我把鑰匙忘了。

　　　　wǒ　　bǎ　　yàoshi　　wàng-le
　　　　1SG　OBJ　key　　　forget-PFV
　　　　'I forgot the keys.'

The pair of sentences in (10) differ only for the position of the object: in (10a) we have a canonical VO sequence, while in (10b) we have a construction in which the object is found in the preverbal position, preceded by 把 *bǎ*. The 把 *bǎ* construction (known in Chinese as 把字句 *bǎ zì jù*) has been the focus of much research in the field of Chinese syntax: nevertheless, many aspects of this construction are not yet fully understood. This topic is extremely complex, and the number of studies on the 把 *bǎ* construction is too large for a review: the reader is referred to Li Audrey Yen-hui (2006; see also Li Audrey Yen-Hui 2017, and the references cited therein) for a general overview. Here, we shall limit ourselves to a few brief remarks only on issues related to word order.

In the past, many linguists believed that 把 *bǎ* is a preposition (see e.g. Mei Kuang 1980; Huang C-T. James 1982; Peyraube 1985, 1996; Li Audrey Yen-hui 1990). However, there are several arguments against a prepositional analysis for this item (see Paul 2015: 29–38), and, actually, many specialists in Chinese syntax now believe that 把 *bǎ* is a functional head, taking a verbal projection as its complement (see e.g. Sybesma 1992, 1999; Zou Ke 1993; Whitman and Paul 2005; Li Audrey Yen-hui 2006; Paul 2015). Paul (2015) remarks that the complement selected by 把 *bǎ* is located to its right, thus implying a head-complement order consistent with VO: if her analysis were correct, the 把 *bǎ* construction would not constitute an exception to the basic VO order.

Moreover, just as seen earlier (§6.1.1) for Old Chinese, negators and auxiliaries are placed before the verb (11a-b) in MSC. The language mostly makes use of prepositions (11c), rather than postpositions, again consistently with the basic VO order (see Dryer 1992):

(11)   a. 我想喝茶 。
      wǒ   xiǎng   hē   chá
      1SG   want   drink   tea
      'I want to drink tea.'

   b. 我不去 。
      wǒ   bù   qù
      1SG   NEG   go
      'I won't go.'

   c. 她在圖書館看報紙 。
      tā   zài   túshūguǎn   kàn   bàozhǐ
      3SG.F   at   library   read   magazine
      'She's reading magazines at the library.'

However, Dryer (2003) highlights that Modern Chinese also has many features which are often associated with OV languages. Firstly, while prepositions are more common, the language makes use of postpositions too, which are typical of OV languages (see Dryer 2013a):

(12)   a. 他（從）明天起上班 。   (Dryer 2003: 48; glosses adapted)
      tā   (cóng)   míngtiān   qǐ   shàng-bān
      3SG.M   from   tomorrow   on   go-work
      'He will go to work from tomorrow on.'

b. 我除夕以前要回家。　　　　(Paul 2015: 306)

wǒ	*Chúxī*	*yǐqián*	*yào*	*huí*	*jiā*
1SG	New.Year's.eve	before	need	return	home

'I need to go home before New Year's Eve.'

Moreover, prepositional phrases tend to follow the verb in VO languages, while in MSC they are often preverbal (11c), just as in OV languages. Indeed, a characteristic of MSC word order which is extremely rare for a VO language is the position of adjuncts (obliques), which precede the verb, just as in (11c). In Dryer and Gensler's (2013) 500-language sample, there are only three VO languages with preverbal oblique phrases: these are Mandarin, Hakka, and Cantonese. Thus, this word order correlation might even be a unique Sinitic feature. However, it must be noted that, actually, while adjunct prepositional phrases are always preverbal, argumental prepositional phrases are always postverbal (just as objects), differently from Old Chinese (13; Paul 2015: 306–7, glosses adapted; see also Dryer 2003: 50–1):

(13)　　他寄了一個包裹給美麗。

tā	*jì-le*	*yī*	*ge*	*bāoguǒ*	*gěi*	*Měilí*
3SG.M	send-PFV	one	CLF	parcel	to	Mary

'He sent a parcel to Mary.'[1]

---

[1] An anonymous reviewer pointed out that (13) may be interpreted as a serial verb construction (see §6.3), in which 給 *gěi* is a verb ('I sent a parcel in order to give it to Mary'). Indeed, the surface structure of the sentence does match a serial verb construction and, hence, (13) could be understood as a serial verb construction with a final intepretation (see Chao Yuen Ren 1968; Huang and Ahrens 1999). However, many scholars believe that, when 給 *gěi* occurs after a direct object, it may be analyzed as a preposition (see e.g. Li and Thompson 1981; Li Audrey Yen-hui 1990; Zhang Shi 1990; Her One-soon 1999, 2006; McCawley 1992; Liu Danqing 2001; Ting and Chang 2004; see also §6.6.1.3).

One of the main arguments proposed by Her One-soon (2006) to support a prepositional analysis for 給 *gěi* in sentences as (13) are alternations as the following examples (adapted from Her One-soon 2006: 1277), where the main verb is a dative ditransitive:

(i)　李四借 / 提供她一棟房子。

Lǐsì	*jiè*	/	*tígōng*	*tā*	*yī*	*dòng*	*fángzi*
Lisi	loan		provide	3SG.F	one	CLF	house

'Lisi will loan/provide her a house.'

(ii)　李四借 / 提供一棟房子給她。

Lǐsì	*jiè*	/	*tígōng*	*yī*	*dòng*	*fángzi*	*gěi*	*tā*
Lisi	loan		provide	one	CLF	house	give / to	3SG.F

a. 'Lisi will loan/provide a house to her'
b. 'Lisi will borrow/provide a house$_i$ to give e_i to her'

Thus, given that there are two possible syntactic positions for prepositional phrases, Paul (2015) observes that this is only partly inconsistent with VO order. Moreover, locative prepositional phrases tend to occur before the verb if they describe the place where an event occurs (14a), while they tend to occur after the verb if they indicate the position of a animate or inanimate entity as the result of an event (14b; adapted from Li and Thompson 1981: 22):

(14)   a. 她在桌子上挑。

tā	zài	zhuōzi	shàng	tiào
3SG.F	at	table	on	jump

'She is jumping (up and down) on the table.'

b. 她挑在桌子上。

tā	tiào	zài	zhuōzi	shàng
3SG.F	jump	at	table	on

'She jumped onto the table.'

According to Sybesma (1992), in cases as (14a) we are dealing with adjunct locative phrases, while in cases as (14b) we are dealing with locative resultative complements.

Dryer (2003) further points out that in MSC manner adverbs are most often placed before the verb, which is unusual for a VO language (but attested also outside Sinitic):

(15)   他很快地走了。

tā	hěn	kuài	de	zǒu-le
3SG.M	very	fast	ADV	leave-PFV

'He left in a hurry.'

Also, MSC has a type of comparative construction which is very rarely found in VO languages, namely 'marker of comparison-standard-adjective':

Her One-soon (2006) argues that if 給 *gěi* were a verb only, the sole interpretation available for (ii) would be b.; besides, we would have to admit that the main verbs in (ii), which are normally trivalent (< agent, goal, theme >), are actually bivalent (< agent, theme >). Her One-soon (2006) highlights that the preferred interpretation for (ii) is a., which is semantically equivalent to (i). This suggests that (i) and (ii) have the same argument structure, which is what we expect if we interpret 給 *gěi* as a prepostion, introducing the goal argument. Thus, according to Her One-soon (2006), (i) and (ii) represent a dative alternation, similarly to Eng. *I gave her a book* vs. *I gave a book to her.* Hence, pairs of sentences as 我送他一本書 *wǒ sòng tā yī běn shū* '1SG give 3SG.M one CLF book' and 我送一本書給他 *wǒ sòng yī běn shū gěi tā* '1SG give one CLF book to 3SG.M' both mean 'I gave him a book [as a present]'. For further details and arguments for a prepositional analysis for 給 *gěi*, the reader is referred to Her One-soon (2006).

(16) 我比他高。
      wǒ   bǐ   tā   gāo
      1SG   compared.to   3SG.M   tall
      'I'm taller than him.'

Dryer highlights that MSC and Hakka are the only VO languages in his database that have this order of constituents in the comparative construction, while the typical order would be 'adjective-marker of comparison-standard'. In fact, the latter is the order which we find in many Sinitic languages, as we shall see in §6.1.3. Moreover, while the construction exemplified in (16) is the most common comparative construction in MSC, another option is available (Paul 2015: 306; glosses adapted):

(17) 他高李四十公分。
      tā   gāo Lǐsì shí   gōngfēn
      3SG.M   tall Lisi ten   centimetre
      'He is ten centimetres taller than Lisi.'

In (17), the order of the constituents is 'adjective-standard', which is consistent for a VO language. Actually, in Old Chinese the comparative construction followed the order 'adjective-marker of comparison-standard', as in 象大於犬 *xiàng dà yú quǎn* 'elephant big than dog, the elephant is bigger than the dog' (Zádrapa 2017). This construction may still be found in MSC, but only in formal registers which tend to imitate the classical language.

One typological 'anomaly' of Sinitic languages which has attracted much attention in the literature is the order of relative clause and noun. While in almost all VO languages the relative clause comes after the noun (phrase) it modifies (Eng. *the book that I bought yesterday*), in MSC relative clauses (18a), as well as all modifiers (18b-c), precede the head noun:

(18) a. 媽媽做的蛋糕
         māma   zuò   de   dàngāo
         mum   make   MOD   cake
         'The cake which mum made'

      b. 老師的書
         lǎoshī   de   shū
         teacher   MOD   book
         'The teacher's book'

c. 一個聰明的姑娘

yī	ge	cōngming	de	gūniang
one	CLF	clever	MOD	girl

'A clever girl'

In Dryer's (2013b) 879-language sample, only five VO languages have postnominal relatives: three of those are Sinitic, and the remaining two are minority languages in Chinese-speaking territories, namely the above-mentioned Bai language (§2.3.1) and Amis, an Austronesian language of Taiwan. Just as said before for the position of adverbial modifier phrases, this seems to be a (nearly-)unique Sinitic correlation.

Some more word order patterns of MSC which are actually typical of OV languages are the use of sentence-final interrogative particles (19), and *in situ* interrogative clauses (20), i.e. clauses in which the interrogative phrase does not appear at the beginning of the sentence but is rather found in the same position in which it appears in the corresponding affirmative sentence:

(19) 你是英國人嗎？

nǐ	shì	Yīngguó-rén	ma
2SG	COP	Britain-person	Q

'Are you British?'

(20) a. 他是誰？

tā	shì	shéi
3SG.M	COP	who

'Who's him?'

b. 他是保羅的朋友。

tā	shì	Bǎoluó	de	péngyou
3SG.M	COP	Paul	MOD	friend

'He's a friend of Paul's.'

However, as pointed out by Dryer (2003: 50–1), most of the inconsistencies in word order of MSC seem to follow a principle, rather than being completely random: arguments come after the verb, while adjuncts come before the verb. Djamouri, Paul, and Whitman (2013; see also Paul 2015) even argue that MSC is more consistent than (Pre-) Archaic Chinese in this respect (see the preceding section), as all adjuncts are restricted to the preverbal position and all (quasi-)arguments are found in the postverbal position. In their view, this means that MSC is actually a consistent VO language, since the order of arguments (rather than adjuncts) with respect to the verb should be the relevant parameter for assessing typological consistency (see Djamouri, Paul, and Whitman 2013 for a theoretical account).

6.1.3 Word order in Chinese dialects

As pointed out before, while the focus of traditional Chinese dialectology has mostly been phonological and lexical variation, there is also much variation at the syntactic level among Chinese dialects. First and foremost, as hinted at earlier (§2.3.1), some very significant differences between Northern and Southern Sinitic are claimed to be due to contact with neighbouring languages: specifically, many OV features of northern Chinese dialects (including MSC) have been interpreted as the product of influence from languages of Northern Asia, while in southern Chinese dialects word order tends to be more consistent with the VO type, just as in the languages of Mainland Southeast Asia (see Dryer 2003).

For instance, differently from MSC, in several dialects of southern China (but also in Shandong and Shaanxi; Yue Anne Oi-kan 2003: 11; Chappell and Peyraube 2015: 143) we find comparative constructions following the 'adjective-(marker)-standard' order, consistently with VO order (see the preceding section), as in the following Cantonese example (Matthews and Yip 2011: 189):

(21) 今日熱過琴日。
      gāmyaht   yiht   gwo   kàhmyaht
      today   hot   surpass yesterday
      'Today is hotter than yesterday.'

The Cantonese comparative construction exemplified in (21) belongs to the so-called 'Exceed Comparatives' type, as the marker of comparison is based on a verb meaning 'surpass' (過 *gwo*; Stassen 2013). Interestingly, an analogous construction may be found also in southern varieties of 普通話 *Pŭtōnghuà* (Ansaldo 2010: 932; glosses adapted):

(22) 你說中文好過我。
      nĭ   shuō   Zhōngwén hăo-guo   wŏ
      2SG   speak   Chinese   good-surpass 1SG
      'You speak Chinese better than me.'

These Exceed Comparatives have close structural and semantic parallels in non-Sinitic languages of Southeast Asia as Lao, Thai, or Vietnamese, and it has been suggested that comparative constructions based on a transitive verb meaning 'surpass' should be added to the list of areal features of EMSEA, again including Southern China but not Northern China (Ansaldo 2010: 937–9). Chappell and Peyraube (2015) suggest that the emergence of Exceed Comparatives in (part of) Sinitic is likely to be an internal development, rather than due to contact. This Sinitic pattern might then have spread to other EMSEA languages. Due to reasons of space, we shall not discuss this any further: the reader is referred to Chappell and Peyraube (2015) for the details of their argumentation.

As to the ditransitive construction, while in MSC the order is verb – indirect object – direct object, in some dialects the direct object comes before the indirect object (though not for all ditrantistive verbs). See the following example of the Xinyu (新余 *Xīnyú*) Gan dialect (Yue Anne Oi-kan 2003: 105):

(23) ŋɔ   pa   pən   sɪ   ɲɪ
      1SG   give CLF   book 2SG
      'I give you a book.'

As said earlier (§2.3.1), the two attested orders for the ditransitive construction have a skewed distribution, once again following the north/south divide: while the indirect object – direct object order is virtually universal in Northern China, the opposite order is found in Southern Sinitic and in a number of Southern Mandarin (i.e. Jianghuai and Southwest Mandarin) and central dialects. Interestingly, some dialects of Central and Southern China (e.g. Suzhounese) allow both orders of direct and indirect object, a feature which could once more be argued to be due to language contact, with the 'northern' pattern borrowed from MSC (Yue Anne Oi-kan 2003: 105–6). Note that, as mentioned before (§2.3.1), Peyraube casts doubts on the idea that the 'southern' pattern is a Tai-Kadai or Austroasiatic borrowing in Sinitic, and believes that it may be analysed as an internal development: this is because the 'southern' order is in fact found in many dialects 'far to the north of this southern border area', making borrowing from non-Sinitic languages of Southern China less likely (Peyraube 2015: 72–3). De Sousa (2015: 184–6) further points out that the Tai-Kadai languages found in the present-day Yue-speaking regions of Southern China do not consistently follow the direct object – indirect object order: some follow the 'northern' pattern, some follow the 'southern' pattern, while yet some others allow both orders. Thus, in agreement with Peyraube, De Sousa argues that the direct object – indirect object order for the ditransitive construction in Sinitic is not necessarily the product of Tai-Kadai influence, but, rather, is likely to be an internal development.

Lastly, while prenominal relative clauses are almost universal in Sinitic, isolated exceptions are apparently attested in Southern China. See the following examples of Hui'an (惠安) Southern Min (24; Chen Weirong 2008: 573; glosses adapted) and of Kaiping (開平) Yue (Yue Anne Oi-kan 1995: 292; no transcription provided in the source):

(24) *lu3* *e0* *hit7–8* *kɔ1* *thak8–4* *tiɔŋ1-bun2* *e0*
girl NOM that CLF study China-language REL
'That girl who studies Chinese.'

(25) *neiŋ²¹* 个 细民 仔著 红 衫 个 系 我
that CLF child wear red shirt NOM COP 1SG
个 妹
POSS younger.sister
'That child who wears a red shirt is my little sister.'

The fact that postnominal relative clauses, consistent with VO order, are found in Southern China, has also been interpreted as a possible case of influence from non-Sinitic languages of the area, which mostly have head-initial relatives (Arcodia 2017: 61–2). Note, however, that while prenominal relative clauses are clearly the default option for MSC and virtually all Sinitic languages, postnominal relative clauses do occur in both written and spoken MSC, although they are much less frequent and are obviously non-canonical (Wang and Wu 2020; ex. from Dong Xiufang 2003: 121).

(26) 司法工作人员私放罪犯的 [...]
sīfǎ *gōngzuò-rényuán* *sī-fàng* *zuìfàn* *de*
judicature working-personnel illicit-release criminal REL
'judiciary staff members who illicitly release a criminal [...]'

The MSC constructions we refer to here are anyway somewhat different from the Hui'an and Kaiping examples seen before, in that the former do not require a nominalizer after the head noun: Arcodia (2017;

see also Liu Danqing 2008) suggests that the noun-relative clause order in Mandarin might be the byproduct of topicalization of the head noun, motivated by the need to avoid the parsing burden of having heavy modifiers (as relative clauses) before the head.

Thus, the cases of variation in word order within Sinitic discussed in this section have all somehow been associated—rightly or wrongly—with the north-south divide proposed by Hashimoto (1976, 1986). However, the area of China where we find the most divergent typological features for a Sinitic language is undoubtedly the above-mentioned (§2.3.1) Qinghai-Gansu (or Amdo) *Sprachbund*. In this language area, where Sinitic, Tibetic, Mongolic, and Turkic languages developed in close contact, some Chinese dialects switched to a basic OV order and adopted other features typical of OV languages (see Slater 2003; Janhunen 2007, 2012; Xu Dan 2017). For instance, differently from the overwhelming majority of Sinitic languages, in the Gangou (甘溝 *Gāngōu*) Mandarin dialect the object comes before the verb in a basic transitive predicate (27; Zhu *et al.* 1997: 440; glosses adapted):

(27) *Wo   nai-cha   huo-liao*
      1SG   milk-tea   drink-PFV
      'I drank milk tea.'

Another typical OV feature which we find in the Sinitic languages of the Qinghai-Gansu area is the use of postpositions to mark case. See the following Linxia (临夏 *Línxià*) Mandarin example (Dwyer 1992: 6; glosses adapted):

(28) *ɲo⁴⁴   tɕia¹³   liaŋkə⁴⁴⁻¹³   pfu²⁴   tsɿ⁵³*
      1SG   3SG   COM   NEG   go
      'I won't go with him.'

In (28), we see the use of the postposition *liaŋkə⁴⁴⁻¹³*, obviously deriving from the numeral 兩 *liǎng* 'two' and the generic classifier 個 *ge*. Dwyer (1992) suggests that *liaŋkə⁴⁴⁻¹³* is a calque of the compound numeral 'two together' found in Mongolic languages of the area (e.g. Baonan *qalə*). While postpositions are rare in VO languages (Dryer 2013a), they are perfectly consistent with the OV typology which has become common to this *Sprachbund*. A very notable variety in the Qinghai-Gansu area is Wutun (五屯話 *Wǔtúnhuà*, lit. 'language of the five villages'), which we might define as a Mandarin-Tibetan-Mongolic mixed language (but cf. Janhunen *et al.* 2008 and Sandman 2016 for a critique of this characterization for Wutun).

The last aspect of word order variation within Sinitic we shall discuss here concerns resultative constructions. In some dialects, resultative constructions have a different order of constituents form MSC. For instance, according to Lien Chinfa (1994), in Taiwanese the object is most often located before the verb in a resultative construction: indeed, in some cases placing the object after the resultative construction results in ungrammaticality. For instance, in 茶斟滇 *tê thîn-tīnn* 'tea pour-full, fill a cup of tea', the object 茶 *tê* 'tea' may not follow the resultative construction 斟滇 *thîn-tīnn* 'pour-full'. Wang and Wu (2015) argue that, when the verb is telic, the object actually must appear in the preverbal positon. Teng Shou-hsin (1995) further remarks that, if the object is a personal pronoun, it is virtually never postverbal (a similar situation is found also in Shanghainese; see Zhu Xiaonong 2006).

Sometimes, in Taiwanese the object (except personal pronouns: Teng Shou-hsin 1995: 14) may be placed between the two constituents of a resultative construction (Chiang Chien-lung 2006: 64; glosses adapted; see also Lien Chinfa 1994):

(29)　伊食飯飽矣。
　　　i　　*tsia̍h*　*pn̄g*　*pá*　*ah*
　　　3SG　eat　　food　full　PFV
　　　'S/he ate to fullness.'

This order, which is actually attested in several dialects of Southern China (Lien Chinfa 1994: 363), is analogous to that of the so-called separable resultative construction, attested in Middle Chinese and then fallen out of use in the modern language (ex. from the 'A New Account of the Tales of the World', qtd. in Shi Yuzhi 2002: 11):

(30)　喚江郎覺！
　　　huàn　*Jiāng Láng*　*jué*
　　　call　　Jiang Lang　　awake
　　　'(Please) wake up Jiang Lang!'

According to Lien Chinfa (1994), this variation in word order for resultative constructions is related to the diachronic development of verb-complement constructions and reflects the coexistence of different historical strata in Min dialects. Specifically, the resultative construction in which the object appears between verb and complement

(29) belongs to the Northern and Southern Dynasties stratum (i.e. the time when the separable resultative construction developed in Chinese). Zhu Xiaonong (2006: 150) also highlights that the Verb-Object-Complement order for the resultative construction in Shanghainese is considered to be 'old-fashioned'.

6.2 Word order, subjecthood, and topichood

In Li and Thompson's (1976) seminal paper, a basic distinction between two language (macro-)types was introduced: 'subject-prominent' *vs.* 'topic-prominent' languages. English, for instance, is a typical subject-prominent language: virtually all sentences have a subject, and it is normally easy to identify the subject in a sentence, as it typically appears before the verb and agrees with it. On the other hand, in Chinese the notion of 'subject' is not nearly as prominent. There is no fixed position for the subject, no agreement with the verb, and no case markers; besides, not all sentences have a subject (Li and Thompson 1981; see §6.2.1). On the other hand, the topic is a very important determinant of sentence structure in Chinese: indeed, the language is usually classified as topic-prominent.

The 'topic' may be defined as 'the thing which the proposition expressed by the sentence is about' (Lambrecht 1994: 118). According to Li and Thompson (1981), the topic always appears in sentence-initial position in Chinese and is always known to the hearer (31a; but see §6.2.2).[2] The topic may be separated from the rest of the sentence (i.e. the comment) by a pause, optionally marked by a particle (31b):

(31)   a. 義大利我已經去過。

        Yìdàlì wǒ yǐjīng   qù- guo
        Italy   1SG already go- EXP
        'I've already been to Italy.'

   b. 這本書啊，我已經念了三遍。

        zhè běn shū   ā   wǒ yǐjīng   niàn-le   sān   biàn
        this CLF book TOP 1SG already read-PFV three time
        'I have already read this book three times.'

---

[2] It has been proposed that sentence-internal topics, which do not appear in the sentence-initial position, are possible in Chinese. For an overview of this issue, see Paul (2015: 233–44).

While the subject should always have a direct semantic relationship with the verb (as e.g. agenthood, i.e. being the volitional entity which initiates the action), this requirement does not apply to the topic (Li and Thompson 1981: 15). From the semantic-pragmatic point of view, subject and topic may coincide, but it is not necessarily so: the topic is not necessarily the (logical) subject, and the subject is not necessarily the topic of the sentence (Lambrecht 1994: 118; on Chinese, see Li and Thompson 1981: 87–92). For instance, in (31a-b), the topic is clearly not a subject. In (32a), on the other hand, topic and subject do overlap, while in (32b) there is a topic, but no subject:

(32)   a. 我喜歡喝綠茶。
       wǒ   xǐhuān   hē   lǜ-chá
       1SG   like   drink   green-tea
       'I like to drink green tea'

    b. 那本書出版了。
       nà   běn   shū   chūbǎn-le
       that   CLF   book   publish-PFV
       'That book has been published'

In (32b), 那本書 *nà běn shū* 'that book' does not appear to be the (logical) subject of the sentence (which is left unexpressed): it may however be analysed as the topic. Paul (2015: 230) points out that, if we choose to adopt a syntactic approach in which the positions for the topic and for the subject are distinct, we cannot speak of 'subject/topic' or of 'topical subjects'. However, this does not exclude that the subject may move to the topic position, and neither that a topic and a subject pronoun may be coreferential. Thus, according to Paul, we should first clarify whether we use the term 'topic' to refer to a specific syntactic position, to the left of the subject (see e.g. Huang, Li, and Li 2009), or in the semantic-pragmatic sense, to refer to the topic of discourse (we will get back to this in §6.2.1).

There are also sentences without a topic, as e.g. imperatives like 進來! *jìnlai!* 'come in!': generally speaking, the topic is often omitted when it is recoverable from the co(n)text. Also, indefinite subjects usually do not occur in the sentence-initial topic position (see §6.2.2), and sentences as (33) are often seen as thetic (all-new) topicless sentences (usually termed 'presentative sentences' in Chinese grammar; Li and Thompson 1981: 91):

(33) 進來了一個人。
  jìn-lai   *le*   *yī*   *ge*   *rén*
  enter-come   PFV   one   CLF   person
  'A person came in.'

For further discussion, see Li and Thompson (1981: 91–2) and LaPolla and Poa (2006: 278–9).

The topic-prominent character of Chinese has important implications for the principles governing word order. While Sinitic languages (with the exception of the Qinghai-Gansu area varieties discussed in §6.1.3) are usually described as SVO, there is actually no universally accepted definition of the subject for Chinese (see the next section), and sentence structure seems to be mainly shaped by pragmatic and semantic factors, rather than by grammatical relations as in English (Morbiato 2018b). Let us now go back to an example presented in Chapter 1 (as Ex. 9; from LaPolla and Poa 2006: 276):

(34) 沒有人可以問問題。
  méi-yǒu   *rén*   *kěyǐ*   *wèn*   *wèntí*
  NEG-exist   person   can   ask   question
  a. '(There is) No one (who) can ask questions.'
  b. 'There is no one to ask questions of.'

The sentence in (34) is an example of what is often analysed as SVO order. However, LaPolla and Poa (2006) highlight that this is misleading: the two possible meanings of (34) are evidence of the fact that the structure is not necessarily 'subject-verb-object'. See also the following examples from Lü Shuxiang (1979), discussed in LaPolla and Poa (2006: 276):

(35) a. 水澆花。
   shuǐ   *jiāo*   *huā*
   water$_N$ water$_V$ flower
   'The water waters the flowers.'

  b. 花澆水。
   huā   *jiāo*   *shuǐ*
   flower   water$_V$ water$_N$
   'The flowers are watered by the water.'

In the English translations of (35a-b), we have two different (grammatical) subjects: 'the water' in (35a), and 'the flowers' in (35b). In Chinese, however, the difference in the interpretation of the two sentences does not involve a change of subject (by means of passivization), but rather a different topic (and focus): in (35a), 水 *shuǐ* 'water' is the topic, and the sentence is framed as being about it; in (35b), 花 *huā* 'flower(s)' is the topic, and the sentence is framed as being about it. Thus, (35a) and (35b) differ in terms of what is presented as being definite (or generic), known to the hearer (the topic), and what is being presented as new information (the comment).

LaPolla (1995: 310) suggests that word order in Chinese is determined by a simple principle of information structure: '[t]opical or non-focal NPs occur preverbally, and focal or non-topical NPs occur postverbally'. This entails a (preferential) given-new order, which is independent from grammatical relations and semantic factors (agenthood, patienthood). LaPolla and Poa (2006: 279–80) highlight that even very common sentence structures in Chinese would be very hard to account for if understood in terms of subject and predicate: they are however very straightforward if analysed on the basis of information structure. Take, for instance, the 'double topic' (also called 'double subject', or 'double nominative') construction, in which there may be different types of semantic relationships between the topical noun phrases: most often, 'possessor-possessed' (36) or 'whole-part'.

(36)　大象鼻子很長。
　　　dàxiàng　*bízi*　*hěn*　*cháng*
　　　elephant　nose　very　long
　　　'The elephant has a long nose.'

In (36), the main (or primary) topic, 大象 *dàxiàng* 'elephant', is the possessor of the secondary topic 鼻子 *bízi* 'nose'.[3] However, the relationship between the two topics is not overtly marked: the secondary topic is simply 'pragmatically incorporated' in the comment. The comment is thus structured as a topic-comment structure, in which the comment is referred to the secondary topic (yielding the structure [topic [topic comment] comment]; LaPolla and Poa 2006: 280).

To sum up, LaPolla and Poa (2006) believe that Chinese cannot be defined as an SVO language, since subject and object are not the main determinants of word order. The fact that agents are often preverbal and patients are often postverbal is due to a general pragmatic principle: agents are most often topical, and patients are most often focal. Thus, in their

---

[3] On the notion of 'secondary topic', see Nikolaeva (2001).

view, it is the pragmatic correlates of agenthood and patienthood, rather than the semantic roles *per se*, which explain the typical associations of agents and patients with, respectively, the preverbal and postverbal position: topical (or non-focal) elements are typically placed before the verb, while focal (or non-topical) elements are typically placed after the verb.

Morbiato (2018b) also maintains that grammatical relations, as subject and object, do not seem to be significant determinants of word order in Chinese, and that topical (frame-setting) elements occupy the sentence-initial position, while focal elements are typically placed after the verb, following the given-new preferred order. However, she also stresses the fact that since 'word order's primary function is to encode the role of participants (who does what to whom)', semantic constraints may take precedence over information structure factors in shaping word order (Morbiato 2018b: 299). Compare the following pairs of allosentences (adapted from Morbiato 2018b: 290):

(37)   a. 他吃了苹果。
   tā *chī-le* *píngguǒ*
   3SG.M eat-PFV apple

  b. 他，苹果吃了。
   tā *píngguǒ* *chī-le*
   3SG.M apple eat-PFV
   'He ate an apple.'

(38)   a. 老虎吃了兔子。
   lǎohǔ *chī-le* *tùzi*
   tiger eat-PFV rabbit

  b. ?老虎，兔子吃了。
   lǎohǔ *tùzi* *chī-le*
   tiger rabbit eat-PFV
   'The tiger ate the rabbit.'

(39)   a. 老虎吃了狮子
   lǎohǔ *chī-le* *shīzi*
   tiger eat-PFV lion

  b. *老虎，狮子吃了
   lǎohǔ *shīzi* *chī-le*
   tiger lion eat-PFV
   'The tiger ate the lion'

In (37–39), we see pairs of sentences with the same structure: (37a–39a) are transitive sentences which follow agent-verb-patient order, while in (37b–39b) the patient is placed in the preverbal position, yielding agent-patient-verb order. This type of permutations in word order are used in MSC, just as in most other languages, to convey differences in terms of information structure (here, different foci). However, while the 'canonical' agent-verb-patient sentences (what is usually interpreted as SVO) are always acceptable, the allosentences with the object in the preverbal position show varying degrees of acceptability, depending on semantic, pragmatic, and world knowledge considerations. (37b) is perfectly fine, since 苹果 *píngguǒ* 'apple' is an inanimate entity, and there can be no doubt as to who eats what. (38b), however, is odd: both arguments are animate, although world knowledge tells us that it is highly unlikely that a rabbit may eat a tiger. On the other hand, (39b) is outright unacceptable, if the intended meaning is 'the tiger ate the lion': this is because both 老虎 *lǎohǔ* and 狮子 *shīzi* are plausible agents and patients, and it is thus unclear 'who does what to whom'. This is taken by Morbiato (2018b) as evidence of the fact that information structure alone may not be enough to account for word order patterns in MSC, and semantic(-pragmatic) considerations may override information structure considerations (see Morbiato 2018b for more examples of animacy-related constraints in Chinese syntax; see also Ex. 46). It is worth remarking here that, as shown by examples (37–39), the default interpretation for a transitive sentence with two overt arguments in MSC is that the preverbal argument is the agent (see also Chappell and Creissels 2019: 480 and the references cited therein; but cf. LaPolla 2009).

6.2.1 On the notion of 'subject' in Chinese

As mentioned in the preceding section, the idea that Chinese has grammatical relations such as 'subject' has been challenged time and again in the literature: indeed, even some linguists who do employ the term 'subject' actually use it to refer to the topic (e.g. Chao Yuen Ren 1968), or to the agent/actor (Li and Thompson 1981; see the overview in LaPolla 2009). However, the idea that MSC and other Sinitic languages do have a subject, which may be distinguished from the topic, is still very much alive and may be found in many (if not most) descriptions of the language, even very recent ones (see e.g. Chappell and Creissels

2019; see also Matthews and Yip 2011 on Cantonese, and Lin Philip T. 2015 on Taiwanese). The definitions of the subject provided in different sources often vary significantly, and a consistent account of subjecthood in Chinese is, perhaps unsurprisingly, lacking (Morbiato 2018b: 25–6).

For instance, topic and subject are often distinguished in formal syntactic approaches. We introduced (§6.1.2) Paul's (2015) view of the topic as the constituent which occupies the position to the left of the subject (i.e. the specifier position in the topic phrase). Thus, according to her analysis, in the following example the constituent 李先生 *Lǐ xiānsheng* 'Mr Li' is a subject which has moved to the topic position (Paul 2015: 230):

(40) 李先生呢認識我。
    Lǐ xiānsheng   ne   rènshi   wǒ
    Li Mr   TOP   know   1SG
    'Mr Li, he knows me.'

Note the presence of the topic marker 呢 *ne* which, according to Paul's analysis, realizes the head of the topic phrase. Paul (2015: 231–3) provides three arguments supporting a distinction between subject and topic in Chinese syntax. Firstly, an interrogative pronoun as 谁 *shéi* 'who' is allowed in subject position (41a), but not in topic position (41b), MSC being a *wh* in-situ language:

(41) a. 誰認識這個人?
      shéi   rènshi   zhèi   ge   rén
      who   know   this   CLF   person

    b. *誰呢認識這個人?
      shéi   ne   rènshi   zhèi   ge   rén
      who   TOP   know   this   CLF   person
      'Who knows this person?'

We will get back to the possible explanations for the ungrammaticality of (41b) in the next section. Secondly, only subjects, but not topics, may be relativized (Huang, Li and Li 2009: 213, qtd. in Paul 2015: 232; glosses adapted):

(42) a. 那些人意外發生了。
      nà-xiē   rén   yìwài   fāshēng-le
      that-CLF   person   accident   happen-PFV
      'As for those people, an accident happened.'

b. *意外發生了的那些人。

yìwài	fāshēng-le	de	nà-xiē	rén
accident	happen-PFV	REL	that-CLF	person

'The people such that an accident happened.'

In (42a), the experiencer 那些人 *nà-xiē rén* 'those people' sits in the topic position, and as such relativization results in ungrammaticality (42b).[4]

Paul's third argument is that prepositional phrases cannot occur in the subject position (43a), but are allowed in the topic position (43b; Paul 2015: 233; glosses adapted):

(43) a. *在屋子裏很乾淨。

zài	wūzi	lǐ	hěn	gānjìng
at	room	in	very	clean

'It is clean in the room.'

b. 在圖書館我可以複印嗎?

zài	túshūguǎn	wǒ	kěyǐ	fùyìn	ma
at	library	1SG	can	copy	Q

'Can I make photocopies in the library?'

The opposite view, namely that Chinese has a topic-comment structure, but no subject, has been supported e.g. by LaPolla (see LaPolla 2009 for a summary of his own work on this issue). In LaPolla's view, as mentioned earlier, Chinese sentences may be best explained as consisting of a topic and comment, and there are no grammatical relations as 'subject' and 'object'. As pointed out by Morbiato (2018a-b), definitions of the subject which rely on positional criteria (as is implicit in the use of the label 'SVO' for Sinitic) or on semantic criteria are clearly inadequate. As to the former, the sentence-initial position may be filled by any element, and is not limited to verbal arguments, including elements which cannot qualify as subjects, as in the following example (Morbiato 2018b: 33; glosses adapted):

---

[4] However, Huang Yan (1994: 170, qtd. in Morbiato 2018b: 45) suggests that even 'hanging topics' (sentence-initial noun phrases which are not arguments of the verb) may be relativized. See the following example, in which the main verb 做主 *zuòzhǔ* 'decide; take responsibility' is monovalent, requiring a single argument (Morbiato 2018b: 45):

[...] 包办企业应该自己做主的事情。

bāobàn	qǐyè	yìnggāi	zìjǐ	zuòzhǔ	de	shìqíng
undertake	company	should	REFL	decide	MOD	matter

'Take care of the matters which the company should decide for.'

(44) 自己的心情，自己做主。
　　　zìjǐ　　*de*　　*xīnqíng*　　　*zìjǐ*　　*zuòzhǔ*
　　　oneself MOD state.of.mind oneself decide
　　　'One's state of mind is one's decision.'

In point of fact, as highlighted in the previous section, the sentence-initial position in Chinese is normally occupied by topics, i.e. frame-setting elements. The semantic criterion, i.e. identifying the subject with the constituent which has a 'doing' or 'being' relationship with the verb (Li and Thompson 1981: 19), is fundamentally flawed, as it equates the subject with the agent or actor: these, however, are semantic roles, rather than grammatical relations (i.e. syntactic notions), and languages with a grammaticalized subject (like English) do have subjects which are not agents/actors (e.g. in passive sentences).

Given the limits of positional and semantic criteria for establishing subjecthood, as well as the already mentioned absence of morphological markers of grammatical relations, Morbiato (2018a-b) carries out a detailed analysis of a wide range of constructions which are usually considered to be sensitive to grammatical relations (i.e. which treat one or more arguments differently from other arguments) in MSC. These include, for instance, relativization site, reflexivization, passivization, topicalization, and conjunction reduction, among others. None of the constructions she examined seem to be controlled by a subject: they either do not impose any restrictions as to which argument is the controller (or 'pivot'), or display role-related restrictions (i.e. semantic restrictions), or display reference-related restrictions. Let us see an example for each of these three categories.

According to Morbiato's analysis, relativization is a good example of a construction which does not seem to impose any restrictions as to the constituent involved, including both arguments and adjuncts: agents, patients, goal/benefactives, locatives, may all be relativized. Indeed, MSC allows so-called 'gapless relative clauses' (Cheng and Sybesma 2006), i.e. relatives in which the head does not correspond to any verbal argument or adjunct (ex. from Cheng and Sybesma 2006: 69, qtd. in Morbiato 2018b: 44; glosses adapted):[5]

---

[5] Note that not everybody agrees that examples as (45) should be interpreted as relative clauses, or even that Sinitic languages have relative clauses at all. For instance, Comrie (2003: 29) uses the term 'general noun-modifying constructions' to indicate any clause-sized modifier of an NP, without any syntactic operation (as gap-filling), and connected to the head by semantic-pragmatic relations (see also Chan, Matthews, and Yip 2011 on analogous constructions in Cantonese).

(45) 他睡觉的姿势。

    tā   *shùijiào*   *de*   *zīshì*

    3SG.M sleep   MOD posture

    'The posture (that he has while) sleeping.'

According to Keenan and Comrie's (1977) well-known 'Accessibility Hierarchy', languages differ as to what constituents can be relativized. If a language may relativize only one type of constituent, that is predicted to be the subject. Since no such restriction applies to the Chinese case, relativization cannot be taken as evidence for the existence of any grammatical relation (but see Ex. 42 and Fn. 4).

Reflexivization, on the other hand, clearly shows role-related restrictions. While in many languages grammatical subjects control reflexives (in terms of reference), in MSC reflexivization rather seems to be sensitive to semantic constraints (ex. from Xu Liejiong 1994, qtd. in Morbiato 2018b: 49–50; glosses adapted):

(46) 李先生的阴谋害了自己。

    Lǐ xiānsheng *de*   *yīnmóu*   *hài-le*   *zìjǐ*

    Li mister   MOD conspiracy harm-PFV REFL

    'Mr Li's conspiracy did harm to him.'

In (46), the first verbal argument, which could arguably be analysed as the subject, is an inanimate entity (阴谋 *yīnmóu* 'conspiracy'), modified by an animate noun (李先生 *Lǐ xiānsheng* 'Mr Li'). The antecedent of the reflexive 自己 *zìjǐ* is not 阴谋 *yīnmóu* 'conspiracy', but rather the modifier 李先生 *Lǐ xiānsheng* 'Mr Li'. This shows that reflexivization is not controlled by the first argument (the 'subject'), or by the the most prominent semantic role (the agent, experiencer, or the external causer, as in the case of 阴谋 *yīnmóu* 'conspiracy'): animacy and pragmatic knowledge play a fundamental role in the interpretation of reflexive constructions, ruling out a purely syntactic account of control in reflexivization (and compare Exx. 37–39).

Lastly, an example of a construction which seems to be sensitive to reference-related restrictions is topicalization. While in many languages topicalization (or topic extraction) is tightly connected with grammatical relations, since it may be the case that only subjects can be topicalized in a given language, in MSC virtually any noun phrase can be a topic: this is certainly not restricted to subjects, nor to arguments in general. The only restriction which seems to apply is related to information structure: the sentence-initial topic position may be occupied only by referents which are given, accessible, or presupposed, and must be recoverable from context (Morbiato 2018b: 92; see §6.2.2). See the following example (Morbiato 2018b: 92–3; glosses adapted):

(47)　她死了一匹马, 便这么哭个不住。
    tā　　*sǐ-le*　　*yī*　*pǐ*　*mǎ*　　*biàn zhème kù*　*ge*　*bú*　*zhù*
    3SG.F die-PFV one CLF horse then so   cry CLF NEG stop
    'She had a horse die on her, and she cannot stop crying.'

In (47), the sentence-initial constituent 她 *tā* 'she' is not an argument of the verb 死 *sǐ* 'die', but it does control coreference with the only argument of the intransitive verb 哭 *kù* in the second clause. Hence, topic extraction is not restricted to specific grammatical relations, but is rather connected to reference- and discourse-related factors (givenness, topic continuity, textual coreference, etc.). Thus, to sum up, Morbiato's (2018a-b) conclusion is that there is no (overt or covert) evidence to support the existence of grammatical relations as subject and object in MSC, and that semantic and pragmatic principles alone are what governs sentence structure (see also the preceding section).

A third, more nuanced stance may be found in Bisang (2016). According to Bisang (2016: 357), there are criteria to distinguish subjects from topics, and also criteria supporting the subject/object asymmetry: however, they 'work in certain contexts but not fully consistently'. Bisang proposes two criteria to distinguish subjects from topics. The first one is relativization, and he uses the same argument and example as Paul (2015): see (42) and Fn. 4 for a counterexample. The second criterion is that since topics must be accessible, indefinite noun phrases cannot be topicalized (48a). However, they may appear in the initial (topic) position in thetic sentences (48b; Bisang 2016: 358; glosses adapted):

(48)　a.　*一个杯子我打碎了。
       yī　　*ge*　　*bēizi*　*wǒ*　*dǎ-suì-le*
       one　CLF　cup　　1SG　hit-shatter-PFV
       'I smashed a cup.'

    b.　一个杯子打碎了。
       yī　　*ge*　　*bēizi*　*dǎ-suì-le*
       one　CLF　cup　　hit-shatter-PFV
       'A cup broke/was broken.'

While in (48a) 打碎 *dǎ-suì* acts as a transitive verb with two arguments, in (48b) it acts as a monovalent verb. Bisang believes that (48b) is acceptable because the indefinite noun phrase 一个杯子 *yī ge bēizi* 'a cup' is a subject, rather than a topic: we will get back in the next section to the issue of the apparent ban on indefinite noun phrases in the topic position. Here, we shall just remark that, as pointed out by Bisang (2016: 358), this criterion has limited applicability, since it may be used only when overt indefinite marking is present: in all other cases, there is no straightforward evidence for the status of the first noun phrase in sequences as (48a-b).

Lastly, Bisang (2016: 361) uses extraction from a relative clause as evidence of subject/object asymmetry. He argues that extraction out of a relative clause modifying an object is allowed only 'if the zero-element in the relative clause is bound by a noun that is inanimate', while if the noun is animate, extraction results in ungrammaticality (ex. from Huang and Li 1996: 82, qtd. in Bisang 2016: 361; glosses adapted):

(49) *张三，我认识很多批评的人。
      Zhāngsān   wǒ   rènshi   hěn   duō   pīpíng   de   rén
      Zhangsan   1SG   know   very   many   criticize   MOD   person
      'Zhangsan, I know many people who criticize him.'

However, Bisang himself points out that the subject/object asymmetry here is not motivated by syntactic principles only, but rather interacts with a non-syntactic criterion, i.e. animacy. According to Morbiato's (2018b: 74) analysis, the reason for the ungrammaticality of a sentence like (49) lies in its ambiguity in terms of the roles of the participants: it is unclear 'who criticized whom'. Ambiguity, on the other hand, is not expected if the binding noun is inanimate. Thus, once again (see Exx. 37–39), the motivation for this restriction has to do more with semantics (role-disambiguation) than with syntax.

6.2.2 Some features of the topic in Chinese

According to Li and Thompson (1981: 85), the topic is 'what the sentence is about' and may be definite (known to the hearer), as in (50a, 50b$_i$), or generic, i.e. referring to a class of entities (50b$_{ii}$). However, an indefinite noun phrase can never be a topic (50b$_{iii}$, 50c), as already pointed out in the preceding section (48a; Li and Thompson 1981: 86; glosses adapted).

(50)   a. 那隻狗我已經看過了。

         nà   zhī   gǒu   wǒ   yǐjīng   kàn-guo   le

         that CLF dog 1SG already see-EXP CRS

         'That dog I have already seen'.

   b. 狗我已經看過了

         gǒu   wǒ   yǐjīng   kàn-guo   le

         dog 1SG already see-EXP CRS

         i. 'The dog I have already seen'.

         ii. 'Dogs I have already seen'.

         iii. *'A dog I have already seen'.

   c. *一隻狗我已經看過了

         yī   zhī   gǒu   wǒ   yǐjīng   kàn-guo   le

         one CLF dog 1SG already see-EXP CRS

         'A dog I have already seen'.

Moreover, as mentioned earlier (§6.2), the topic is often characterized as given information (LaPolla and Poa 2006). However, as pointed out by Paul (2015: 201), 'given' or 'old' information is actually used to refer to different statuses: information may be defined as 'given' because it has been mentioned or is implicitly present in the discourse, or because it is 'expected' or 'plausible' in the (extralinguistic) context, or even just because it may be considered as general world knowledge, as in the case of generic topics (50b$_{ii}$). Paul suggests that by adopting such a broad definition of givenness, then almost anything can be construed as given, based on 'contextual appropriateness': this view has actually been defended e.g. by Büring (2003) and Roberts (2012), according to whom 'any assertion in a discourse (except completely 'out of the blue' sentences) provides the answer to a possibly implicit 'question under discussion', thus accounting for its relevance to the current discourse' (Paul 2015: 201). On the other hand, if we use the term 'given' in the narrow sense, i.e. to refer to information which has been already mentioned, or is anyway implicitly present in the previous discourse, then we have to admit that the topic may also convey new information (see Reinhart 1982). See the following examples (Paul 2015: 196, 201; glosses adapted):

(51)   a. 你的博士論文怎麼樣？

         nǐ   de   bóshì   lùnwén   zěnmeyàng

         2SG mod PhD dissertation how

         'How is your thesis going?'

b. 我還要寫結論、書目; 答辯呢我不知道李教授有没有空。

wǒ	hái	yào	xiě	jiélùn	shūmù
1SG	still	have.to	write	conclusions	bibliography

dábiàn	ne	wǒ	bù	zhīdào	Lǐ	jiàoshòu	yǒu
defence	TOP	1SG	NEG	know	Li	professor	have

méi	yǒu	kòng
NEG	have	time

'I still have to write the conclusion and the bibliography. Concerning the defence, I don't know yet whether Prof Li is available.'

(52)   隔壁的商店, 他們什麼時候開門？

gébì		de	shāngdiàn	tā-men	shénme	shíhou
neighbouring	MOD	shop	3M-PL	what		time

kāi-mén
open-door

'The shop next door, when do they open?'

As highlighted by Paul (2015), in (51b) the topic 答辯 *dábiàn* 'defence' (followed by the topic particle 呢 *ne*) provides a partial answer to the question in (51a). The same goes for 結論 *jiélùn* 'conclusions' and 書目 *shūmù* 'bibliography', which are however postverbal objects. The topic 答辯 *dábiàn* 'defence', according to Paul, is new information: all the three elements mentioned are only some of the many possible aspects connected with writing a thesis. As to (52), Paul (2015: 201) observes that the item in the topic position 隔壁的商店 *gébì de shāngdiàn* 'shop next door' may not be interpreted as 'partially expected' if uttered, for instance, in a butcher shop.

Thus, according to Paul (2015: 202–8), the topic in Chinese does not necessarily convey given/old information. This is further proven by non-nominal topics, as e.g. conditional clauses, or prepositional phrases indicating topic shift, as those headed by the preposition 至於 *zhìyú* 'as for', used to introduce a different topic (see Lü Shuxiang 1980), i.e a topic conveying new information. As highlighted by Paul (2015: 206), topics introduced by 至於 *zhìyú* may be new not only 'with respect to a previous topic', but also 'with respect to the general subject matter in the preceding discourse' (example from Lü Shuxiang 1980, qtd. in Paul 2015: 206; glosses adapted):[6]

---

[6] Lü Shuxiang (1980) points out that 至於 *zhìyú* may not be substituted by 關於 *guānyú* 'about, concerning' as a preposition introducing a new topic. This entails that there are two types of topics: those carrying new information *vs.* those carrying old information.

(53)　熊是雜食動物，吃肉吃果實塊根，至於熊貓則是完全素食。

xióng   shì   záshí   dòngwu   chī   ròu   chī   guǒshí
bear   COP   omnivorous   animal   eat   meat   eat   fruit
kuàigēn   zhìyú   xióngmāo   zé   shì   wánquán
root.tuber   as.for   panda   then   COP   completely
sùshí
vegetarian
'Bears are omnivorous animals, they eat meat, they eat fruit and
root tuber; as for pandas, they are completely vegetarian.'

The fact that a topic may also convey new information has been
reported also for Romance and Germanic languages: Bianchi and
Frascarelli (2010) highlight that the so-called 'aboutness topics' are not
necessarily associated with old information and, in fact, they often
involve a shift to a new topic ('aboutness-shift topics').

Besides, Paul (2015) points out that the topic is not necessarily 'what
the sentence is about', and, hence, the relationship between topic and
comment is not always connected with the notion of 'aboutness'. See the
following examples (Paul 2015: 208–9; glosses adapted):

(54)　a. 中國，大城市，上海，交通比較亂。

Zhōngguó   dà   chéngshì   Shànghǎi   jiāotōng   bǐjiào
China   big   town   Shanghai   traffic   rather
luàn
chaotic
'In China, among the big towns, in Shanghai, the traffic is
rather chaotic.'

b. 半個小時的時間，我只能給你們講個大概。

bàn   ge   xiǎoshí   de   shíjiān   wǒ   zhǐ   néng   gěi
half   CLF   hour   MOD   time   1SG   only   can   to
nǐ-men   jiǎng   ge   dàgài
2-PL   talk   CLF   outline
'In half an hour time, I can only give you a broad outline.'

Paul remarks that in multiple topic structures as (54a), it is unclear
which topic is the one the sentence 'is about'. Moreover, topics that are

Moreover, 至於 *zhìyú* may not be used at the beginning of a conversation, without a preceding discourse (Liu Charles A. 1977: 205, qtd. in Paul 2015: 206–7): topic shift 'is only possible
against the background of already established information' (Paul 2015: 207).

not referential expressions, as e.g. adverbs, quantifier phrases, and conditional clauses, do not seem to indicate 'what the sentence is about', as 半個小時的時間 *bàn ge xiǎoshí de shíjiān* 'half an hour time' in (54b).

Thus, Paul (2015) suggests that Chafe's (1976: 50–1) definition of the topic as the 'frame within which a sentence holds', having the function of 'limit[ing] the applicability of the main predication to a certain restricted domain', is more appropriate than those relying on 'aboutness'. In her view, the topic may 'convey an aboutness relation', including topic shift, or set up the above-mentioned 'frame within which a sentence holds': in both cases, the topic is not restricted to given/old information (Paul 2015: 211).[7] This is obviously at odds with the idea that in Chinese focus, and thus new information, is always found after the main verb (see §6.2).

As hinted at before (§6.2, 6.2.1), Morbiato (2018b) also believes that Chinese topics are better characterized as frame-setting, rather than 'aboutness' topics. However, her analysis of topichood is significantly different from Paul's: she believes that Paul's suggestion that topics are not necessarily associated with any particular information value (as e.g. given/old) is incorrect. We mentioned in the preceding section that, according to Morbiato, topics must be given, accessible, or presupposed. However, Morbiato (2018b: 229–43) also concedes that Chinese topics may in fact not always be given and/or definite. What is crucial is that they must at least be 'locatable': namely, the set to which the referent belongs must be identifiable. *Contra* Bisang (2016; see §6.2.1), she shows that indefinite noun phrases may be topics, as long as they are locatable (Morbiato 2018b: 240; glosses adapted):

(55) 候机室里一片混乱。一位旅客起来维持秩序。
 hòujīshì   lǐ yī   piàn hùnluàn
 airport.lounge in one CLF disorder
 yī   wèi lǚkè   qǐlái wéichí zhìxù
 one CLF passenger rise keep order
 'The airport waiting room is in disorder. One waiting passenger gets up to keep order.'

In (55), the indefinite noun phrase 一位旅客 *yī wèi lǚkè* 'one passenger' is found in the topic position. Indeed, according to Morbiato

---

[7] Due to space constraints, here we omit the discussion of other types of topics, as contrastive topics, often treated as focus constructions in the literature. For an overview, see Shyu (2014) and Paul (2015).

(2018b), specificity (i.e. the referent is identifiable by the speaker) could be sufficient to license topics, although in most cases we expect the topic to be given (i.e. known to the hearer). In (55), however, both a specific and a non-specific reading are actually possible. Note that, without a context, the sentence becomes ungrammatical (and compare Ex. 48a):

(56) *一位旅客起来维持秩序。

  yī wèi lǚkè   *qǐlái wéichí zhìxù*
  one CLF passenger rise keep order
  'One waiting passenger gets up to keep order.'

(55) is said to be acceptable only if 'the speaker wants to emphasize that the number of passengers she is talking about is just one', or in a context in which 'one passenger keeps order, another helps people' (Morbiato 2018b: 240). Besides, the mention of 候机室 *hòujīshī* 'airport waiting room' makes the referent 'one passenger' locatable: it is implicit that the latter refers to a passenger in the aforementioned room. Morbiato (2018b: 242) also argues that Paul's examples (54a-b, 51) may be analysed in terms of locatability: the referents 'big cities' and 'Shanghai' are all locatable in the context of the initial topic 'China', 'defence' is locatable with respect to the thesis (and the speaker), and 'the shop next door' is 'locatable with respect to the contextual location where the conversation occurs'.

Thus, in Morbiato's analysis, locatability is the main restriction in terms of information status for Chinese topics: information status is hence not irrelevant, but 'given/old' is not the proper label for characterizing the restrictions they are subject to. Given that Bisang provides no context for example (48b), it is unclear whether the sentence-initial noun phrase 一个杯子 *yī ge bēizi* might be interpreted as locatable too. As to the ungrammaticality of sentences like (41b), it might also be explained by the lack of locatability of interrogative pronouns as 谁 *shéi*, the referents of which do not belong to an identifiable set. Indeed, Paul (2015: 199, Fn. 5), quoting Yuan and Dugarova (2012), highlights that a plain *wh-* pronoun may appear in the topic position if a 'discourse-linked' interpretation may be imposed 'by mentioning the set among which to choose and/or by using a predicate that implies the existence of such a set': this condition is pretty much equivalent to Morbiato's 'locatability'.

6.3 Serial verb constructions

A prominent typological characteristic of Sinitic, as well as of other EMSEA languages (see §2.3.1), is the use of serial verb constructions (henceforth: SVCs), i.e. 'a sequence of verbs which act together as a single predicate, without any overt marker of coordination, subordination, or syntactic dependency of any other sort', and which 'describe what is conceptualised as a single event' (Aikhenvald 2006: 1). See the following Cantonese example (O'Melia 1966 [1938]: 3, qtd. in Matthews 2006: 69):

(57)　佢入去坐。
　　　kéuih　yahp　heui　chóh
　　　3SG　　enter　come　sit
　　　'He went in and sat down.'

SVCs have been the subject of a huge number of studies, and it is not possible to provide an overview of the relevant literature here, due to space constraints. We shall just mention the construction types which may be analysed as SVCs in Sinitic, focussing on some controversial issues. Our presentation is mainly based on Li and Thompson (1973, 1978, 1981), which take into consideration a wide range of constructions.

Li and Thompson (1978, 1981) define SVCs as sentences which contain 'two or more verbs or clauses juxtaposed without any marker indicating what the relationship is between them' (Li and Thompson 1981: 594). Despite having different interpretations, all SVCs share the same (surface) structure: namely, (NP) V (NP) (NP) V (NP) (noun phrases are optional). Based on the possible interpretations of the relationship between the verbs, Li and Thompson identify four types of SVCs.

The first type of SVC singled out by Li and Thompson includes sentences composed of two or more separate events. These may be further divided into four subtypes (Li and Thompson 1981: 595, 597; glosses adapted):

(58)　a.　Consecutive: one event occurs after the other
　　　　我買票進去。
　　　　wǒ　mǎi　piào　jìn-qù
　　　　1SG　buy　ticket　enter-go
　　　　'I bought a ticket and went in.'

b. Purpose: the purpose of the first event is achieving the second
我們開會討論那個問題。

wǒ-men	kāi-huì	tǎolùn	nà	ge	wèntí
1-PL	hold-meeting	discuss	that	CLF	problem

'We'll hold a meeting to consider that problem.'

c. Alternating: the subject alternates between two actions
她天天唱歌寫信。

tā	tiān~tiān	chàng-gē	xiě	xìn
3SG.F	day~day	sing-song	write	letter

'Everyday she sings songs and writes letters.'

d. Circumstance: the first verb describes the circumstances of
the second event
他們用手吃飯。

tā-men	yòng	shǒu	chī-fàn
3M-PL	use	hand	eat-food

'They eat with their hands.'

The second type of SVCs includes sentences in which the second verb phrase is the object of the first verb (59a), or the first verb phrase is the subject of the second verb (59b; Li and Thompson 1981: 600, 603; glosses adapted):

(59) a. 我們禁止抽煙。

wǒ-men	jìnzhǐ	chōu-yān
1-PL	prohibit	draw-smoke

'We prohibit smoking.'

b. 大聲念課文可以幫助發音。

dà-shēng	niàn	kè-wén	kěyǐ	bāngzhù	fāyīn
big-voice	read	lesson-text	can	help	pronunciation

'Reading the lesson aloud can help one's pronunciation.'

The third type of SVC includes the so-called 'pivotal constructions', i.e. constructions which contain 'a noun phrase that is simultaneously the subject of the second verb and the object of the first verb' (acting as a 'pivot' relating the two verbs; Li and Thompson 1981: 607; glosses adapted):

(60) 我勸他念醫。

wǒ	quàn	tā	niàn	yī
1SG	advise	3SG.M	study	medicine

'I advised him to study medicine.'

Lastly, Li and Thompson (1981: 611, 618) list as a type of SVCs the so-called 'descriptive clauses', i.e constuctions in which there is a transitive verb, and its direct object is 'described' by the following clause:

(61) a. 他有一個妹妹很喜歡看電影 。

    tā   *yǒu*   *yī*   *ge*   *mèimei*   *hěn*   *xǐhuan*   *kàn*

    3SG.M   have   one   CLF   sister   very   like   watch

    diànyǐng

    film

    'He has a younger sister who likes to see movies.'

  b. 我們種那種菜吃 。

    wǒ-men   *zhòng*   *nà*   *zhǒng*   *cài*   *chī*

    1-PL   raise   that   CLF   vegetable   eat

    'We raise that kind of vegetable to eat.'

The interpretation of SVCs may be ambiguous: this is often the case for the first subtype (58a-d). For instance, while (58a) is translated here as 'I bought a ticket and went in' (consecutive), it may be also understood as 'I bought a ticket to go in' (purpose; Li and Thompson 1981: 595). While Li and Thompson believe that the correct interpretation depends on the context, Paul argues that Li and Thompson's identification of four types of SVC is not correct, and that SVCs do not generally tolerate the degree of ambiguity they suggest. In Paul's view (2008), a sequence of verbs without any overt marker of coordination or subordination is not normally interpreted as a coordinating structure (as implied e.g. by the characterization of 58c): it may however be interpreted as a construction in which the first verb (phrase) is the main verb, and the second verb is a purpose clause, or as a construction in which the first verb is an adjunct of the second verb (Paul 2008: 387–8). See the following example:

(62)   他打電話叫車 。

    tā   *dǎ-diànhuà*   *jiào*   *chē*

    3SG.M   hit-telephone   call   car

    a. 'He phoned to call a taxi.' (main verb – purpose clause)

    b. 'He called a taxi. (with the phone)' (adjunct – main verb)

Thus, there appears to be a wide range of syntactic structures which have been described with the label 'SVC' in the literature. While these share the same surface structures, they seem to differ significantly in terms of structure and properties: hence, treating them as instantiations of a single construction type is not uncontroversial (see Paul 2008). Paul (2008: 376) highlights that Li and Thompson's (1981) second type of SVC, namely when one verb/clause is the object or subject of the other verb, actually includes sentences with very different structures: one in which the first verb 'is contained in a sentential subject' (59b), and one in which the first verb 'selects a complement clause' (59a). These two structures are not only different from each other, but they are also different from purpose (62a) and adjunct (62b) structures (see Paul 2008: 376–9 for the details). Moreover, Paul (2008: 379) argues that pivotal constructions are not really different from object control constructions, in which 'the matrix object controls, i.e. determines the reference of, the null subject in the embedded nonfinite clause'. The object control construction is however neither typical of Chinese, nor of languages with SVCs.

To sum up, the label 'SVC' for Chinese could be argued to be in fact a descriptive term for any sequence of verbs without overt markers of their syntactic relationship, rather than a 'construction' sharing structural and semantic properties. This might explain why there is no agreement among specialists as to the definition and delimitation of the SVC in Chinese (see e.g. Zhu Dexi 1982; Li Linding 1986; Chang Claire Hsunhuei 1991; Dai John Xiang-Ling 1990; Wang Xin 2007; Paul 2008).

6.3.1 Serial verb constructions and grammaticalization

As mentioned earlier (§2.3.1), the notion of SVC is often employed in Chinese historical linguistics to account for the grammaticalization of prepositions and other grammatical morphemes. For instance, it has been proposed (see Shi Yuzhi 2002) that aspect markers evolved from constituents in SVCs: in this section, we shall briefly illustrate the case of the 把 bǎ construction (see §6.1.2).

The traditional account for the evolution of 把 bǎ into an object marker, first proposed by Zhu Minche (1957) and Wang Li (1980 [1958]), and further developed by Peyraube (1985), may be summarized as follows. Before the second century BC 把 bǎ, just as 將 jiāng, 持 chí, and 捉 zhuō, was a verb meaning 'take, grab': between the second and the fifth century AD, 把 bǎ began to appear in SVCs of the form 'V$_1$-Object-V$_2$' and then grammaticalized into an object marker between the seventh and ninth century (Peyraube 1996). However, a careful analysis of the data reveals that, in fact, between the second and the sixth century AD, *two* distinct SVCs in which the first verb meant 'take, grab' emerged; both constructions were still attested in the Tang period (Peyraube 1996; Paul 2015):

(63)　巴粟與雞呼朱朱。(洛陽伽藍紀 *Luòyáng Qiélánjì*; Peyraube
　　　　1985: 197)
　　　　bǎ　　sù　　yǔ　　jī　　　hū　　zhūzhū
　　　　take　grain　give　chicken　call　zhuzhu
　　　　'While taking the grains and giving them to the chicken, he called out *zhuzhu*.'

(64)　於是即將雌劍往見楚王。(搜神記 *Sōu shén jì*; in Peyraube
　　　　1996: 169)
　　　　yúshì　jí　　　　jiāng　cí　　　jiàn　wǎng　jiàn　Chǔ
　　　　thus　immediately　take　female　sword　go　　see　Chu
　　　　Wáng
　　　　Prince
　　　　'(He) immediately took the female sword to go to see the Prince of Chu.'

In (63) we see an example of an object sharing SVC (see Collins 1997), in which 粟 *sù* 'grain' is both the object of the verb 巴 (把) *bǎ* 'take' and of the verb 與 *yǔ* 'give'. According to Paul (2015: 27–8), this should be analysed as a complementation structure, in which the verb 巴 (把) *bǎ* 'take' selects the second verb phrase, the head of which is 與 *yǔ* 'give', as its complement. This construction is argued to be the source of the Modern Chinese 把 *bǎ* construction (see e.g. Zhu Minche 1957; Peyraube 1996), which is also a complementation structure (see §6.1.2). Example (64) is however different: it does not appear to be an object sharing construction, as 雌劍 *cí jiàn* 'female sword' is the object of the verb 將 *jiāng* 'take' but not of the verb 往 *wǎng* 'go'. Constructions as (64) are analysed by Paul (2015) as adjunction structures, in which 將 *jiāng* 'take' is the verb in an adjunct clause modifying the second verb: if a second object is present, it is the object of the second verb. This second pattern evolved into the instrumental construction (Peyraube 1996: 169), as in the following ninth century example (Paul 2015: 27):

(65)　輕將玉杖敲花片。　(公子行 *Gōng zǐ xíng*)
　　　　qīng　　jiāng　yù-zhàng　qiāo　huā-piàn
　　　　lightly　take　jade-stick　tap　　flower-petal
　　　　'Taking a stick of jade, she lightly tapped on the flower petals.'

Thus, according to Peyraube (1996), two diachronic changes occurred, which led to the conventionalization of two different constructions: the modern 把 *bǎ* construction, marking a preverbal object, and the instrumental 把 *bǎ* construction, which is no longer in use in Modern Chinese. Peyraube (1988, 1989, 1996) believes that these changes are the result of a process of grammaticalization (dating to the seventh century) in which 把 *bǎ*, as well as all other 'take' verbs mentioned here, gradually lost their lexical meaning, becoming object or instrument markers: this arguably happened because the second verb in the SVC was, in a sense, more important than the first verb. Moreover, Peyraube (1996) suggests that, besides the grammaticalization process, the analogy with Archaic Chinese (tenth–seconnd century BC) constructions based on 以 *yǐ* 'take, use' had a role in the development of the 把 *bǎ* construction: see Peyraube (1996: 171–4) for further details and for an overview of competing hypotheses on the development of the 把 *bǎ* construction.

6.4 Tense and aspect

Languages use different strategies to locate events in time. Some languages have grammaticalized tense markers (e.g. the English regular past tense marker -*ed*), while others do not use inflection to express time reference. MSC, and Sinitic languages in general, are normally described as 'tenseless', since they do not seem to possess obligatory grammatical markers of tense (see e.g. Li and Thompson 1981; Norman 1988; Klein, Li, and Hendriks 2000; Lin Jo-wang 2003, 2006, 2012; Smith and Erbaugh 2005; Matthews and Yip 2011).

However, the debate concerning the tenseless nature of Chinese has not settled yet (for an overview, see Soh Hooi Ling 2014). In contemporary syntactic theories, tense markers sit in a functional node in the tense projection: while some believe that Chinese does have a tense projection, albeit with a null head (e.g. Sybesma 2007), others argue that there is no tense projection at all (e.g. Lin Jo-wang 2003, 2006, 2010; Smith and Erbaugh 2005). For those which do not posit a tense projection for Chinese, the interpretation of time reference relies on other factors, as aspect, modal verbs, and the use of time expressions.

Lin Jo-wang (2003, 2006, 2010, 2012) proposes that in 'simple' sentences (i.e. without any time expression or aspect marker), time reference is established by lexical aspect (*Aktionsart*; see §6.4.1) and by grammatical aspect (viewpoint aspect). Specifically, sentences describing perfective telic states of affairs[8] are interpreted by default as located in the past, while sentences describing imperfective atelic states of affairs are intepreted by default as located in the present. Thus, for instance, (66), with a stative predicate, is interpreted as located in the present, and (67), with an activity (atelic) verb, is normally interpreted as expressing generic or habitual present:

(66)　我很忙。
　　　 wǒ　hěn　máng
　　　 1SG　very　busy
　　　 'I am very busy.'

(67)　她踢足球。
　　　 tā　　tī　　zúqiú
　　　 3SG.F　kick　football
　　　 'She plays football.'

On the other hand, the main verbs in (68a-b) are telic, and hence both sentences are by default interpreted as located in the past:

(68)　a.　他打破一個花瓶。
　　　　　 tā　　　dǎ-pò　　yī　　ge　　huā-píng
　　　　　 3SG.M　hit-break　one　CLF　flower-bottle
　　　　　 'He broke a vase.'

　　　 b.　她在北京出生。
　　　　　 tā　　　zài　Běijīng　chūshēng
　　　　　 3SG.F　at　Beijing　be.born
　　　　　 'She was born in Beijing.'

However, if time expressions are present, they determine the temporal location of the state of affairs:

(69)　a.　我昨天很忙。
　　　　　 wǒ　zuótiān　hěn　máng
　　　　　 1SG　yesterday　very　busy
　　　　　 'Yesterday I was very busy.' (compare Ex. 66)

---

[8] The generic label 'state of affairs' is used here as a cover term for situation, event, process, and action (see Dik 1997; Mauri 2008).

b. 我明天去羅馬。

wǒ   míngtiān   qù   Luómǎ
1SG   tomorrow   go   Rome
'I'm going to Rome tomorrow.'

c. 我去年在羅馬工作。

wǒ   qù-nián   zài   Luómǎ   gōngzuò
1SG   past-year   at   Rome   work
'I was working in Rome last year.'

Time reference, as already mentioned, may also be conveyed by modal verbs. A 'future' tense modal which has attracted much attention in the literature is 會 *huì*,[9] the function of which is indicating the possibility that an event occurs. However, while in some cases 會 *huì* is required when talking about a future event (70a), in other future-time contexts it is simply not allowed (70b; Lin Jo-wang 2012: 674–5):

(70) a. 明天會下雨。

míngtiān   huì   xiàyǔ
tomorrow   will   rain
'It will rain tomorrow.'

b. 火車三點(*會)開。

huǒchē   sān   diǎn   (*huì)   kāi
train   three hour   (*will)   leave
'The train leaves at three o' clock.'

The use of 會 *huì* in (70b) results in ungrammaticality because the event described by the verb is already planned, and unlikely to change. (70a), on the other hand, formulates a prediction, concerning a non-controllable event (rain): the prediction has a significant chance of being wrong. The difference between (70a) and (70b), hence, lies in the degree of uncertainty: 會 *huì* basically indicates that something is more or less likely, but not certain. See also the following sentence (Lin Jo-wang 2012: 675; glosses adapted):

(71) 我下午不（會）在辦公室。

wǒ   xiàwǔ   bù   （huì）   zài   bàngōngshì
1SG   afternoon   NEG   (will)   stay   office
'I will not be in my office in the afternoon.'

---

[9] Other modals for which a future tense interpretation has been proposed are 將 *jiāng* and 要 *yào* (see Lin Jo-wang 2012: 675).

The meaning of (71) slightly changes if 會 *huì* is present. While the bare verb, again, indicates something which is already scheduled, the addition of 會 *huì* turns it into 'a prediction about a future eventuality' (Lin Jo-wang 2012: 675).

Thus, Lin Jo-wang (2012: 676–7) highlights that 會 *huì* is not a real future tense marker, as proven by the fact that it is not obligatory (and sometimes even unacceptable) in future time contexts. Moreover, 會 *huì* is used also in non-future contexts. It can, for instance, be used for a state of affairs that occurs on a regular basis:

(72) 這裡夏天常（會）下雨。
      zhèlǐ   *xiàtiān*   *cháng*   *(huì)*   *xiàyǔ*
      here   summer   often   will   rain
      'It often rains here in summer.'

Hence, 會 *huì* is perhaps best understood as an irrealis marker, rather than as a future marker (see Lin Jo-wang 2012: 677 and the references cited therein).

In some cases, time reference may be determined by aspectual markers. For instance, the perfective marker 了 *-le* in (73a) and the experiential marker 過 *-guo* in (73b) locate the event in the past:

(73)   a. 我買了一本書。
          wǒ   *mǎi-le*   *yī*   *běn*   *shū*
          1SG   buy-PFV   one   CLF   book
          'I bought a book.'

    b. 他去過北京。
          tā   *qù-guo*   *Běijīng*
          3SG.M   go-EXP   Beijing
          'He has been to Beijing (in the past).'

The perfective marker 了 *-le* in (73a) is generally interpreted as indicating the endpoint of the event described by the verb, thus suggesting a past interpretation. The function of experiential 過 *-guo* is indicating that the state of affairs has been experienced in the past, thus, again, suggesting a past interpretation. Without 過 *-guo*, (73b) would by default be understood as having present time reference. Indeed, the experiential aspect marker 過 *-guo* may be used with verbs belonging to any aspectual (i.e. *Aktionsart*) class and always implies that the entire state of affairs is in the past, as an experience located before a certain reference time (see Xiao and McEnery 2004: 143–6).

As to perfective 了 -*le*, it suggests a default past time interpretation when combined with activities and accomplishments, as it indicates that the event occurred before speech time (73a). Not all stative verbs may combine with this aspect marker: 了 -*le* is allowed only for those statives which, in specific contexts, may have an eventive reading, as e.g. 知道 *zhīdào* 'know', 相信 *xiāngxìn* 'believe', 有 *yǒu* 'have, exist', but not 認為 *rènwéi* 'believe, think', 屬於 *shǔyú* 'belong', 佩服 *pèifu* 'admire' (see Sybesma 1992: 17; Lin Jo-wang 2006: 13). The addition of 了 -*le* to a stative verb imposes an inchoative reading, turning them into achievements (type-coercion): thus for instance, 我知道了這件事 *wǒ zhīdao-le zhè jiàn shì* 'I learned this matter' implies a change of state, from not knowing to knowing (Lin Jo-wang 2006: 13).

Lastly, Lin Jo-wang (2006: 13) highlights that, when 了 -*le* occurs with an achievement verb (including resultatives), the resulting state must hold at the 'evalutation time' (which is often, though not necessarily, the same speech time). Compare:

(74)   a. 李四跌斷了左腿。
        Lǐsì   diē-duàn-le   zuǒ-tuǐ
        Lisi   fall-break-PFV   left-leg
        'Lisi has broken his left leg.'

        b. 李四跌斷過左腿。
        Lǐsì   diē-duàn-guo   zuǒ-tuǐ
        Lisi   fall-break-EXP   left-leg
        'Lisi broke his left leg before.'

The difference between (74a) and (74b) is that the former implies that the event occurred before speech time, and Lisi's leg is still broken, while the latter implies that Lisi's leg has now healed.[10] However, note

[10] Chappell (2004a) interprets 过 -*guo*, as well as other experiential markers found in Sinitic languages, as exponents of evidentiality (a modal category), rather than as 'true' aspect markers. She convincingly argues that the use of 过 -*guo* necessarily involves 'discontinuity', namely that 'the result state associated with an event or situation no longer holds' (Chappell 2004a: 82), just as in Ex. (74b), and, also, that the event must be repeatable (thus, for instance, 'die' is not normally used with 过 -*guo*). In her analysis, this is tightly connected with the semantics of evidentiality: 过 -*guo* expresses 'that the speaker is certain of the truth of the proposition', based on inference or on witnessing the event; if the event is occurring at speech time, 'the use of the evidential would be rendered superflous' (Chappell 2004a: 67–8, 71).

that if we had a past time indication in (74a), as e.g. 上個月 *shàng ge yuè* 'last month', then the event must necessarily be located in that time frame (last month), but it is not implied that the result state still holds at speech time: the leg could be cured or still broken. In that case, what is being stated is that Lisi broke his leg last month (event time) and that the leg was still broken (result state) at that time, but nothing is said about speech time (Lin Jo-wang 2006: 14).

Sybesma (2007) believes that the perfective marker 了 *-le* is actually required when talking about a telic event in the past. Sybesma's argument is based on sentences as (73a), in which, without 了 *-le*, the sentence receives a present time reading: indeed, without 了 *-le*, a past time reading is odd even if an overt time expression is present (e.g. ?我昨天買一本書 *wǒ zuótiān mǎi yī běn shū* 'I bought a book yesterday'). Thus, the presence of 昨天 *zuótiān* 'yesterday' does not appear to be enough to imply past time reference in this context, and perfective 了 *-le* is necessary. However, Lin Jo-wang (2010) remarks that 了 *-le* is actually required for telic events in the past only in certain constructions: mostly, with accomplishment verbs, when the verb is followed by a quantized object (e.g. 寫一本書 *xiě yī běn shū* 'write a book'). Other types of telic predicates, as e.g. resultative compounds, do not necessarily require the perfective marker (see 68a). Moreover, the use of 了 *-le* is not limited to past time contexts:

(75) a. 下了課我就回宿舍。
       xià-le   kè   wǒ   jiù   huí   sùshè
       finish-PFV class 1SG then return dormitory
       'Once classes are over, I'll go back to the dorm.'

      b. 媒體的整体水平, 一定程度上反映了社會的整體素質。
       méitǐ   de   zhěngtǐ   shuǐpíng   yīdìng   chéngdù   shàng
       media MOD overall   level   certain   degree   on
       fǎnyìng-le   shèhuì   de   zhěngtǐ   sùzhì
       reflect-PFV   society MOD overall   quality
       'The overall level of mass media reflects, to a certain degree, the overall quality of the society.'

Thus, in short, neither 過 *-guo* nor 了 *-le* may be understood as tense markers: they are not obligatory in past time contexts; besides, the use of 了 *-le* is not limited to past time reference. However, Lin Jo-wang (2006) also argues that the meaning of the aspect markers 過 *-guo* and 了 *-le* includes a relationship between 'topic time' (i.e. the time within which the predication holds) and 'evaluation time'. Thus, these markers are not purely aspectual, but also include 'semantic tense' as part of their meaning: they may be both analysed as having 'a component of relative past' (but, crucially, not *deictic* past; Lin Jo-wang 2006: 19, Fn. 18).

MSC also has two markers of imperfective aspect: progressive (正)在 *(zhèng)zài*, found in preverbal position, and durative 著 *-zhe*, which comes after the verb.[11]

The marker (正)在 *(zhèng)zài* is akin to the progressive construction in English but is restricted to dynamic durative verbs, being incompatible with telic predicates (achievements and accomplishments followed by a quantized object): hence the ungrammaticality of *他在死 *tā zài sǐ* 'he is dying' (see Xiao and McEnery 2004; Lin Jo-wang 2006). In a simple sentence with no overt time expressions, (正)在 *(zhèng)zài* triggers an episodic present reading:

(76) 他在踢足球。

    tā   *zài*   *tī*   *zúqiú*

    3SG.M PROG kick football

    'He is playing football.' (compare Ex. 67)

However, 在 *zài* is not restricted to present time contexts: indeed, it can be used also with past or future time reference. See the following example, with a past tense adverbial:

(77) 我昨天去他家的時候，他在做作業。

    wǒ *zuótiān* *qù* *tā* *jiā* *de* *shíhou* *tā*

    1SG yesterday go 3SG.M house MOD time 3SG.M

    zài   *zuò* *zuòyè*

    PROG do homework

    'Yesterday, when I went to his place, he was doing his homework.'

Lin Jo-wang (2006) shows that the semantics of progressive 在 *zài* is not deictic, but rather relative (just as for 過 *-guo* and 了 *-le*), since topic time does not necessarily correspond to speech time, as proven by sentences as 李四十分鐘前說他在洗澡 *Lǐsì shí fēnzhōng qián shuō tā zài xǐzǎo* 'Lisi said ten minutes ago that he was taking a bath', in which the time of the event 洗澡 *xǐzǎo* 'take a bath' includes the time of 說 *shuō* 'say'.[12]

---

[11] For other aspect markers in MSC, see Xiao and McEnery (2004).

[12] On the temporal interpretation of embedded and relative clauses, see Lin Jo-wang (2006).

The marker 著 -*zhe* combines with atelic predicates, and its function is indicating that a dynamic or static state of affairs is durative (see Xiao and McEnery 2004; Lin Jo-wang 2006):

(78)   a.   她嘴裡嚼著口香糖。
        tā   zuǐ   lǐ   jiáo-zhe   kǒuxiāngtáng
        3SG.F mouth in chew-DUR chewing-gum
        'He is chewing chewing-gum (in his mouth).'

     b.   門開著。
        mén   kāi-zhe
        door open-DUR
        'The door is open.'

If no time expressions are present, the verbs marked by durative 著 -*zhe* are understood as having present time reference. According to Lin Jo-wang's (2006: 17) analysis, (78a) refers to the present because the activity of chewing must be occurring at speech time. The semantics of 著 -*zhe* is relative, and not deictic, just as for the other aspect markers seen before: for instance, in 李四昨天說桌子上放著一杯茶 *Lǐsì zuótiān shuō zhuōzi shàng fàng-zhe yī bēi chá* 'Lisi said yesterday that a cup of tea was placed on the table', 'the time of the embedded state overlaps the matrix event time' (Lin Jo-wang 2006: 14).

Lastly, there are some sentence-final particles which seem to play a role in the temporal interpretation of the sentence: namely, 來著 *láizhe*, (sentence-final) 了 *le* (see §4.2.1, Fn. 29), and 呢 *ne*. Zhu Dexi (1982: 208–9) argues that these particles are connected to the category of tense. See the following examples (Zhu Dexi 1982: 209, qtd. in Paul 2015: 257; glosses adapted):

(79)   a.   下雨呢。
        xiàyǔ   ne
        rain   SFP
        'It's (still) raining.' (implication: it was raining before)

     b.   下雨了。
        xiàyǔ   le
        rain   CRS
        '(Look,) it's raining.' (implication: it wasn't raining before)

c. 下雨來著。

xiàyǔ   *láizhe*

rain   REC.PST

'It just rained.' (implication: it was raining a moment ago)

Zhu Dexi (1982) suggests that 來著 *láizhe* indicates that the event occurred in the recent past (it is often paired with adverbs like 剛才 *gāngcái* 'a moment ago'), 了 *le* indicates a new state of affairs, while 呢 *ne* indicates the continuity of a state of affairs (on sentence-final particles, see also Paul 2015). Li and Thompson (1981: 240) proposed that the main function of 了 *le* is that of indicating 'current relevance', similarly to a perfect (Li, Thompson, and McMillan 1982). Thus, again, the meaning and functions of these particles appear to be more akin to aspect than to tense: just as the aspect markers discussed before, they however play a role in the temporal interpretation of the sentence. As to 來著 *láizhe* (also 來的 *laide*), Chirkova (2003: 30) remarks that this particle has often been seen as a feature of Beijing Mandarin (see Chao Yuen Ren 1968: 810; Iljic 1983: 65): in the corpus she collected, 來著 *láizhe* is the (tense/) aspect particle with the lowest number of occurrences. Paul (2015: 259) highlights that 來著 *láizhe* is incompatible with telic verbs: these verbs presuppose a result state which still holds at speech time, which is in contradiction with the very notion of recent past, excluding speech time.

To sum up, what emerges from the discussion in this section is that MSC has no dedicated tense markers, and that aspect (both grammatical and lexical), temporal expressions, and modal verbs are the primary determinant of time reference. Unfortunately, due to space constraints, here we just discussed the situation of MSC, ignoring the variation within Sinitic: we shall just briefly mention that, according to Yue Anne Oi-Kan (2003: 90–1), some Southern Sinitic languages do distinguish between perfective aspect and past tense. In these dialects, she suggests, past tense is marked by a construction based on the existential verb, as e.g. Cantonese 有 *yáuh* 'have, exist' (vs. 冇 *móuh* 'not have, not exist'). Furthermore, Sybesma (2004) and Cheng Lisa Lai-Shen (2010) suggests that there are sentence-final particles in Cantonese which possess tense semantics (see the sources for the details).

6.4.1 Lexical aspect

The topic of lexical aspect has been the object of much debate in Chinese linguistics (see e.g. Tai and Chou 1975; Chu Chauncey Cheng-hsi 1976;

Tai James Hao-yi 1984; Sybesma 1997; Lin Jimmy 2004; Soh and Kuo 2005; for an overview, see Soh Hooi Ling 2014; Basciano 2017d). While the existence of the Vendlerian verb classes[13] state (e.g. 恨 *hèn* 'hate') and activity (e.g. 跑 *pǎo* 'run') is generally accepted, there is no agreement as to whether Chinese also has achievements and accomplishments. See the following examples:

(80)   a. 張三殺了李四兩次，李四都沒死。

      Zhāngsān shā-le   Lǐsì liǎng cì   Lǐsì dōu méi sǐ

      Zhangsan kill-PFV Lisi two   time Lisi still NEG die

      'Zhangsan killed Lisi twice, but Lisi didn't die.'

   b. 我昨天寫了一封信，可是沒寫完。

      wǒ zuótiān   xiě-le   yī   fēng xìn   kěshì méi

      1SG yesterday write-PFV one CLF letter but   NEG

      xiě-wán

      write-finish

      'Yesterday I wrote a letter, but I didn't finish it.'

Tai James Hao-yi (1984) proposes that, in order to convey that a result has been achieved, Chinese makes use of complex verbs: specifically, resultative compounds (see §5.1.3.1). For instance, while the English verb *kill* does imply that the result has been achieved (i.e. terminating a life), the MSC verb 殺 *shā* by itself should be classified as an activity, in Vendlerian terms (i.e. perform an action aimed at killing someone): thus, (80a) does not necessarily imply that Lisi died, and the perfective marker 了 -*le* indicates the conclusion of the action, but not its completion (Smith 1994; Soh and Gao 2006, 2007). If we want to convey that

---

[13] Vendler (1957, 1967) proposes that verbs may be divided into four *Aktionsart* classes: a. 'states', i.e. static, non-dynamic, and durative states of affairs (e.g. *know, love*); b. 'activities', i.e. dynamic, durative states of affairs without an endpoint (e.g. *run, drive*); c. 'accomplishments', i.e. dynamic, durative states of affairs with an endpoint (e.g. *build* (a house), *drink* (a glass of milk); d. 'achievements', i.e. punctual, non-durative states of affairs with an endpoint (e.g. *die, arrive*). A fifth class was later added, namely 'semelfactives', i.e. instantaneous (like achievements) but atelic states of affairs (e.g. *knock, sneeze: she knocked on the door for five minutes*; see Smith 1991). The class to which a verb belongs may predict its behaviour.

However, it has been suggested that, in order to assess the telicity of a predicate, we must take into consideration the whole verb phrase: compare *he built houses for years/*in a year* (activity) and *he built two houses *for years/in a year* (accomplishment; see e.g. Verkuyl 1972; Dowty 1979; Rothstein 2004). Thus, a verb as *build* may be telic or atelic, depending on its object: generally speaking, 'for X time' adverbials are compatible with atelic states of affairs (*she ran for hours*), while 'in X time' adverbials are compatible with telic states of affairs (*she fixed her car in an hour*).

the result has been achieved, we must use a resultative compound, adding the verb 死 sǐ 'die' to 殺 shā: (80a) would indeed be ungrammatical, if we substitute 殺 shā with 殺死 shā-sǐ (as it implies that Lisi is dead). Sybesma (1997: 225) believes that Chinese has no inherently telic verbs, and hence there are no monomorphemic verbs which may translate English verbs as *see*, *hear*, or *find*: again, we need resultative compounds (看到 kàn-dào 'look-arrive, see', 聽見 tīng-jiàn 'listen-see, hear', 找到 zhǎo-dào 'search-arrive, find').[14]

However, despite the fact that Chinese very often makes use of compound verbs to express the achievement of a result, there are indeed some inherently telic (achievement) monomorphemic verbs, as 死 sǐ 'die', 到 dào 'arrive', 去 qù 'go'. Tai James Hao-yi (1984: 294) includes those verbs, as well as resultative compounds, in the category 'results'. He proposes that there are three aspectual classes in Chinese: states, activities, and results. Tai's 'results' are basically equivalent to Vendler's achievements (they are incompatible with the progressive; see §6.4), and, hence, we may say that Chinese does have both simple (e.g. 死 sǐ 'die') and compound (resultatives) achievements (see also Soh Hooi Ling 2014).

As for accomplishments, the situation is even more complex. Typical accomplishment verbs include creation verbs, as *build*, *write*, and *paint*, and consumption verbs, as *drink*, *eat*, and *read*: they may be telic or atelic, depending on the properties of the direct object (also known as 'incremental theme'). Krifka (1998) highlights that these verbs describe telic situations when the object is quantized, as e.g. *two books*, *a cup of tea*. However, it seems that, in Chinese, these verbs do not imply completion even if a quantized object is present (80b). According to some scholars, this implies that Chinese lacks accomplishments (see Tai James Hao-yi 1984; Sybesma 1997): again, if we want to convey completion in a sentence as (80b), we must use a resultative compound (寫完 xiě-wán 'write-finish').

Smith (1991, 1994) believes that the above-mentioned characteristics are not explained by the lack of some aspectual classes in Chinese, but rather by the properties of the perfective marker 了 -le. As hinted at before, 了 -le indicates the conclusion of the action, but not its completion: according to Smith, an accomplishment-type predicate with the

---

[14] The second constituent of these compounds is often referred to as 'phase complement' (see Chao Yuen Ren 1968; Li and Thompson 1981).

perfective marker may be interpreted as concluded (with an arbitrary endpoint) without reaching its 'true' endpoint. This is the reason why (80b) is acceptable.

However, Soh and Kuo (2005) offer an alternative account. They argue that the telicity of a predicate depends both from the type of verb and (again) from the type of object. Soh and Kuo distinguish between creation verbs and 'non-creation' verbs: non-creation verbs, like 吃 *chī* 'eat' and 喝 *hē* 'drink', if followed by objects modified by numerals, imply completion; however, if the object is modified by a demonstrative, there is no such implication.[15] Thus, (81) becomes ungrammatical if an object with a numeral is present, but it is acceptable if a demonstrative is present instead (Soh and Kuo 2005: 204; glosses adapted):

(81) 他吃了那個蛋糕/*兩個蛋糕，但是沒吃完。

    tā   *chī-le*   *nà*   *ge*   *dàngāo* / **liǎng* *ge*   *dàngāo*
    3SG.M eat-PFV that CLF   cake   two   CLF cake
    dànshì *méi* *chī-wán*
    but   NEG   eat-finish
    'He ate that cake/* two cakes, but he did not finish eating it/*them.'

As for objects modified by 一 *yī* 'one', Soh and Kuo (2005: 202) argue that, when 一 *yī* is interpreted as a numeral, the event must be completed, while when it is interpreted as an indefinite determiner, the event is not necessarily completed:

(82) 我昨天看了一本書，可是沒看完 。

    wǒ   *zuótiān* *kàn-le*   *yī*   *běn* *shū*   *kěshì*   *méi*
    1SG   yesterday read-PFV one   CLF   book   but   NEG
    kàn-wán
    read-finish
    'Yesterday I read a book, but I did not finish it.'

With creation verbs, as 寫 *xiě* 'write' and 畫 *huà* 'draw, paint', however, telicity depends on the type of object: Soh and Kuo (2005) distinguish between 'No Partial Objects' (NPO) and 'Allows Partial Objects' (APO). Objects belonging to the former class, as e.g. 一個蛋糕 *yī ge*

---

[15] This is said to depend from the [±bounded] feature: quantified objects possess the [+bounded] feature, while demonstrative objects can be either [+bounded] or [-bounded] (Soh and Kuo 2005; see also Jackendoff 1991).

dàngāo 'a cake', 一個字 *yī ge zì* 'a character', may not be regarded as relevant objects until the process of creation has reached its inherent endpoint (i.e. it must be completed). Objects belonging to the APO class, as 一封信 *yī fēng xìn* 'a letter' or 一幅畫 *yī fú huà* 'a painting', however, may be considered to be relevant even if the process of creation is interrupted before reaching its inherent endpoint: if I am writing a letter and just write a few lines, without completing it, the created object may still be defined as a 'letter'. If, however, I mix the ingredients for a cake, but I do not put it in the oven and wait until it is ready, the resulting object may not be defined as a 'cake' (NPO). Thus, with NPO objects, the event must necessarily be completed, and a sentence like (83) is anyway unacceptable, no matter what modifies the object (Soh and Kuo 2005: 205; glosses adapted; compare Exx. 81, 82):

(83) *他做了一個蛋糕 / 兩個蛋糕 / 那個蛋糕, 可是沒做好 。
     tā   *zuò-le*   *yī*   *ge*   *dàngāo* / *liǎng ge*   *dàngāo* /
     3SG.M make-PFV one CLF cake   two   CLF   cake
     nà   *ge*   *dàngāo kěshì méi*   *zuò-hǎo*
     that   CLF   cake   but   NEG   make-finish
     'He made a cake/two cakes/that cake, but he did not finish it/
     them.'

Soh and Kuo (2005) remark that, in this type of sentence, the use of perfective 了 *-le* does imply the completion of the event.

However, when a creation verb is followed by an APO object, the final endpoint must not necessarily be reached, as already mentioned. Thus, (84) is unacceptable if the object is modified by a numeral, but not if it is modified by a demonstrative (Soh and Kuo 2005: 205; glosses adapted):

(84) 他畫了 *兩幅畫 / 那幅畫, 可是沒畫完 。
     tā   *huà-le*   *liǎng fú*   *huà* /   *nà*   *fú*   *huà*
     3SG.M paint-PFV two   CLF painting/ that CLF painting
     kěshì   *méi*   *huà-wán*
     but   NEG   paint-finish
     'He painted *two paintings/that painting, but he did not finish
     painting them/it.'

This explains the acceptability of (80b): 寫 *xiě* is a creation verb followed by an APO object, 信 *xìn* 'letter', modified by the numeral 一 *yī* 'one'. If we interpret the numeral 'one' as a definite determiner, the completion of the event is not a requirement. If, however, we substitute

信 *xìn* 'letter' with 字 *zì* 'character' (NPO), the event must be completed, and, hence, the sentence becomes unacceptable (Soh and Kuo 2005: 202; glosses adapted):

(85) 我昨天寫了一封信／＊一個字，可是沒寫完。
    *wǒ   zuótiān   xiě-le   yī   fēng   xìn /   *yī   ge*
    1SG   yesterday   write-PFV   one   CLF   letter   one   CLF
    zì   kěshì   méi   xiě-wán
    character   but   NEG   write-finish
    'Yesterday I wrote a letter /*a character, but I did not finish writing it.'

According to Soh and Kuo, the differences between Chinese and English as for the interaction between perfective aspect and accomplishments depend on the different noun systems of the two languages: while English distinguishes between count and mass nouns, in Chinese there are only mass nouns (Chierchia 1988; Cheng and Sybesma 1999). This has consequences for the boundedness of the nominal expression and, thus, for the telicity of the phrase or sentence (see also Soh Hooi Ling 2014).

Thus, if we consider the verb phrase in its entirety, we may say that Chinese has all four Vendlerian verb classes. This seems to be confirmed also by standard telicity tests: creation and consumption verbs, as 畫 *huà* 'paint' and 喝 *hē* 'drink', are compatible both with 'for X time' and with 'in X time' expressions (see Fn. 13):

(86) a. 我畫了十年的畫。
        wǒ   huà-le   shí   nián   de   huà
        1SG   paint-PFV   ten   year   MOD   painting
        'I painted paintings for years.'

    b. 我在一個星期裡畫了兩幅畫。
        wǒ   zài   yī   ge   xīngqī   lǐ   huà-le   liǎng   fú
        1SG   in   one   CLF   week   in   paint-PFV   two   CLF
        huà
        painting
        'I painted two paintings in a week.'

6.4.1.1 Aspect in resultative compounds

It has been observed that 'for X time' expressions may be used with resultative constructions, but not with resultative compounds (Li Yafei 2005: 58; glosses adapted):

(87) a. 李逵累得哭了兩天。

      Lǐ Kuí lèi-de   *kū-le*   *liǎng*   *tiān*

      Li Kui tired-RES   cry-PFV   two   day

      'Li Kui was so tired he wept for two days.'

    b. 李逵累哭了（＊兩天）。

      Lǐ Kuí lèi-kū-le   (**liǎng*   *tiān*)

      Li Kui tired-cry-PFV   two   day

      'Li Kui was so tired he wept (*for two days).'

According to Li Yafei (2005), resultative compounds are accomplishments with an inherent endpoint and, thus, are incompatible with duration adverbials, regardless of their morphological structure. Li Yafei believes that resultative compounds behave as a single lexical item, and thus the temporal expression may not have scope only over the action verb (as is instead the case for the resultative construction; see Ex. 87a).

However, resultative compounds do not form a coherent category in terms of aspectual properties: different resultatives interact in different ways with aspect markers. Yong Shin (1997) divides resultatives into two classes: 'simple change resultatives' and 'complex change resultatives'. Simple change resultatives include, for instance, verbs as 打破 *dǎ-pò* 'hit-break, break', 學會 *xué-huì* 'study-be.able, learn': they behave as achievements, since they describe an instantaneous change of state, but, differently from English achievements, they do not allow a detachable preliminary process. Complex change resultatives, as 拉長 *lā-cháng* 'pull-long, lengthen', 放大 *fàng-dà* 'expand-large, enlarge', in contrast, are unlike achievements, i.e. they are not instantaneous, and allow a gradual development of the action: they are however also different from accomplishments, as they describe an action which leads to a predetermined termination (Yong Shin 1997: 17). According to Yong Shin, in complex change resultatives the process leading to the endpoint is characterized by a development with culminating stages. Complex change resultatives thus resemble degree achievements, as e.g. Eng. *widen, lengthen, dry* (Dowty 1979; Hay, Kennedy, and Levin 1999; Kearns 2007; Rothstein 2008).

The difference between simple and complex change resultatives becomes obvious if we observe their interaction with imperfective aspect markers. While all resultative compounds are incompatible with the durative aspect marker 著 *-zhe* (e.g. *喝醉著 *hē-zuì-zhe* 'drink-drunk-DUR', *吃飽著 *chī-bǎo-zhe* 'eat-full-DUR', 洗乾淨著 *xǐ-gānjìng-zhe* 'wash-clean-DUR' (Yong Shin 1997; Xiao and McEnery 2004; but cf. Basciano 2019), not all of them are incompatible with the progressive aspect marker 在 *zài*. Yong Shin (1997) highlights that simple change resultatives are incompatible with the progressive, just as achievements, while complex change resultatives do allow 在 *zài*. See the following example (Tham Shiao Wei 2009: 13; glosses adapted):

(88) 三毛在擦乾那隻盤子。
 Sān Máo *zài* *cā-gān* *nà* *zhī* *pánzi*
 San Mao PROG wipe-dry that CLF plate
 'San Mao is wiping that plate dry.'

The use of the progressive is allowed with complex change resultatives precisely because these verbs, while having an endpoint, describe a gradual process with stages (Smith 1991; Yong Shin 1997). Tham Shiao Wei (2009) argues that the reason why some resultatives may be marked for the progressive aspect is that their result constituents are degree achievements, which may describe a gradual change of state: for instance, 長 *cháng* 'long', 短 *duǎn* 'short', 大 *dà* 'big', 小 *xiǎo* 'small', 濕 *shī* 'wet', 寬 *kuān* 'wide' (see also Basciano 2010, 2019).[16]

Just as for degree achievements, the telicity of resultatives which tolerate the progressive may arise contextually or by adding a bounded measure of change, as e.g. 有一米多 *yǒu yī mǐ duō* 'about a metre' in the following sentence (adapted from Basciano 2019: 212):

(89) 我一口氣挖了大約有五分鐘，通道被我挖寬了大概有一米多
 wǒ *yīkǒuqì* *wā-le* *dàyuē* *yǒu* *wǔ* *fēnzhōng*
 1SG without.a.break dig-PFV about have five minute
 tōngdào *bèi* *wǒ* *wā-kuān-le* *dàgài* *yǒu* *yī*
 passageway PASS 1SG dig-wide-PFV about have one
 mǐ *duō*
 metre much
 'I dug without a break for about five minutes, and I widened the passageway by a little more than a metre.'

---

[16] Indeed, these items, may be argued to have both adjectival and verbal properties: they may be used as intransitive change of state verbs, as e.g. in 碗盤剛乾，你又要用了 *wǎnpán gāng gān, nǐ yòu yào yòng le* 'the dishes have just dried, and you want to use them again' (Tham Shiao Wei 2009: 5); 路面寬了 (但是還不太寬) *lùmiàn kuān-le (dànshì hái bù tài kuān)* 'the road has widened (but it still isn't very wide)'.

Thus, not all verbs which are usually classified as resultatives imply the achievement of a result state. Based on their aspectual properties, we may in fact divide resultatives into at least two groups, characterized by different event structures (see Basciano 2019).

6.5 Argument structure: the case of resultative compounds

In the preceding section, we dealt with the aspectual properties of resultative compounds. Resultatives are one of the most debated topics in Chinese linguistics: indeed, due to the syntactic and semantic peculiarities of resultatives, the research on them contributed to improve our understanding of the argument structure of verbs (for an overview, see Basciano 2010, 2017c, 2019).

Resultative compounds may be both transitive and intransitive. Transitive resultatives may in turn be divided into four distinct construction types:

a. V_1 is a transitive verb, and the object is selected by the verb itself (i.e. it is the object of V_1):

(90) 張三搖醒了李四 。
  Zhāngsān   *yáo-xǐng-le*   *Lǐsì*
  Zhangsan   shake-wake-PFV   Lisi
  'Zhangsan woke up Lisi (by shaking him).'

b. V_1 is an unergative (intransitive) verb and, hence, the object of the construction is not selected by V_1:

(91) 她跑丟了一隻鞋 。
  tā   *pǎo-diū-le*   *yī*   *zhī*   *xié*
  3SG.F   run-lose-PFV   one   CLF   shoe
  'She lost a shoe (while) running.'

c. V_1 is a transitive verb, but the object is not the object of V_1:

(92) 他踢破了球鞋 。
  tā   *tī-pò-le*   *qiúxié*
  3SG.M   kick-break-PFV   sneakers
  'He broke his sneakers by kicking (i.e. playing football).'

d. V_1 is a transitive verb, and the object is not the object of V_1, but rather an inalienable noun (often, a body part):

(93)　他看花了眼睛。

tā　　*kàn-huā-le*　　　*yǎnjīng*
3SG.M　read-blurred-PFV　eye
'His eyes got blurred by reading.'

In all four types of resultatives the result is predicated of the object: in (90), it is Lisi who woke up; in (91), it is the shoe which was lost; in (92), it is the shoes which broke; in (93), it is the eyes (vision) which got blurred. However, there are also cases in which the result state is predicated of the 'subject' (here, mostly, the agent; see §6.2.1), in violation of the Direct Object Restriction (henceforth: DOR; Simpson 1983; Levin and Rappaport Hovav 1995):[17]

(94)　a.　他喝醉了酒。

tā　　*hē-zuì-le*　　　*jiǔ*
3SG.M　drink-drunk-PFV　wine
'He got drunk (by drinking wine).'

　　　b.　她學會了日語。

tā　　*xué-huì-le*　　　*Rìyǔ*
3SG.F　study-know-PFV　Japanese
'She learned Japanese (= she studied Japanese and learned it as a result).'

In (94a) it is the subject/agent 他 *tā* 'he' who got drunk, and in (94b) it is the subject/agent 她 *tā* 'she' who learned Japanese. There are however restrictions on the type of object which may appear in constructions as (94a): they are mostly dummy, non-referential objects, as e.g. 飯 *fàn* 'food' (吃飯 *chī-fàn* 'eat-food, eat'), 看書 *kàn-shū* 'read-book, read, study' (see Huang C-T. James 2006, 2010). It appears that, generally speaking, the more the object is generic, the more it is perceived as acceptable in this construction type, although grammaticality judgements vary from speaker to speaker, and examples with rather specific objects are also attested (see Basciano 2010). As for (94b), 會 *huì* 'be able to' is a transitive stative verb (compare 他會日語 *tā huì Rìyǔ* 'he

---

[17] The DOR predicts that, in a resultative construction, the result must be predicated of the object, but not of the subject, and that the resultative phrase may not be predicated of noun phrases which are not direct objects. In English, when there is no object, the reflexive acts as a 'fake' object: see e.g. *he played himself tired*, in which the result state (*tired*) is predicated of the object *himself*. For a syntactic analysis of Chinese resultative constructions in which the result is predicated of the subject, see Huang James Cheng-te (1992), Sybesma (1999), Zhang Niina Ning (2007).

knows Japanese'): in this case, the result may be predicated of the subject because the object in the construction is actually the object of V$_2$ (see Basciano 2010 for further details).

Since sometimes the result state may be predicated either of the subject or of the object, there may be ambiguous sentences. See the following examples:

(95)   張三騎累了馬。
     Zhāngsān   qí-lèi-le   mǎ
     Zhangsan   ride-tired-PFV   horse
     a. 'Zhangsan rode the horse tired.'
     b. 'Zhangsan rode a horse and got tired.'

While (95a) is the preferred reading, (95b) is indeed a possible interpretation. This ambiguity is due to the fact that the object 馬 *mǎ* 'horse' in (95b) may be interpreted as non-referential (cf. Cheng Lisa Lai-Shen 1997), i.e. as a 'weak' non-referential object part of the compound verb 騎馬 *qí-mǎ* 'ride a horse': thus, it may be seen as equivalent to the dummy objects mentioned before. In fact, if we substitute 馬 *mǎ* 'horse' with 那匹馬 *nà pǐ mǎ* 'that horse', i.e. a referential object, the only possible interpretation is that the result is predicated of the object (as in Ex. 95a), i.e. it is the horse who got tired. The same holds also if we substitute 馬 *mǎ* 'horse' with 豬 *zhū* 'pig' (see Lin Jimmy 2004): since 'pig' may not be interpreted as a dummy or weak object, only the first reading (i.e. the result is predicated of the object) is available. Moreover, (95) becomes ungrammatical if we substitute 馬 *mǎ* 'horse' with 自行车 *zìxíngchē* 'bicycle':

(96)   *張三騎累了自行车。
     Zhāngsān   qí-lèi-le   zìxíngchē
     Zhangsan   ride-tired-PFV   bicycle

Since 自行车 *zìxíngchē* 'bicycle' may only be interpreted as a referential object, the only available reading is that the result is predicated of the object. However, the result state 累 *lèi* 'tired' is not normally associated with inanimate entities: hence the ungrammaticality of (96). Compare the following sentences (Shi Chunhong 2008: 254):

(97)   a. 爷爷开累了车。
        yéye   kāi-lèi-le   chē
        grandfather   drive-tired-PFV   car
        'My grandfather got tired driving.'

b. *爷爷开累了桑塔纳。

yéye   kāi-lèi-le   Sāngtǎnà
grandfather   drive-tired-PFV   Santana
'My grandfather got tired driving a Santana.'

Both (97a) and (97b) contain an inanimate object. However, (97a) is acceptable, as 車 *chē* may be interpreted as a dummy object (as in 開 車 *kāi-chē* 'operate-car, drive'), and, thus, the result may be predicated of the subject. (97b), on the other hand, is ungrammatical, as the object 桑塔納 *Sāngtǎnà* 'Santana' is referential: the result must be predicated of the object, but a car cannot become tired (Shi Chunhong 2008: 254).

In intransitive constructions, however, the result is always predicated of the 'subject'. There are two types of intransitive constructions, exemplified by (98) and (99):

(98)   瓶子破碎了。

      píngzi pò-suì-le
      bottle   break-shatter-PFV
      'The bottle shattered.'

(99)   他跑累了。

      tā   *pǎo-lèi-le*
      3SG.M   run-tired-PFV
      'He got tired running.'

The first type (98) is non-causative and contains a change of state verb (V_1): thus, V_1 already conveys a result, and V_2 further specifies the result (compare Eng. *the window broke into pieces*). Constructions as (98) do not constitute a violation to the DOR (see Fn. 17), since the subject of an unaccusative verb may be analysed as an underlying object (see Levin and Rappaport Hovav 2005): thus, in (98) the result is predicated of an (underlying) object. Constructions as (99), however, do violate the DOR, since the result does not refer to an object: they are akin to resultatives with a 'fake' object in English, as e.g. *he ran himself tired*, in which, from the syntactic point of view, the result is predicated of the object *himself*.

Resultative compounds may also be used in causative constructions like those exemplified in (100a-d) (see Cheng and Huang 1994; Zou Ke 1993; Her One-soon 2006; Basciano 2010, 2017c):

(100) a. 青草吃肥了羊儿。(Xiong and Liu 2006: 123)
      qīngcǎo   chī-féi-le   yángr
      grass   eat-fat-PFV sheep
      'Grass made the sheep get fat (= grass made the sheep eat
      until it got fat).'

   b. 那瓶酒喝醉了他。(adapted from Xiong and Liu 2006: 123)
      nà   píng jiǔ   hē-zuì-le   tā
      that   CLF   wine   drink-drunk-PFV   3SG.M
      'That bottle of wine made him get drunk (= that bottle of
      wine made him drink until he got drunk).'

   c. 這件事哭累了張三。(Sybesma 1999: 43)
      zhè   jiàn   shì   kū-lèi-le   Zhāngsān
      this   CLF   matter cry-tired-PFV Zhangsan
      'This made Zhangsan cry until he got tired.'

   d. 這件事累死了他。(Sybesma 1999: 43)
      zhè   jiàn   shì   lèi-sǐ-le   tā
      this   CLF   matter tired-die-PFV   3SG.M
      'This made him become tired to death.'

As shown in the examples above, this process of causativization may
be applied to any resultative, independently from the characteristics of
V_1 (see Basciano 2010).[18] However, there are some constraints this
construction is subject to. First of all, the initial position in this causative construction may not be occupied by entities which can control
the event (i.e. initiators). Thus, rather than an initiator, the entity in the
sentence-initial position is a condition which makes the event possible
(an 'enabling condition'; see Wolff 2003): for instance, in (100a) the availability of grass is what makes it possible for the sheep to eat and, hence,
get fat; in (100b), the bottle of wine makes it possible for 'him' to get

---

[18] In English, for instance, this is possible only if V_1 in the causative construction is a
change of state verb (Huang James Cheng-te 2006: 9):
(i)   a. *The river froze solid.*
       b. *An unusually cold winter froze the river solid.*
(ii)   a. *Mary cried herself sad.*
       b. **That event cried Mary sad.*
(iii) a. *She quickly kicked free.*
       b. **The threat of death quickly kicked her free.*

drunk. Indeed, Huang Han-Chun (2006: 28) remarks that in this construction type, the phrase in the sentence-initial position does not directly participate in the event described by the verb, but it is still required for the event to occur.[19] As for the noun phrase in the postverbal position (i.e. the causee), it is either the agent of V_1 (the sheep in Ex. 100a, 'him' in 100b, Zhangsan in 100c) or the entity undergoing the change of state ('him' in 100d). At the same time, the result state must be predicated of the postverbal noun phrase.

Given these restrictions, sentences like those in (101) are ungrammatical:

(101)   a. *李四喝醉了張三。

        Lǐsì   hē-zuì-le   *Zhāngsān*

        Lisi   drink-drunk-PFV   Zhangsan

        'Lisi made Zhangsan drink until he got drunk.'

      b. *這件事哭濕了手帕。

         zhè jiàn shì   kū-shī-le   shǒupà

         this CLF matter cry-wet-PFV handkerchief

         'This made the handkerchief get wet (as a result of somebody's crying).'

In (101a), Lisi controls the event, thus directly participates in it. As for (101b), while in the initial position we find a possible enabling condition for 哭濕 *kū-shī* 'cry-wet, make wet by crying', the sentence is anyway ungrammatical since the postverbal noun, 手帕 *shǒupà* 'handkerchief', is not a possible participant to the event described by V_1 (哭 *kū* 'cry'): thus, what is lacking is an entity which may perform the action, which is required for the structure of the event.

6.6 Word classes

Word classes, or parts of speech (詞類 *cílèi*), are groups of lexical items which share a number of phonological, morphological, syntactic, and semantic properties (Anward, Moravcsik, and Stassen 1997; Anward 2001). Thus, a word class groups together words which share a set of those properties. The introduction of word classes in the Western philosophical and grammatical tradition is usually attributed to Dionysius

---

[19] For a syntactic analysis of this type of resultatives, see Sybesma (1992).

Thrax, in his grammar of the Greek language *Téchnē Grammatikḗ* (end of the second century BC): in the *Téchnē*, Dionysius first proposes a distinction into eight 'parts of speech' (Greek *mérē lógou*).

However, the characterization of word classes based on the classical (Greek and Latin) grammatical tradition has been the object of much controversy. The criteria for the definition of word classes vary significantly in different theoretical approaches, and many more issues arise in their application to languages which are typologically distant from 'European' languages (known as 'Standard Average European'; Haspelmath 2001). Indeed, because of the wide range of variation in the way lexical items behave in the languages of the world, the universality of parts of speech has been often called into question. Some suggest that word classes are a viable concept for some languages, but not for others (see Croft 2000: 65), while others believe that at least the distinction between nouns and verbs is universal, and that there are always criteria for distinguishing them in any language (Croft 2003; Evans and Osada 2005). The universality of adjectives, on the other hand, is often questioned, and they are sometimes grouped with nouns or with verbs (Croft 2000: 67).

However, Croft (2000: 65) believes that the categories of noun, verb, and adjective are indeed universal, in the sense that there are 'typological prototypes' which may be termed 'noun', 'verb', and 'adjective'. According to Croft (2000: 85), word classes, just as any other syntactic category, derive from the constructions which define them. While the prototypes for each part of speech are universal, the structures and borderlines of a word class are language-specific. In this perspective, the 'noun' is the prototype of a thing-denoting word class, mostly acting as the subject or object of a sentence. The 'verb' is the prototype of an action-denoting word class, mostly acting as a predicate. The 'adjective' is the prototype of a property-denoting word class, mostly acting as a modifier (Anward 2001: 727–8; Croft 2001: 87–8). 'Minor' word classes may also be defined in prototypical terms, although this may be less straightforward for them (Zádrapa 2017).

Given the difficulties associated with the definition of word classes, especially in cross-linguistic perspective, some scholars adopted a 'lumping' approach, suggesting that there are languages in which some word classes are missing, or even without any word class distinction: parts of speech are thus 'lumped' in a single major class (see Croft 2000: 67–72; Bisang 2010). For instance, according to Hengeveld (1992) there are 'flexible' languages, which combine the function of two or more parts of speech in a single class, and 'rigid' languages, which lack one or more parts of speech; 'specialized' languages, on the other hand, have all the major parts of speech. Other scholars prefer a 'splitting' approach, based on distributional analysis (see Croft 2000: 72–83): however, this may potentially lead to a proliferation of word classes, which are then hard to associate with the 'traditional' major parts of speech.

The issues related to the definition and delimitation of word classes are particularly relevant for Sinitic languages. Chinese is a very good example of a language in which the identification of parts of speech is indeed problematic. However, while word classes in modern Sinitic (mostly, in MSC) have been extensively discussed in the literature (at least) since the 1950s, the research on earlier stages of Chinese is still not very developed, especially on the period between the end of the Han dynasty and the Song dynasty (Zádrapa 2011, 2017).

In traditional Chinese philology, two major word classes are distinguished: namely, 實字 *shízì* (now 實詞 *shící*) 'full words', and 虛字 *xūzì* (虛詞 *xūcí*) 'empty words'. This distinction is roughly equivalent to that between content words and function words. Content words, i.e. nouns, verbs, adjectives (and also adverbs, although this is controversial), are words with a lexical meaning, which typically name things, events, or properties. Function words, i.e. conjunctions, prepositions, articles, etc., are words with a more abstract/grammatical meaning, which are often used also to indicate the relationships between content words (Ježek 2015).

Besides the distinction between 'full' and 'empty' words, in the Song period we find the first mention of the terms 死字 *sǐzì* '(lit.) dead words' and 活字 *huózì* 'living words', used to indicate, respectively, nouns (as well as adjectives, sometimes) and verbs. Some authors, as e.g. Jia Changzhao (賈昌朝, 997/8–1065), distinguish between 動字 *dòngzì* 'action words', i.e. (transitive) verbs, and 靜字 *jìngzì* 'still words', i.e. adjectives or intransitive and passive verbs (occasionally, also nouns). Note, however, that the terminology used to refer to word classes is not consistent, and its usage varies considerably from author to author. Besides, these terms were not systematically used in the description of the lexicon or grammar of Chinese, except for philological works discussing characters with multiple readings (depending on their function) in ancient texts (Zádrapa 2017).

The explanation of function words later became an independent branch of linguistic research, and several works on the topic were published.

However, a Western-style distinction into word classes was not introduced in China before the nineteenth century: the first work which proposes a systematic classification of parts of speech for (Classical) Chinese is Ma Jianzhong's (马建忠, 1844–1900) 馬氏文通 *Mǎshì wéntōng* 'Mr Ma's Grammar' (1898). This grammar draws extensively from the above-mentioned native philological tradition, as proven by the use of terms like 實字 *shízì* and 虛字 *xūzì* (Peyraube 2001: 349). However, the classification of parts of speech is essentially based on the Western tradition of grammatical description, including both grammars of Sinitic languages by Western missionaries (and sinologists) and grammars of Indo-European languages. Specifically, according to Peyraube (2001), Ma Jianzhong's main model is the well-known *Grammaire de Port-Royal* of 1660. In the 馬氏文通 *Mǎshì wéntōng*, the following parts of speech are listed:

a. 名字 *míngzì* 'nouns'
b. 代字 *dàizì* 'pronouns'
c. 動字 *dòngzì* 'verbs' (compare the above-mentioned 'action words')
d. 靜字 *jìngzì* 'adjectives' (compare the above-mentioned 'still words')
e. 狀字 *zhuàngzì* 'adverbs'
f. 介字 *jièzì* 'prepositions'
g. 連字 *liánzì* 'conjunctions'
h. 助字 *zhùzì* 'particles'
i. 嘆字 *tànzì* 'interjections'

Note, also, that the 馬氏文通 *Mǎshì wéntōng* distinguishes between 字 *zì* 'parts of speech' and 詞 *cí* 'syntactic functions' (e.g. 詞起 *cíqǐ* 'subject', 止詞 *zhǐcí* 'object'). The system of word classes introduced by Ma Jianzhong is particularly important for the development of the native tradition of linguistic analysis, as most of the labels are still in use nowadays (Peyraube 2001): however, the morpheme 字*zì* '(lit.) character' in the names of parts of speech has been substituted with 詞 *cí* 'word' (e.g. 名詞 *míngcí* 'noun', 動詞 *dòngcí* 'verb', 介詞 *jiècí* 'preposition').

The classification of parts of speech of the 馬氏文通 *Mǎshì wéntōng* is largely based on semantic criteria, and Ma Jianzhong's approach has been often criticized by Chinese scholars, who believe it represents a mechanical application of Western categories, inadequate for Chinese.

Nevertheless, this was the dominant model for a very long time (Zádrapa 2017). In Western works on the topic of word classes, on the other hand, we find a variety of criteria for the identification of word classes, and some specialists actually question the relevance of word classes for Chinese (especially for the classical language; Zádrapa 2017). Generally speaking, three types of criteria have been used for the identification of word classes (Evans 2000):

a. syntactic criteria, based on the distribution of words and on their compatibility with other elements in the sentence
b. morphological criteria, based on word structure (e.g. in some languages, nouns are inflected for gender and number, etc.)
c. semantic criteria, based on the meaning of words (e.g. nouns denote entities, while verbs denote actions, etc.)

Moreover, functional criteria have also been proposed in the literature (see e.g. Hopper and Thompson 1984; Hengeveld 1992).

Semantic criteria appear inadequate if we look at a broad range of typologically diverse languages. For instance, basic kinship terms as 'mother' or 'father' may be seen as typical examples of nouns: however, there are languages in which they 'behave as' verbs ('be the mother of', 'be the father of'; see Dixon 2004). Besides, words with very similar meanings, as e.g. 突然 *tūrán* and 忽然 *hūrán*, both meaning 'suddenly', have a different syntactic behaviour: 突然 *tūrán* may be both a predicative adjective and an adverb, while 忽然 *hūrán* may only be used as an adverb (Basciano 2017e). Thus, according to Xing Fuyi (2003), despite the semantic similarity, these two words belong to different classes: 突然 *tūrán* is an adjective, while 忽然 *hūrán* is an adverb (see also Zhu Dexi 1982: 37).

In languages with a rich inflectional morphology, parts of speech may be distinguished (also) on the basis of word structure. However, this does not apply to Chinese, in which words have a single, invariant form: thus, a verb like 走 *zǒu* 'walk' is not different from the noun 書 *shū* 'book', from the structural point of view. There are indeed exceptions, as e.g. the words containing the suffixes 子 *-zi* (刷子 *shuāzi* 'brush$_N$'; compare 刷 *shuā* 'brush$_V$') and 頭 *-tou* (想頭 *xiǎngtou* 'idea'; compare 想 *xiǎng* 'think'), which are always nouns (see Zhu Dexi 1982; Tai James Hao-yi 1997; Yan Mai 2007; see also §5.1.3.2). However, beside these exceptions, there is nothing in the structure of a word which may be used to classify it as a noun or as a verb. This appears to be true also for earlier historical stages of the language, in which we find no productive morphology which is systematically associated with a word class, even if we take into account reconstructed derivational morphology (§5.1.2): there are few well-established paradigms, and even the better understood affixes, as e.g. the suffix *-s, have a broad range of functions. In addition to that, most reconstructed derivational processes seem to be vestiges of a previous stage of the language, and many words derived from the same lexical root became associated with different characters, thus losing their connection (Zádrapa 2017).

In the absence of morphosyntactic clues, the only criteria which we may apply to distinguish parts of speech in Chinese are syntactic: word classes may be defined on the basis of their syntactic function and distribution (see Jin Zhaozi 1983 [1922]; Chao Yuen Ren 1948, 1968; Zhu Dexi 1982; Norman 1988; McCawley 1992; Tai James Hao-yi 1997; Xing Fuyi 2003; Yan Mai 2007). Zádrapa (2017) highlights that the best approach to the issue of word classes in Chinese is adopting a functionalist perspective, focussing on the interaction between syntactic and semantic aspects. This approach, widely accepted among specialists in the past few decades, is in line with some recent trends in general and typological linguistics.

As highlighted by Lü Shuxiang (1980), dividing words into a number of classes does not exclude the possiblity of overlaps among distinct parts of speech: the same word may simply appear in different syntactic slots (Basciano 2017e). Indeed, in Modern Chinese it is often the case that lexical items may be ambiguous in terms of part of speech identity: especially, nouns and verbs (see Kwong and Tsou 2003). For instance, the word 領導 *lǐngdǎo* may be both a verb ('lead') and a noun ('leader'), without any change in its structure (Kwong and Tsou 2003: 116). The same goes for 鎖 *suǒ*, which, again, may be a verb ('lock$_V$') or a noun ('lock$_N$'). An even more interesting case is that of 麻煩 *máfan* 'inconvenient, trouble, bother', which may be used as an adjective (102a), as a verb (102b), or as a noun (102c):[20]

(102) a. 这件事很麻烦。

       zhè *jiàn* *shì*   *hěn*   *máfan*

       this   CLF   matter very   inconvenient

       'This is very inconvenient.'

---

[20] Examples from the *Centre for Chinese Linguistics PKU corpus* < http://ccl.pku.edu.cn:8080/ccl_corpus/> (last access: 9 January 2020).

b. 他不愿麻烦别人。

tā	bù-yuàn	máfan	biérén
3SG.M	NEG-desire	bother	other

'He does not want to bother other people.'

c. 你们在路上会遇到一些麻烦。

nǐ-men	zài	lù-shang	huì	yùdào	yīxiē	máfan
2-PL	at	road-on	FUT	meet	some	trouble

'You might meet some trouble on the road.'

Should we treat these different usages as distinct (homophone) lexemes or as occurrences of a single multicategorial word? The very notion of 'multicategorial word' (兼類詞 *jiānlèicí*) is very controversial (see Hu Mingyang 1996b; Guo Rui 2002a; Liang and Feng 2006). According to some scholars, words as 麻煩 *máfan* (102a-c) do belong to more than one word class, i.e. they are multicategorial (Lu and Zhu 2005 [1951]: 10; Guo Rui 2002b; Kwong and Tsou 2003).[21] Others, however, believe that e.g. 鎖 *suǒ* 'lock$_N$' and 鎖 *suǒ* 'lock$_V$' are in fact two distinct words, since their meaning is different: the former describes an object, while the latter describes an action (Zhu Dexi 1982; Lu Jianming 1994). Yet other specialists propose that an item as 鎖 *suǒ* 'lock$_N$' is actually derived from 鎖 *suǒ* 'lock$_V$' through a process of nominalization (conversion or zero derivation; Tai James Hao-yi 1997; see also Shi Dingxu 2004). It has been claimed that conversion was quite common in Classical Chinese (see Zádrapa 2017): for instance, names of instruments could also be used as denominal verbs, as e.g. 鞭 *biān* 'whip$_N$' > 'whip$_V$', 法 *fǎ* 'model, law' > 'follow the model of'. Also, nouns indicating social or professional roles were quite systematically used as verbs, with the meaning 'acting as X', 'become X': e.g. 相 *xiàng* 'prime minister' > 'to become/be the prime minister' (Zádrapa 2017). If we look at the MC forms of these words, we see that they rarely contained an overt marker of derivation (as e.g. the *-s* suffix or the voiced-voiceless alternation; Zádrapa 2017; see §2.3.1, 5.1.2).

Note, also, that even words which are not normally ambiguous in terms of word class assignment may occasionally be found in different syntactic slots. Kwong and Tsou use the label 'innovative ambiguity' to describe cases as (103), in which the noun 小丑 *xiǎochǒu* 'clown' is used as an adjective (Kwong and Tsou 2003:116; glosses adapted).

---

[21] On multicategorial lexical items in Classical Chinese, see Zhang Shuangdi (1989: 206–9), Zhang Wenguo (2005: 354), and Zádrapa (2017).

(103)　他很小丑。

    tā　　*hěn*　　*xiǎochǒu*
    3SG.M　very　clown
    'He is very clown(ish).'

According to Kwong and Tsou (2003), (103) is not a case of 'regular ambiguity',[22] as those seen before, since here the word 小丑 *xiǎochǒu* 'clown' is used on purpose to obtain a particular effect. These innovative uses may be regarded as instances of 'true' ambiguity only when they become quite common. See also the examples of innovative ambiguity in (104), where 高興 *gāoxìng* 'happy' and 來 *lái* 'come' are used as nouns:

(104)　　a.　赵群德心里有说不出的高兴。[23]

      Zhāo　*Qúndé*　*xīn-li*　　*yǒu*　*shuō-bù-chū*　*de*
      Zhao　Qunde　heart-LOC　have　say-NEG-exit　MOD
      gāoxìng
      happy
      'Zhao Qunde felt an unspeakable joy in his heart.'

    b.　他的来使大家很高兴。　(Guo Rui 2002a: 66)
      tā　　　*de*　　*lái*　　*shǐ*　　*dàjiā*　　*hěn*　　*gāoxìng*
      3SG.M　MOD　come　CAUS　everybody　very　happy
      'His coming made everybody very happy.'

According to Zádrapa (2017), in Chinese it is not possible to distinguish between prototypical and non-prototypical uses of a word based on its shape. However, what may be perceived is a 'functional strain' ('pragmatic markedness' in Bisang 2008), due to typological markedness: this always leads to a 'semantic shift' (Croft 2001: 73), which may be more syntactic in nature or more lexical (Anward 2001: 731–2; on Classical Chinese, see Yin Guoguang 1997: 30–1).

Different approaches have been proposed in the literature to account for the polyfunctionality of words in Chinese. A first approach, which may be traced back to the earlier-mentioned 馬氏文通 *Mǎshì wéntōng*, is based on the notion of 'category borrowing' (假借 *jiǎjiè*): words change their word class depending on their position in the sentence. Thus, for instance, if a verb is placed in the syntactic slot of the direct

---

[22] On systematic and non-systematic polysemy in Classical Chinese, see Zádrapa (2011, 2017).

[23] Example from the *Centre for Chinese Linguistics PKU corpus* <http://ccl.pku.edu.cn:8080/ccl_corpus/> (last access: 9 January 2020).

object, it becomes a noun (Guo Rui 2002a; Liang and Feng 2006). Chen Chengze (1982 [1922]) and Jin Zhaozi (1983 [1922]) propose instead that lexical categories may have 'flexible usage' (活用 *huóyòng*; on word class flexibility in Classical Chinese, see Wang Kezhong 1989; Zádrapa 2011, 2017). Li Jinxi (2001 [1924]) suggests that parts of speech should be identified 'based on syntax' (依句辯品 *yī jù biàn pǐn*; see Guo Rui 2002a; Yan Mai 2007): thus, according to him, words by themselves are categorially indefinite, and they may be assigned to a specific word class only on the basis of their position and function in the sentence. A similar proposal may be found in Marosán (2006), according to whom Chinese is a flexible language in which words are 'acategorial', i.e. their lexical category becomes apparent only in actual use (on 'acategoriality', see also Hopper and Thompson 1984). Note, also, that Bisang (2008) defines Late Archaic Chinese as a 'precategorial' language, i.e. a language in which lexical items are not 'preclassified' as nouns or verbs: thus, in his view, the interpretation of each occurrence of a word depends on the syntactic environment in which it is found.

Some scholars go as far as to cast doubts on the very existence of word classes in Chinese. Gao Mingkai (1953) highlights that parts of speech should be defined on the basis of their morphological structure: thus, since Chinese has no inflection (and little derivation), lexical items simply may not be classified into word classes. Gao Mingkai (1960) further argues that word classes may be assigned to an item only on the basis of its use: in Chinese, however, the same lexical item may be sometimes used as a noun, verb, or adjective (i.e. it may be found in the position of the subject, predicate, or object). Thus, according to him, every word belongs to more than one word class, which entails that there are no categories (see Guo Rui 2002a; see also Mártonfi 1977). According to Xu Tongqiang (1994), a classification of words into parts of speech is necessary for Indo-European languages, in which there is a correspondence between word classes and syntactic functions (see also Sasse 1993), but not for Chinese, in which there is no such correspondence.

In 暫擬漢語教學語法系統 *Zànnǐ Hànyǔ jiàoxué yǔfǎ xìtǒng* 'Proposal for a System for Teaching Chinese Grammar' (1956; presented in Zhang Zhigong 1956), drafted by a team of experts with the aim of finding a common system for teaching, cases as (104a-b) are treated as nominalizations (名物化 *míngwùhuà*): the adjective 高興 *gāoxìng* 'happy' and the verb 來 *lái* 'come' lose (part of) their verbal features and acquire nominal features (see also Kwong and Tsou 2003: 116), leading to nominalization (compare Guo Rui 2002a; for a critique of the nominalization-based approach, see Zhu, Lu, and Ma 1961).

Chen Aiwen (1986) argues that the notion of word class may be interpreted in two ways: as a syntax-based notion, in which the word class of an item may change depending on the syntactic context, and as a meaning-based notion, in which the word class of an item does not change (see also Guo Rui 2002b). Thus, for instance, the word 出版 *chūbǎn* 'publish' in (105) has 'nominal nature' (名詞性 *míngcíxìng*) from the syntactic point of view, but meaning-wise it is still a verb (動基詞 *dòngjīcí*; ex. adapted from Chen Aiwen 1986: 79).

(105)　　这个部门专搞美术出版。
　　　　zhè　ge　bùmén　　zhuān gǎo měishù　chūbǎn
　　　　this　CLF　department　special do　art　　publications
　　　　'This department specializes in art publishing.'

To sum up, it appears that the idea of having clearly distinct lexical categories in Chinese does not find much support nowadays (Zádrapa 2017; for Classical Chinese, see Harbsmeier 1998: 138; for Modern Chinese, see Guo Rui 2002b; Yuan Yulin 2010), and that the idea of Chinese as a language without parts of speech is now marginal. Moreover, as pointed out by Zádrapa (2017), the degree of word class flexibility which we see in the pre-Qin period was first reduced by a gradual functional specialization of lexemes, already apparent in the Han period (Zhang Wenguo 2005), and later on by the development of compounding: this is because compound words tend to be less flexible than simple words in terms of word class. Thus, in the modern language, true word class flexibility is not very common (Zádrapa 2017).

6.6.1 Proposed criteria for establishing word classes in Chinese

As seen in the preceding section, the classification of parts of speech laid out in the 馬氏文通 *Mǎshì wéntōng* dominated the field for a long time, and much of its terminology is still in use today. Since the publication of Ma Jianzhong's grammar, scholars have proposed other parts of speech, not mentioned in the 馬氏文通 *Mǎshì wéntōng*: for instance, Lü Shuxiang (2002 [1942]) defines the class of 語氣詞 *yǔqìcí* 'modal particles', which include 語氣副詞 *yǔqì fùcí* 'modal adverbials' and 感嘆詞 *gǎntàncí* 'interjections'. Wang Li (1985 [1943]) mentions 數詞 *shùcí* 'numerals' and 語氣詞 *yǔqìcí* 'modal particles'; moreover, he proposes three special subclasses of nouns, namely 時間詞 *shíjiāncí* 'time nouns', 處所詞 *chùsuǒcí* 'place nouns', and 方位詞 *fāngwèicí* 'localizers' (see Huang, Li, and Li 2009 on localizers; for an overview, see Guo Rui 2002a).

In the already mentioned 'Proposal for a System for Teaching Chinese Grammar' (§6.6), we find eleven word classes:

    a. 名詞 *míngcí* 'nouns'
    b. 量詞 *liàngcí* 'classifiers'
    c. 代詞 *dàicí* 'pronouns'
    d. 動詞 *dòngcí* 'verbs'
    e. 形容詞 *xíngróngcí* 'adjectives'
    f. 數詞 *shùcí* 'numerals'
    g. 副詞 *fùcí* 'adverbs'
    h. 介詞 *jiècí* 'prepositions'
    i. 連詞 *liáncí* 'conjunctions'
    j. 助詞 *zhùcí* 'particles'
    k. 嘆詞 *tàncí* 'interjections'

This system was later revised in 中學教學語法系統提要 *Zhōngxué jiàoxué yǔfǎ xìtǒng tíyào* 'Outline of a System for Teaching Grammar in Middle School' (1984), in which an additional word class is included: namely, 擬聲詞 *nǐshēngcí* 'onomatopoeias' (also 象聲詞 *xiàngshēngcí*; see Guo Rui 2002a).

Current dictionaries mostly follow this partition into twelve word classes, although some works distinguish between 語氣詞 *yǔqìcí* 'modal particles' and 助詞 *zhùcí* 'particles'. We may also find further distinctions into subclasses (小類 *xiǎo lèi*), as e.g. different subclasses of pronouns, or even additional word classes (附類 *fù lèi*): for instance, 方位詞 *fāngwèicí* 'place names/localizers' and 時間詞 *shíjiāncí* 'time words', or 助動詞 *zhùdòngcí* 'auxiliary verbs' and 趨向動詞 *qūxiàng dòngcí* 'directional verbs' (see e.g. the XHCD).

Due to space constraints, here we cannot discuss in detail all word classes. Thus, in what follows, we focus on the three major word classes of nouns, verbs, and adjectives (§6.6.1.1, 6.6.1.2); we include also prepositions (§6.6.1.3), a particularly controversial category in Chinese.

6.6.1.1 Nouns and verbs

In Chinese, nouns and verbs may be distinguished based on their syntactic distribution. Nouns have the following distribution in

Chinese syntax (see e.g. Tai James Hao-yi 1997; Norman 1998; Xing Fuyi 2003):

a. they may follow a number/demonstrative-classifier combination, as e.g. 兩本書 *liǎng běn shū* 'two CLF book, two books'
b. they may follow the particle 的 *de* (marking modification and/or subordination), as e.g. 爸爸的毛衣 *bàba de máoyī* 'dad MOD sweater, dad's sweater'
c. they may not follow adverbs, as shown e.g. by the ungrammaticality of *都書 *dōu shū* 'all book', *不書 *bù shū* 'not book', *忽然飛機 *hūrán fēijī* 'sudden airplane'

For more syntactic criteria which may be used to define nouns, see e.g. Hu Mingyang (1996a) and Huang, Li, and Li (2009).

Xing Fuyi (2003: 10) notes that, in fact, there are some cases of nouns which directly follow adverbs, as e.g. 僅僅一個人 *jǐnjǐn yī ge rén* 'only one CLF person, only one person', 大約三輛汽車 *dàyuē sān liàng qìchē* 'about three CLF car, about three cars', 共兩块錢 *gòng liǎng kuài qián* 'altogether two CLF money, two Yuan altogether'. However, this type of sentences always seem to imply a covert verb. Xing Fuyi further remarks that time words may be preceded by adverbs, as e.g. 今天已經星期五了 *jīntiān yǐjīng xīngqīwǔ le* 'today already Friday CRS, today is already Friday': however, we may note that these time words belong to the subclass of nouns which may act as nominal predicates in Chinese (for further examples, see Xing Fuyi 2003: 10; for other exceptions, see Huang, Li, and Li 2009).

Verbs, on the other hand, may be defined as words which (Tai James Hao-yi 1997; Norman 1988):

a. may follow adverbs, as e.g. 不去 *bù qù* 'not/don't go', 都去 *dōu qù* 'all go'
b. may be followed by verbal classifiers, as e.g. 來一次 *lái yī cì* 'come one time'
c. may be followed by aspect markers as 了 *-le*, 著 *-zhe*, 過 *-guo*, e.g. 吃了 *chī-le* 'eat-PFV'
d. may not follow nominal classifiers, as shown e.g. by the ungrammaticality of *一個踢 *yī ge tī* 'one CLF kick_v'

However, we must stress the fact that not all lexical items which are usually classified as verbs do satisfy all the criteria listed here. For instance, the copula 是 *shì* and the verb 在 *zài* 'be at' may not be followed by aspect markers, but they are treated as verbs in most theoretical frameworks and descriptions (Tai James Hao-yi 1982).

Moreover, nouns and verbs may be distinguished on the basis of their functions (see e.g. Zhu Dexi 1982; Hu Mingyang 1996a). For instance, nouns may not be predicates, while verbs may not act as noun modifiers, unless the (modification/subordination) particle 的 *de* is added (see Croft 2000).

6.6.1.2 Adjectives

We mentioned earlier (§6.6) that the universality of the category of adjectives has often been questioned in the typological literature. As for Chinese, indeed many scholars propose that adjectives are not an independent word class but, rather, a subclass of verbs (Li and Thompson 1981; Ross 1984; Hengeveld 1992; McCawley 1992; Lin Jimmy 2004). For instance, Li and Thompson (1981) use the label 'adjectival verbs' since, according to them, most adjectives may act as verbs. The main argument in support of a verbal analysis for Chinese adjectives is that they may be used as predicates, without a copula (see also Tai James Hao-yi 1982; Tang Ting-chi 1988; Li Yafei 1990: 177, Fn. 2):

(106) 她真 / 不漂亮。
      tā   *zhēn / bù*   *piàoliang*
      3SG.F really / NEG beautiful
      'She is really/not beautiful.'

McCawley (1992: 232), based on a list of universals of adjectives and verbs, also argues that Chinese has no adjectives and that those items which are usually translated as adjectives in English are, in fact, verbs. Hengeveld (1992) describes Chinese as a 'rigid' language (see §6.6) as far as adjectives (i.e. property-denoting words) and verbs (i.e. action-denoting words) are concerned. Neither properties nor actions require any overt structural coding when used as predicates, but they do require the particle 的 *de* when used as modifiers. Hence, they both belong to the verbal category, according to Hengeveld. See the following examples:

(107) a. 聰明的姑娘
        cōngming   *de*   *gūniang*
        clever   MOD   girl
        'clever girl'

b. 一些吃的東西

yīxiē	chī	de	dōngxi
some	eat	MOD	thing

'some things to eat'

In fact, modifiers followed by 的 *de* have also been analysed as relative clauses (see e.g. Sproat and Shih 1988, 1991; Duanmu San 1998), or as small clauses, deriving each modifier from an underlying predicate (den Dikken and Singhapreecha 2004).

However, some scholars argue that it is indeed possible to define an independent class of adjectives, distinct from verbs, for Chinese. Paul (2010) highlights that not all adjectives may act as predicates by themselves: there is indeed a subclass of non-predicative adjectives, which may act as modifiers, but not as predicates (see Lü and Rao 1981; Li Yuming 1996a),[24] like 方 *fāng* 'square', 共同 *gòngtóng* 'common', 原來 *yuánlái* 'original': see e.g. 一個方的桌子 *yī ge fāng de zhuōzi* 'one CLF square MOD table, a square table'. Within this subset, we find 'intersective' adjectives, as 方 *fāng* 'square', which may act as predicates only within the '是 *shì* (copula)...的 *de*' construction: for instance, 這個桌子*(是)方*(的) *zhè ge zhuōzi *(shì) fāng *(de)* 'this CLF table *(COP) square *(MOD), this table is square'. However, among non-predicative adjectives we find also non-intersective adjectives as 共同 *gòngtóng* 'common', which are completely excluded from the predicative function (Paul 2010: 118–19). Besides, non-predicative adjectives may not be modified by 很 *hěn* 'very', while predicative adjectives are very often preceded by this degree adverb, which neutralizes their inherent comparative value (when used as predicates; Lü Shuxiang 1980).[25]

[24] Another subclass of adjectives which has been proposed in the literature is that of 'non-attributive' or 'predicative-only' adjectives (非定形容詞 *fēidìng xíngróngcí*; Hu Mingyang 1979; Deng, Wang, and Li 1996), as e.g. 妥 *tuǒ* 'appropriate'. However, Arcodia (2014) argues that this subclass is far from homogeneous and that many of the adjectives labelled as 'non-attributive' are indeed often used as modifiers, generally with the particle 的 *de*. Arcodia highlights that some of the so-called 'predicative-only' adjectives are in fact 'ordinary' predicative adjectives, while some others behave more or less as stative verbs. Thus, each member of this alleged subclass should rather be assigned either to the adjectival or to the verbal category, as they do not constitute a coherent set.

[25] While in English the positive degree is the unmarked form of adjectives, and the comparative is somehow overtly marked (e.g. *tall* > *taller*), the opposite is true for Chinese: the unmarked form of the adjective is mostly understood as comparative. For instance, a sentence as 這個教室大 *zhè ge jiàoshì dà* 'this CLF classroom big', would normally be interpreted as 'this classroom is big*ger* (as opposed to a smaller one, present in the universe of discourse)'. The addition of the adverb 很 *hěn* 'very' is generally required for the positive degree: 這個教室很大 *zhè ge jiàoshì hěn dà* 'this CLF classroom very big, this classroom is (very) big'. If 很 *hěn* 'very' is emphasized in the intonation, then it actually conveys the meaning 'very' (see Sybesma 1992; Liu Luther Chen-sheng 2010).

Moreover, differently from verbs, adjectives may actually modify a noun phrase without the addition of the particle 的 *de* (*contra* Hengeveld 1992; compare Ex. 107a): this criterion can be used to distinguish (predicative) adjectives from (stative) verbs. Paul shows that 的 *de*-less modification is possible not only with monosyllabic adjectives (cf. Sproat and Shih 1988, 1991) but also with disyllabic ones (Paul 2010: 123; glosses adapted):

(108) 一件髒／漂亮／乾淨（的）衣服。

  yī jiàn zāng / piàoliang / gānjìng (de) yīfu
  one CLF dirty pretty   clean MOD dress
  'A dirty / pretty / clean dress.'

Besides, both predicative (108) and non-predicative (109) adjectives may act as modifiers with and without 的 *de* (see Paul 2010: 128 for an account of the cases in which 的 *de*-less modification is not acceptable):

(109) 一張方(的)桌子。

  yī zhāng fāng (de) zhuōzi
  one CLF square MOD table
  'A square table.'

However, if we analyse modifiers followed by 的 *de* as relative clauses, as hinted at before, then we would expect to see predicative adjectives always marked by 的 *de* when acting as modifiers (as is necessary for relative clauses), while non-predicative adjectives, on the contrary, should be found only in 的 *de*-less modification.

According to Arcodia's (2014) analysis, the characteristics of Chinese adjectives are consistent with Croft's prototype (see §6.6), in terms of structural markedness. Both predicative adjectives and verbs may act as predicates without any overt marking (106), while non-predicative adjectives need overt marking in this function (namely, the above-mentioned '是 *shì*...的 *de*' construction): thus, verbs are not more marked than adjectives, when used in this prototypical verbal function (predication). On the other hand, modification, the prototypical adjectival function, necessarily involves overt marking for verbs (107b), but not for adjectives (108, 109): thus, again, adjectives are not more marked than verbs in their prototypical function.

Moreover, Huang, Li, and Li (2009) highlight that some adjectives involve two participants, one of which is the 'semantic object'. However, differently from verbs, this object must be introduced by the preposition

對 *duì* 'to, for' (adapted from Huang, Li, and Li 2009: 22; see also McCawley 1992: 233):

(110) a. 這個工作對你很合適。

    zhè   ge   gōngzuò duì nǐ   hěn   héshì
    this CLF job   for 2SG (very) suitable
    'This job is suitable for you.'

    b. 這個工作很適合/*合適你。

    *zhè   ge   gōngzuò hěn   shìhé / *héshì nǐ*
    this CLF job   (very) suit   suitable 2SG
    'This job suits you well.'

Another proposed criterion for the definition of the adjectival category is based on reduplication patterns (Paul 2010). In MSC, both transitive and intransitive verbs reduplicate as a whole (see §5.1.3.3): e.g. 學習 *xuéxí* 'study' → 學習學習 *xuéxí~xuéxí* ([AB]$_V$ [AB]$_V$). For adjectives, in contrast, each syllable is reduplicated: e.g. 高興 *gāoxìng* 'happy' → 高高興興 *gāo~gāo-xìng~xìng* ([AABB]$_A$). While in the case of mono-syllabic items there is no difference between verbs and adjectives at the segmental level, the patterns of reduplication may be different at the suprasegmental level: according to some scholars, in verbal reduplication the second instantiation is always in the neutral tone, while for adjectives it is always in the first tone (Dragunov 1960; Tang Ting-chi 1988: 282; Paul 2010: 120). Others, however, suggest that the second syllable is in the neutral tone also for reduplicated adjectives (Li and Thompson 1981: 33). Moreover, as said earlier (§5.1.3.3), the morpheme 一 *yī* 'one' may be inserted between the base and the reduplicant in the case of reduplicated monosyllabic verbs (e.g. 看一看 *kàn yi kàn* 'look one look, have a look'), but not in the case of adjectives. Lastly, as seen before (§5.1.3.3), reduplication conveys a different meaning for verbs and adjectives: while verbal reduplication adds a temporal boundary to the event, and marks the so-called 'tentative' (Chao Yuen Ren 1968: 204) or 'delimitative' aspect (Li and Thompson 1981: 29, 232–6), adjectival reduplication conveys a higher degree of intensity or vividness (Chao Yuen Ren 1968: 209; Li and Thompson 1981; Tang Ting-chi 1988; Li Yuming 1996b).

From the point of view of their basic features, adjectives, differently from verbs, are typically (though not always) gradable, and, as already mentioned, their prototypical function is modification. Thus, the possibility of appearing in a comparative construction may be understood as evidence for adjectival status: compare 我比你高 *wǒ bǐ nǐ gāo* 'I am taller than you' and *我比你走 *wǒ bǐ nǐ zǒu* '(intended meaning:) I walk more than you'. According to Zádrapa (2017), the fact that some items which are normally seen as verbs, as e.g. 愛 *ài* 'love' and 喜歡 *xǐhuan* 'like', may be modified by degree adverbs depends from the fact that word classes may overlap to some extent and may have blurred boundaries: see e.g. 我很喜歡唱歌 *wǒ hěn xǐhuān chàng-gē* 'I like singing very much'; 我比他喜歡唱歌 *wǒ bǐ tā xǐhuān chàng-gē* 'I like singing more than he does'.

As for Classical Chinese, Zádrapa (2017), based on the data in Yin Guoguang (1997: 28) on the 呂氏春秋 *Lǚshì Chūnqiū* (ca. 239 BC), argues that adjectives show a strong affinity with verbs, since they are often used as non-nominal predicates. Moreover, the most common adnominal modifiers are nouns rather than adjectives. However, Zádrapa (2017) also highlights that verbs are very rarely used as adnominal or adverbial modifiers, while adjectives may freely modify nouns and predicates. Besides, the typical derivational patterns for the two word classes are different: while adjectives may be used in the absolute sense (大 *dà* 'big' > 'someone who is big'), in the causative sense ('make s.o. become big'), and in the putative sense ('consider to be big'), intransitive verbs may be used only in the causative construction. Both the differences in their distribution and in the derivational patterns associated with them constitute arguments in favour of a distinction between verbs and adjectives also for Classical Chinese.

Thus, to sum up, while property-denoting words (i.e. adjectives) have much in common with verbs, they are fundamentally different from intransitive verbs. These differences support the proposal that adjectives do constitute an independent word class in Chinese, separate from verbs. Again, due to space constraints, here we took into consideration only the situation of MSC: however, some criteria, as e.g. reduplication patterns, may not apply in the same way to the verb-adjective distinction in other Sinitic languages. See, for instance, Francis and Matthews (2005) for a discussion of the verb-adjective distinction in Cantonese.

6.6.1.3 Prepositions

In Chinese, prepositions are one of the most debated word classes (Huang, Li, and Li 2009), especially since virtually all the lexical items analysed as prepositions derive from verbs (Mei Tsulin 2004; Guo

Xiliang 2005, among others) and are thus often treated as 'coverbs' (Chao Yuen Ren 1968; Li and Thompson 1981).

However, Djamouri and Paul (2009) provide several arguments supporting the status of prepositions as an independent word class not only in Modern Chinese, but rather since the earliest attestations of the language. First and foremost, while the fact that prepositions may follow adverbs (including negators) is often taken as evidence of their verbal nature, Djamouri and Paul argue that this is possible only when prepositions are in the adjunct position of the verb phrase (111a). In all other positions, as e.g. in the sentence-initial topic position, prepositions may not follow adverbs (111b; Djamouri and Paul 2009: 204–5; glosses adapted):

(111)   a. 我已經給瑪麗打了半個小時的電話。

wǒ	*yǐjīng*	*gěi*	*Mǎlì*	*dǎ-le*	*bàn*	*ge*	*xiǎoshí*
1SG	already	to	Mary	make-PFV	half	CLF	hour
de	*diànhuà*
MOD	telephone

'I have already talked on the phone to Mary for half an hour.'

    b. (*已經)給瑪麗，我已經打了半個小時的電話。

(*yǐjīng*)	*gěi*	*Mǎlì*	*wǒ*	*yǐjīng*	*dǎ-le*	*bàn*
already	to	Mary	1SG	already	make-PFV	half
ge	*xiǎoshí*	*de*	*diànhuà*
CLF	hour	MOD	telephone

'To Mary, I have already talked on the phone for half an hour.'

Moreover, prepositions may never act as predicates (112) and may not be followed by aspect markers (Djamouri and Paul 2009: 207):

(112)   *他從北京。

tā	*cóng*	*Běijīng*
3SG.M	from	Beijing

'(intended meaning:) He comes from Beijing.'

Besides, while it is true that prepositions do resemble verbs since, differently from nouns and adjectives, they may be directly followed by a noun phrase (e.g. 從南方到北方 *cóng nánfāng dào běifāng* 'from south to north'; Huang, Li, and Li 2009: 26–7), they always require a complement: differently from verbs, they do not allow an empty object position (Djamouri and Paul 2009: 208). Thus, the object of a verb may be unexpressed, if recoverable from the context (113a), but this is not possible for the object of a preposition (113b; Djamouri and Paul 2009: 208):

(113)　a. 我剛才去了一趟，他没在（家）。

　　　wǒ gāngcái qù-le yī tàng tā méi zài (jiā)
　　　1SG just　　go-PFV one time 3SG.M NEG be (home)
　　　'I just went there, he wasn't at home.'

　　　b. 他每天在＊（家）睡午覺。

　　　tā měi-tiān zài ＊(jiā) shuì wǔjiào
　　　3SG.M every-day at (home) sleep nap
　　　'He takes a nap at home every day.'

Thus, by applying these criteria, it is possible to argue that prepositions are an independent word class in Chinese. We may also remark that, in MSC, there are actually prepositions which are no longer connected with a verb (except perhaps in some fossilized expressions), as e.g. 從 *cóng* 'from' (originally, 'follow'; see Djamouri and Paul 2009; Huang, Li, and Li 2009).

However, there are several lexical items which may be used both as verbs and as prepositions in MSC: for instance, 給 *gěi* 'give/for/to', or 在 *zài* 'be at/at, in' (see Exx. 111, 113). The word 給 *gěi* appears to have all the features usually associated with verbs: it may act as a predicate, and it may be followed by aspect markers (e.g. 我給了她一本書 *wǒ gěi le tā yī běn shū* '1SG give-PFV 3SG.F one CLF book, I gave her a book'. However, when found in the preverbal or in the postverbal position, 給 *gěi* is usually analysed as a preposition (Li Audrey Yen-hui 1990; Sybesma 1992, 1999; Her One-soon 2006). Djamouri and Paul (2009) highlight that while 'verbal' 給 *gěi* takes two complements, 'prepositional' 給 *gěi* may only take one complement, as is generally the case for prepositions. Moreover, while the goal of the process described by the double object verb 給 *gěi* 'give' must be [+human], the constraint does not hold for prepositional 給 *gěi* 'for, to' (Djamouri and Paul 2009: 209).

Another criterion which can be used to distinguish 給 *gěi*$_v$ from 給 *gěi*$_p$ is the different range of semantic roles which are available for the prepositional phrase introduced by 給 *gěi*$_p$. Prepositional 給 *gěi* may introduce a beneficiary, a recipient, or the so-called 'ethical dative' (Djamouri and Paul 2009: 209–10).[26] There are also cases in which the

---

[26] The item 給 *gěi* may also be used as a passive marker (Her One-soon 2006: 1286).

interpretation of the referent of the prepositional phrase may be ambiguous between beneficiary and recipient (adapted from Her One-soon 2006: 1288; see also Huang, Li, and Li 2009: 31):

(114) 李四給老師寄了一份文件。

Lǐsì gěi lǎoshī jì-le yī fèn wénjiàn
Lisi to/for teacher post-PFV one CLF document
'Lisi posted a document to/for the teacher.'

Her One-soon (2006: 1288–90) highlights that with some prepositional dative verbs the goal argument may appear both postverbally and preverbally. However, with ditransitive verbs as e.g. 賣 *mài* 'sell', 借 *jiè* 'borrow', 還 *huán* 'return' (i.e. double-object verbs), the goal argument may appear only in the postverbal position (adapted from Her One-soon 2006: 1289):

(115) 張三賣了一棟房子給李四 。

Zhāngsān mài-le yī dòng fángzi gěi Lǐsì
Zhangsan sell-PFV one CLF house to Lisi
'Zhangsan sold a house to Lisi.'

If the prepositional phrase introduced by 給 *gěi* in (115) is placed in the preverbal position, then it is interpreted as a beneficiary (i.e. 'Zhangsan sold a house *for* Lisi'; Her One-soon 2006: 1289).[27]

According to Djamouri and Paul (2009), 給 *gěi*$_v$ and 給 *gěi*$_p$ are actually homophones. They argue that prepositions are an independent word class in Chinese, independently from the fact that they may be connected to a homophonous verb (like 給 *gěi* and 在 *zài*) or not (like 從 *cóng* 'from' and 關於 *guānyú* 'about'). Huang, Li, and Li (2009: 30), believe that lexical items as 給 *gěi* are different from other prepositions, since they have a 'double status': namely, they are both verbs and prepositions.

---

[27] Her One-soon (2006: 1277–88) analyzes postverbal 給 *gěi* in example (115), as well as locative 在 *zài* 'at, in' in the postverbal position, as a preposition, while others (e.g. Li Audrey Yen-hui 1990; Huang and Ahrens 1999) believe it is a verb.

References

Abbiati, Magda (2012). *La Scrittura Cinese nei Secoli. Dal Pennello alla Tastiera.* Roma: Carocci.

Aikhenvald, Alexandra Y. (2006). 'Serial Verb Constructions in a Typological Perspective', in A.Y. Aikhenvald and R. M. W. Dixon (eds.), *Serial Verb Constructions: A Cross-linguistic Typology.* Oxford: Oxford University Press, 1–68.

Aldridge, Edith (2010). 'Clause-internal Wh Movement in Archaic Chinese', *Journal of East Asian Linguistics* 19(1): 1–36.

Aldridge, Edith (2013a). 'Survey of Chinese Historical Syntax Part I: Pre-Archaic and Archaic Chinese', *Language and Linguistics Compass* 7(1): 39–57.

Aldridge, Edith (2013b). 'Survey of Chinese Historical Syntax Part II: Middle Chinese', *Language and Linguistics Compass* 7(1): 58–77.

Alves, Mark J. (2001). 'What's so Chinese about Vietnamese?', in G. W. Thurgood (ed.), *Papers from the Ninth Annual Meeting of the Southeast Asian Linguistic Society.* Arizona State University: Program for Southeast Asian Studies, 221–42.

Alves, Mark J. (2009). 'Loanwords in Vietnamese', in M. Haspelmath and U. Tadmor (eds.), *Loanwords in the World's Languages: A Comparative Handbook.* Berlin-New York: Mouton de Gruyter, 617–37.

Ansaldo, Umberto (2010). 'Surpass Comparatives in Sinitic and Beyond: Typology and Grammaticalization', *Linguistics* 48(4): 919–50.

Ansaldo, Umberto, and Lisa Lim (2004). 'Phonetic Absence as Syntactic Prominence: Grammaticalization in Isolating Tonal Languages', in O. Fischer, M. Norde, and H. Perridon (eds.), *Up and Down the Cline. The Nature of Grammaticalization.* Amsterdam-Philadelphia: John Benjamins, 345–61.

Anward, Jan (2001). 'Typology of Morphological and Morphosyntactic Categories: Parts of Speech', in M. Haspelmath, E. König, W. Oesterreicher, and W. Raible (eds.), *Language Typology and Language Universals. Volume 1.* Berlin-New York: Mouton de Gruyter, 726–35.

Anward, Jan, Edith Moravcsik, and Leon Stassen (1997). 'Parts of Speech: A Challenge for Typology', *Linguistic Typology* 1(2), 167–84.

Arcodia, Giorgio F. (2011). 'A Construction Morphology Account of Derivation in Mandarin Chinese', *Morphology* 21: 89–130.

Arcodia, Giorgio F. (2012). *Lexical Derivation in Mandarin Chinese.* Taipei: Crane.

Arcodia, Giorgio F. (2013). 'Grammaticalisation with Coevolution of Form and Meaning in East Asia? Evidence from Sinitic', *Language Sciences* 40: 148–67.

Arcodia, Giorgio F. (2014). 'The Chinese Adjective as a Word Class', in R. Simone and F. Masini (eds.), *Word Classes: Nature, Typology and Representations*. Amsterdam-Philadelphia: John Benjamins, 95–117.

Arcodia, Giorgio F. (2015). 'More on the Morphological Typology of Sinitic', *Bulletin of Chinese Linguistics* 8(1): 5–35.

Arcodia, Giorgio F. (2017). 'Towards a Typology of Relative Clauses in Sinitic: Headedness and Relativisation Strategies', *Cahiers de Linguistique Asie Orientale* 46(1): 33–72.

Arcodia, Giorgio F., and Bianca Basciano (2012). 'On the Productivity of the Chinese Affixes –兒 –r, –化 –huà and –頭 –tou', *Taiwan Journal of Linguistics* 10: 89–118.

Arcodia, Giorgio F., and Bianca Basciano (2014 [2012]). 'Neoclassical Compounding Beyond Europe: The Case of East Asia' *Verbum* 34(2): 233–56.

Arcodia, Giorgio F., and Bianca Basciano (2018). 'The CxM Analysis of Chinese Word Formation', in G. Booij (ed.), *The Construction of Words. Advances in Construction Morphology*. Berlin: Springer, 219–53.

Arcodia, Giorgio F., Bianca Basciano, and Chiara Melloni (2015). 'Areal Perspectives on Total Reduplication of Verbs in Sinitic', *Studies in Language* 39(4): 795–831.

Basciano, Bianca (2010). 'Verbal Compounding and Causativity in Mandarin Chinese', PhD dissertation, University of Verona.

Basciano, Bianca (2013). 'Causative Light Verbs in Mandarin Chinese (and beyond)', in N. Hathout, F. Montermini, and J. Tseng (eds.), *Morphology in Toulouse. Selected Proceedings of Décembrettes 7*. Munich: Lincom, 57–89.

Basciano, Bianca (2017a). 'Brand Names', in R. Sybesma, W. Behr, Y. Gu, Z. Handel, C.-T. J. Huang, and J. Myers (eds.), *Encyclopedia of Chinese Language and Linguistics. Volume 1*. Leiden: Brill, 311–18.

Basciano, Bianca (2017b). 'Causative Constructions', in R. Sybesma, W. Behr, Y. Gu, Z. Handel, C.-T. J. Huang, and J. Myers (eds.), *Encyclopedia of Chinese Language and Linguistics. Volume 1*. Leiden: Brill, 345–52.

Basciano, Bianca (2017c). 'Resultatives', in R. Sybesma, W. Behr, Y. Gu, Z. Handel, C.-T. J. Huang, and J. Myers (eds.), *Encyclopedia of Chinese Language and Linguistics. Volume 3*. Leiden: Brill, 571–82.

Basciano, Bianca (2017d). 'Vendlerian Verb Classes', in R. Sybesma, W. Behr, Y. Gu, Z. Handel, C.-T. J. Huang, and J. Myers (eds.), *Encyclopedia of Chinese Language and Linguistics. Volume 4*. Leiden: Brill, 484–8.

Basciano, Bianca (2017e). 'Word Classes, Modern', in R. Sybesma, W. Behr, Y. Gu, Z. Handel, C.-T. J. Huang and J. Myers (eds.), *Encyclopedia of Chinese Language and Linguistics. Volume 4*. Leiden: Brill, 554–66.

Basciano, Bianca (2019). 'On the Event Structure of Chinese Resultative Compounds', *Cahiers de Linguistique Asie Orientale* 48(2): 173–241.

Basciano, Bianca, and Antonella Ceccagno (2009). 'The Chinese Language and Some Notions from Western Linguistics', *Lingue e Linguaggio* 8(1): 105–35.

Basciano, Bianca, and Chiara Melloni (2017). 'Event Delimitation in Mandarin: The Case of Diminishing Reduplication'. *Rivista di Linguistica* 29: 143–66.

Basciano, Bianca, Nancy Kula, and Chiara Melloni (2011). 'Modes of Compounding in Bantu, Romance and Chinese', *Italian Journal of Linguistics* 23(2): 203–49.

Bauer, Laurie (2006). 'Compound', in K. Brown (ed.), *Encyclopedia of Language and Linguistics. Volume 2*. Oxford: Elsevier, 719–26.

Bauer, Robert S. (1996). 'Identifying the Tai Substratum in Cantonese', in *The Fourth International Symposium on Language and Linguistics*. Bangkok: Institute of Language and Culture for Rural Development, Mahidol University, 1806–44.

Bauer, Robert S. (2000). 'The Chinese-based Writing System of the Zhuang Language', *Cahiers de Linguistique Asie Orientale* 29(2): 223–53.

Bauer, Robert S. (2018). 'Cantonese as Written Language in Hong Kong', *Global Chinese* 4(1): 103–42.

Bauer, Robert S., and Paul K. Benedict (1997). *Modern Cantonese Phonology*. Berlin-New York: Mouton de Gruyter.

Baxter, William H. (1992). *A handbook of Old Chinese Phonology*. Berlin-New York: Mouton de Gruyter.

Baxter, William H. (1999). 'Reconstructing Proto-"Mandarin" Retroflex Initials', in R. VanNess Simmons (ed.), *Issues in Chinese Dialect Description and Classification*. Berkeley: Project on Linguistic Analysis, 1–35.

Baxter, William H. (2000). 'Did Proto-Mandarin Exist?', *Journal of Chinese Linguistics* 28(1): 100–15.

Baxter, William H. (2006). 'Mandarin Dialect Phylogeny', *Cahiers de Linguistique Asie Orientale* 35(1): 71–114.

Baxter, William H., and Laurent Sagart (1998). 'Word Formation in Old Chinese', in J. Packard (ed.), *New Approaches to Chinese Word Formation*. Berlin-New York: Mouton de Gruyter, 35–75.

Baxter, William H., and Laurent Sagart (2014). *Old Chinese. A New Reconstruction*. Oxford: Oxford University Press.

Behr, Wolfgang (2010). 'Role of Language in Early Chinese Constructions of Ethnic Identity', *Journal of Chinese Philosophy* 37(3): 567–87.

Behr, Wolfgang (2017). 'The Language of the Bronze Inscriptions', in E. L. Shaughnessy (ed.), *Imprints of Kinship. Studies of Recently Discovered Bronze Inscriptions from Ancient China*. Hong Kong: The Chinese University Press, 9–32.

Bennett, Paul (1979). 'A Critique of the Altaicization Hypothesis'. *Cahiers de Linguistique Asie Orientale* 6: 91–104.

Bianchi, Valentina, and Mara Frascarelli (2010). 'Is Topic a Root Phenomenon?', *Iberia: An International Journal of Theoretical Linguistics*, 2(1): 43–88.

Bickel, Balthasar, and Johanna Nichols (2007). 'Inflectional Morphology', in T. Shopen (ed.), *Language Typology and Syntactic Description. Volume III: Grammatical Categories and the Lexicon*. Cambridge: Cambridge University Press, 169–240.

Bisang, Walter (1996). 'Areal Typology and Grammaticalization: Processes of Grammaticalization Based on Nouns and Verbs in East and Mainland South East Asian Languages', *Studies in Language* 20(3): 519–97.

Bisang, Walter (1998). 'Grammaticalization and Language Contact, Constructions and Positions', in A. Giacalone Ramat and P. J. Hopper (eds.), *The Limits of Grammaticalization*. Amsterdam-Philadelphia: John Benjamins, 13–58.

Bisang, Walter (2001a). 'Areality, Grammaticalization and Language Typology: On the Explanatory Power of Functional Criteria and The Status of Universal Grammar', in W. Bisang (ed.), *Aspects of Typology and Universals*. Berlin: Akademieverlag, 175–223.

Bisang, Walter (2001b). 'Syntax/morphology Asymmetry in Vietnamese - A Consequence of Contact by Writing Between Vietnamese, Chinese and Standard Average European Languages', in B. Igla and T. Stolz (eds.), *Was Ich Noch Sagen Wollte…A Multilingual Festschrift for Norbert Boretzky*. Berlin, Akademieverlag: 189–201.

Bisang, Walter (2004). 'Grammaticalization without Coevolution of Form and Meaning: The Case of Tense-Aspect-Modality in East and Mainland Southeast Asia', in, W. Bisang, N. P. Himmelmann and B. Wiemer (eds.), *What Makes Grammaticalization? A Look From its Fringes and its Components*. Berlin-New York: Mouton de Gruyter, 109–38.

Bisang, Walter (2008). 'Grammaticalization and the Areal Factor – The Perspective of East and Mainland South East Asian Languages', in M. J. López-Cousa and E. Seoane (eds.), *Rethinking Grammaticalization*. Amsterdam-Philadelphia: John Benjamins, 15–35.

Bisang, Walter (2009). 'Serial Verb Constructions', *Language and Linguistics Compass* 3: 792–814.

Bisang, Walter (2010). 'Word Classes', in J. J. Song (ed.), *The Oxford Handbook of Linguistic Typology*. Oxford: Oxford University Press, 280–302.

Bisang, Walter (2016). 'Chinese Syntax', in S.-w. Chan (ed.), *The Routledge Encyclopedia of the Chinese Language*. Oxford: Routledge, 354–77.

Bisetto, Antonietta, and Sergio Scalise (2005). 'Classification of Compounds', *Lingue e Linguaggio* 4(2): 319–32.

Blust, Robert (1995). 'An Austronesianist Looks at Sino-Austronesian', in W. S.-Y. Wang (ed.), *The Ancestry of the Chinese Language*. Berkeley: Project on Linguistic Analysis, 283–98.

Boltz, William G. (1993). 'Shuo Wen Chieh Tzu 說文解字', in M. Loewe (ed.). *Early Chinese Texts: A Bibliographical Guide*. Berkeley: The Society for the Study of Early China and The Institute of East Asian Studies, University of California, 429–42.

Boltz, William G. (1994). *The Origin and Early Development of the Chinese Writing System*. New Haven: American Oriental Society.

Boltz, William G. (1999). 'Language and Writing', in M. Loewe and E. L. Shaughnessy (eds.), *The Cambridge History of Ancient China: From the Origins of Civilization to 221 B.C.* Cambridge: Cambridge University Press, 74–123.

Branner, David P. (1999). 'The Classification of Longyan', in R. VanNess Simmons (ed.), *Issues in Chinese Dialect Description and Classification*. Berkeley: Project on Linguistic Analysis, 36–83.

Branner, David P. (2000). *Problems in Comparative Chinese Dialectology: The Classification of Miin and Hakka*. Berlin-New York: Mouton de Gruyter.

Branner, David P. (2002). 'Common Chinese and Early Chinese Morphology', *Journal of the American Oriental Society* 122(4): 706–21.

Branner, David P. (2006a). 'Appendix II: Comparative Transcriptions of Rime Table Phonology', in D. P. Branner, *The Chinese Rime Tables: Linguistic Philosophy and Historical-Comparative Phonology*. Amsterdam-Philadelphia: John Benjamins, 265–302.

Branner, David P. (2006b). 'Introduction: What Are Rime Tables, and What Do They Mean?', in D. P. Branner, *The Chinese Rime Tables: Linguistic Philosophy and Historical-Comparative Phonology*. Amsterdam-Philadelphia: John Benjamins, 1–36.

Bulfoni, Clara (2009). 'Lexical Borrowing of English in the Internet Era: How to Preserve Chinese Identity?', in G. Garzone and P. Catenaccio (eds.), *Identities across Media and Modes: Discursive Perspectives*. Bern: Peter Lang, 215–34.

Bulfoni, Clara (2010). 'Il Cinese della Computer-Mediated Communication', in E. Lupano (ed.), *Media in Cina Oggi. Testimonianze e Orientamenti*. Milan: Franco Angeli, 93–107.

Büring, Daniel (2003). 'On D-trees, Beans and B-accents', *Linguistics and Philosophy* 26: 511–45.

Campbell, Lyle (2004). *Historical Linguistics. Second Edition*. Edinburgh: Edinburgh University Press.

Cao, Guangshun, and Hsiao-Jung Yu (2015). 'Language Contact and its Influence on the Development of Chinese Syntax', in W. S. Wang, and

C. Sun (eds.), *The Oxford Handbook of Chinese Linguistics*. Oxford: Oxford University Press, 203–14.

Cao, Zhiyun [曹志耘] *et al.* (2008). 汉语方言地图集. 词汇卷 [Linguistic Atlas of Chinese Dialects. Volume 2: Lexicon]. Beijing: The Commercial Press.

Casacchia, G. (2006). 'Chinese Linguistic Tradition', in K. Brown (ed.), *Encyclopedia of Language and Linguistics. Volume 2*. Oxford: Elsevier, 358–62.

Ceccagno, Antonella, and Bianca Basciano (2007). 'Compound Headedness in Chinese: An Analysis of Neologisms', *Morphology* 17: 207–31.

Ceccagno, Antonella, and Bianca Basciano (2009). *Shuobuchulai: La Formazione delle Parole in Cinese*. Bologna: Serendipità.

Ceccagno, Antonella, and Sergio Scalise (2006). 'Classification, Structure and Headedness of Chinese Compounds', *Lingue e Linguaggio* 5(2), 233–60.

Ceng, Haiping [曾海萍] (2009). '网络语言与方言' [Netspeak and Dialects], *Meili Zhongguo* 22: 139–40.

Chafe, Wallace (1976). 'Givenness, Contrastiveness, Definiteness, Subjects and Topics', in C. N. Li (ed.), *Subject and Topic*. New York: Academic Press, 25–55.

Chambers, John K., and Peter Trudgill (2004). *Dialectology. Second Edition*. Cambridge: Cambridge University Press.

Chan, Abraham (2006). 'On the Principle of the Four Grades', in D. P. Branner, *The Chinese Rime Tables: Linguistic Philosophy and Historical-Comparative Phonology*. Amsterdam-Philadelphia: John Benjamins, 37–46.

Chan, Angel, Stephen Matthews, and Virginia Yip (2011). 'The Acquisition of Relative Clauses in Cantonese and Mandarin', in E. J. Kidd (ed.), *The Acquisition of Relative Clauses: Processing, Typology and Function*. Amsterdam-Philadelphia: John Benjamins, 197–225.

Chang, Claire Hsun-huei (1990). 'On Serial Verbs in Mandarin Chinese: VV Compounds and Coverbial Phrases', in B. D. Joseph and A. M. Zwicky (eds.), *When the Verbs Collide. Papers from the Ohio State Mini-Conference on Serial Verbs. Ohio State Working Papers in Linguistics* 39, 288–315.

Chao, Yuen Ren (1930). 'A System of Tone-Letters', *Le Maître Phonétique* 45: 24–7.

Chao, Yuen Ren (1948). *Mandarin Primer*. Cambridge, MA: Harvard University Press.

Chao, Yuen Ren (1967). 'The Contrastive Aspect of the Wu dialect', *Language* 43(1): 92–101.

Chao, Yuen Ren (1968). *A Grammar of Spoken Chinese*. Berkeley: University of California Press.

Chappell, Hilary (2001). 'Language Contact and Areal Diffusion in Sinitic Languages', in A. Y. Aikhenvald and R. M. W. Dixon (eds.), *Areal Diffusion and Genetic Inheritance: Problems in Comparative Linguistics.* Oxford: Oxford University Press, 328–57.

Chappell, Hilary (2004a). 'A Typology of Evidential Markers in Sinitic Languages', in H. Chappell (ed.), *Chinese Grammar: Synchronic and Diachronic Perspectives.* Oxford: Oxford University Press, 56–84.

Chappell, Hilary (2004b). *Synchrony and Diachrony of Sinitic Languages: A Brief History of Chinese Dialects*, in H. Chappell (ed.), *Chinese Grammar: Synchronic and Diachronic Perspectives.* Oxford: Oxford University Press, 3–28.

Chappell, Hilary (2015a). 'Introduction: Ways of Tackling Diversity in Sinitic Languages', in H. Chappell (ed.), *Diversity in Sinitic Languages.* Oxford: Oxford University Press, 3–12.

Chappell, Hilary (2015b). 'Linguistic Areas in China for Differential Object Marking, Passive, and Comparative Constructions', in H. Chappell (ed.), *Diversity in Sinitic Languages.* Oxford: Oxford University Press, 13–52.

Chappell, Hilary, and Denis Creissels (2019). 'Topicality and the Typology of Predicative Possession', *Linguistic Typology* 23(3): 467–532.

Chappell, Hilary, and Christine Lamarre (2005). *A Grammar and Lexicon of Hakka. Historical Materials from the Basel Mission Library.* Paris: École des Hautes Études en Sciences Sociales.

Chappell, Hilary, and Alain Peyraube (2015). 'The Comparative Construction in Sinitic Languages: Synchronic and Diachronic Variation', in H. Chappell (ed.), *Diversity in Sinitic Languages.* Oxford: Oxford University Press, 134–54.

Chappell, Hilary, Ming Li, and Alain Peyraube (2007). 'Chinese Linguistics and Typology: The State of the Art', *Linguistic Typology* 11(1): 187–211.

Chen, Aiwen [陈爱文] (1986). 汉语词类研究和分类实验 [The Research on Word Classes in Chinese and Attempts at their Classification]. Beijing: Beijing Daxue Chubanshe.

Chen, Chengze [陈承泽] (1982 [1922]). 国文法草创 [Foundations for a Grammar of the National Language]. Beijing: The Commercial Press.

Chen, Jidong (2008). 'The Acquisition of Verb Compounding in Mandarin Chinese', PhD dissertation, Vrije Universiteit Amsterdam.

Chen, Mengjia [陳夢家] (1956). 殷墟卜辭綜述 [An Overview of Yinxu Oracle Bone Inscriptions]. Beijing: Kexue Chubanshe.

Chen, Ning [陈宁] (2006). 山东博山方言的子变韵及相关问题 [Derivational Rhyme Change in the Boshan Dialect of Shandong and Related Issues], *Fangyan*: 316–22.

Chen, Ping (1999). *Modern Chinese: History and Sociolinguistics.* Cambridge: Cambridge University Press.

Chen, Weirong (2008). 'Relative Clauses in Hui'an Dialect', in M. K. M Chan and H. Kang (eds.), *Proceedings of the 20th North American Conference on Chinese Linguistics.* Columbus, OH: The Ohio State University, 567–82.

Chen, Zhong [陈忠] (2007). '现代汉语连动式研究的一部力作 — 读高增霞《现代汉语连动式的语法化视角》' [A Masterpiece of Research on Serial Verb Constructions in Chinese: Reading Gao Zengxia's 'Chinese Serial Verb Constructions from the Perspective of Grammaticalisation'], *Xueshu Tansuo* 3: 142–9.

Cheng, Chin-Chuan (1996). 'Quantifying Dialect Mutual Intelligibility', in C.-T. J. Huang and A. Y.-h. Li (eds.), *New Horizons in Chinese Linguistics*. Dordrecht: Kluwer, 269–92.

Cheng, Lisa, and Rint Sybesma (2006). 'A Chinese Relative', in H. Broekhuis, N. Corver, R. Huijbregts, U. Kleinhenz, and J. Koster (eds.), *Organizing Grammar. Linguistic Studies in Honor of Henk van Riemsdijk*. Berlin-New York: Mouton de Gruyter, 69–76.

Cheng, Lisa L.-S. (1997). 'Resultative Compounds and Lexical Relational Structures', in F.-f. Tsao and H. S. Wang (eds.), *Chinese Languages and Linguistics III: Morphology and Lexicon*. Taipei: Academia Sinica, 167–97.

Cheng, Lisa L.-S. (2010). 'Cantonese as a Tense-Second Language', in J. W. Wouter and M. de Vries (eds.), *Structure Preserved, Studies in Syntax for Jan Koster*. Amsterdam-Philadelphia: John Benjamins, 73–9.

Cheng, Lisa L.-S., and C.-T. James Huang (1994). 'On the Argument Structure of Resultative Compounds', in M. Y. Chenand and O. L. Tzeng (eds.), *In Honour of William S-Y. Wang: Interdisciplinary Studies on Language and Language Change*. Taipei: Pyramid Press, 187–221.

Cheng, Lisa L.-S., and Rint Sybesma (1999). Bare and Not-so-bare Nouns and the Structure of NP, *Linguistic Inquiry* 30(4): 509–42.

Cheng, Xiangqin [程湘清] (1992). '先秦双音词研究' [Studies on Pre-Qin Disyllabic Words], in X. Cheng [程湘清] (ed.), *先秦汉语研究* [Studies on Pre-Qin Chinese]. Jinan: Shandong Jiaoyu Chubanshe, 44–112.

Chi, Telee R. (1985). *A Lexical Analysis of Verb-Noun Compounds in Mandarin Chinese*. Taipei: Crane.

Chiang, Chien-lung (2006). 'Causative and Inchoative Alternation in Taiwanese Southern Min: in Comparison with Mandarin and English', MA dissertation, National Tsinghua University.

Chierchia, Gennaro (1998). 'Reference to Kinds across Languages', *Natural Language Semantics* 6: 339–405.

Chirkova, Katia (2003). *In Search of Time in Peking Mandarin*. Leiden: Leiden University Press.

Chirkova, Katia (2013). 'On Principles and Practices of Language Classification', in G. Cao, H. Chappell, R. Djamouri, and T. Wiebusch (eds.), *Breaking Down the Barriers: Interdisciplinary Studies in Chinese Linguistics and Beyond*. Taipei: Academia Sinica, 715–34.

Chirkova, Katia, and Yiya Chen (2017). 'Běijīng, The Language of', in R. Sybesma, W. Behr, Y. Gu, Z. Handel, C.-T. J. Huang, and J. Myers (eds.),

Encyclopedia of Chinese Language and Linguistics. Volume 1. Leiden: Brill, 275–83.

Chiu, Hsiang-Yun [邱湘雲] (2008). '客家話"打"字語法化初探' [Preliminary Remarks on the Grammaticalisation of '*dǎ*' in Hakka], *Zhanghua Shida Guowen Xuezhi* 16: 75–103.

Chu, Chauncey C. (1976). 'Some Semantic Aspects of Action Verbs', *Lingua* 40(1): 43–54.

Chuang, Hui-ju (2007). 'Verbal Reduplication in Taiwan Southern Min'. MA dissertation, National Chung Cheng University.

Coblin, Weldon S. (1983). *A Handbook of Eastern Han Sounds Glosses*. Hong Kong: The Chinese University Press.

Coblin, Weldon S. (1994). *A Compendium of Phonetics in Northwest Chinese*. Berkeley: Project on Linguistic Analysis.

Coblin, Weldon S. (1996). 'Northwest Reflections on the Yunjing', *T'oung Pao* 82(4/5): 349–63.

Coblin, Weldon S. (1997). 'Palatalization of Velars in the Nanking Dialect', *Bulletin of the School of Oriental and African Studies* 60(3): 533–7.

Coblin, Weldon S. (1999). 'Thoughts on the Identity of the Chinese 'Phags-pa Dialect', in R. VanNess Simmons (ed.), *Issues in Chinese Dialect Description and Classification*. Berkeley: Project on Linguistic Analysis, 84–144.

Coblin, Weldon S. (2000a). 'A Brief History of Mandarin', *Journal of the American Oriental Society* 120(4): 537–52.

Coblin, Weldon S. (2000b). 'A Diachronic Study of Míng *Guānhuà* Phonology', *Monumenta Serica* 48(1): 267–335.

Coblin, Weldon S. (2000c). 'The Phonology of Proto-Central Jiang-Huai: An Exercise in Comparative Reconstruction', in P.-S. Ting and A. O.-K. Yue (eds.), *In Memory of Professor Li Fang-Kuei: Essays of Linguistic Change and the Chinese Dialects*. Taipei: Academia Sinica, 73–140.

Coblin, Weldon S. (2001). 'Phags-pa Chinese and the Standard Reading Pronunciation of Early Míng: A Comparative Study', *Language and Linguistics* 2(2): 1–62.

Coblin, Weldon S. (2002a). 'Migration History and Dialect Development in the Lower Yangtze Watershed', *Bulletin of the School of Oriental and African Studies*, 65(3): 529–43.

Coblin, Weldon S. (2002b). 'Reflections on the Study of Post-Medieval Chinese Historical Phonology', in D.-a. Ho (ed.), *Dialect Variation in Chinese. Papers from the Third International Conference on Sinology, Linguistics Section*. Taipei: Academia Sinica, 23–50.

Coblin, Weldon S. (2002c). 'Review of: Problems in Comparative Chinese Dialectology: The Classification of Miin and Hakka', *T'oung Pao* 88(3): 198–210.

Coblin, Weldon S. (2003). 'A Sample of Eighteenth Century Spoken Mandarin from North China', *Cahiers de Linguistique Asie Orientale* 32(2): 195–244.

Coblin, Weldon S. (2006). 'Zhang Linzhi on the Yunjing', in D. P. Branner, *The Chinese Rime Tables: Linguistic Philosophy and Historical-Comparative Phonology*. Amsterdam-Philadelphia: John Benjamins, 123–49.

Coblin, Weldon S. (2007a). *A Handbook of 'Phags-pa Chinese*. Honolulu: University of Hawai'i Press.

Coblin, Weldon S. (2007b). 'The Roots of Modern Standard Chinese Pronunciation', in W. S. Coblin (ed.), *Modern Chinese Phonology: From Guānhuà to Mandarin*. Paris: EHESS-CRLAO, 53–72.

Coblin, Weldon S. (2007c). 'The Southern Role in the Formation of Northern Guānhuà Phonology', in W. S. Coblin (ed.), *Modern Chinese Phonology: From Guānhuà to Mandarin*. Paris: EHESS-CRLAO, 23–42.

Coblin, Weldon S. (2007d). 'Thoughts on the Nature and Origin of the *Nányīn* Pronunciation of *Guānhuà*', in W. S. Coblin (ed.), *Modern Chinese Phonology: From Guānhuà to Mandarin*. Paris: EHESS-CRLAO, 7–22.

Coblin, Weldon S. (2011). *Comparative Phonology of the Central Xiāng Dialects*. Taipei: Academia Sinica.

Coblin, Weldon S., and Joseph Levi (2000). *Francisco Varo's Grammar of the Mandarin Language, 1703: An English Translation of 'Arte de la Lengua Mandarina'*. Amsterdam-Philadelphia: John Benjamins.

Collins, Chris (1997). 'Argument Sharing in Serial Verb Constructions', *Linguistic Inquiry* 28(3): 461–97.

Comrie, Bernard (2003). 'Typology and Language Acquisition: The Case of Relative Clauses', in A. Giacalone Ramat (ed.), *Typology and Second Language Acquisition*. Berlin-New York: Mouton de Gruyter, 19–38.

Comrie, Bernard (2007). 'Areal Typology of Mainland Southeast Asia: What we Learn from the WALS Maps', in P. Kullavanijaya (ed.), *Trends in Thai Linguistics*. Bangkok: Chulalongkorn University, 18–47.

Comrie, Bernard (2008). 'The Areal Typology of Chinese: between North and Southeast Asia', in R. Djamouri, B. Meisterernst, and R. Sybesma (eds.), *Chinese Linguistics in Leipzig*. Paris: EHESS - CRLAO, 1–21.

Coseriu, Eugenio (1980). ' "Historische Sprache" und "Dialekt" ', in J. Göschel, I. Pavle, and K. Kehr (eds.), *Dialekt und Dialektologie*. Wiesbaden: Steiner, 106–22.

Coulmas, Florian (2003). *Writing Systems*. Cambridge: Cambridge University Press.

Croft, William (2000). 'Parts of Speech as Typological Universals and as Language Particular Categories', in G. Bossong and B. Comrie (eds.), *Approaches to the Typology of Word Classes*, Berlin-New York: Mouton de Gruyter, 65–102.

Croft, William (2001). *Radical Construction Grammar*. Oxford: Oxford University Press.

Croft, William (2003). *Typology and Universals. Second Edition*. Cambridge: Cambridge University Press.

Dai, John X.-L. (1990). 'Syntactic Constructions in Serial Verb Expressions in Chinese', in B. D. Joseph and A. M. Zwicky (eds.), *When the Verbs Collide: Papers from the Ohio State Mini-Conference on Serial Verbs (Ohio State Working Papers in Linguistics 39)*. Columbus, OH: The Ohio State University, 316–39.

Dai, John X.-L. (1992). 'Chinese Morphology and its Interface with the Syntax', PhD dissertation, The Ohio State University.

De Boer, Elisabeth M. (2005). 'The Historical Development of Japanese Pitch Accent; Part I: The Accent Patterns of the Modern Dialects. Part II: The Introduction and Adaptation of the Middle Chinese Tones in Japan', PhD dissertation, Leiden University.

De Boer, Elisabeth M. (2008). 'The Middle Chinese Tones through Japanese Eyes', in R. Djamouri, B. Meisterernst, and R. Sybesma (eds.), *Chinese Linguistics in Leipzig*. Paris: EHESS - CRLAO, 71–86.

De Dominicis, Amedeo (2013). *Fonologie Comparate*. Rome: Carocci.

De Sousa, Hilário (2015). 'Language Contact in Nanning: Nanning Pinghua and Nanning Cantonese', in H. Chappell (ed.), *Diversity in Sinitic Languages*. Oxford: Oxford University Press, 157–89.

DeFrancis, John (1984). *The Chinese Language: Facts and Fantasy*. Honolulu: University of Hawai'i Press.

DeFrancis, John (1989). *Visible Speech: The Diverse Oneness of Writing Systems*. Honolulu: University of Hawai'i Press.

DeLancey, Scott (2010). 'Language Replacement and the Spread of Tibeto-Burman', *Journal of the Southeast Asian Linguistics Society* 3(1): 40–55.

DeLancey, Scott (2015). 'The Historical Dynamics of Morphological Complexity in Trans-Himalayan', *Linguistic Discovery* 13(2): 60–79.

Demattè, Paola (2010). 'The Origins of Chinese Writing: The Neolithic Evidence', *Cambridge Archaelogical Journal* 20(2): 211–28.

Den Dikken, Marcel, and Pornsiri Singhapreecha (2004). 'Complex Noun Phrases and Linkers', *Syntax* 7(1): 1–54.

Deng, Xiaoyong, Qilong Wang, and Jian Li (1996). 'A Statistical Study of Special Adjectives', in *Pan-Asiatic Linguistics: Proceedings of the Fourth International Symposium on Languages and Linguistics*. Bangkok: Mahidol University, 232–41.

Dik, Simon (1997). *The Theory of Functional Grammar. Part I: The Structure of the Clause. Second Edition*. Berlin-New York: Mouton de Gruyter.

Dixon, Robert M. W. (2004). 'Adjective Classes in Typological Perspective', in R. M. W. Dixon and A. Y. Aikhenvald (eds.), *Adjective Classes: A Cross-linguistic Typology*. Oxford: Oxford University Press, 1–49.

Dixon, Robert M. W. (1997). *The Rise and Fall of Languages*. Cambridge: Cambridge University Press.

Dixon, Robert M. W., and Alexandra Y. Aikhenvald (2002). 'Word: a Typological Framework', in R. M. W. Dixon and A. Y. Aikhenvald (eds.),

Word: A Cross-Linguistic Typology. Cambridge: Cambridge University Press, 1–41.

Djamouri, Redouane (1988). 'Etude des Formes Syntaxiques dans les Écrits Oraculaires Gravés Sur Os et Écaille de Tortue (Chine 14e-11e s. av. J.-C.)', PhD dissertation, Ecole des Hautes Etudes en Sciences Sociales, Paris.

Djamouri, Redouane (1991). 'Particules de Négation dans les Inscriptions sur Bronze de la Dynastie des Zhou', *Cahiers de Linguistique Asie Orientale* 20(1): 5–76.

Djamouri, Redouane (2004). 'Markers of Predication in Shang Bone Inscriptions', in H. Chappell (ed.), *Chinese Grammar: Synchronic and Diachronic Perspectives.* Oxford: Oxford University Press, 143–71.

Djamouri, Redouane, and Waltraud Paul (1997). 'Les Syntagmes Prépositionnels *Yu* et *Zai* en Chinois Archaïque', *Cahiers de Linguistique Asie Orientale* 26(2): 221–48.

Djamouri, Redouane, and Waltraud Paul (2009). 'Verb-to-Preposition Reanalysis in Chinese', in P. Crisma and G. Longobardi (eds.), *Historical Syntax and Linguistic Theory.* Oxford: Oxford University Press, 194–211.

Djamouri, Redouane, Waltraud Paul, and John Whitman (2013). 'Syntactic Change in Chinese and the Argument-Adjunct Asymmetry', in G. Cao, H. Chappell, R. Djamouri, and T. Wiebusch (eds.), *Breaking Down the Barriers: Interdisciplinary Studies in Chinese Linguistics and beyond. Volume 2.* Taipei: Academia Sinica, 577–94.

Dong, Hongyuan (2014). *A History of the Chinese Language.* London: Routledge.

Dong, Xiufang [董秀芳] (2003). '"的" 字短语做后置关系从句的用法—兼评法律文献中的"的"字短语的用法' [The Use of '*de*'-marked Phrases as Postnominal Relatives – an Analysis of their Usage in Legal Texts]. *Yuyan Wenzi Yinyong* 4: 120–6.

Dong, Xiufang [董秀芳] (2004). 汉语的词库与词法 [The Lexicon and Morphology of Chinese]. Beijing: Beijing Daxue Chubanshe.

Dowty, David R. (1979). *Word Meaning and Montague Grammar.* Dordrecht: Reidel.

Dryer, Matthew S. (1992). 'The Greenbergian Word Order Universals', *Language* 68(1): 81–138.

Dryer, Matthew S. (2003). 'Word Order in Sino-Tibetan Languages from a Typological and Geographical Perspective', in G. Thurgood and R. J. LaPolla (eds.), *The Sino-Tibetan Languages.* London: Routledge, 43–55.

Dryer, Matthew S. (2013a). 'Relationship between the Order of Object and Verb and the Order of Adposition and Noun Phrase', in M. S. Dryer and M. Haspelmath (eds.), *The World Atlas of Language Structures Online.* Leipzig: Max Planck Institute for Evolutionary Anthropology, chapter 95.

Dryer, Matthew S. (2013b). 'Relationship between the Order of Object and Verb and the Order of Relative Clause and Noun', in M. S. Dryer and

M. Haspelmath (eds.), *The World Atlas of Language Structures Online*. Leipzig: Max Planck Institute for Evolutionary Anthropology, chapter 96.

Dryer, Matthew S., and Orin Gensler (2013). 'Order of Object, Oblique, and Verb', in M. S. Dryer and M. Haspelmath (eds.), *The World Atlas of Language Structures Online*. Leipzig: Max Planck Institute for Evolutionary Anthropology, chapter 84.

Duanmu, San (1998). 'Wordhood in Chinese', in J. Packard (ed.), *New Approaches to Chinese Word Formation*. Berlin-New York: Mouton de Gruyter, 135–95.

Duanmu, San (2007). *The Phonology of Standard Chinese. Second Edition*. Oxford: Oxford University Press.

Duanmu, San (2008). *Syllable Structure: The Limits of Variation*. Oxford: Oxford University Press.

Duanmu, San (2011). 'Chinese Syllable Structure', in M. van Oostendorp, C. J. Ewen, E. Hume, and K. Rice (eds.), *The Blackwell Companion to Phonology, Volume 5*. Oxford: Blackwell, 2151–777.

Dwyer, Arienne (1992). 'Altaic Elements in the Línxià dialect [of NW Chinese]: Contact-induced Change on the Yellow River Plateau', *Journal of Chinese Linguistics* 20(1): 160–79.

Enfield, Nick (2005). 'Areal Linguistics and Mainland Southeast Asia', *Annual Review of Anthropology* 34: 181–206.

Enfield, Nick (2006). 'Heterosemy and the Grammar-Lexicon Trade-Off', in F. K. Ameka, A. Dench, and N. Evans (eds.), *Catching Language: The Standing Challenge of Grammar Writing*. Berlin-New York: Mouton de Gruyter, 297–320.

Enfield, Nick (2007). *A grammar of Lao*. Berlin-New York: Mouton de Gruyter.

Evans, Nicholas, and Toshiki Osada (2005). 'Mundari: The Myth of a Language Without Word Classes', *Linguistic Typology* 9(3): 351–90.

Feng, Shengli (1996). 'Prosodically Constrained Syntactic Changes in Early Archaic Chinese', *Journal of East Asian Linguistics* 5(4): 323–71.

Feng, Shengli (1998). 'Prosodic Structure and Compound Words in Classical Chinese', in J. Packard (ed.), *New Approaches to Chinese Word Formation*. Berlin-New York: Mouton de Gruyter, 196–259.

Feng, Shengli [冯胜利] (2001). '论汉语"词"的多维性' [On the multidimensionality of the 'word' in Chinese], *Dangdai Yuyanxue* 3(3): 161–74.

Ferlus, Michel (2009). 'What Were the Four Divisions of Middle Chinese?', *Diachronica* 26(2): 184–213.

Fetscherin, Marc, Ilan Alon, Romie Littrell, and Allan Chan (2012). 'In China? Pick Your Brand Name Carefully', *Harvard Business Review* September issue: 26.

Francis, Elaine J., and Stephen Matthews (2005). 'A Multi-Dimensional Approach to the Category "Verb" in Cantonese', *Journal of Linguistics* 41(2): 269–305.

François, Alexandre (2014). 'Trees, Waves and Linkages: Models of Language Diversification', in C. Bowern and B. Evans (eds.), *The Routledge Handbook of Historical Linguistics*. London: Routledge, 161–89.

Frellesvig, Bjarke (2010). *A History of the Japanese Language*. Cambridge: Cambridge University Press.

Gao, Liwei (2012). *Synchronic Variation or Diachronic Change: A Sociolinguistic Study of Chinese Internet Language*, in J. Liu and H. Tao (eds.), *Chinese Under Globalization. Emerging Trends in Language Use in China*. Singapore: World Scientific, 7–28.

Gao, Mingkai [高名凯] (1953). '关于汉语的词类分别' [On Word Class Distinctions in Chinese], *Zhongguo Yuwen* 10: 13–16.

Gao, Mingkai [高名凯] (1960). '在北京大学 1959年五四科学讨论会上的发言' [Talk given at the 4th May 1959 scientific colloquium at Peking University], in Beijing Daxue Zhongwenxi Yuyanxue Luncong Bianjibu [北京大学中文系语言学论丛编辑部] (eds.), 语言学论丛 4 [Collection of Essays in Lingusitics - 4]. Shanghai: Shanghai Jiaoyu Chubanshe, 35–40.

Gao, Xuesong (2012). '"Cantonese is Not a Dialect": Chinese Netizens' Defence of Cantonese as a Regional Lingua Franca', *Journal of Multilingual and Multicultural Development* 33(5): 449–64.

Gil, David (2013). 'Numeral Classifiers', in M. S. Dryer and M. Haspelmath (eds.), *The World Atlas of Language Structures Online*. Leipzig: Max Planck Institute for Evolutionary Anthropology, chapter 55.

Goddard, Cliff (2005). *The Languages of East and Southeast Asia*. Oxford: Oxford University Press.

Guan, Xiechu [管燮初] (1953). 殷墟甲骨刻辞的语法研究 [Studies on the Grammar of Yinxu Oracle Bone Inscriptions]. Shanghai: Guojia Kexue.

Guo, Rui [郭锐] (2002a). '汉语词类研究' [Studies on Word Classes in Chinese], in T. Lin [林焘] (ed.), 世纪中国学术大典：语言学 [A Collection of Academic Research in China: Linguistics]. Fuzhou: Fujian Jiaoyu Chubanshe, 65–71.

Guo, Rui [郭锐] (2002b). 现代汉语词类研究 [Studies on Word Classes in Modern Chinese]. Beijing: The Commercial Press.

Guo, Xiliang [郭锡良] (2005). '汉语介词'于'起源与汉藏语说商榷' [The Origin of the Chinese Preposition '*yú*' and the Debate on Sino-Tibetan], *Zhongguo Yuwen* 4: 341–5.

Handel, Zev (2003a). 'A Concise Introduction to Old Chinese Phonology', in J. A. Matisoff (ed.), *Handbook of Tibeto-Burman Phonology: System and Philosophy of Sino-Tibetan Reconstruction*. Berkeley: University of California Press, 543–74.

Handel, Zev (2003b). 'Northern Min Tone Values and the Reconstruction of "Softened Initials"', *Language and Linguistics* 4(1): 47–84.

Handel, Zev (2008). 'What is Sino-Tibetan? Snapshot of a Field and a Language Family in Flux', *Language and Linguistics Compass* 2(3): 422–41.

Handel, Zev (2010). 'Old Chinese and Min', *Chūgoku Gogaku* 257: 34–68.

Handel, Zev (2014). 'Historical Phonology of Chinese', in C.-T. J. Huang, A. Y.-h. Li, and A. Simpson (eds.), *The Handbook of Chinese Linguistics*. Oxford: Wiley-Blackwell, 576–98.

Handel, Zev (2019). *Sinography: The Borrowing and Adaptation of the Chinese Script*. Leiden: Brill.

Hannas, William C. (1997). *Asia's Orthographic Dilemma*. Honolulu: University of Hawai'i Press.

Hansell, Mark (2003). 'Chinese Writing', in G. Thurgood and R. J. LaPolla (eds.), *The Sino-Tibetan Languages*. London: Routledge, 156–65.

Harbsmeier, Christoph (1998). *Language and Logic in Traditional China*. Cambridge: Cambridge University Press.

Harbsmeier, Christoph (2001). 'May Fourth Linguistic Orthodoxy and Rhetoric: Some Informal Comparative Notes', in M. Lackner, I. Amelung, and J. Kurtz (eds.), *New Terms for New Ideas: Western Knowledge and Lexical Change in Late Imperial China*. Leiden: Brill, 373–410.

Harbsmeier, Christoph (2016). 'Irrefutable Conjectures. A Review of William H. Baxter and Laurent Sagart, Old Chinese. A New Reconstruction', *Monumenta Serica* 64(2): 445–504.

Harrison, Shelly P. (2003). 'On the limits of the comparative method', in B. D. Joseph and R. D. Janda (eds.), *The Handbook of Historical Linguistics*. Oxford: Blackwell, 213–43.

Hashimoto, Mantaro (1976). 'Language Diffusion on the Asian Continent: Problems of Typological Diversity in Sino-Tibetan', *Computational Analyses of Asian and African Languages* 3: 49–65.

Hashimoto, Mantaro (1986). 'The Altaicization of Northern Chinese', in J. McCoy and T. Light (eds.), *Contributions to Sino-Tibetan Studies*. Leiden: Brill, 76–97.

Haspelmath, Martin (2001). 'The European Linguistic Area: Standard Average European', in M. Haspelmath, E. König, W. Oesterreicher, and W. Raible (eds.), *Language Typology and Language Universals*. Berlin: Walter de Gruyter, 1492–510.

Haudricourt, André-G. (1954a). 'Comment Reconstruire le Chinois Archaïque', *Word* 10(2-3): 351–64.

Haudricourt, André-G. (1954b). 'De l'origine des Tones en Vietnamien', *Journal Asiatique* 242: 69–82.

Hay, Jennifer, Christopher Kennedy, and Beth Levin (1999). 'Scalar Structure Underlies Telicity in "Degree Achievements"', in T. Matthews and D. Strolovitch (eds.), *Proceedings of SALT IX*. Ithaca: CLC Publications, 127–44.

He, Wei [贺巍] (1989). 获嘉方言研究 [The Huojia Dialect]. Beijing: The Commercial Press.

He, Yuanjian (2004). 'The Word-and-rules Theory: Evidence from Chinese Morphology', *Taiwan Journal of Linguistics* 2(2), 1–26.

Hengeveld, Kees (1992). 'Parts of Speech', in M. D. Fortescue, P. Harder, and L. Kristoffersen (eds.), *Layered Structure and Reference in a Functional Perspective*. Amsterdam: John Benjamins, 29–56.

Her, One-Soon (1999). 'Interaction of Thematic Structure and Syntactic Structures: On Mandarin Dative Alternations', in Y. M. Yin, I.-L. Yang, and H.-C. Chan (eds.), *Languages and Linguistics V: Interactions in Language*. Taipei: Academia Sinica, 373–412.

Her, One-Soon (2004). 'Argument-function Linking in Resultatives', *Concentric: Studies in Linguistics* 30(2), 1–34.

Her, One-Soon (2006). 'Justifying Part-Of-Speech Assignments for Mandarin *gei*', *Lingua* 116(8): 1274–302.

Her, One-Soon (2007). 'Argument-function Mismatches in Mandarin Chinese: A Lexical Mapping Account', *Lingua* 117(1): 221–46.

Ho, Dah-an [何大安] (1981). '澄邁方言的文白異讀' [Colloquial and Literary Readings in the Chengmai Dialect], *Zhongyang Yanjiuyuan Lishi Yuyan Yanjiusuo Jikan* 52(1): 101–52.

Ho, Dah-an (2003). 'The Characteristics of Mandarin Dialects', in G. Thurgood and R. J. LaPolla (eds.). *The Sino-Tibetan Languages*. London: Routledge, 126–30.

Hock, Hans H. (1991). *Principles of Historical Linguistics*. Berlin-New York: Mouton de Gruyter.

Holm, David (2008). 'The Old Zhuang Script', in A. V. N. Diller, J. A. Edmondson and Y. Luo (eds.), *The Tai-Kadai Languages*. London: Routledge, 415–28.

Holm, David (2013). *Mapping the Old Zhuang Character Script: A Vernacular Writing System from Southern China*. Leiden: Brill.

Hong, Bo (2005). 立體化古代漢語教程 [A Consolidation Course in Classical Chinese]. Beijing: Gaodeng Jiaoyu Chubanshe.

Hong, Miao [洪淼] (2004). '现代汉语连动结构方式构词研究' [On Resultative Verb Compounds in Modern Chinese], *Xuzhou Shifan Daxue Xuebao* 30: 57–60.

Hopper, Paul J., and Sandra A. Thompson (1984). 'The Discourse Basis for Lexical Categories in Universal Grammar', *Language* 60(4): 703–52.

Hou, Jingyi [侯精一] (1999). 现代晋语的研究 [The Research on Modern Jin Dialects]. Beijing: The Commercial Press.

Hou, Jingyi [侯精一], and Duanzheng Wen [温端政] (1993). 陕西方言调查研究报告 [Report on the Survey of Shaanxi Dialects]. Taiyuan: Shanxi Gaoxiao Lianhe Chubanshe.

Hsiau, A-chin (2000). *Contemporary Taiwanese Cultural Nationalism*. London: Routledge.

Hu, Mingyang [胡明扬] (1979). 北京话初探 [Preliminary Remarks on the Beijing Dialect]. Beijing: The Commercial Press.

Hu, Mingyang [胡明扬] (1996a). '现代汉语词类问题考察' [An Investigation of the Issue of Word Classes in Modern Chinese], in M. Hu [胡明扬] (ed.), 词类问题考察 [An Investigation of the Issue of Word Classes]. Beijing: Beijing Yuyan Wenhua Daxue Chubanshe, 1–21.

Hu, Mingyang [胡明扬] (1996b). '兼类问题' [The Issue of Multicategoriality], in M. Hu [胡明扬] (ed.), 词类问题考察 [An Investigation of the Issue of Word Classes]. Beijing: Beijing Yuyan Wenhua Daxue Chubanshe, 215–57.

Hu, Peijun [胡培俊] (2012). 常用字字源字典 [An Etymological Dictionary of Frequently-Used Characters]. Wuhan: Chongwen Shuju.

Hu, Xiaobin [胡孝斌] (2006). '动词重叠AABB式的语法化' [The Grammaticalization of the AABB Pattern of Verb Reduplication], Hanyu Xuexi 4: 18–25.

Hua, Xuecheng [華學誠] (2007). 周秦漢晉方言研究史. 修订本 [History of the Research on Jin Dialects in the Zhou, Qing, and Han periods. Revised edition]. Shanghai: Fudan Daxue Chubanshe.

Huang, Borong [黄伯荣], and Xudong Liao [廖序东] (2002). 现代汉语: 增订三版. 上册 [Modern Chinese: Third revised and expanded edition. Volume 1]. Beijing: Gaodeng Jiaoyu Chubanshe.

Huang, Chu-Ren and Kathleen Ahrens (1999). 'The Function and Category of Gei in Mandarin Ditransitive Constructions', Journal of Chinese Linguistics 27(2): 1–26.

Huang, C.-T. James (1982). 'Logical Relations in Chinese and the Theory of Grammar', PhD dissertation, Massachusetts Institute of Technology.

Huang, C.-T. James (1984). 'Phrase Structure, Lexical Integrity, and Chinese Compounds', Journal of the Chinese Language Teachers Association 19(2): 53–78.

Huang, C.-T. James (1992). 'Complex Predicates in Control', in R. K. Larson, S. Latridou, U. Lahiri, and J. Higginbotham (eds.), Control and Grammar. Dordrecht: Kluwer, 109–47.

Huang, C.-T. James (2006). 'Resultatives and Unaccusatives: A Parametric View', Bulletin of the Chinese Linguistic Society of Japan 253: 1–43.

Huang, C.-T. James (2010). Between Syntax and Semantics. London: Routledge.

Huang, C.-T. James, and Audrey Yen-hui Li, (1996). 'Recent Generative Studies in Chinese Syntax', in C.-T. J. Huang and A. Y.-h. Li (eds.), New Horizons in Chinese Linguistics. Dordrecht: Kluwer, 49–95.

Huang, C.-T. James, Audrey Yen-hui Li, and Yafei Li (2009). The Syntax of Chinese. Cambridge: Cambridge Unversity Press.

Huang, Han-Chun (2006). 'A Constructional Approach to Argument Realization of Chinese Resultatives', UST Working Papers in Linguistics 2: 13–31.

Huang, Jack K. T., and Timothy D. Huang (1989). *An Introduction to Chinese, Japanese and Korean Computing.* Singapore: World Scientific.

Huang, Yan (1994). *The Syntax and Pragmatics of Anaphora: A Study with Special Reference to Chinese.* Cambridge: Cambridge University Press.

Huang, Yingqiong [黄映琼] (2006). 梅县方言语法研究 [Research on the Grammar of the Meixian Dialect]. MA dissertation, Southwest University.

Iljic, Robert (1983). 'Le Marqueur *Laizhe*', *Cahier de Linguistique Asie Orientale* 12(2): 65–102.

Jackendoff, Ray (1991). 'Parts and Boundaries', *Cognition* 41: 9–45.

Jacques Guillaume (2017a). 'The Genetic Position of Chinese', in R. Sybesma, W. Behr, Y. Gu, Z. Handel, C.-T. J. Huang, and J. Myers (eds.), *Encyclopedia of Chinese Language and Linguistics. Volume 2.* Leiden: Brill, 297–306.

Jacques Guillaume (2017b). 'Traditional Chinese Phonology', in R. Sybesma, W. Behr, Y. Gu, Z. Handel, C.-T. J. Huang, and J. Myers (eds.), *Encyclopedia of Chinese Language and Linguistics. Volume 4.* Leiden: Brill, 376–91.

Janhunen, Juha (2007). 'Typological Interaction in the Qinghai Linguistic Complex', *Studia Orientalia* 101: 85–103.

Janhunen, Juha, Marja Peltomaa, Erika Sandman, and Dongzhou Xiawu (2008). *Wutun.* Munich: Lincom.

Janhunen, Juha (2012). 'On the Hierarchy of Structural Convergence in the Amdo Sprachbund', in P. Suihkonen, B. Comrie, and V. Solovyev (eds.), *Argument Structure and Grammatical Relations: A Crosslinguistic Typology.* Amsterdam-Philadelphia: John Benjamins, 177–89.

Ježek, Elisabetta (2015). *The Lexicon: An Introduction.* Oxford: Oxford University Press.

Jin, Zhaozi [金兆梓] (1983 [1922]). 国文法之研究 [Research on the Grammar of the National Language]. Beijing: The Commercial Press.

Kang, Shiyong [亢世勇], and Hairun Liu [刘海润] (2015). 新世纪新词语大辞典 [New Century Comprehensive Dictionary of Neologisms]. Shanghai: Shanghai Cishu Chubanshe.

Karlgren, Bernhard (1940). 'Grammata Serica: Script And Phonetics in Chinese and Sino-Japanese', *Bulletin of the Museum of Far Eastern Antiquities* 12, 1–471.

Karlgren, Bernhard (1957). *Grammata Serica Recensa.* Stockholm: Museum of Far Eastern Antiquities.

Kaske, Elisabeth (2004). 'Mandarin, Vernacular, and National Language: China's Emerging Concept of a National Language in Early Twentieth-century China', in M. Lackner and N. Vittinghoff (eds.), *Mapping Meanings: The Field of New Learning in Late Qing China.* Leiden: Brill, 265–304.

Kaske, Elisabeth (2008). *The Politics of Language in Chinese Education, 1895–1919.* Leiden: Brill.

Kearns, Kate (2007). *Telic Senses of Deadjectival Verbs, Lingua* 117(1): 26–66.

Kibrik, Andrej A. (2001). 'Reference Maintenance in Discourse', in M. Haspelmath, E. Konig, W. Oesterreicher, and W. Raible (eds.), *Language Typology and Language Universals. Volume 2*. Berlin-New York: Mouton de Gruyter, 1123–41.

Kim, Tae Eun (2012). 'A Study of Mandarin Loanwords: Lexical Stratification, Adaptation and Factors', PhD dissertation, University of Wisconsin-Madison.

Klein, Wolfgang, Ping Li, and Henriette Hendriks (2000). 'Aspect and Assertion in Mandarin Chinese', *Natural Language and Linguistic Theory* 18, 723–70.

Klöter, Henning (2005). *Written Taiwanese*. Wiesbaden: Harassowitz.

Klöter, Henning (2017). 'Táiwān: Language Situation', in R. Sybesma, W. Behr, Y. Gu, Z. Handel, C.-T. J. Huang, and J. Myers (eds.), *Encyclopedia of Chinese Language and Linguistics. Volume 4*. Leiden: Brill, 263–7.

Krifka, Manfred (1998). 'The Origins of Telicity', in S. Rothstein (ed.), *Events and Grammar*. Dordrecht: Kluwer, 197–235.

Kurpaska, Maria (2010). *Chinese Language(s). A Look through the Prism of The Great Dictionary of Modern Chinese Dialects*. Berlin-New York: Mouton de Gruyter.

Kwong, Oi Yee, and Benjamin K. Tsou (2003). 'Categorial Fluidity in Chinese and its Implications for Part-of-speech Tagging', in A. Copestake and J. Hajič (eds.), *EACL '03: Proceedings of the Tenth Conference on European Chapter of the Association for Computational Linguistics*. Stroudsburg, PA: Association for Computational Linguistics, 115–18.

Lamarre, Christine [柯理思] (2009). ' 论北方方言中位移终点标记的语法化和句位义的作' [On the Grammaticalization of Markers of Displacement in Northern Chinese Dialects and on their Syntactic Use], in F. Wu [吴福祥] and X. Cui [崔希亮] (eds.), 语法化与语法研究 – 四 [Studies on Grammaticalization and Grammar – Volume 4]. Beijing: The Commercial Press, 145–87.

Lambrecht, Knud (1994), *Information Structure and Sentence Form: Topic, Focus, and the Mental Representation of Discourse Referents*. Cambridge: Cambridge University Press.

LaPolla, Randy J. (1994) 'On the Change to Verb-medial Order in Proto-Chinese: Evidence from Tibeto-Burman', in H. Kitamura, T. Nishida, and Y. Nagano (eds.). *Current Issues in Sino-Tibetan Linguistics*. Osaka: National Museum of Ethnology, 98–104.

LaPolla, Randy J. (1995). 'Pragmatic Relations and Word Order in Chinese', in P. A. Downing and M. Noonan (eds.), *Word Order in Discourse*. Amsterdam: Benjamins, 297–332.

LaPolla, Randy J. (2001). 'The Role of Migration and Language Contact in the Development of the Sino-Tibetan Family', in A. Y. Aikhenvald and

R. M. W. Dixon (eds.). *Areal Diffusion and Genetic Inheritance*. Oxford: Oxford University Press, 225–54.

LaPolla, Randy J. (2003). 'Overview of Sino-Tibetan Morphosyntax', in G. Thurgood and R. J. LaPolla (eds.). *The Sino-Tibetan Languages*. London: Routledge, 126–30.

LaPolla, Randy J. (2009). 'Chinese as a Topic-Comment (Not Topic-Prominent and Not SVO) Language', in J. Z. Xing (ed.), *Studies of Chinese Linguistics: Functional Approaches*. Hong Kong: Hong Kong University Press, 9–22.

LaPolla, Randy J. (2017). 'Overview of Sino-Tibetan Morphosyntax', in G. Thurgood, and R. J. LaPolla (eds.), *The Sino-Tibetan Languages*. London: Routledge, 40–8.

LaPolla, Randy J., and Dorothy Poa (2006). 'On Describing Word Order', in F. K. Ameka, A. Dench, and N. Evans (eds.), *Catching Language: The Standing Challenge of Grammar Writing*. Berlin-New York: Mouton de Gruyter, 269–96.

Lau, Chun-Fat [劉鎮發] (2002). '漢語方言的分類標準與'客家話'在漢語方言分類上的問題' [The Criteria for the Classification of Chinese Dialects and the Problem of the Position of Hakka], *Journal of Chinese Linguistics* 30(1): 90–1.

Lau, Helena Yang Ping, and Sophia Yat Mei Lee (2015). 'A Comparative Study on Mandarin and Cantonese Resultative Verb Compounds', in H. Zhao (ed.), *Proceedings of the 29th Pacific Asia Conference on Language, Information and Computation*. Shanghai, 231–9.

Lee, James, and Bin R. Wong (1991). 'Population Movements in Qing China and their Linguistic Legacy', in W. S.-Y. Wang (ed.), *Languages and Dialects of China*. Berkeley: Project on Linguistic Analysis, 52–77.

Lee, Ki-Moon, and S. Robert Ramsey (2011). *A History of the Korean Language*. Cambridge: Cambridge University Press.

Lee, Yeon-Ju, and Laurent Sagart (2008). 'No Limits to Borrowing: The Case of Bai and Chinese', *Diachronica* 25(3): 357–85.

Lehmann, Christian (2015). *Thoughts on Grammaticalization. Third Edition*. Berlin: Language Science Press.

Leong, Che Kan (2006). 'Making Explicit Children's Implicit Epilanguage in Learning to Read Chinese', in P. Li, H. T. Li, E. Bates, and O. J. L. Tzeng (eds.), *The Handbook of East Asian Psycholinguistics*. Cambridge: Cambridge University Press, 70–80.

Leung, Chi Hong (2010). 'Code-Mixing in Print Advertisement and its Cultural Implications in Hong Kong', *European Journal of Social Sciences* 12(3): 417–29.

Levin, Beth, and Malka Rappaport Hovav (1995). *Unaccusativity: At the Syntax-Lexical Semantics Interface*. Cambridge, MA: MIT Press.

Li, Ai-jun, Qiang Fang, Ruiyuan Xu, Xuxia Wang, and Yunzhong Tang (2005). 'A Contrastive Study between Minnan-accented Chinese and Standard Chinese', *Report of Phonetic Research* 18: 86–92.

Li, Audrey Yen-hui (1990). *Order and Constituency in Mandarin Chinese.* Dordrecht: Kluwer.

Li, Audrey Yen-hui (2006). 'Chinese *Ba*', in M. Everaert and H. van Riemsdijk (eds.), *The Blackwell Companion to Syntax. Volume 1.* Oxford: Blackwell, 374–468.

Li, Audrey Yen-hui (2017). 'Bǎ 把-Construction', in R. Sybesma, W. Behr, Y. Gu, Z. Handel, C.-T. J. Huang, and J. Myers (eds.), *Encyclopedia of Chinese Language and Linguistics. Volume 1.* Leiden: Brill, 249–57.

Li, Charles N., and Sandra A. Thompson (1973). 'Serial Verb Constructions in Mandarin Chinese: Coordination or Subordination?', in C. Corum and C. Smith-Stark (eds.), *You Take the High Node and I'l Take the Low Node: Papers from the Comparative Syntax Festival.* Chicago: Chicago Linguistic Society, 96–103.

Li, Charles N., and Sandra A. Thompson (1974). 'An Explanation of Word Order Change SVO > SOV', *Foundations of Language* 12(2): 201–14.

Li, Charles N., and Sandra A. Thompson (1976). 'Subject and Topic: A New Typology of Language', in C. N. Li (ed.), *Subject and Topic.* New York: Academic Press, 457–89.

Li, Charles N., and Sandra A. Thompson (1978). 'An Exploration of Mandarin Chinese', in W. P. Lehmann (ed.), *Syntactic Typology: Studies in the Phenomenology of Language.* Austin: University of Texas Press, 233–66.

Li, Charles N., and Sandra A. Thompson (1981). *Mandarin Chinese. A Functional Reference Grammar.* Berkeley: University of California Press.

Li, Charles N., Sandra A. Thompson, and R. McMillan Thompson (1982). 'The Discourse Motivation for the Perfect Aspect: The Mandarin Particle *le*', in P. J. Hopper (ed.), *Tense-aspect: Between Semantics and Pragmatics.* Amsterdam-Philadelphia: John Benjamins, 19–44.

Li, Fang-Kuei (1973 [1937]). 'Languages and Dialects of China', *Journal of Chinese Linguistics* 1(1): 1–13.

Li, Fang-Kuei [李芳桂] (1980 [1971]). 上古音研究 [Old Chinese Phonology]. Beijing: The Commercial Press.

Li, Jia (2019). 'New Trends in the Protection of Dialects', in Y. Li and W. Li (eds.), *The Language Situation in China. Volume 5,* Berlin-New York: Mouton de Gruyter, 59–70.

Li, Jie (1996). 'Das Chinesische Schriftsystem', in G. Hartmut and O. Ludwig (eds.), *Schrift und Schriftlichkeit/Writing and Its Use. Volume 2.* Berlin-New York: Mouton de Gruyter, 1404–12.

Li, Jinxi [黎锦熙] (2001 [1924]). 新著国语文法 [A New Grammar of the National Language]. Beijing: The Commercial Press.

Li, Linding [李临定] (1986). 现代汉语句型 [Modern Chinese Sentence Patterns]. Beijing: The Commercial Press.

Li, Paul Jen-kuei (1995). 'Is Chinese Genetically Related to Austronesian?', in W. S.-Y. Wang (ed.), *The Ancestry of the Chinese Language.* Berkeley: Project on Linguistic Analysis, 93–112.

Li, Rong [李荣] (1985). '官话方言的分区' [The Classification of Mandarin Dialects], *Fangyan* 1: 2–5.

Li, Rong [李荣] (1987). '汉语方言的分区' [The Classification of Chinese Dialects], in S. A. Wurm, R. Li, T. Baumann, and M. W. Lee (eds.), *Language Atlas of China - 中国语言地图集*. Hong Kong: Longman, A2.

Li, Rong [李荣] (1989). '汉语方言的分区' [The Classification of Chinese Dialects], *Fangyan* 4: 241–59.

Li, Rulong [李如龙] (2001). *汉语方言学* [Chinese Dialectology]. Beijing: Gaodeng Jiaoyu Chubanshe.

Li, Rulong [李如龙], and Shuangqing Zhang [张双庆] (1992). *客赣方言调查报告* [Report on a Survey of Hakka and Gan Dialects]. Xiamen: Xiamen Daxue Chubanshe.

Li, Xiaofan [李小凡] (2006). '汉语方言分区方法再认识' [New Reflections on the Methods for the Classification of Chinese Dialects], *Fangyan* 4: 356–63.

Li, Yafei (1990). 'On V-V Compounds in Chinese', *Natural Language and Linguistic Theory* 8: 177–207.

Li, Yafei (1995). 'The Thematic Hierarchy and Causativity', *Natural Language and Linguistic Theory* 13: 255–82.

Li, Yafei (2005). *A Theory of the Morphology-Syntax Interface*. Cambridge, MA: MIT Press.

Li, Yuming [李宇明] (1996a). '非谓形容词的词类地位' [The Word Class Identity of Non-predicative Adjectives], *Zhongguo Yuwen* 1: 3–11.

Li, Yuming [李宇明] (1996b). '论词语重叠的意义' [On the Meaning of Reduplication], *Shijie Hanyu Jiaoxue* 1: 10–19.

Liang, Dandan [梁丹丹], and Shiwen Feng [封世文] (2006). '再论兼类词处理——并以神经语言学研究为证据' [More on the Treatment of Multicategorial words: Evidence from Neurolinguistic Research], *Jiangxi Shehui Kexue* 10: 230–7.

Lieber, Rochelle, and Pavol Štekauer (2009). 'Introduction: Status and Definition of Compounding', in L. Rochelle and P. Štekauer (eds.), *The Oxford Handbook of Compounding*. Oxford: Oxford University Press, 3–18.

Lieber, Rochelle, and Sergio Scalise (2006). 'The Lexical Integrity Hypothesis in a New Theoretical Universe', *Lingue e Linguaggio* 5(1): 7–32.

Lien, Chinfa (1994). 'The Order of "Verb-Complement" Constructions in Taiwan Southern Min', *The Tsing Hua Journal of Chinese Studies* 24(3): 345–69.

Light, Timothy (1979). 'Word Order and Word Order Change in Mandarin Chinese', *Journal of Chinese Linguistics* 7(2): 149–80.

Lin, Hua (2001). *A Grammar of Mandarin Chinese*. Munich: Lincom.

Lin, Jimmy (2004). 'Event Structure and the Encoding of Arguments: The Syntax of the Mandarin and English Verb Phrase', PhD dissertation, Massachusetts Institute of Technology.

Lin Jo-wang (2003). 'Temporal Reference in Mandarin Chinese', *Journal of East Asian Linguistics* 12: 259–311.

Lin Jo-wang (2006). 'Time in a Language without Tense: The Case of Chinese', *Journal of Semantics* 23(1): 1–53.

Lin Jo-wang (2010). 'A Tenseless Analysis of Mandarin Chinese Revisited: A Response to Sybesma 2007', *Linguistic Inquiry* 41(2): 305–29.

Lin Jo-wang (2012). 'Tenselessness', in R. I. Binnick (ed.), *The Oxford Handbook of Tense and Aspect*. Oxford: Oxford University Press, 669–95.

Lin, Philip T. (2015). *Taiwanese Grammar*. Leipzig: Greenhorn Media.

Lin, Tiansong [林天送], and Ying Fan [范莹] (2010). '闽方言的词源统计分类' [A Statistical Classification of Word Etymology in Min Dialects], *Yuyan Kexue* 9(6): 661–9.

Liu, Charles A. (1977). 'On Two Topic Markers in Chinese', *Journal of the Chinese Language Teachers' Association* 12(3): 204–9.

Liu, Cunhan [刘村汉] (1987). '广西壮族自治区的汉语方言' [Chinese Dialects in the Guangxi Zhuang Autonomous Region], in S. A. Wurm, R. Li, T. Baumann, and M. W. Lee (eds.), *Language Atlas of China - 中国语言地图集*. Hong Kong: Longman, B14.

Liu Danqing [刘丹青] (2001). '汉语给予类双及物结构的类型学考察' [A Typological Study of Chinese Ditransitive Dative Verbs], *Zhongguo Yuwen* 5: 387–97.

Liu, Danqing (2008). '汉语名词性短语的句法类型特征' [Typological Syntactic Features of Noun Phrases in Chinese], *Zhongguo Yuwen* 1: 3–18.

Liu, Luther Chen-sheng (2010). 'The Positive Morpheme in Chinese and the Adjectival Structure', *Lingua* 120(4): 1010–56.

Liu, Lydia H. (1995). *Translingual Practice: Literature, National Culture and Translated Modernity: China, 1900–1937*. Stanford, CA: Stanford University Press.

Lock, Graham, and Gary S. Linebarger (2018). *Chinese Buddhist Texts. An Introductory Reader*. Oxford: Routledge.

Lu, Jianming [陆俭明] (1994). '关于词的兼类问题' [On the Issue of Multicategorial Words], *Zhongguo Yuwen* 1: 28–34.

Lü, Shuxiang [吕叔湘], and Changrong Rao [饶长溶] (1981). '试论非谓形容词' [Tentative remarks on non-predicative adjectives], *Zhongguo Yuwen* 2: 81–5.

Lü, Shuxiang [吕叔湘] (1979). *汉语语法分析问题* [Issues in the Analysis of Chinese Grammar]. Beijing: The Commercial Press.

Lü, Shuxiang [吕叔湘] (1980). *现代汉语八百词* [Eight Hundred Words of Modern Chinese]. Beijing: The Commercial Press.

Lü, Shuxiang [吕叔湘] (1981). *语文常谈* [A Conversation on Language]. Beijing: Sanlian Shudian.

Lü, Shuxiang [吕叔湘] (1985). *近代汉语指代词* [Demonstrative Pronouns in Early Mandarin]. Shanghai: Xuelin Chubanshe.

Lü, Shuxiang [呂叔湘] (2002 [1942]). 中国文法要略 [An Outline of Chinese Grammar]. Shenyang: Liaoning Jiaoyu Chubanshe.

Lü, Shuxiang [呂叔湘], and Dexi Zhu [朱德熙] (2005 [1951]). 语法修辞讲话 [Introduction to Grammar and Rhetoric]. Shenyang: Liaoning Jiaoyu Chubanshe.

Luo, Kangning [罗康宁] (1987). 信宜方言志 [Xinyi Dialect Gazetteer]. Guangzhou: Zhongshan Daxue Chubanshe.

Luo, Yongxian (2008). 'Zhuang', in A. V. N. Diller, J. A. Edmondson, and Y. Luo (eds.), *The Tai-Kadai Languages*. London: Routledge, 317–77.

Ma, Qingzhu [马庆株] (1995). '现代汉语词缀的性质、范围和分类' [The Nature, Scope and Classification of Modern Chinese Affixes], *Zhongguo Yuyanxuebao* 6: 101–37.

Mair, Victor H. (1991). 'What Is a Chinese "Dialect/Topolect"? Reflections on Some Key Sino-English Linguistic Terms', *Sino-Platonic Papers* 29: 1–31.

Mair, Victor H. (1994). 'Buddhism and the Rise of the Written Vernacular in East Asia: The Making of the National Languages', *The Journal of Asian Studies* 53(3): 707–51.

Mair, Victor H. (1997). 'Ma Jianzhong and the Invention of Chinese Grammar', in S. Chaofen (ed.), *Studies on the History of Chinese Syntax*. Berkeley, CA: Project on Linguistic Analysis, 5–26.

Marosán, Lajos (2006). *The Meaning of Word Classes*. Bern: Peter Lang.

Mártonfi, Ferenc (1977). 'On Conceptions of "Parts of Speech" in Chinese and Generative Grammar (Parts of Speech to Be Buried)', *Acta Orientalia Hungarica* 31(3): 279–310.

Masini, Federico (1993). *The Formation of Modern Chinese Lexicon and Its Evolution Towards a National Language: The Period from 1840 to 1898*. Berkeley: Project on Linguistic Analysis.

Maspero, Henri (1920). 'Le Dialecte de Tchang-ngan sous les T'ang', *Bulletin de l'Ecole française d'Extrême-Orient* 20(1): 1–124.

Matisoff, James A. (1991). 'Sino-Tibetan Linguistics: Present State and Future Prospects', *Annual Review of Anthropology* 20: 469–504.

Matisoff, James A. (2001). 'Genetic versus Contact Relationship: Prosodic Diffusibility in South-East Asian Languages', in A. Y. Aikhenvald and R. M. W. Dixon (eds.), *Areal Diffusion and Genetic Inheritance: Problems in Comparative Linguistics*. Oxford: Oxford University Press, 291–326.

Matisoff, James A. (2003). *Handbook of Tibeto-Burman Phonology: System and Philosophy of Sino-Tibetan Reconstruction*. Berkeley: University of California Press.

Matthews, Stephen (1996). 'Ditaxia and Hybridization in Chinese Dialect Grammar', in I. Thongde *et al.* (eds.), *Pan-Asiatic Linguistics: Proceedings of the Fourth International Symposium on Language and Linguistics*. Salaya: Mahidol University, 1274–83.

Matthews, Stephen (1999). 'Y. R. Chao and Universal Chinese Grammar', in D. Cram, A. R. Linn, and E. Nowak (eds.), *History of Linguistics 1996*. Amsterdam: John Benjamins, 217–24.

Matthews, Stephen (2006). 'On Serial Verb Constructions in Cantonese', in A. Y. Aikhenvald and R. M. W. Dixon (eds.), *Serial Verb Constructions: A Cross-Linguistic Typology*. Oxford: Oxford University Press, 69–87.

Matthews, Stephen, and Virginia Yip (2011). *Cantonese. A Comprehensive Grammar. Second Edition.* London: Routledge.

Mauri, Caterina (2008). *Coordination Relations in the Languages of Europe and Beyond.* Berlin-New York: Mouton de Gruyter.

McBride-Chang, Catherine, and Yiping Zhong (2006). 'Emerging Literacy Skills in Chinese', in P. Li, H. T. Li, E. Bates, and O. J. L. Tzeng (eds.), *The Handbook of East Asian Psycholinguistics*. Cambridge: Cambridge University Press, 81–9.

McCawley, James D. (1992). 'Justifying Part-of-Speech Assignment in Mandarin Chinese', *Journal of Chinese Linguistics* 20(2): 211–45.

McWhorter, John (2007). *Language Interrupted. Signs of Non-Native Acquisition in Standard Language Grammars.* Oxford: Oxford University Press.

Mei, Kuang (1980). 'Is modern Chinese Really a SOV language?', *Cahiers de Linguistique Asie Orientale* 7: 23–45.

Mei, Tsu-lin (1970). 'Tones and Prosody in Middle Chinese and the Origin of the Rising Tone', *Harvard Journal of Asiatic Studies* 30: 86–110.

Mei, Tsu-lin [梅祖麟] (1989). '上古漢語 *S- 前綴的構詞功用' [The Functions of the Old Chinese Prefix *S-], in *Proceedings of the Second International Conference on Sinology: Section on Linguistics and Paleography. Volume 2.* Taipei: Academia Sinica, 33–52.

Mei, Tsu-lin [梅祖麟] (1991). '从汉代 "动、杀"、"动、死" 来看动补结构的发展 – 兼论中古时期起词的施受关系的中立化' [The Han Dynasty 'verb-*shā*' and 'verb-*sǐ*'' Constructions and the Development of the Resultative Construction: On the Neutralization of the Agent-patient Relation in Middle Chinese], in Beijing Daxue Zhongwenxi 'Yuyanxue Luncong' Bianweihui [北京大学中文系'语言学论丛'编委会] (eds.), *语言学论丛* 16 [Collection of Essays on Linguistics 16]. Beijing: The Commercial Press, 112–36.

Mei, Tsu-lin [梅祖麟] (1994). '唐代、宋代共同语的语法和现代方言的语法' [The Grammar of the Common Language in the Tang and Song Periods and the Grammar of Modern Dialects], in P. J.-k. Li [李壬癸], C.-R. Huang [黃居仁], and C.-C. J. Tang [湯志真] (eds.), *中國境內語言暨語言學 (第二輯) – 歷史語言學* [Language and Linguistics in China 2: Historical Linguistics]. Taipei: Academia Sinica, 61–97.

Mei, Tsu-lin [梅祖麟] (2004). '介词'于'在甲骨文和汉藏语里的起源' [The Preposition '*yú*' in Oracle Bone Inscriptions and its Sino-Tibetan Origins], *Zhongguo Yuwen* 4: 323–32.

Meisterernst, Barbara (2010). 'Object Preposing in Classical and Pre-Medieval Chinese', *Journal of East Asian Linguistics* 19: 75–102.

Melloni, Chiara, and Bianca Basciano (2018). 'Reduplication Across Boundaries: The Case of Mandarin', in O. Bonami, G. Boyé, G. Dal, H. Giraudo, and F. Namer (eds.), *The Lexeme in Descriptive and Theoretical Morphology*. Berlin: Language Science Press, 339–80.

Michaud, Alexis (2012). 'Monosyllabicization: Patterns of Evolution in Asian Languages', in N. Nau, T. Stolz, and C. Stroh (eds.), *Monosyllables: From Phonology to Typology*. Berlin: Akademie Verlag, 115–30.

Miyake, Marc H. (2003). *Old Japanese: A Phonetic Reconstruction*. London: Routledge.

Morbiato, Anna (2018a). 'How Subjective is the Subject?', *Annali Di Ca' Foscari. Serie Orientale* 54(1): 319–48.

Morbiato, Anna (2018b). 'Word Order and Sentence Structure in Mandarin Chinese: New Perspectives', PhD dissertation, Ca' Foscari University of Venice and The University of Sydney.

Myers, James (2006). 'Processing Chinese Compounds: A Survey of the Literature', in Gary Libben and Gonia Jarema (eds.), *The Representation and Processing of Compound Words*. Oxford: Oxford University Press, 169–96.

Nguyen, Dinh-Hoa (1997). *Vietnamese*. Amsterdam-Philadelphia: John Benjamins.

Nikolaeva, Irina (2001). 'Secondary Topic as a Relation in Information Structure', *Linguistics* 39(1): 1–49.

Norman, Jerry (1973). 'Tonal Development in Min', *Journal of Chinese Linguistics* 1(2): 222–38.

Norman, Jerry (1974). 'The Initials of Proto-Min', *Journal of Chinese Linguistics* 2(1): 27–36.

Norman, Jerry (1981). 'The Proto-Min Finals', in *Proceedings of the International Conference on Sinology. Section on Linguistics and Paleography*. Taipei: Academia Sinica, 35–73.

Norman, Jerry (1988). *Chinese*. Cambridge: Cambridge University Press.

Norman, Jerry (1989). 'What Is a *Kèjiā* Dialect?', in *Proceedings of the Second International Conference on Sinology: Section on Linguistics and Paleography. Volume 1*. Taipei: Academia Sinica, 323–44.

Norman, Jerry (1994). 'Pharyngealization in Early Chinese', *Journal of the American Oriental Society* 114(3): 397–408.

Norman, Jerry (1999). 'Vocalism in Chinese Dialect Classification', in R. VanNess Simmons (ed.), *Issues in Chinese Dialect Description and Classification*. Berkeley: Project on Linguistic Analysis, 193–203.

Norman, Jerry (2003). *The Chinese Dialects: Phonology*, in G. Thurgood and R. J. LaPolla (eds.), *The Sino-Tibetan Languages*. London: Routledge, 72–83.

Norman, Jerry (2005). '闽方言中的来母字和早期汉语' [The *lái* Initial in Min Dialects and Old Chinese], *Minzu Yuwen* 4: 1–5.

Norman, Jerry (2006). 'Modern Chinese and the Rime Tables', in D. P. Branner (ed.), *The Chinese Rime Tables: Linguistic Philosophy and Historical-Comparative Phonology*. Amsterdam-Philadelphia: John Benjamins, 183–8.

Norman, Jerry, and Weldon S. Coblin (1995). 'A New Approach to Chinese Historical Linguistics', *Journal of the American Oriental Society* 115(4): 576–84.

O'Melia, Thomas (1966 [1938]). *First Year Cantonese: Revised edition. Volume 2.* Hong Kong: Catholic Truth Society.

Osterkamp, Sven (2017). 'Sinoform writing', in R. Sybesma, W. Behr, Y. Gu, Z. Handel, C.-T. J. Huang, and J. Myers (eds.), *Encyclopedia of Chinese Language and Linguistics. Volume 4.* Leiden: Brill, 115–24.

Ōta, Tatsuo [太田辰夫] (1987). *中国语历史文法* [A Historical Grammar of Chinese]. Beijing: Beijing Daxue Chubanshe.

Packard, Jerome (1998). 'Introduction', in J. Packard (ed.), *New Approaches to Chinese Word Formation.* Berlin-New York: Mouton de Gruyter, 3–34.

Packard, Jerome (2000). *The Morphology of Chinese.* Cambridge: Cambridge University Press.

Packard, Jerome (2006). 'Chinese as an Isolating Language', in K. Brown (ed.), *Encyclopedia of Language and Linguistics. Volume 2.* Oxford: Elsevier, 355–9.

Pan, Wenguo [潘文国], Po-Ching Yip [叶步青], and Yang Han [韩洋] (2004). *汉语的构词法研究* [Research on Word Formation in Chinese]. Shanghai: Huadong Shifan Daxue Chubanshe.

Pan, Wuyun (1991). 'An Introduction to the Wu Dialects', in W. S.-Y. Wang (ed.), *Languages and Dialects of China.* Berkeley: Project on Linguistic Analysis, 237–93.

Pan, Wuyun [潘悟云] (1995). '对华奥语系假说的若干支持材料' [Some Supporting Evidence for the Sino-Austric Hypothesis], in W. S.-Y. Wang (ed.), *The Ancestry of the Chinese Language.* Berkeley: Project on Linguistic Analysis, 113–44.

Pan, Wuyun [潘悟云] (2000). *汉语历史音韵学* [Chinese Historical Phonology]. Shanghai: Shanghai Jiaoyu Chubanshe.

Pan, Wuyun (2017). 'Xiéshēng 諧聲 (Phonetic Series)', in R. Sybesma, W. Behr, Y. Gu, Z. Handel, C.-T. J. Huang, and J. Myers (eds.), *Encyclopedia of Chinese Language and Linguistics. Volume 4.* Leiden: Brill, 623–5.

Pan, Yunzhong [潘允中] (1989). *汉语词汇史概要* [Outline of the History of the Chinese Lexicon]. Shanghai: Shanghai Guji Chubanshe.

Paris, Marie-Claude (2007). 'Un aperçu de la Réduplication Nominale et Verbale en Mandarin', *Faits des Langues* 29(1): 63–76.

Paul, Waltraud (2008). 'The Serial Verb Construction in Chinese: A Tenacious Myth and a Gordian Knot', *The Linguistic Review* 25(3-4): 367–411.

Paul, Waltraud (2010). 'Adjectives in Mandarin Chinese: The Rehabilitation of a Much Ostracized Category', in P. Cabredo-Hofherr and O. Matushansky (eds.), *Adjectives: Formal analyses in Syntax and Semantics*. Amsterdam-Philadelphia: John Benjamins, 115–52.

Paul, Waltraud (2015). *New Perspectives on Chinese Syntax*. Berlin-New York: Mouton De Gruyter.

Paul, Waltraud, and John Whitman (2008). 'Shi . . . de Focus Clefts in Mandarin Chinese', *The Linguistic Review* 25(3-4): 413–51.

Perfetti, Charles A., and Ying Liu (2006). 'Reading Chinese Characters: Orthography, Phonology, Meaning, and the Lexical Constituency Model', in P. Li, H. T. Li, E. Bates and O. J .L. Tzeng (eds.), *The Handbook of East Asian Psycholinguistics*. Cambridge: Cambridge University Press, 225–36.

Peyraube, Alain (1985). 'Les Structures en *BA* en Chinois Mediéval et Moderne', *Cahiers de Linguistique Asie Orientale* 14(2): 193–213.

Peyraube, Alain (1988). *Syntaxe Siachronique du Chinois: Évolution des Constructions Datives du 14. Siècle av. J.-C. au 18. Siècle*. Paris: Collège de France - Institut des Hautes Études Chinoises.

Peyraube, Alain (1989). '早期"把"字句的几个问题' [Some Issues Regarding the Early *bǎ* Construction], *Yuwen Yanjiu* 1: 1–9.

Peyraube, Alain (1996). 'Recent Issues in Chinese Historical Syntax', in C.-T. J. Huang and A. Y.-h. Li (eds.), *New Horizons in Chinese linguistics*. Dordrecht: Kluwer, 161–213.

Peyraube, Alain (1997). 'On Word Order in Archaic Chinese', *Cahiers de Linguistique Asie Orientale* 26(1): 3–20.

Peyraube, Alain (2001). 'Some Reflections on the Sources of the *Mashi Wentong*', in M. Lackner, I. Amelung, and J. Kurtz (eds.), *New Terms for New Ideas: Western Knowledge and Lexical Change in Late Imperial China*. Leiden: Brill, 341–56.

Peyraube, Alain (2015). 'Grammatical Change in Sinitic Languages and its Relation to Typology', in H. Chappell (ed.), *Diversity in Sinitic Languages*. Oxford: Oxford University Press, 53–80.

Pirani, Laura (2008). 'Bound Roots in Mandarin Chinese and Comparison with European "Semi-words"', in M. K. M. Chan and H. Kang (eds.), *Proceedings of the 20th North American Conference on Chinese Linguistics (NACCL-20)*. Columbus, OH: Ohio State University, 261–77.

Plag, Ingo (2003). *Word-Formation in English*. Cambridge: Cambridge University Press.

Pulleyblank, Edwin G. (1962a). 'The Consonantal System of Old Chinese', *Asia Major* 9: 58–144.

Pulleyblank, Edwin G. (1962b). 'The Consonantal System of Old Chinese, Part II', *Asia Major* 9: 206–65.

Pulleyblank, Edwin G. (1973). 'Some New Hypotheses Concerning Word Families in Chinese', *Journal of Chinese Linguistics* 1(1): 111–25.

Pulleyblank, Edwin G. (1978). 'The Nature of the Middle Chinese Tones and their Development to Early Mandarin', *Journal of Chinese Linguistics* 6(2): 173–203.

Pulleyblank, Edwin G. (1984). *Middle Chinese: A study in Historical Phonology.* Vancouver: University of British Columbia Press.

Pulleyblank, Edwin G. (1991). *Lexicon of Reconstructed Pronunciation in Early Middle Chinese, Late Middle Chinese, and Early Mandarin.* Vancouver: University of British Columbia Press.

Pulleyblank, Edwin G. (1995a). *Outline of Classical Chinese Grammar.* Vancouver: University of British Columbia Press.

Pulleyblank, Edwin G. (1995b). 'The Historical and Prehistorical Relationships of Chinese', in W. S.-Y. Wang (ed.), *The Ancestry of the Chinese Language.* Berkeley: Project on Linguistic Analysis, 145–94.

Pulleyblank, Edwin G. (1998). '*Qieyun* and *Yunjing*: The Essential Foundation for Chinese Historical Linguistics', *Journal of the American Oriental Society* 118(2): 200–16.

Pulleyblank, Edwin G. (2004). 'From Archaic Chinese to Mandarin', in G. Booij, C. Lehmann, and J. Mugdan (eds.), *Morphologie/Morphology. 2. Halbband.* Berlin-New York: Mouton de Gruyter, 1730–40.

Qian, Cengyi [钱曾怡] (1993). 博山方言研究 [The Boshan Dialect]. Beijing: Shehui Kexue Wenxian Chubanshe.

Qiao, Quansheng [乔全生] (2008). 晋方言语音史研究 [The Historical Phonology of Jin Dialects]. Beijing: Zhonghua Shuju.

Qiu, Xigui (2000). *Chinese Writing.* Berkeley: University of California Press.

Raini, Emanuele (2010). 'Sistemi di Romanizzazione del Cinese Mandarino nei Secoli XVI-XVIII', PhD dissertation, Sapienza University of Rome.

Rankin, Robert L. (2003). 'The Comparative Method', in B. D. Joseph and R. D. Janda (eds.), *The Handbook of Historical Linguistics.* Oxford: Blackwell, 183–212.

Reinhart, Tanya (1982). *Pragmatics and Linguistics: An Analysis of Sentence Topics.* Bloomington, IN: Indiana University Linguistics Club.

Ringe, Don (2003). 'Internal Reconstruction', in B. D. Joseph and R. D. Janda (eds.), *The Handbook of Historical Linguistics.* Oxford: Blackwell, 244–61.

Roberts, Craige (2012). 'Information Structure in Discourse: Towards an Integrated Formal Theory of Pragmatics', *Semantics and Pragmatics* 5: 1–69.

Rohsenow, John S. (2004). 'Fifty Years of Script and Written Language Reform in the P.R.C.: The Genesis of the Language Law of 2001', in M. Zhou and H. Sun (eds.), *Language Policy in the People's Republic of China: Theory and Practice since 1949.* Boston: Kluwer, 21–44.

Ross, Claudia (1984). 'Grammatical Categories in Mandarin Chinese', *Journal of the Chinese Language Teachers' Association* 19(2): 1–22.

Rothstein, Susan (2004). *Structuring Events: A Study in the Semantics of Lexical Aspect*. Oxford: Blackwell.

Rothstein, Susan (2008). 'Two Puzzles for a Theory of Lexical Aspect: Semelfactives and Degree Achievements', in J. Dölling, T. Heyde-Zybatow, and M. Schäfer (eds.), *Event Structures in Linguistic Form and Interpretation*. Berlin: Walter de Gruyter, 175–98.

Ryding, Karin C. (2011). 'Modern Standard Arabic', in S. Weninger (ed.), *The Semitic Languages. An International Handbook*. Berlin-New York: Mouton de Gruyter, 844–50.

Sagart, Laurent (1988). 'On Gan-Hakka', *Tsinghua Journal of Chinese Studies* 18(1): 141–60.

Sagart, Laurent (1993). *Les Dialectes Gan*. Paris: Langages Croisés.

Sagart, Laurent (1998). 'On distinguishing Hakka and Non-Hakka Dialects', *Journal of Chinese Linguistics* 26(2): 281–302.

Sagart, Laurent (1999a). 'The Origin of Chinese Tones', in S. Kaji (ed.). *Proceedings of the Symposium/Cross-Linguistic Studies of Tonal Phenomena/ Tonogenesis, Typology and Related Topics*. Tokyo: Institute for the Study of Languages and Cultures of Asia and Africa (ILCAA), Tokyo University of Foreign Studies, 91–104.

Sagart, Laurent (1999b). *The Roots of Old Chinese*. Amsterdam-Philadelphia: John Benjamins.

Sagart, Laurent (2002). 'Gan, Hakka and the Formation of Chinese Dialects', in D.-a. Ho (ed.), *Dialect Variations in Chinese. Papers from the Third International Conference on Sinology, Linguistics Section*. Taipei: Academia Sinica, 129–54.

Sagart, Laurent (2004a). 'The Higher Phylogeny of Austronesian and the Position of Tai-Kadai', *Oceanic Linguistics* 43(2): 411–44.

Sagart, Laurent (2004b). 'Vestiges of Archaic Chinese Derivational Affixes in Modern Chinese Dialects', in H. Chappell (eds.), *Chinese Grammar: Synchronic and Diachronic Perspectives*. Oxford: Oxford University Press, 123–42.

Sagart, Laurent (2005a). 'Sino-Tibetan-Austronesian: An Updated and Improved Argument', in L. Sagart, R. Blench, and A. Sanchez-Mazas (eds.), *The Peopling of East Asia: Putting together Archaeology, Linguistics and Genetics*. London : Routledge, 161–76.

Sagart, Laurent (2005b). 'Tai-Kadai as a Subgroup of Austronesian', in L. Sagart, R. Blench, and A. Sanchez-Mazas (eds.), *The Peopling of East Asia: Putting together Archaeology, Linguistics and Genetics*. London : Routledge, 177–81.

Sagart, Laurent (2006). 'L'Emploi des Phonetiques dans l'Ecriture Chinoise', in F. Bottero and R. Djamouri (eds.), *Ecriture Chinoise: Données, Usages et Représentations*. Paris: EHESS-CRLAO, 35–53.

Sagart, Laurent (2007). 'Introduction', in W. S. Coblin (ed.) *Modern Chinese Phonology: From Guānhuà to Mandarin*. Paris: EHESS-CRLAO, 1–6.

Sagart, Laurent (2017). 'A candidate for a Tibeto-Burman Innovation', *Cahiers de Linguistique Asie Orientale* 46(1): 101–19.

Sagart, Laurent, Guillaume Jacques, Lai Yunfan, Robin J. Ryder, Valentin Thoizeau, Simon J. Greenhill, and Johann-Mattis List (2019). 'Dated Language Phylogenies Shed Light on the Ancestry of Sino-Tibetan', *Proceedings of the National Academy of Sciences* 116(21): 10317–22.

Saillard, Claire (2004). 'On the Promotion of Putonghua in China: How a Standard Language Becomes a Vernacular', in M. Zhou and H. Sun (eds.), *Language Policy in the People's Republic of China: Theory and Practice since 1949*. Boston: Kluwer, 153–76.

San, Duanmu (2014). 'Syllable Structure and Stress', in C.-T. J. Huang, A. Y.-h. Li, and A. Simpson (eds.), *The Handbook of Chinese Linguistics*. Oxford: Wiley-Blackwell, 422–42.

Sandman, Erika (2016). 'A Grammar of Wutun', PhD dissertation, University of Helsinki.

Sasse, Hans-Jürgen (2003). 'Syntactic Categories and Subcategories', in J. Jacobs, A. von Stechow, W. Sternefeld, and T. Vennemann (eds.), *Syntax: Ein internationales Handbuch zeitgenössischer Forschung/An International Handbook of Contemporary Research. 1. Halbband*. Berlin-New York: Mouton de Gruyter, 646–86.

Scalise, Sergio, and Irene Vogel (2010). 'Why Compounding?', in S. Scalise and I. Vogel (eds.), *Cross-Disciplinary Issues in Compounding*. Amsterdam-Philadelphia: John Benjamins, 1–18.

Schuessler, Axel (2007). *ABC Etymological Dictionary of Old Chinese*. Honolulu: University of Hawai'i Press.

Schuessler, Axel (2009). *Minimal Old Chinese and Later Han Chinese: A Companion to Grammata Serica Recensa*. Honolulu: University of Hawai'i Press.

Shi, Chunhong [施春宏] (2008). '动结式"V 累"的句法语义分析及其理论蕴涵' [A Semantic and Syntactic Analysis of the Resultative 'V-*lèi*' Construction and its Theoretical Implications], *Yuyan Kexue* 7(3): 242–58.

Shi, Dingxu [石定栩] (2004). '名物化、名词化与"的"字结构' [Nominalization and the "*de*" Construction], in C.-T. J. Huang [黄正德] (ed.), 中国言学论丛 3 [Collection of Essays in Chinese Linguistics]. Beijing: Beijing Yuyan Daxue Chubanshe, 78–92.

Shi, Yuzhi (2002). *The establishment of Modern Chinese Grammar. The Formation of the Resultative Construction and its Effects*. Amsterdam-Philadelphia: John Benjamins.

Shi, Yuzhi [石毓智] (2007). '汉语方言中动词重叠的语法意义和功能的差别' [Differences in Meaning and Function of Verb Reduplication across Chinese Dialects], *Hanyu Xuebao* 4: 59–63.

Shibatani, Masayoshi (1990). *The Languages of Japan*. Cambridge: Cambridge University Press.

Shyu, Shu-Ing (2014). 'Topic and Focus', in C.-T. J. Huang, A.Y.-h. Li, and A. Simpson (eds.), *The Handbook of Chinese Linguistics*. Oxford: Blackwell, 100–25.

Simons, Gary F., and Charles D. Fennig (eds.) (2018). *Ethnologue: Languages of the World*. Twenty-first edition. Dallas, TX: SIL International.

Simpson, Jane (1983). 'Resultatives', in L. Levin, M. Rappaport Hovav, and A. E. Zaenen (eds.), *Papers in Lexical-Functional Grammar*. Bloomington, IN: Indiana University Linguistics Club, 143–57.

Slater, Keith W. (2003). *A Grammar of Mangghuer*. London: Routledge.

Smith, Carlota S. (1991). *The Parameter of Aspect*. Dordrecht: Kluwer.

Smith, Carlota S. (1994). 'Aspectual Viewpoint and Situation Type in Mandarin Chinese', *Journal of East Asian Linguistics* 3(2): 107–46.

Smith, Carlota S., and Mary S. Erbaugh (2005). 'Temporal Interpretation in Mandarin Chinese', *Linguistics* 43(4): 713–56.

Snow, Don (2004). *Cantonese as Written Language: The Growth of a Written Chinese Vernacular*. Hong Kong: Hong Kong University Press.

Snow, Don, Senyao Shen, and Xiayun Zhou (2018). 'A Short History of Written Wu, Part II: Written Shanghainese', *Global Chinese* 4(2): 217–46.

Snow, Don, Xiayun Zhou, and Senyao Shen (2018). 'A Short History of Written Wu, Part I: Written Suzhounese', *Global Chinese* 4(1): 143–66.

Soh, Hooi Ling (2014). 'Aspect', in C.-T. J. Huang, A. Y.-h. Li, and A. Simpson (eds.), *The Handbook of Chinese Linguistics*. Oxford: Blackwell, 126–55.

Soh, Hooi Ling, and Jenny Y.-C. Kuo (2005). 'Perfective Aspect and Accomplishment Situations in Mandarin Chinese', in A. van Hout, H. de Swart, and H. Verkuyl (eds.), *Perspectives on Aspect*. Dordrecht: Springer, 199–216.

Sohn, Ho-Min (1999). *The Korean Language*. Cambridge: Cambridge University Press.

Sproat, Richard, and Chilin Shih (1988). *Prenominal Adjectival Ordering in English and Mandarin*, in J. Blevins and J. Carter (eds.), *Proceedings of the North Eastern Linguistics Society 18. Volume 2*. Amherst, MA: GLSA, 465–89.

Sproat, Richard, and Chilin Shih (1991). 'The Cross-linguistic Distribution of Adjective Ordering Restrictions', in C. Perkins Georgopoulos and R. Lynn Ishihara (eds.), *Interdisciplinary Approaches to Language: Essays in Honor of S.-Y. Kuroda*. Dordrecht: Kluwer, 565–92.

Sproat, Richard, and Chilin Shih (1996). 'A Corpus-Based Analysis of Mandarin Nominal Root Compound', *Journal of East Asian Linguistics* 5(1): 9–71.

Starosta, Stanley (2005). 'Proto-East Asian and the Origin and Dispersal of the Languages of East and Southeast Asia and the Pacific', in L. Sagart, R. Blench, and A. Sanchez-Mazas (eds.), *The Peopling of East Asia: Putting together Archaeology, Linguistics and Genetics*. London: Routledge, 182–97.

Stassen, Leo (2013). 'Comparative Constructions', in M. S. Dryer and M. Haspelmath (eds.), *The World Atlas of Language Structures Online*. Leipzig: Max Planck Institute for Evolutionary Anthropology, chapter 121.

Steffen Chung, Karen (2006). *Mandarin Compound Verbs*. Taipei: Crane.

Steffen Chung, Karen (2014). 'Sino-Tibetan: Chinese', in R. Lieber and P. Štekauer (eds.), *The Oxford Handbook of Derivational Morphology*. Oxford: Oxford University Press, 609–20.

Sun, Chaofen (1996). *Word-order Change and Grammaticalization in the History of Chinese*. Stanford: Stanford University Press.

Sun, Chaofen (2006). *Chinese: A Linguistic Introduction*. Cambridge: Cambridge University Press.

Sun, Chaofen, and T. Givón (1985). 'On the So-Called SOV Word Order in Mandarin Chinese: A Quantified Text Study and its Implications', *Language* 61(2): 329–51.

Sun, Jingtao (1999). 'Reduplication in Old Chinese', PhD dissertation, University of British Columbia.

Suthiwan, Titima (2009). 'Thai Vocabulary', in M. Haspelmath, and U. Tadmor (eds.), *World Loanword Database*. Leipzig: Max Planck Institute for Evolutionary Anthropology.

Sybesma, Rint P. E. (1992). 'Causatives and Accomplishments: The Case of Chinese BA', PhD dissertation, Leiden University.

Sybesma, Rint P. E. (1997). 'Why Chinese Verb-le is a Resultative Predicate'. *Journal of East Asian Linguistics* 6(3): 215–61.

Sybesma, Rint P. E. (1999). *The Mandarin VP*. Dordrecht: Kluwer.

Sybesma, Rint P. E. (2004). 'Exploring Cantonese Tense', in L. Cornips and J. Doetjes (eds.), *Linguistics in the Netherlands 2004*. Amsterdam: John Benjamins, 169–80.

Sybesma, Rint P. E. (2007). 'Whether We Tense-Agree Overtly or Not', *Linguistic Inquiry* 38(3): 580–7.

Szeto, Pui Yiu, Umberto Ansaldo, and Stephen Matthews (2018). 'Typological Variation across Mandarin Dialects: An Areal Perspective with a Quantitative Approach', *Linguistic Typology* 22(2): 233–75.

Tadmor, Uri (2009), 'Loanwords in the World's Languages: Findings and Results', in M. Haspelmath and U. Tadmor (eds.), *Loanwords in the World's languages: A Comparative Handbook*, Berlin-New York, Mouton de Gruyter, 55–75.

Taft, Marcus (2006). 'Processing of Characters by Native Chinese Readers', in P. Li, H.T. Li, E. Bates, and O. J. L. Tzeng (eds.), *The Handbook of East Asian Psycholinguistics*. Cambridge: Cambridge University Press, 237–49.

Tai, James Hao-yi (1982). 'Relevant Categorial Distinctions in Chinese', in K. Tuite, R. Schneider, and R. A. Chametzky (eds.), *Papers from the Eighteenth Regional Meeting of the Chicago Linguistic Society*. Chicago: Chicago Linguistic Society, 495–506.

Tai, James Hao-yi (1984). 'Verbs and Times in Chinese: Vendler's Four Categories', in D. Testen, V. Mishra, and J. Drogo (eds.), *Papers from the Parasession on Lexical Semantics*. Chicago: Chicago Linguistic Society, 289–96.

Tai, James Hao-yi (1997). 'Category Shifts and Word-Formation Redudancy Rules in Chinese', in F.-f. Tsao and S. H. Wang (eds.), *Chinese Language and Linguistics III: Morphology and Lexicon*. Taipei, Academia Sinica Institute of History and Philology, 435–68.

Tai, James Hao-yi, and Marjorie K.-M. Chan (1999). 'Some Reflections on the Periodization of the Chinese Language', in A. Peyraube and C. Sun (eds.), *In Honor of Mei Tsu-Lin. Studies on Chinese Historical Syntax and Morphology*. Paris: EHESS-CRLAO, 223–39.

Tai, James Hao-yi, and Jane Yang Chou (1975). 'On the Equivalent of "Kill" in Mandarin Chinese', *Journal of the Chinese Language Teachers Association* 10(2): 48–52.

Talmy, Leonard (2000). *Toward a Cognitive Semantics: Typology and Process in Concept Structuring. Volume 2*. Cambridge, MA: MIT Press.

Tan, Yuanxiong [覃远雄] (2012). '平话和土话' [Pinghua and *Patois*], in Institute of Linguistics of the Chinese Academy of Social Sciences, Institute of Ethnology and Anthropology of the Chinese Academy of Social Sciences, Language Information Sciences Research Centre of the Chinese University of Hong Kong [中国社会科学院语言研究所，中国社会科学院民族学与人类学研究所，香港城市大学语言资讯科学研究中心] (eds.), *中国语言地图集. 第2版. 汉语方言卷* [*Language Atlas of China. Second Edition. Chinese Dialects*]. Beijing: The Commercial Press, 152–9.

Tang, Ting-chi [湯廷池] (1988). *漢語詞法句法論集* [Collection of Essays on Chinese Morphology and Syntax]. Taipei: Student Book Company.

Tao, Hongyin, and Jin Liu (2016). 'Chinese Language in a Global Context', in W.-S. Chan (ed.), *The Routledge Encyclopedia of the Chinese Language*. Oxford: Routledge, 119–36.

Taylor, Insup, and M. Martin Taylor (2014). *Writing and Literacy in Chinese, Korean and Japanese. Revised Edition*. Amsterdam-Philadelphia: John Benjamins.

Teng, Shou-hsin (1995). 'Verb Compounding in Taiwanese', *Cahiers de Linguistique Asie Orientale* 24(1): 3–28.

Tham, Shiao Wei (2009). 'Building Resultatives in Mandarin (from the Result)', unpublished conference paper, Tenth Stanford Semantics Fest, Stanford University, March 2009.

Thompson, Laurence C. (1987 [1965]). *A Vietnamese Reference Grammar*. Honolulu: University of Hawai'i Press.

Thurgood, Graham (2003). 'A Subgrouping of the Sino-Tibetan Language: The Interaction between Language Contact, Change, and Inheritance', in

G. Thurgood and R. J. LaPolla (eds.), *The Sino-Tibetan Languages*. London: Routledge, 3–21.

Thurgood, Graham (2017). 'Sino-Tibetan Languages: Genetic and Areal Subgroups'. In G. Thurgood and R. J. LaPolla (Eds.), *The Sino-Tibetan Languages*. London: Routledge, 3–39.

Ting, Jen, and Miller Y.-L. Chang (2004). 'The Category of *Gei* in Mandarin Chinese and Grammaticalization', *Taiwan Journal of Linguistics* 2(2): 45–74.

Ting, Pang-hsin (1991). 'Some Theoretical Issues in the Study of Mandarin Dialects', in W. S.-Y. Wang (ed.), *Languages and Dialects of China*. Berkeley: Project on Linguistic Analysis, 187–236.

Ting, Pang-hsin (1996). 'Tonal Evolution and Tonal Reconstruction in Chinese', in James C.-t. Huang and A. Y.-h. Li (eds.), *New Horizons in Chinese Linguistics*. Dordrecht: Kluwer, 141–59.

Tsao, Feng-fu (2004). 'Semantics and Syntax of Verbal and Adjectival Reduplication in Mandarin and Taiwanese Southern Min', in H. Chappell (ed.), *Chinese Grammar: Synchronic and Diachronic Perspectives*. Oxford: Oxford University Press, 285–308.

Tsao, Feng-fu (2008). 'The Language Planning Situation in Taiwan with an Update', in R. B. Kaplan and R. B. Baldauf Jr. (eds.), *Language Planning and Policy in Asia, Vol. 1: Japan, Nepal and Taiwan and Chinese Characters*. Bristol: Multilingual Matters, 237–300.

Tung, T'ung-ho [董同龢] (1944). 上古音韻表稿 [Draft for a Table of the Sounds of Old Chinese]. Taipei: Academia Sinica.

Unger, James M. (2004). *Ideogram: Chinese Characters and the Myth of Disembodied Meaning*. Honolulu: University of Hawai'i Press.

Van Driem, George (1997). 'Sino-Bodic', *Bulletin of the School of Oriental and African Studies* 60(3): 455–88.

Van Driem, George (2005a). 'Sino-Austronesian vs. Sino-Caucasian, Sino-Bodic vs. Sino-Tibetan, and Tibeto-Burman as Default Theory', in Y. P. Yadava, G. Bhattarai, R. R. Lohani, B. Prasain, and K. Parajuli (eds.), *Contemporary Issues in Nepalese Linguistics*. Kathmandu: Linguistic Society of Nepal, 285–338.

Van Driem, George (2005b). 'Tibeto-Burman vs. Indo-Chinese: Implications for Population Geneticists, Archaeologists and Prehistorians', in L. Sagart, R. Blench, and A. Sanchez-Mazas (eds.), *The Peopling of East Asia: Putting together Archaeology, Linguistics and Genetics*. London: Routledge, 81–106.

VanNess Simmons, Richard (1997). 'A Second Look at the *Tōwa Sanyō*: Clues to the Nature of the Guanhuah Studied by Japanese in the Early Eighteenth Century', *Journal of the American Oriental Society* 117(3): 419–26.

VanNess Simmons, Richard (1999a). *Chinese Dialect Classification. A Comparative Approach to Harngjou, Old Jintarn, and Common Northern Wu*. Amsterdam-Philadelphia: John Benjamins.

VanNess Simmons, Richard (1999b). 'On Chinese Dialect Classification: A Case Study Examining the Relationship of the Harngjou and Jennjiang Dialects', in R. VanNess Simmons (ed.), *Issues in Chinese Dialect Description and Classification*. Berkeley: Project on Linguistic Analysis, 204–34.

VanNess Simmons, Richard (2006). 'Common Dialect Phonology in Practice: Y. R. Chao's Field Methodology'. Amsterdam-Philadelphia: John Benjamins, 189–208.

Vendler, Zeno (1957). 'Verbs and Times', *The Philosophical Review* 66(2): 143–60.

Vendler, Zeno (1967). *Linguistics in Philosophy*. Ithaca, NY: Cornell University Press.

Verkuyl, Henk J. (1972), *On the Compositional Nature of the Aspects*. Dordrecht: Kluwer.

Wang, Chyan-an Arthur, and Hsiao-hung Iris Wu (2015). 'Inner Aspect and Object Displacement: Telicity in Taiwanese Southern Min', unpublished conference paper, 9th Conference of the European Association of Chinese Linguistics, Stuttgart University, 24–16 September 2015.

Wang, Fang [王芳] (2011). 温州话动词和形容词重叠研究 [Verbal and Adjectival Reduplication in Wenzhounese], MA dissertation, National University of Singapore and Peking University.

Wang, Fang, and Fuyun Wu (2020). 'Postnominal Relative Clauses in Chinese', *Linguistics* 58(6): 1501–1542.

Wang, Feng (2005). 'On the Genetic Position of the Bai Language', *Cahiers de Linguistique Asie Orientale* 34(1): 102–37.

Wang, Fu-chang (2014), *A Reluctant Identity: The Development of Holo Identity in Taiwan*, *Taiwan in Comparative Perspective* 5: 79–119.

Wang, Fusheng (1998). *La Formazione delle Parole nella Lingua Cinese Contemporanea*. Trieste: Università degli Studi di Trieste.

Wang, Futang [王福堂] (1999). 汉语方言语音的演变和层次 [Evolution and Strata in the Phonology of Chinese Dialects]. Beijing: Yuwen Chubanshe.

Wang, Hui (2013). '*Putonghua* in Hong Kong', in Y. Li and W. Li (eds.), *The Language Situation in China. Volume 1*. Berlin-New York: Mouton de Gruyter, 311–24.

Wang, Kezhong [王克仲] (1989). 古汉语词类活用 [Word Class Flexibility in Old Chinese]. Changsha: Hunan Renmin Chubanshe.

Wang, Li [王力] (1980 [1958]). 漢語史稿 [A Draft History of Chinese]. Beijing: Zhonghua Shuju.

Wang, Li [王力] (1985 [1943]). 现代汉语语法 [Modern Chinese Grammar]. Beijing: The Commercial Press.

Wang, Li [王力] (1989). 汉语语法史 [A History of Chinese Grammar]. Beijing: The Commercial Press.

Wang, Ping [汪平], and Zhiyun Cao [曹志耘] (2012). '吴语' [The Wu Dialects], in Institute of Linguistics of the Chinese Academy of Social Sciences,

Institute of Ethnology and Anthropology of the Chinese Academy of Social Sciences, Language Information Sciences Research Centre of the Chinese University of Hong Kong [中国社会科学院语言研究所，中国社会科学院民族学与人类学研究所, 香港城市大学语言资讯科学研究中心] (eds.), *中国语言地图集. 第2版. 汉语方言卷* [Language Atlas of China. Second Edition. Chinese Dialects]. Beijing: The Commercial Press, 103–9.

Wang, William S.-Y. (1995). 'The Ancestry of Chinese: Retrospect and Prospect', in W. S.-Y. Wang (ed.), *The Ancestry of the Chinese Language*. Berkeley: Project on Linguistic Analysis, I–XI.

Wang, Xin (2007). 'Notes about Serial Verb Construction in Chinese', *California Linguistic Notes* 32(1): 1–15.

Wang, Yunlu [王云路] (2005). '谈谈词缀在古汉语构词法中的地位' [On the Position of Affixes in Old Chinese Word Formation], in Q. Zhu [朱庆之] (ed.), *中古汉语研究 (二)* [Research on Middle Chinese]. Beijing: The Commercial Press, 286–98.

Wen, Duanzheng [温端政] (1997). '试论晋语的特点与归属' [On the Characteristics and Affiliation of Jin Dialects], *Yuwen Yanjiu* 2: 1–12.

Whitman, John, and Waltraud Paul (2005). 'Reanalysis and Conservancy of Structure in Chinese', in M. Batllori, M.-L. Hernanz, C. Picallo, and F. Roca (eds.), *Grammaticalization and Parametric Change*. Oxford: Oxford University Press, 82–94.

Wiebusch, Thekla, and Uri Tadmor (2009). 'Loanwords in Mandarin Chinese', in M. Haspelmath and U. Tadmor (eds.), *Loanwords in the World's Languages*. Berlin-New York: Mouton de Gruyter, 575–98.

Wiedenhof, Jeroen (2017). 'Names for the Chinese Language', in R. Sybesma, W. Behr, Y. Gu, Z. Handel, C.-T. J. Huang, and J. Myers (eds.), *Encyclopedia of Chinese Language and Linguistics. Volume 3*. Leiden: Brill, 136–9.

Wiersma, Grace (2003). 'Yunnan Bai', in G. Thurgood and R. J. LaPolla (eds.), *The Sino-Tibetan Languages*. London: Routledge, 651–73.

Wu, Chuanfei [吴传飞] (2003). '中国网络语言研究概观' [An Overview of the Research on Chinese Internet Language], *Hunan Shifan Daxue Shehui Kexue Xuebao* 32(6): 102–5.

Wu, Ming-Hsuan (2009). 'Language Planning and Policy in Taiwan: Past, Present and Future', *Working Papers in Educational Linguistics* 24(2): 99–118.

Wu, Wei [伍巍] (2012). '粤语' [The Yue Dialects], in Institute of Linguistics of the Chinese Academy of Social Sciences, Institute of Ethnology and Anthropology of the Chinese Academy of Social Sciences, Language Information Sciences Research Centre of the Chinese University of Hong Kong [中国社会科学院语言研究所, 中国社会科学院民族学与人类学研究所, 香港城市大学语言资讯科学研究中心] (eds.), *中国语言地图集. 第2版. 汉语方言卷* [Language Atlas of China. Second Edition. Chinese Dialects]. Beijing: The Commercial Press, 125–33.

Wu, Yunji (2005). *A Synchronic and Diachronic Study of the Grammar of the Chinese Xiang Dialects.* Berlin-New York: Mouton de Gruyter.

Xiao, Richard, and Tony McEnery (2004). *Aspect in Mandarin Chinese. A Corpus-Based Study.* Amsterdam-Philadelphia: John Benjamins.

Xie, Liuwen [谢溜文] (2012). '赣语' [The Gan Dialects], in Institute of Linguistics of the Chinese Academy of Social Sciences, Institute of Ethnology and Anthropology of the Chinese Academy of Social Sciences, Language Information Sciences Research Centre of the Chinese University of Hong Kong [中国社会科学院语言研究所, 中国社会科学院民族学与人类学研究所, 香港城市大学语言资讯科学研究中心] (eds.), *中国语言地图集. 第2版. 汉语方言卷* [Language Atlas of China. Second Edition. Chinese Dialects]. Beijing: The Commercial Press, 141–5.

Xie, Liuwen [谢溜文] and Xuezhen Huang [黄雪贞] (2012). '客家话' [The Kejia Dialects], in Institute of Linguistics of the Chinese Academy of Social Sciences, Institute of Ethnology and Anthropology of the Chinese Academy of Social Sciences, Language Information Sciences Research Centre of the Chinese University of Hong Kong [中国社会科学院语言研究所, 中国社会科学院民族学与人类学研究所, 香港城市大学语言资讯科学研究中心] (eds.), *中国语言地图集. 第2版. 汉语方言卷* [Language Atlas of China. Second Edition. Chinese Dialects]. Beijing: The Commercial Press, 116–24.

Xin, Yongfen [辛永芬] (2006). *浚县方言研究* [The Shunxian Dialect]. Beijing: Zhonghua Shuju.

Xing, Fuyi [邢福义] (2003). *词类辩难* [The Debate on Word Classes]. Beijing: The Commercial Press.

Xing, Janet Zhiqun (2006). *Teaching and Learning Chinese as a Foreign Language.* Hong Kong: Hong Kong University Press.

Xiong, Zhongru [熊仲儒], and Liping Liu [刘丽萍] (2006). '动结式的论元实现' [The realization of argument structure in resultatives], *Xiandai Waiyu* 29(2): 120–10.

Xu, Dan (2006). *Typological Change in Chinese Syntax.* Oxford: Oxford University Press.

Xu, Dan (2012). 'Introduction: Plurality and Classifiers across Languages of China', in D. Xu (ed.), *Plurality and Classifiers across Languages in China.* Berlin-New York: Mouton de Gruyter, 1–19.

Xu, Dan (2017). *The Tangwang Language. An Interdisciplinary Case Study in Northwest China.* Cham: Springer.

Xu, Hui Ling (2007). *Aspects of Chaozhou Grammar: A Synchronic Description of the Jieyang Variety.* Berkeley: Project on Linguistic Analysis.

Xu, Liejiong (1994). 'The Antecedent of "Ziji"', *Journal of Chinese Linguistics* 22(1): 115–37.

Xu, Tongqiang [徐通锵] (1994). '"字"和汉语研究的方法论 —— 兼评汉语研究中的"印欧语的眼光"' [The 'Character' and the Methodology of Research on Chinese: With a Discussion of the 'Indo-European Perspective' in the Research on Chinese], *Shijie Hanyu Jiaoxue* 3: 3–16.

Xu, Zhaohui [徐朝晖] (2013). 当代流行语研究 [Research on Contemporary Buzzwords]. Guangzhou: Jinan Daxue Chubanshe.

Yan, Mai [颜迈] (2007). '词类划分标准的回顾和选择' [A Review of the Criteria for the Definition of Word Classes and their Choice], *Guizhou Minzu Xueyuan Xuebao* 1: 129–32.

Yan, Margaret Mian (2006). *Introduction to Chinese Dialectology*. Munich: Lincom.

Yan, Sen [颜森], and Houxing Bao [鲍厚星] (1987). '江西省与湖南省的汉语方言' [The Chinese Dialects of Jiangxi and Hunan], in S. A. Wurm, R. Li, T. Baumann, and M. W. Lee (eds.), *Language Atlas of China - 中国语言地图集*. Hong Kong: Longman, B11.

Yang, Chunsheng (2007). 'Chinese Internet Language: A Sociolinguistic Analysis of Adaptations of Chinese Writing Systems', *Language@Internet* 4: article 2.

Yang, Ji [杨季] (2013). '「囧」的前世今生——从《说文》到网络,考释「囧」之音形义' [The Past and Present of '*jiǒng*': A Philological Study of the Sound, Shape and Meaning of '*jiǒng*' from the *Shuōwén* to the Internet,], *Changchun Ligong Daxue Xuebao* 1: 70–1.

Yang, Xipeng [杨锡彭] (2003). 汉语语素论 [A Theory of the Chinese Morpheme]. Nanjing: Nanjing Daxue Chubanshe.

Ye, Baokui [叶宝奎] (2001). 明清官话音系 [The Phonology of Ming-Qing Mandarin]. Xiamen: Xiamen Daxue Chubanshe.

Yi, Dan [易丹] (2007). '关于补充式与连动式复合词的区分' [The Distinction between Verb-complement and Serial Verb Compounds], *Xiandai Yuwen* 6: 7–11.

Yin, Binyong (1994). *Modern Chinese Characters*. Beijing: Sinolingua.

Yin, Guoguang [殷国光] (1997). 吕氏春秋词类研究 [Research on Word Classes in the *Lǚshì Chūnqiū*]. Beijing: Huaxia Chubanshe.

Yip, Moira (2002). *Tone*. Cambridge: Cambridge University Press.

Yip, Po-Ching (2000). *The Chinese Lexicon: A Comprehensive Survey*. London: Routledge.

Yong, Shin (1997). 'The Grammatical Functions of Verb Complements in Mandarin Chinese', *Linguistics* 35(1): 1–24.

You, Rujie [游汝杰] (1992). 汉语方言学导轮 [Introduction to Chinese Dialectology]. Shanghai: Shanghai Jiaoyu Chubanshe.

Yu, Alan Ji-Leun (2007). 'Understanding Near Mergers: The Case of Morphological Tone in Cantonese', *Phonology* 24(1): 187–214.

Yu, Zhiqiang (1999). 'Issues in Selecting Features for Genetic Classification of the Wu Dialect Group', in R. VanNess Simmons (ed.), *Issues in Chinese Dialect Description and Classification*. Berkeley: Project on Linguistic Analysis, 235–63.

Yu, Zhiwei [余志伟], and Liming Chen [陈立明] (2013). 网络新语漫谈 [A Discussion of Internet Neologisms]. Beijing: Zhongguo Shehui Kexue Chubanshe.

Yuan, Boping, and Esuna Dugarova (2012). '*Wh*-topicalization at the Syntax-Discourse Interface in English Speakers' L2 Chinese Grammars', *Studies in Second Language Acquisition* 34(4): 533–60.

Yuan, Hui [袁晖] (2002). '前言' [Preface], in H. Yuan [袁晖] and X. Ruan [阮显忠] (eds.), 现代汉语缩语词典 [Dictionary of Modern Chinese Abbreviations]. Beijing: Yuwen Chubanshe, 1–13.

Yuan, Jiahua [袁家骅] *et al.* (2001). 汉语方言概要. 第二版 [Outline of Chinese Dialects. Second Edition]. Beijing: Yuwen Chubanshe.

Yuan, Yulin [袁毓林] (2010). 汉语词类的认知研究和模糊划分 [Cognitive Research on Chinese Word Classes and Fuzzy Classification]. Shanghai: Shanghai Jiaoyu Chubanshe.

Yue, Anne Oi-Kan (1991). 'The Yue Dialects', in W. S.-Y. Wang (ed.), *Languages and Dialects of China*. Berkeley: Project on Linguistic Analysis, 294–324.

Yue, Anne Oi-Kan [余霭芹] (1995). '广东开平方言的 "的" 字结构' [The '*de*' Construction in the Kaiping Dialect of Guangdong], *Zhongguo Yuwen* 247: 289–97.

Yue, Anne Oi-Kan (2003). 'Chinese Dialects: Grammar', in G. Thurgood and R. J. LaPolla (eds.), *The Sino-Tibetan Languages*. London: Routledge, 84–125.

Yue, Anne Oi-Kan, and Ken-ichi Takashima (2000). 'Evidence of Possible Dialect Mixture in Oracle-Bone Inscriptions', in P.-S. Ting and A. O.-K. Yue (eds.), *In Memory of Professor Li Fang-Kuei: Essays of Linguistic Change and the Chinese Dialects*. Taipei: Academia Sinica and University of Washington, 1–52.

Zádrapa, Lukas (2011). *Word-Class Flexibility in Classical Chinese. Verbal and Adverbial Uses of Nouns*. Leiden: Brill.

Zádrapa, Lukas (2017). *Word Classes, Premodern*, in R. Sybesma, W. Behr, Y. Gu, Z. Handel, C.-T. J. Huang, and J. Myers (eds.), *Encyclopedia of Chinese Language and Linguistics. Volume 4*. Leiden: Brill, 566–76.

Zee, Eric, and Wai-sum Lee (2007). 'Vowel Typology in Chinese', in J. Trouvain and W. J. Barry (eds.), *Proceedings of the 2007 International Congress of Phonetic Sciences (ICPhS 2007)*. Saarbrücken: Universtät des Saarlandes, 1429–32.

Zhang, Niina Ning (2007). 'A Syntactic Account of the Direct Object Restriction in Chinese', *Language Research* 43(1): 53–75.

Zhang, Niina Ning (2014). 'Expressing Number Productively in Mandarin Chinese', *Linguistics* 52(1): 1–34.

Zhang, Shi (1990). 'Correlations between the Double Object Construction and Preposition Stranding', *Linguistic Inquiry* 21(2): 312–16.

Zhang, Shuangdi [张双棣] (1989). 吕氏春秋词汇研究 [Research on the Lexicon of the *Lǚshì Chūnqiū*]. Jinan: Shandong Jiaoyu Chubanshe.

Zhang, Wenguo [张文国] (2005). *古汉语的名动词类转变及其发展* [Category Change between Nouns and Verbs in Old Chinese and its Development]. Beijing: Zhonghua Shuju.

Zhang, Yunhui [张云辉] (2007). '网络语言的词汇语法特征' [Lexical and Grammatical features of Internet Language], *Zhongguo Yuwen* 6: 531–5.

Zhang, Zhanshan [张占山], and Rulong Li [李如龙] (2007). '虚化的终极: 合音' [The Endpoint of Grammaticalization: Fusion], *Ludong Daxue Xuebao* 24: 95–100.

Zhang, Zhenxing [张振兴] (1987). '闽语' [Min Dialects], in S. A. Wurm, R. Li, T. Baumann, and M. W. Lee (eds.), *Language Atlas of China - 中国语言地图集*. Hong Kong: Longman, B12.

Zhang, Zhigong [张志公] (ed.) (1956). *语法和语法教学－介绍'暂拟汉语教学语法系统'* [Grammar and the Pedagogy of Grammar: Introducing the 'Proposal for a System for Teaching Chinese Grammar']. Beijing: Renmin Jiaoyu Chubanshe.

Zhao, Rixin [赵日新] (2012). '徽语' [The Hui Dialects], in Institute of Linguistics of the Chinese Academy of Social Sciences, Institute of Ethnology and Anthropology of the Chinese Academy of Social Sciences, Language Information Sciences Research Centre of the Chinese University of Hong Kong [中国社会科学院语言研究所, 中国社会科学院民族学与人类学研究所, 香港城市大学语言资讯科学研究中心] (eds.), *中国语言地图集. 第2版. 汉语方言卷* [Language Atlas of China. Second Edition. Chinese Dialects]. Beijing: The Commercial Press, 146–51.

Zhengzhang, Shangfang [郑张尚芳] (1987). '安徽南部的方言分布' [The distribution of Dialects in Southern Anhui], in S. A. Wurm, R. Li, T. Baumann, and M. W. Lee (eds.), *Language Atlas of China - 中国语言地图集*. Hong Kong: Longman, B10.

Zhengzhang, Shangfang [鄭張尚芳] (1995). '漢語與親屬語同源根詞及附綴成分比較上的擇對問題' [The Issue of Selection in the Comparison of Cognate Roots and Affixes in Chinese and in Related Languages], in W. S.-Y. Wang (ed.), *The Ancestry of the Chinese Language*. Berkeley: Project on Linguistic Analysis, 269–82.

Zhengzhang, Shangfang [郑张尚芳] (2003). *上古音系* [The Phonology of Old Chinese]. Shanghai: Shanghai Jiaoyu Chubanshe.

Zhengzhang, Shangfang [郑张尚芳] (2008). *温州方言志* [Wenzhou Dialect Gazetteer]. Beijing: Zhonghua Shuju.

Zhou, Changji [周长楫] (2012). '闽语' [The Min Dialects], in Institute of Linguistics of the Chinese Academy of Social Sciences, Institute of Ethnology and Anthropology of the Chinese Academy of Social Sciences, Language Information Sciences Research Centre of the Chinese University of Hong Kong [中国社会科学院语言研究所，中国社会科学院民族学与人类学研究所，香港城市大学语言资讯科学研究中心] (eds.), *中国语言*

地图集. 第2版. 汉语方言卷 [Language Atlas of China. Second Edition. Chinese Dialects]. Beijing: The Commercial Press, 110–15.

Zhou, Minglang (2012). 'Introduction: The Contact between Putonghua (Modern Standard Chinese) and Minority Languages in China', *International Journal of the Sociology of Language* 215: 1–17.

Zhou, Zhenhe (1991). 'Migrations in Chinese History and their Legacy on Chinese Dialects', in W. S.-Y. Wang (ed.), *Languages and Dialects of China*. Berkeley: Project on Linguistic Analysis, 29–51.

Zhou, Zhenhe [周振鹤], and Rujie You [游汝杰] (1986). 方言与中国文化 [Dialects and Chinese Culture]. Shanghai: Shanghai Renmin Chubanshe.

Zhu, Dexi [朱德熙] (1982). 语法讲义 [Lectures on Grammar]. Beijing: The Commercial Press.

Zhu, Dexi [朱德熙], Jiawen Lu [盧甲文], and Zhen Ma [馬真] (1961). '關於動詞形容詞"名物化"的問題' [On the 'Nominalization' of Verbs and Adjectives], *Beijing Daxue Xuebao* 4: 51–64.

Zhu, Jianjun 祝建军 (2003). '近代汉语动词前缀"打-"演变探析' [An Exploration of the Prefix '*dǎ*' in Pre-Modern Mandarin'], *Yantai Daxue Xuebao* 16(4): 470–6.

Zhu, Jingtao [朱景松] (2003). '形容词重叠式的语法意义' [The Grammatical Meaning of Adjectival Reduplication], *Yuwen Yanjiu* 3: 9–17.

Zhu, Minche [祝敏彻] (1957). '論初期處置式' [On Early Attestations of the Object Marking Construction], *Yuyanxue Luncong* 1: 17–33.

Zhu, Qingshi, and Bohan Li (2018). 'The Language of Chinese Buddhism. From the Perspective of Chinese Historical Linguistics', *International Journal of Chinese Linguistics* 5(1): 1–32.

Zhu, Yongzhong, Üjiyediin Chuluu, Keith Slater, and Kevin Stuart (1997). 'Gangou Chinese dialect. A Comparative Study of a Strongly Altaicized Chinese Dialect and its Mongolic Neighbour', *Anthropos* 92: 433–50.

Zhu, Xiaonong (2006). *A Grammar of Shanghai Wu*. Munich: Lincom.

Zou, Ke (1993). 'The Syntax of the Chinese *Ba* Construction', *Linguistics* 31(4): 715–36.

Zu, Shengli [祖生利] (2013). '清代旗人汉语的满语干扰特征初探 – 以【清文启蒙】等三种兼汉满会话教材为研究的中心' [A Preliminary Survey of Linguistic Interference Observed in the Sino-Manchu Bilingual Texts of the Qing Period, Based on the '*Qīngwén Qǐméng*' and Two More Sino-Manchu Bilingual Dialogue Textbooks]. *Lishi Yuyanxue Yanjiu* 6: 187–227.

Index of languages and language families

Subject index